™

References for the Rest of Us!™

BESTSELLING BOOK SERIES

Do you find that traditional reference books are overloaded with technical details and advice you'll never use? Do you postpone important life decisions because you just don't want to deal with them? Then our *...For Dummies*® business and general reference book series is for you.

...For Dummies business and general reference books are written for those frustrated and hard-working souls who know they aren't dumb, but find that the myriad of personal and business issues and the accompanying horror stories make them feel helpless. *...For Dummies* books use a lighthearted approach, a down-to-earth style, and even cartoons and humorous icons to dispel fears and build confidence. Lighthearted but not lightweight, these books are perfect survival guides to solve your everyday personal and business problems.

> *"...Dummies books consistently live up to their brand-name promise to transform 'can't into can.' "*
> — *Ottawa Citizen*

> *"...clear, straightforward information laced with a touch of humour."*
> — *The Toronto Star*

> *"...set up in bits and bites that are easy to digest, full of no-nonsense advice."*
> — *The Calgary Herald*

Already, millions of satisfied readers agree. They have made *...For Dummies* the #1 introductory level computer book series and a best-selling business book series. They have written asking for more. So, if you're looking for the best and easiest way to learn about business and other general reference topics, look to *...For Dummies* to give you a helping hand.

™

CDG BOOKS
C A N A D A

8/99

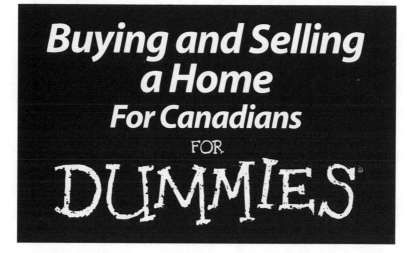

Buying and Selling a Home
For Canadians
FOR
DUMMIES®

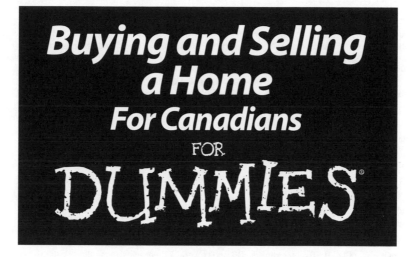

Buying and Selling a Home
For Canadians
FOR DUMMIES®

by **Tony Ioannou**
Moira Bayne
Wendy Yano

CDG BOOKS CANADA

CDG Books Canada, Inc.

◆ Toronto, ON ◆

Buying and Selling a Home For Canadians For Dummies®

Published by
CDG Books Canada, Inc.
99 Yorkville Avenue
Suite 400
Toronto, ON M5R 3K5
www.cdgbooks.com (CDG Books Canada Web Site)
www.idgbooks.com (IDG Books Worldwide Web Site)
www.dummies.com (Dummies Press Web Site)

Canadian Cataloguing in Publication Data

Ioannou, Tony

Buying and selling a home for Canadians for dummies

Includes index.
ISBN. 1-894413-06-7

1. House buying — Canada. 2. House selling — Canada. I. Bayne, Moira. II. Yano, Wendy. III. Title.

HD1379.I52 2000   643'.12'0971   C00-930701-X

Printed in Canada

2 3 4 5 6 TRI 04 03 02 01 00

Distributed in Canada by CDG Books Canada, Inc.

For general information on CDG Books, including all IDG Books Worldwide publications, please call our distribution center: HarperCollins Canada at 1-800-387-0117. For reseller information, including discounts and premium sales, please call our Sales department at 1-877-963-8830.

This book is available at special discounts for bulk purchases by your group or organization for resale, premiums, fundraising and seminars. For details, contact CDG Books Canada, Special Sales Department, 99 Yorkville Avenue, Suite 400, Toronto, ON, M5K 3K5; Tel: 416-963-8830; Email: spmarkets@cdgbooks.com.

For press review copies, author interviews, or other publicity information, please contact our Marketing department at 416-963-8830, fax 416-923-4821, or e-mail publicity@cdgbooks.com.

For authorization to photocopy items for corporate, personal, or educational use, please contact Cancopy, The Canadian Copyright Licensing Agency, One Yonge Street, Suite 1900, Toronto, ON, M5E 1E5; Tel: 416-868-1620; Fax: 416-868-1621; www.cancopy.com.

is a trademark under exclusive license to CDG Books Canada, Inc., from International Data Group, Inc.

About the Authors

Moira Bayne is a writer and editor at the Toronto-based publishing services company, Colborne Communications. She writes on topics as diverse as investing and healthcare, gardening and home decorating. A passionate do-it-yourselfer, she is committed to convincing other people that they can too.

Wendy Yano, also a writer and editor with Colborne Communications, has worked on books ranging from the *Lemon-Aid* car guides to *The Canadian Encyclopedia.* Wendy recently bought her first home in Toronto's Riverdale area and obsesses over home renovations and maintenance.

Tony Ioannou is currently a senior associate with Dexter Properties Inc., and has been interviewed many times in the Vancouver media, to comment on the state of the Vancouver real estate market. He has lived in Vancouver's Kitsilano neighbourhood for the last 15 years and is an avid mountain biker and golfer.

Tony obtained his real estate licence in 1984, and has consistently been a top producing salesperson with NRS Block Bros, and with Dexter Properties Inc since 1990. In 1990, he obtained his agents (brokers) licence, but continues to enjoy working as a residential real estate salesperson primarily on the West Side of Vancouver. He has also worked as a division director for the Real Estate Board of Greater Vancouver.

Tony Ioannou was and born and raised in Sydney, Australia and immigrated with his family to Vancouver in 1973. He completed high school in Vancouver and obtained a Bachelor of Arts degree in Urban Geography from the University of British Columbia.

ABOUT CDG BOOKS CANADA, INC. AND IDG BOOKS WORLDWIDE, INC.

Welcome to the world of IDG Books Worldwide and CDG Books Canada.

IDG Books Worldwide, Inc., is a subsidiary of International Data Group, Inc., the world's largest publisher of computer-related information and the leading global provider of information services on information technology. IDG was founded more than 30 years ago and now employs more than 9,000 people worldwide. IDG publishes more than 295 computer publications in over 75 countries (see listing below). More than 90 million people read one or more IDG publications each month.

Launched in 1990, IDG Books Worldwide is today the #1 publisher of best-selling computer books in North America. IDG Books Worldwide is proud to be the recipient of eight awards from the Computer Press Association in recognition of editorial excellence and three from *Computer Currents'* First Annual Readers' Choice Awards. Our best-selling *...For Dummies®* series has more than 55 million copies in print with translations in 31 languages. In record time, IDG Books Worldwide has become the first choice for millions of readers around the world who want to learn how to better manage their businesses.

In 1998, IDG Books Worldwide formally partnered with Macmillan Canada, a subsidiary of Canada Publishing Corporation, to create CDG Books Canada, a dynamic new Canadian publishing company. CDG Books Canada is now Canada's fastest growing publisher, bringing valuable information to Canadians from coast to coast through the introduction of Canadian *...For Dummies®* and *CliffsNotes™* titles.

Every one of our books is designed to bring extra value and skill-building instructions to the reader. Our books are written by experts who understand and care about our readers. The knowledge base of our editorial staff comes from years of experience in publishing, education, and journalism — experience we use to produce books to carry us into the new millennium. In short, we care about books, so we attract the best people. We devote special attention to details such as audience, interior design, use of icons, and illustrations. And because we use an efficient process of authoring, editing, and desktop publishing our books electronically, we can spend more time ensuring superior content and spend less time on the technicalities of making books.

You can count on our commitment to deliver high-quality books at competitive prices on topics you want to read about. At IDG Books Worldwide and CDG Books Canada, we continue in the IDG tradition of delivering quality for more than 30 years. You can learn more about IDG Books Worldwide and CDG Books Canada by visiting www.idgbooks.com, www.dummies.com, and www.cdgbooks.com.

Eighth Annual Computer Press Awards ≥ 1992

Ninth Annual Computer Press Awards ≥ 1993

Tenth Annual Computer Press Awards ≥ 1994

Eleventh Annual Computer Press Awards ≥ 1995

Authors' Acknowledgements

At CDG Books, editor Kim Herter rallied us through the tough spots, flexed the schedule, and laughed at our jokes. Without her good humour and perseverance, this book would never have been finished. Thanks also to Melanie Rutledge, Joan Whitman, Lisa Berland, and Pam Erlichman.

Thank you to everyone who reviewed the manuscript and provided all sorts of helpful advice and information: Reeves Coleman at Homelife/Experience Realty Inc; Hugh McLean of PrivateList; Catherine Gordon of Remax West/Annex; Steve Gilmour of Remax Realty Specialists; Joaquim Pinheiro, Associate Broker with Canada Group Realty Corporation; Roman Sydor and Terry Di Carlo of Sydor and Associates; Vance Pitre of the Canadian Real Estate Association; Trevor Weeden; and Mitsu Yano. Thank you also to Robin Hill at British Columbia Real Estate Association for assistance with agency description, Paula Siemens at the Mortgage Group for answering a zillion questions concerning mortgages, Edmund Wong at Ken K. Wong and Assoc. for their Strata plan, Bob Kinnear at the Ontario Real Estate Association for use of the Agreement of Purchase and Sale, and Jeff Clarke of Baker Street Home Inspections Services Inc. for use of the sample inspection report.

Thanks also to everyone who shared their stories from the trenches: David Akins, Catharine Haggert, Andrew Johnston, Arthur Johnson, Sandra and Chris Seney, Anne Wraggett, Jim Bayne, Melissa Bayne, and Steve Langendyk. A big thank-you to Michal Tarnowski, who not only bought a home and shared stories, but also acted as courier, chauffeur, and support pillar. Thanks also to Chris Coker for all the great meals and for making us laugh every day.

Finally, the author credit on this book should really go to "The Team," the talented group of writers and researchers at Colborne Communications: Sarah Kisilevsky, Eva Blank, Rosanne Green, Jennifer Warren, and Ilana Weitzman. Thank you also to Dave Peerless and Brian Thompson at Dexter Properties for their assistance and guidance. Thanks especially to Greg Ioannou for support and encouragement throughout.

Publisher's Acknowledgments

We're proud of this book; please register your comments through our IDG Books Worldwide Online Registration Form located at `http://my2cents.dummies.com`.

Some of the people who helped bring this book to market include the following:

Acquisitions and Editorial

Acquisitions Editor: Joan Whitman

Assistant Editors: Melanie Rutledge, Kim Herter

Substantive Editor: Lisa Berland

Copy Editor: Pamela Erlichman

Editorial Assistants: Stella Partheniou, Jennifer Findlay

Production

Production Manager: Donna Brown

Production Editor: Rebecca Conolly

Layout and Graphics: Kim Monteforte, Heidy Lawrance Associates

Proofreader: Kelli Howey

Indexers: Ilana Weitzman and Jennifer Warren

Special Help: Amy Black, Michael Kelly

General and Administrative

IDG Books Worldwide, Inc.: John Kilcullen, CEO; William Barry, President

CDG Books Canada, Inc.: Ron Besse, Chairman; Tom Best, President; Robert Harris, Vice President and Publisher

IDG Books Technology Publishing Group: Richard Swadley, Senior Vice President and Publisher; Walter Bruce III, Vice President and Associate Publisher; Steven Sayre, Associate Publisher; Joseph Wikert, Associate Publisher; Mary Bednarek, Branded Product Development Director; Mary Corder, Editorial Director

IDG Books Consumer Publishing Group: Roland Elgey, Senior Vice President and Publisher; Kathleen A. Welton, Vice President and Publisher; Kevin Thornton, Acquisitions Manager; Kristin A. Cocks, Editorial Director

IDG Books Internet Publishing Group: Brenda McLaughlin, Senior Vice President and Publisher; Diane Graves Steele, Vice President and Associate Publisher; Sofia Marchant, Online Marketing Manager

IDG Books Production for Dummies Press: Michael R. Britton, Vice President of Production; Debbie Stailey, Associate Director of Production; Cindy L. Phipps, Manager of Project Coordination, Production Proofreading, and Indexing; Tony Augsburger, Manager of Prepress, Reprints, and Systems; Laura Carpenter, Production Control Manager; Shelley Lea, Supervisor of Graphics and Design; Debbie J. Gates, Production Systems Specialist; Robert Springer, Supervisor of Proofreading; Kathie Schutte, Production Supervisor

Dummies Packaging and Book Design: Patty Page, Manager, Promotions Marketing

◆

The publisher would like to give special thanks to Patrick J. McGovern, without whom this book would not have been possible.

◆

Contents at a Glance

Table of Contents

Introduction

. . . .

*B*uying or selling a home is an incredibly enormous undertaking, not recommended for the faint of heart, the short of memory, or the big of debt. These are the biggest financial and lifestyle choices you'll ever make: so choose wisely. Actually, it's not that bad — especially with this book in hand. Armed with information about everything from mortgages to heating systems, you can calmly face the real estate world and see how it works. You'll learn what fixed rate, open term mortgages are. You'll use the word *chattel* in everyday conversation. And, most important, you'll discover what your priorities are, and how to match them with a home — a home of your own.

If you're considering buying a home, read this book! Self promotion aside, we'll tell you what you need to think about before making that huge decision, how to make your choices in a realistic and informed way, and how to avoid unexpected problems, crumbling foundations, and street parking.

If you're selling, you'll find all kinds of information about what your buyer expects from you, how to get the most money for your home, and how to manage the details so you don't overlook anything. If you're thinking about selling your home yourself, you'll find lots of tips to help you out. Coordinating a home sale is a long, intense process that many people do as a full-time job; we'll try to help you see whether you're ready for that kind of do-it-yourself challenge.

Buying a new home or leaving an old and cherished one involves a lot of decisions and considerations. In this book, we outline them all, setting you on the path to your new life, wherever that may be.

Are You Buying or Are You Selling?

Some of us are buyers and some of us are sellers, and some of us are both at the same time. We divide the book into easy-to-use parts: read the first half if you're looking to buy a home, and the second half if you're trying to sell one. We cover diverse topics like mortgages, shopping for a new home, and assembling your selling team: your real estate agent and lawyer. Wherever you start reading, we guarantee you can find information that's useful and easy to absorb. If you're struggling with mortgage and real estate jargon, don't worry, we have a full glossary at the back to help you figure out all the fancy terms too. We do our best to keep it simple, but sometimes you just can't get around using the A-word (amortization).

Why Should You Read This Book?

If you're hemming and hawing over whether you're ready to be a homeowner, read this book. We go through the pros and cons of both buying and renting and explain the financial benefits you can realize from investing in your own home. If you already have a home, this book is a great refresher course on how to handle all the details involved in choosing a new home. If this is your first time on the home-buying market, we take you through all the key decisions to make and steps to take to get yourself into the right home at the right price.

Selling your current home is often a very tough decision, and we don't ignore the fact that you may not feel completely ready to slap a "for sale" sign on the front lawn. This book helps you determine whether you're ready to say goodbye to your present home. If you've already made up your mind to move on to a bigger and better (or a smaller and less expensive) home, we take you through the nuts and bolts of getting your home sold. We include pointers on working with a selling agent, or handling the sale yourself. Everything from writing your listing, to making your home irresistible to buyers, to negotiating the best selling conditions — it's all here.

How to Find What You Need

Each part of this book focuses on a specific stage in the buying or selling process. Buyers and sellers are concerned with some of the same things, like the price of the home in question. We investigate your buying and selling options from each point of view separately. For example, you'll approach the negotiating table quite differently if you're buying a home than if you're selling. You might find it helpful to read up on your "opponent's" probable tactics, or you may just want to focus on your own questions and concerns. Either way, we've got plenty of information for you.

Part I: Deciding to Buy

This section looks at making the decision to buy a home. We start with the basic question: "Is now the right time?" and provide guidelines to help you answer it truthfully. Next, you need to look at your finances, to see what you can afford to buy. We give you all the tools necessary to paint a truthful financial picture. Then you need to think about mortgages, and understand the different financing options. Finally, it's time for some soul searching: what kind of home is right for you?

Part II: Discovering Your Perfect Home

At some point, you have to set your priorities and be certain that you're making the right choice when you make an offer on a new home. In this part, we help you choose the right professionals to help you buy a home — not to mention keep you informed, safe, and sane. Then you need to prioritize what you want in a home into a usable set of criteria. Armed with this list, it's time to go shopping. We tell you how to find potential homes and evaluate the homes you see. And just in case you get carried away dreaming about home entertainment centres and sunken living rooms, we provide a dose of reality by letting you in on all sorts of potential problems you may not notice right away when you're touring prospective houses, and what to look for (and in) as you investigate.

Part III: Getting the House You Want

This section deals with the paperwork involved in buying a home. Look to this part for information on offers (just what do all those conditions in the sale contract mean?), terms, and negotiating tips . . . everything you need to close the deal. Professional home inspections, surveys, and new-home warranties are also covered in this part. Speaking of paperwork, we put together a "Moving Timeline" starting two months (yes, two months) before you move all the way through to the blissful day after. Read up! It's time to get organized.

Part IV: Deciding to Sell

It's decision time again, but this time, from the seller's perspective. In this part, you figure out whether the timing's right to sell your home. It might make more sense to stay put and renovate. And what about the money? How much can you get for your home? And (an often-overlooked point), how much will it cost you to move? We also suggest ways to balance the selling of one house with the buying of another, focussing on what to do with your mortgage and on timing the closing properly.

Part V: Preparing Yourself and Your House to Sell

This part gives you advice on how to market and present your home to potential buyers. We include all the information you need to find the right real estate agent for you — *or* to decide that you want to be your *own* real estate agent and sell your house yourself. There is more paperwork involved on the selling side of the equation than on the buying side. This part outlines sale contracts, commissions, and disclosure statements. We also take a look at inspections and appraisals from the seller's point of view, so you can make sure your home is ready to sell.

Part VI: Sealing the Deal

The first chapter in this part is Marketing 101 for homesellers, with tips on advertising your home to potential buyers — whether you're selling with an agent or on your own. Then it's time to face more paperwork (but this book makes it much more bearable). This part covers offers and counteroffers, as well as transferring deeds and titles. Turn to the last chapter in this part for advice on negotiating from the seller's side of the table.

Part VII: The Part of Tens

Here you'll find extra tidbits we just couldn't fit into the body of the book. Of special interest is the section on regional home-buying concerns; Canada is a large and diverse country, and each region and province has some particular considerations you may want to read up on. We also provide some special tips for condominium owners, and some valuable maintenance advice to help you protect the value of your real estate investment.

Part VIII: Appendixes

Here you'll find a glossary of all those indecipherable real estate and mortgage terms, as well as a sample inspection report, so you'll know what to expect when your house gets checked out. And if you *still* want more information, there's a list of real estate resources, as well.

Icons Used in This Book

Extra-helpful information to help you survive in the real estate jungle.

A heads-up about potential problems and pitfalls in your path.

Reminders of important information that you shouldn't lose sight of in your home hunt or purchasing pursuit.

Places where you may want to look deeper and ask for further information. We don't have the space to explain *everything*, you know . . .

Definitions of terms, technical information, stuff that you don't necessarily *need* to know, but may *want* to anyway.

Part I
Deciding to Buy

The 5th Wave   By Rich Tennant

"I'M ENTERING ALL THE BANK'S REQUIREMENTS FOR A MORTGAGE, AND I EITHER HAVE TO BUY A COMPUTER WITH MORE MEMORY OR START LOOKING FOR A SMALLER HOUSE."

In this part . . .

When will you be ready to buy a home? What kind of home should you buy? What neighbourhoods should you look in? Whose help should you enlist? How are you going to come up with the cash?

Why are you panicking? Relax, kick back with a cup of tea, and read this first part. You won't actually find the answers to these questions, but you *will* find advice on how to figure out the answers for yourself.

Chapter 1

Looking to Buy a Home?

● ●

In This Chapter

▶ Becoming a homeowner — what's in it for you?

▶ Deciding that you're ready to buy

▶ Owning versus renting

▶ Learning about common homeowning concerns

● ●

Dorothy said it best: There's no place like home. You may be a jet-setting entrepreneur or a stay-at-home parent, but we're willing to bet where you live is your most cherished space. You need a place to wind down, to relax, and to rejuvenate. Whether you own or rent (or mooch off your parents), the place you call home is the foundation of your life.

We all want our homes to be perfect — even though our definitions of perfect change over time. Maybe as a teenager, your perfect bedroom was all black with huge speakers in every corner of the room. Twenty years, three children, two dogs, and a father-in-law later, your idea of perfect is an ensuite bathroom with good water pressure, a Jacuzzi, and a lock on the door. We all need a living space that can adapt to our changing needs and wants, and, of course, what better way to have that living space than to own it?

The idea of owning a home can be scary: your water pipes could freeze and break, your basement could flood, your electrical system could need a complete overhaul. People can put thousands of dollars into their homes for renovations, thousands more for emergency repairs, and then there's daily upkeep, seasonal maintenance, taxes. . . . But ask homeowners if it's worth it, and they'll nod their heads vigorously and show you their Zen rock garden, the self-designed workshop in the basement, and the "Elvis room" with white and gold sequined walls, blue suede curtains, and pink Cadillac couch.

Even though owning your home can dictate how much money you have for other things and leave you constantly worrying about finances, researching and planning will help you stay in control. You can and should decide how much home you can afford, and that's why this section of the book is geared toward getting you the home you want — at a price that doesn't leave you eating macaroni and cheese three times a day for the next 20 years. After all, you want your home to complement your lifestyle, not overrun it. You want enough money left over to create that "Elvis" room you've dreamed of.

Joys of Ownership

We probably don't even need to write this section: If you're reading this book, the idea of owning obviously appeals to you. But as a helpful reminder, we'd like to suggest to you some of the advantages of owning a home.

- **More stability, less stress.** Stability is a wonderful thing — it means that there will be less on your mind. Moving, according to some, is the third most stressful activity in life (after death and divorce). Owning a home means you don't have to worry about moving from one rental apartment to the next, about how much rent will go up next year, about what happens if the landlord decides to sell the place, or even about keeping the landlord happy enough so that you can re-sign the lease. Homeowning also means that you acquire a major investment, which will make you feel more secure when thinking about the future.

- **It's yours.** It's yours to do with what you want! You too can have an "Elvis" room! On a more sane note, you can change even the small things you don't like: the dripping faucets, the ugly shag rug, and the showerhead that goes only as high as your belly button. And all your time, effort, and money go into *your* investment, not someone else's. You no longer have to deal with landlords not fixing things or spending small amounts of money when they do. Of course, many building owners and managers out there respect their tenants and respond quickly to the tenants' and the building's needs. However, good landlords are hard to find, and chances are that your house or apartment simply won't be their priority; their own homes will.

- **Your sense of community deepens.** Even if you're more anti-social than Mr. Scrooge, owning a home encourages you to appreciate the surrounding community. After all, protecting the value of your property requires you to protect the general area, too. You may start grudgingly by organizing the neighbourhood protest against your local park being turned into a dumpsite (which would mean horrible things for your investment), but hopefully, you'll start to actually like your neighbours. Belonging to a community can be a wonderful feeling. We recommend that you buy a home in an area where the majority of people are homeowners — they tend to care more about the neighbourhood than tenants do.

Making an investment

Although mortgages may be uppermost in your mind, buying a house isn't just a financial investment. It's a lifestyle investment. What and where you buy will ultimately dictate how you will live. Bought a fixer-upper with the intention of doing all the renovations yourself? Five years later, you may still be devoting all your time and money to it. Bought a home in the distant suburbs, but work in the heart of the city? You may spend more time in heavy traffic than at home. On the other hand, maybe you've become a gourmet cook because your wonderful kitchen deserves to be used constantly, and the once-rec-room, now-home-theatre means you can host the big Grey Cup bash every year.

You will have to make sacrifices when you buy a home — but you can make them *informed* sacrifices. This means you'll have to do some creative brainstorming to imagine the upsides and downsides of various features of the home you're considering. For instance, you may buy a house on a corner lot, knowing that you'll have a lot of snow shovelling and leaf raking to do. You may not mind these tasks too much because you decided before you bought the house that its unobstructed south-facing kitchen windows and bigger garden were well worth the effort.

✔ **You're a better person.** Or at least, people think you are. Ownership of a home often translates into people thinking wonderful things about you: you're mature, you're dependable, and you're stable. And paying your mortgage on time every month (with banks encouraging "direct withdrawal" this is really easy) does wonders for your credit rating.

✔ **You can benefit financially.** Even with a mortgage that may seem overwhelming, there are definite advantages to owning a home. Think of a mortgage as a forced savings plan, in which you (usually) cannot skip a deposit or withdraw money, and each payment gives you a slightly bigger part of your asset. Home ownership is also generally considered a good investment — one that grows over time. Another great thing about investing in a home is that if it's your principal residence, you don't pay tax on the amount you earn. The increase in your home's value, similar to other types of investments, is called a *capital gain*. On other investments, you would normally pay tax on these gains, but you're exempted from paying this tax if the capital gain is on your principal residence. (More on capital gains in Chapter 14.)

Should You Buy Right Now?

Although you may think researching real estate markets and waiting for the right time to buy are the only ways to get a good deal, your personal situation is what should really determine your decision to buy. Are you able to pay your mortgage, utilities, taxes, insurance, and whatever maintenance comes up, not only for the next year, but also for the next 5, or 25? (We show you how to get a picture of your financial situation in Chapter 2.)

Are you willing to remain in the same place for the next five years? Considering the closing costs involved whether you're a seller or a buyer (more on closing costs in Chapter 2), you should be prepared to keep your home for at least a few years. It's a good idea to avoid having to sell your home quickly, because chances are you would have to sell at a lower price. So even if the market is at an all-time low and interest rates are way down, buying a home could be a huge mistake if you're in the middle of a career change or planning a move to Luxembourg in a year.

Maintaining a house requires a big commitment — of money and time. Each season presents a list of chores to maintain your home's integrity and efficiency. Overlooking the overflowing eaves or the leaky roof may lead to significant water damage; neglecting your furnace could cause hundreds of dollars in repairs to it and your frozen home. There are many situations in which a little neglect can transform into expensive repairs and sometimes irreversible damage, resulting in huge losses when it's time to sell. If you don't budget the time and money for regular upkeep, be prepared to invest more time and money down the line.

Knowing your finances

Home buying is an investment. Although it is cheaper in the long run to buy than to rent, that initial outlay of cash is enough to send anyone's heart racing. You'll need to take a careful look at your current expenditures in order to evaluate your readiness to take on mortgage payments and home maintenance. Chapter 2 helps you determine whether you're financially ready to buy.

Knowing where your money goes now is a crucial first step. Suppose that after you've accounted for what you spend on food, clothes, transportation, and vacations, you still have a $15,000 surplus. You're not really sure where it went last year but figure it should be all the cushion you need to cover the new costs of being a homeowner. Once your pipes freeze and you need to call in a plumber, you don't want to discover that you've already spent most of that $15,000 surplus on gifts for your friends and family as well as regular rounds of drinks for all your pals down at the local pub, and large bouquets of flowers for your partner once you can see straight again.

Have a plan for the future, too. Know what you want to spend on RRSPs and your kids' education. Tuition is only going up. Being clear on where you want your financial life to be in five years and ten years will help you make smart decisions now about how much to put into a down payment and how much to carry in monthly mortgage payments.

Don't buy your dream home without leaving enough money to replace the 25-year-old couch that you picked up when you first moved out on your own.

Renting versus buying

Owning your home instead of renting almost always makes more sense in the long run, especially if you settle in one area. The biggest advantage of owning over renting is that your monthly payments are an investment (and they'll eventually cease!). The most common complaint about buying a home is having to pay the mortgage, and more specifically, the interest on the mortgage. You can live with your parents until you've made enough money to buy a home outright, but your parents may not want to live with you for that long!

Renting your home instead of owning it does have advantages, and there are times in your life when owning isn't the best option for you. One of the biggest reasons to buy a home is for stability, but if you like your flexible lifestyle, this may be a burden to you. Owning a home is a serious commitment, and if your priorities aren't geared to maintaining a 25-year debt, or having a permanent address, it may be better to rent.

If you're in one of the following situations you should probably wait a while to buy a home:

- **Having financial woes:** Although you can leap into home ownership with as little as a 5 percent down payment in some cases, you still have to come up with that amount. And you'll have to be prepared to make those regular mortgage payments for what may seem like an eternity, not to mention all the other costs of being a homeowner. Getting a mortgage also might be tricky if you've neglected other loans, or have significant debts.

- **Living in transition:** You haven't decided to live in one place. Saddling yourself with a chunk of property and debt if you think you're really going to want to spend the next year island-hopping around Greece is not the best move.

- **Lacking job security:** If you end up relocating for employment, you may have to get rid of your home in a hurry. If you don't have a reliable or steady source of income, lenders may not be willing to authorize a mortgage because you can't guarantee you'll have more freelance work in the coming years.

✔ **Space uncertainty:** Although you can't really predict having triplets, there's no sense in buying a two-bedroom bungalow if you're pretty sure that your brother-in-law's family of seven and their three dogs will move in with you for an unspecified amount of time. Unless this is your way of ensuring they can't live with you, you may find you have to change houses sooner than you'd like. If you are considering setting up a home office or starting a home-based business in the future, make sure you have a spare bedroom or room in the basement to expand.

✔ **Facing a bad housing market:** Generally speaking, you should focus on your own situation rather than the real estate market. But there may be a time when interest rates skyrocket and yet homes sell for twice as much as their listing prices — in these circumstances, it's probably better to wait until the market cools down to buy a home. If a monthly cost analysis shows that buying a home would be 20 to 30 percent more than renting a comparable home, think twice about buying. (We show you how to analyze monthly costs in Chapter 3.)

✔ **Waiting for the gravy train:** You and your friend are starting a new dot.com company that will revolutionize the Internet, and you need some start-up capital. You decide to invest all your savings in the company instead of real estate. If your company takes off, you may be able to buy an estate in the south of France instead of a bungalow in the suburbs.

Common homeowning concerns

You may be skeptical about the complications of buying a home. There are many different kinds of homes and ownership of homes, however, so you don't have to let your hatred of shovelling snow stop you from owning. The following are the most common reservations about home owning:

✔ **Unexpected costs:** One of the main arguments for renting is that you know what your monthly costs are, and they don't change. When you own a house, and the furnace breaks down, you have to fix it. But consider that when you rent, your landlord may not get around to fixing things right away, or he may be in Florida for the holidays and you may be stuck in the cold for a while. Although living in the same building as your landlord may guarantee some things are fixed in a hurry, your concern about a missing screen on your bedroom window may not be her priority. And maybe she likes the house at 18°C during the winter and 30°C in the summer. Sometimes paying the money to get things fixed is worth the hassle, but if you pay for a repair in your rented home, you may never see that money again.

So, though the responsibility for repairs in your home will fall on your own shoulders, the main point is that you have the control. And with a mortgage you know from the beginning how much you'll be paying each month for the length of your mortgage; with renting, it's hard to get that guarantee.

✔ **Extra work:** Don't like doing lawn work, shovelling snow, fixing leaks? Your partner or child refuses to do your dirty work for you? Instead of renting to avoid such chores, you might prefer to buy a condominium where someone else takes care of the maintenance. If you buy an apartment-style condo, you won't even have a sidewalk to worry about!

Keep in mind that once you move into a new home, you'll have new rates for some monthly expenses like utilities (heating, hydro, water). You may be taking on new costs such as property taxes and home and garden maintenance. New homeowners should also prepare for the worst by ensuring they have a reserve fund for emergency repairs. Make sure you have enough monthly income left over after your mortgage payments to cover these costs as well.

Typical costs for a new homeowner

Okay, so you want a better idea of exactly what kind of costs a new homeowner faces? Here goes.

✔ **Maintenance:** You may have a high-maintenance relationship or a low-maintenance relationship with the home you buy. Be sure your finances can handle the costs of regular repairs. Also, keep an emergency fund for unexpected repairs, and contribute to it on a regular basis. If you dip into it to help pay your way to Tahiti, that's your call, but be aware that your basement could be flooded when you return, and then you may not have the cash to pay the plumber.

✔ **Insurance:** You will need proof of fire and extended coverage insurance before you can finalize the purchase of your new home, since the property itself is the *only* security against the loan. If your new home burns down . . . well, you understand. Insurance costs vary, depending on your deductible, the value of your home and its contents, and the type of coverage you get, as well as each insurer's rates. Shop around for an affordable policy that covers you for replacement of your personal property and grants you a living allowance if your home is destroyed. A policy with public liability insurance is also a good idea, as it protects you if someone is harmed on your property. (You'll find more on insurance in Chapter 10.)

✔ **Utilities:** When you buy a home, you assume all the heating, cooling, water, and electricity bills for the property. If you live in the colder, draftier parts of this country, you already know that heat is the most important utility there is. And if you've ever rented a house and paid the hydro bill separately for electric heat, you've already been walloped by the biggest bill you've ever experienced. If the house you're buying is new, you'll probably pay less for utilities because of better insulation and construction quality. If you're buying a resale home, ask the owners for copies of their utility bills so you can figure out average heating costs. In Chapter 7 we go over the costs and benefits of various heating systems commonly found in Canadian homes.

✔ **Taxes:** Property taxes are calculated based on your home's assessed value and the local tax rates. Unfortunately, property tax rates can fluctuate yearly, and they vary from region to region. Some real estate listings will state the amount of the previous year's taxes for the property being sold. When you're looking at new homes, find out from the selling agent or the owners what the previous year's taxes were. If you need a high-ratio mortgage to buy a new home, your lender may insist that property tax installments be added to your monthly mortgage payments. (See Chapter 3 for more details on high-ratio mortgages.)

✔ **Condo fees:** The great thing about living in a condo is that someone else looks after all the pesky maintenance and landscaping stuff. The flip side is you have to pay for it in your condo fees. In addition to your mortgage payments, condo fees alone can cost as much as rent in a decent apartment.

Understanding the market

The housing market fluctuates, experiencing both strong and weak periods. History has shown, however, that the market will rise in the long run. So don't focus too much on waiting for the "right time" to buy. It's nearly impossible to predict how the market will go, and if you wait around forever for the market to be perfect you'll waste tonnes of potential investment money on rent! Generally speaking, after you've bought your first home you'll continue to own it for years to come, and its value will increase. It's your personal situation that really should matter, because that will determine whether you have to sell the home in a hurry, and whether you can really afford to buy in the first place.

Having said all this, chances are you still want to know how the market works, because there are periods when it's best to be a buyer (and conversely, times when it's best to be a seller). You can see what the current market is like by checking out the prices in the local paper and asking your real estate agent how the current market compares to the last 12 months. Your agent can tell you how homes have been selling in the past year, what the *median sales price* was (the *median* sales price is the actual middle price between the highest and lowest selling prices, not the average price), and sometimes even how long homes were on the market, the types of homes sold, and their neighbourhoods.

A good overall economy will naturally produce a stronger market with more people looking to buy. Chances are, of course, there will be more sellers, because with more money, owners may decide to "trade up" and buy bigger homes. A strong economy also produces more construction and housing developments, opening up the market to more new homes.

To understand the housing market, there are a couple of terms and effects that you should know about.

- **Buyer's market:** Ideally you'll want to buy when many sellers want to sell, but few buyers are looking to buy. Homes take longer to sell and so buyers can take more time to make decisions. To sell a home in this market, the seller will have to list at a really good price, and sometimes even offer other incentives, such as secondary financing (see Chapter 3 for a discussion of financing options).

- **Seller's market:** The opposite of a buyer's market is a seller's market. Few homes are on the market, but buyers are plentiful, which results in fast home sales at prices close to, or even above, the listing prices. Some homes will sell even before they're listed. Because of the rise in sales, a lot of owners may sell their homes themselves. In a seller's market, buyers have less negotiating power, less time to decide, and may even find themselves in a bidding war for homes. So if you're buying in a seller's market, be prepared to make quick decisions. Have all your homework done and your financing arranged. (See Chapter 2 for details on mortgage pre-approval.)

- **Seasonal influences:** Winter in Canada is notorious for being cold and unpleasant everywhere but the south coast of B.C. People don't like to venture out much, unless for necessities like groceries and hockey games (and skiing). Besides, who wants to look for a home when they're busy buying Christmas presents? Frostbite aside, the winter months also tend to be slower for the real estate market because people with children don't like to move during the school year. A lot of homes won't be on the market simply because sellers know their homes look best in the summer with the flowers, the leaves, and the sunshine. This means, of course, that the homes on the market at this time of year probably have to be sold urgently, and so you might find a good bargain. You just might have to deal with snowdrifts and –40°C temperatures on moving day. The exception to the rule is Toronto. Although the whole city seems to grind to a halt whenever there's a big snowstorm, for the last few years there's been no seasonal slowdown in the real estate market.

- **Interest rates:** If you need a mortgage to purchase your home (lucky you, if you don't!), you'll find that interest rates make a big difference in how much home you can afford. When interest rates are high, fewer buyers tend to be in the market for a new home. You can see the logic: A 6.5 percent interest rate on a $200,000 mortgage loan will cost you approximately $13,000 in interest in one year; while the same $200,000 loan at a 10 percent interest rate will cost you about $20,000 interest! Different types of mortgages can increase or decrease your interest rate from what banks consider the current standard. Have a look at Chapter 3 for more information.

Chapter 2

Understanding Your Finances

· ·

· ·

*A*s you step into the world of being a homeowner, you're going to have to get up close and personal with your financial life. Maybe you have a long and close history together. Maybe there is some distance between you . . . a "That is where my finances are, and this is where I bury my head in the sand" relationship. Either way, we have collected all the information we think you'll need to buy your next home confidently, and with your eyes wide open.

Armed with a clear (and honest!) picture of your financial situation, you're ready to look at more specific costs associated with buying a home, like getting a mortgage. We help you figure out what size mortgage your bank is likely to give you — and encourage you to get your mortgage pre-approved before you start home shopping. The chapter wraps up with a look at closing-day costs, such as insurance and legal fees, so you know exactly what to anticipate before the seller hands you the keys. Trust us, we've been there! Just when you think you're ready to move in, you face a few last expenses that can really add up.

Getting Up Close And Personal with Your Finances

Although it can be depressing to examine your meagre income next to your substantial expenses, you'll be even more depressed if you can't make your mortgage payments on your new home. In assessing what size mortgage you're eligible for, your lender (usually a bank) takes into account only those debts you *have* to pay. The really expensive food you buy for your 16 cats, or the trips to Aruba you take every other month to work on your tan are not accounted for. If you don't want to find yourself with hungry rebellious felines, then you should examine your real monthly expenses to calculate how much of your income you can realistically put toward your mortgage payments. Take a look at Table 2-1: Once you've deducted your total monthly expenses from your total monthly income, the remaining amount is what you can afford to pay towards your mortgage each month.

Table 2-1	Monthly Budget Worksheet	
Income		**Monthly Amount**
Net income after taxes	_____	_____
Partner's net income after taxes	_____	_____
Other income: investments, gifts, annuity, trust fund, pension, etc.	_____	_____
Total Income	_____	_____
Expenses		**Monthly Amount**
Investments		
RRSP	_____	_____
Education funds	_____	_____
Other	_____	_____
Debts		
Credit cards	_____	_____
Lines of credit	_____	_____
Student loans	_____	_____
Other loans/debt	_____	_____
Transportation		
Auto loan or lease payments	_____	_____
Insurance	_____	_____
Registration	_____	_____
Repairs/maintenance	_____	_____
Fuel	_____	_____
Parking	_____	_____
Public transit	_____	_____

Expenses	Monthly Amount	
Household Costs		
Groceries	_____	_____
Utilities	_____	_____
Hydro/electricity	_____	_____
Water	_____	_____
Gas	_____	_____
Home insurance	_____	_____
Telephone	_____	_____
Cable television	_____	_____
Internet	_____	_____
Health		
Medication	_____	_____
Glasses/contacts	_____	_____
Dental/orthodontics	_____	_____
Therapist	_____	_____
Special needs items	_____	_____
Miscellaneous		
Life insurance	_____	_____
Education	_____	_____
Tuition fees	_____	_____
Books/supplies	_____	_____
Daycare	_____	_____
Entertainment	_____	_____
Restaurant meals	_____	_____
Vacation	_____	_____
Clothing/accessories	_____	_____
Recreation/sports	_____	_____
Membership fees	_____	_____
Equipment	_____	_____
Pets	_____	_____
Gifts	_____	_____
Other		
Total Expenses	_____	_____

However, before you even think about mortgage costs, you need to have a lump sum amount in your bank to make the down payment on a new home. (See later in this chapter for more details.) Your down payment can amount to as little as 5 percent of the purchase price of the home you want to buy. And one more thing: In addition to the down payment, you need another chunk of money (a couple of thousand dollars at least) to pay the closing costs on a new home. We take you through these costs later in the chapter. Chapter 12 gives you all the details on closing a home sale.

Determining What Size Mortgage You Can Carry

After you have gone through the above calculations, you may realize that you qualify for a larger mortgage than you initially considered. At this point, you are faced with two scenarios: what you can comfortably afford and what amount you can absolutely financially stretch yourself to in order to buy your dream house. Banks will be more than happy to give you a larger mortgage if you can afford the payments, but you should remember what monthly payment amounts comfortably fit within your budget. You don't want to be saddled with a large mortgage and not be able to afford those cherished trips to Aruba.

Financial institutions have two typical approaches to determine how big a mortgage they're willing to give you. One method involves calculating your *Gross Debt Service Ratio*. This is calculated as the percentage of gross annual or gross monthly income needed to cover all housing-related costs (including principal and interest payments on your mortgage, property taxes, hydro, water, and heating). It should not be more than approximately 30 percent of your gross annual or gross monthly income. The other method is to calculate your *Total Debt Service Ratio*. This is calculated as the percentage of gross annual or monthly income required to cover all your housing-related costs *plus any other debts* (e.g., student loan, car, and credit card payments). This should be no more than 40 percent of your gross annual or monthly income.

You can use a calculation like this to determine your Gross Debt Service (GDS):

Gross monthly income (pre-tax):	$6,000
Multiplied by 30% available for housing:	$0.3 \times \$6,000 = \$1,800$
Minus deduction for estimated monthly property taxes ($200):	$\$1,800 - \$200 = \$1,600$
Monthly income available for mortgage payments:	$1,600

(Note: figures are approximate and have been rounded.)

However, your GDS can be a very misleading guide in deciding what size mortgage you can carry, particularly if you have a lot of other debts. This is where knowing your Total Debt Service (TDS) comes in handy. You can use this method to calculate your TDS:

Gross monthly income:	$6,000
Multiplied by 40% available for housing and other debts:	$0.4 \times \$6,000 = \$2,400$
Minus current monthly debt payments ($400 for car payment, $200 for credit cards, $150 for student loan)	$2,400 – $400 – $200 – $150 $1,650
Minus estimated monthly property taxes ($200):	$1,650 – $200 = $1,450
Monthly income available for mortgage payments:	$1,450

As you can see, the Total Debt Service presents a much more accurate picture of what is left over to spend on housing.

On the Internet, several online calculators total your GDS and TDS automatically when you fill in a table similar to the one above. See Appendix C for our list of Canadian mortgage resources available on the Internet. You'll also find lots of good advice on the Web about financing sources to consider and options to bargain for when you're negotiating a mortgage.

Using GDS and TDS calculations can help you determine a reasonable price range for a new home, but they only factor in the official debt you carry — not the other obligations you may prefer to forget about. So don't forget to factor in the other costs you worked out in the Monthly Budget Worksheet earlier in this chapter (Table 2-1).

Getting a Head Start with a Pre-Approved Mortgage

Most financial institutions offer to *pre-approve* your mortgage loan before you even start looking at homes. Getting a pre-approved mortgage is highly recommended because it means your financial position is clear before you make an offer on a home. Because getting pre-approval is the same process you have to go through to get an actual mortgage, it makes sense to do it in advance, and because institutions want your business, it's free. Similar to applying for an actual mortgage, when you apply for pre-approval you answer questions and provide documents based on your financial position, debt load, and credit history. (Details about the mortgage process appear in Chapter 3.) There is usually a fixed time period (either 60 or 90 days) for which lenders will offer a certain size mortgage at a specific interest rate, and they will confirm this in writing. The advantages to being pre-approved are:

- ✔ **You know your price limit.** Before you set your heart on the mansion up the road it's a good idea to know your financial limitations.

- ✔ **Your offers are taken more seriously by sellers.** Sellers prefer to accept an offer from someone who has started to arrange their financing. After all, there's a chance the buyer may not be able to get financing at all. As a buyer, you don't have to worry about rushing to arrange a loan when you find that perfect home — having pre-approval means you've done everything in advance.

- ✔ **You're protected from any rise in interest rates.** As long as you close your sale within the time period of the pre-arranged mortgage (typically 60 or 90 days), you can rest assured that your mortgage will be at the rate stated in your pre-approval even if bank interest rates have risen since you initially obtained the pre-approval.

Even with pre-approval, you still have to secure the mortgage once you've negotiated the buying of a home. Your final mortgage approval is subject to a full check of your finances and an appraisal of the market value of the property you want to buy, but pre-approval means most of the paperwork has been done beforehand, which speeds up the process significantly.

If you're applying for a high-ratio mortgage (your down payment amounts to less than 25 percent of the purchase price of the home you're buying), you're also subject to the approval of the *Canada Mortgage and Housing Corporation* (CMHC), a federal Crown corporation that administers national housing programs and insures mortgages under the provisions of the National Housing Act. Your application for CMHC approval can't be processed until you have an accepted offer to purchase contract from your seller. (See Chapter 9 for details concerning contracts of purchase and sale.)

Just because you're pre-approved for a mortgage doesn't mean you can make an unconditional offer to buy a home. Write into your offer to purchase contract a "subject to financing" clause (a very common procedure) so you have at least a couple of days to complete your mortgage approval. A mortgage is a contract. It's a legally binding document and you must uphold it. Make sure you know what you're getting into. Read all the details and ask your lender to explain anything you don't understand. You're trying to buy a house here, not make a deal with the devil.

Anticipating the Closing Costs

The last big hurdle in the home-buying process is your *closing day* — this is the day that you complete all the paperwork to buy your house. It's also the day that you finalize all the really boring details that need to be covered when you buy a house. For example, the property has to be transferred into your name, obviously enough; but first, your lawyer or real estate agent must check that no one else has any claims against the house or property. You have municipal taxes to pay, land transfer taxes to pay, accounts to settle with the previous owners, mortgage details to finalize, and so on. (We walk you through closing day in Chapter 11.)

Each one of the closing day items outlined in this section costs you money. You don't want to find yourself short of cash on that final important day. We recommend you set aside at least a couple thousand dollars to pay for your closing costs.

Deposit and down payment

You will be required to pay a deposit of around 5 percent of the purchase price of the house, and you pay it in stages. Your first offer on a house will include an initial deposit, typically between $500 and $1,000. You pay this with a regular or certified cheque, payable to your real estate agent's brokerage. Generally, this amount is only deposited once your offer has been accepted. The deposit, which is a negotiated amount, is held in your real estate agent's trust account. If you are not using an agent, your lawyer holds your deposit in trust.

When all conditions in your agreement of purchase and sale have been settled (see Chapter 9 for information on these items), you increase the deposit, often to around 5 percent of the purchase price, although this amount is negotiable. Again, the deposit increase is payable to your real estate agent's brokerage by certified cheque or bank draft and is held with the earlier deposit in your real estate agent's trust account. The deposit forms part of the down payment — you pay off the balance of the down payment on the closing date (also known as the completion date). A certified cheque or bank draft payable to your lawyer or notary public is the most common way to pay the balance of your down payment. Your lawyer will advise you of the exact amount you have to bring in and the preferred method of payment.

If you make a minimal down payment (perhaps 5 percent on a super-affordable house), the amount of the deposit held by the real estate agent may also represent the total down payment. In this case, your agent will convey the money to your lawyer or notary public on your behalf.

Three key closing fees

To sew up your mortgage deal you need financing, insurance, and the services of a good lawyer. Of course, lining up all of these details costs money, so get your chequebook ready to make further withdrawals at closing time.

Financing fees

If you use the services of a mortgage broker, the lender will probably pay the brokerage fee. However, if you have had past financial difficulties, you may be required to pay this fee yourself; it will likely be about 2 percent of the total mortgage. Ask early in the process what to expect.

Most lenders charge an application fee when you apply for a mortgage. You can usually have these fees waived, so don't be shy about asking for these savings from your lender.

Insurance fees

If you have a high-ratio mortgage, you must obtain mortgage loan insurance. Insurance costs range between 0.5 percent and 3.75 percent of your total mortgage amount. For convenience, you can incorporate your insurance fee into your monthly mortgage payments. You may have to pay taxes on your insurance as well: in some provinces GST is charged, and in others PST is charged as well.

An application fee is also payable on your mortgage loan insurance. The fees will range from $75 to $235 depending on whether an appraisal is required. You can find more on mortgage insurance in Chapter 3.

Legal fees and disbursements

You need a lawyer (or a notary, if you are buying in Quebec) to review the offer to purchase, perform a title search, draw up your mortgage documents, and tend to the closing details. Your lawyer also takes care of any reimbursements owed the previous owner (for items such as prepaid hydro and water bills, and property taxes). You'll find more information on the lawyer's role, and how to find one, in Chapter 5.

You pay only the applicable portion of the expenses from the date that you take possession of the home you're buying. (If you're buying a resale condo, and the condo fees are prepaid, they too will be pro-rated.) How much all this will cost depends on how complicated your deal is, but you can count on about $500 to $1,000 to cover legal fees. The pro-rated fees for property taxes, condo fees, and any other prepaid expenses will be outlined in the Statement of Adjustments prepared by your lawyer. You'll find more on Statements of Adjustments in Chapter 10.

Appraisals, surveys, inspections, and condominium certificates

Here are four more items that you may have to pay for before closing day.

- ✔ **Appraisal:** You'll probably need to get an appraisal for your lender. An *appraisal* is an independent confirmation that the purchase price is of fair market value. A basic appraisal fee is about $150 to $250, but that figure will go up if you're buying a large home or a home located in a neighbourhood with very little turnaround. Appraisals are done on a comparison basis, and if there's nothing to compare with, more work is involved, hence the higher fee. (See Chapter 5 for more on appraisals.)

- ✔ **Survey:** The Land Titles Office, or your lender, may require an up-to-date survey in order to approve your mortgage. A *survey* verifies the boundaries of your property and ensures that there are no encroachments either by you onto your neighbour's property or vice versa. The price of surveys varies widely, depending on the location and type of property. Your real estate agent should be able to give you an idea of what to expect. (You'll find more on surveys in Chapter 11.)

- ✔ **Inspection:** Take our advice: Get a professional home *inspection* done on the home you're going to buy. An inspection is a report on the presence and apparent condition of the structural and operational systems of a home. (See Chapter 11 for details.) The cost of an inspection ranges from $150 to $500. If your property is very large or unusual in its construction, count on a higher fee. If you're moving to a rural area where wells or septic tanks are involved, you should get certification that both systems are in good condition, and this will cost you about another $50 to $100.

- ✔ **Condominium certificate:** If you're buying a condo, you'll need a document confirming the seller has fulfilled all obligations to the condominium corporation. This information is contained in a document variously known as the *condominium certificate*, *estoppel certificate, information certificate*, or *status certificate*, to name a few of its incarnations. Ask your real estate agent what the local alias is. This certificate and its supporting documents will cost you up to $50, although if you're buying in Québec, you don't need it (C'est bon, non?).

Taxes

Of course, your new home-owning adventure wouldn't be complete without taxes. Get ready for these additions to your closing costs, too.

- ✔ **Property tax:** As we mentioned above, if the previous owners of your new home paid any property taxes in advance, the tax paid is pro-rated to the closing date, and you have to reimburse the sellers. The reimbursement you make is called an *adjustment*. (See Chapter 10 for more information on adjustments.) Once you take possession of your new home, all bill payments become your responsibility.

✔ **Land transfer tax:** Depending on where you live, you may also have to pay a land transfer tax. The calculation and applicability of this tax varies across Canada. Provinces with a land transfer tax are: British Columbia, Manitoba, Ontario, Quebec, New Brunswick, and Nova Scotia. Your real estate agent or lawyer will be able to tell you what to expect. Generally, the amount of the land transfer tax works out to between 1 percent and 4 percent of the purchase price of your home. Some provinces will waive part or all of the provincial land transfer tax for first-time buyers. Your agent, lawyer, or bank can tell you about the rules (and exceptions) governing the land transfer tax in your province.

✔ **Goods and Services Tax:** If you're buying a new house, you will pay 7 percent GST on the price. This will also apply if you purchase a house that has been substantially renovated. If your home costs less than $450,000, you may be rebated up to 2.5 percent of the GST amount charged if the home will be your principal residence; ask your agent or lawyer for details.

Don't forget you pay GST on all services for all parties concerned: your lawyer, your agent, your inspector, your appraiser, and so on.

Little extras you may not have considered

We don't have to tell you Canada is a big country. Especially if you're moving from one province to another, keep the following points in mind:

✔ **Local oddities:** Ranging from the obvious to the unexpected, there are probably as many obscure local closing costs in various parts of Canada as there are regional accents. Your real estate agent and/or lawyer will advise which of the following might apply to your purchase: garbage/recycling charges, dyking fee if the area is below sea level, meter hook-up, tree planting, education development fees — the list goes on. If you're buying a resale house, the fees are pro-rated to your closing date.

✔ **Moving costs:** Do some research to arrive at a reasonable budget for your move. Of course, the exact amount will vary depending on how much stuff you have to move, how far you have to move it, and how much you're willing to move on your own. Expect moving rates to be higher at the end of a month or during the summer, as these are high-traffic times for moving companies. Try to plan ahead. Make some calls and request moving cost estimates. If you decide to rent a van or truck, reserve it in advance.

✔ **Utility charges:** Be prepared to pay connection fees for the hook-up of your telephone, cablevision, and hydro, and don't forget it costs $30 to get your mail re-directed by the post office.

Chapter 3

Your Mortgage Options

*I*n this chapter we introduce you to some of the finer points of mortgage options so that you can personalize your mortgage to fit your needs. We explain the various kinds of mortgages available: portable, assumable, vendor take back (VTB), and builder/developer interest rate buy down. Knowing the main features of each mortgage type helps you choose the right kind of financing to buy a home. We also give you advice for smooth sailing through the financing process: who to talk to, what you need to tell them, and what you should ask your lender. This chapter will help you secure the mortgage you need with the terms you want.

Addressing Your Mortgage Needs

If you want a mortgage, you just have to ask. And then your lender will ask you for a list of information about as long as your arm (keep reading for a comprehensive list). We'll help you to be prepared with your own list of questions to find out which lender you want to award your business. We'll also fill you in on all the financial terms and various options available so you'll be able to negotiate a mortgage with terms and conditions that suit your needs.

Types of mortgages

Mortgages break down into two types based on the amount of the down payment and therefore the amount of risk the lender is assuming by advancing you the money.

✔ **Conventional mortgages:** A *conventional mortgage* covers not more than 75 percent of the purchase price of the house or the appraised value, whichever is lower. (See Chapter 5 for more information on home appraisals.) So if you want to buy a $200,000 house, you need a $50,000 down payment (25 percent of purchase price) if you're applying for a conventional mortgage.

✔ **High-ratio mortgages:** *High-ratio mortgages* account for between 75 and 95 percent of the purchase price of a house or its appraised value, whichever is lower. So you can still buy the $200,000 house, even if you only have a $10,000 down payment (just 5 percent of the purchase price). High-ratio mortgages must be insured by either the Canada Mortgage and Housing Corporation (CMHC) or GE Capital Mortgage Insurance. This insurance protects the lender if you default on your mortgage payments. An insurance premium ranging from 0.5 percent to 3.75 percent of the mortgage amount, pre-determined by a sliding scale, will be added to your mortgage. You'll find more on different kinds of mortgage insurance later in this chapter.

Mortgage basics and jargon 101

One cool thing about getting a mortgage (unlike a computer, for example) is that every element has a clear purpose. Once you sit down with a pen and paper and calculator, or simply open your spreadsheet program on your computer and start plugging in numbers, it all starts to make sense really, really quickly. There are five chief elements to every mortgage:

✔ *Mortgage principal:* the amount of the loan

✔ *Interest:* the amount you pay for borrowing the money

✔ *Blended payments:* regular payments made toward the principal and the interest

✔ *Amortization period:* the period of time over which the calculation of the size of the required payments is based

✔ *Mortgage term:* the time period over which you agree to make payments to your lender under certain conditions — for example, at a specific interest rate

Mortgage principal

The total amount of the loan you get is called the *principal*. So if you need to borrow $150,000 to buy a house, then your principal is $150,000. The principal will become smaller and smaller as you pay off the loan.

Interest

Interest is the money you pay a lender in addition to repaying the principal of your loan — a sort of compensation so your lender profits from giving you a loan. The *interest rate*, calculated as a percentage of the principal, determines how much interest you pay the lender in each scheduled payment — the cost of borrowing the money.

People like to buy houses when interest rates are low because they can either buy a more expensive house than if the rates were higher, or they can pay off the mortgage more quickly. For example, at a 5 percent interest rate, a $100,000 principal would cost you approximately $5,000 in interest each year. At a 7 percent interest rate, you would pay approximately $7,000 in interest in a year on a principal of $100,000. That's a difference of approximately $2,000 a year that would go to paying off your principal in the low-interest-rate scenario rather than being gobbled up by interest.

Because interest rates rise and fall, some times are better than others for taking out a mortgage. To give yourself some stability, you can choose a *fixed rate mortgage* that allows you to lock in at a specific interest rate for a certain period of time (*mortgage term*). If interest rates are rising, you may want to lock in at a fixed rate so you know what your monthly costs will be over the term of your mortgage. Once a mortgage term expires, you can renegotiate your interest rate and the length of time (term) that you will make payments at the new rate. As you shop for mortgages, you can see that each lender specifies a certain interest rate for a certain term: Under most market conditions, the lower the fixed interest rate, the shorter the time period you can lock in to pay that rate. Take a look in the financial pages of the newspaper and you'll see a chart of mortgage rates that will look something like Table 3-1.

Table 3-1	Mortgage Rates						
Banks	**Variable Rate**	**6-month**	**1-year**	**2-year**	**3-year**	**4-year**	**5-year**
Banks "r" Us	6.5	7.5	7.9	8.1	8.3	8.4	8.5
Mr. Bank	6.45	7.45	7.5	7.75	7.8	8.9	8.0
Mortgage Trust	6.75	7.5	7.45	7.7	7.9	8.05	7.95

The first option you see in Table 3-1 is a *variable rate mortgage* that rises and falls alongside regular market rates. As you can see, a variable interest rate is usually significantly lower than the interest rate you could get for a longer period, such as a four- or five-year term. If interest rates are dropping and you don't mind a certain amount of risk, a variable interest rate may be a good option for you. However, if you take on a $100,000 mortgage at 6.5 percent and then interest rates double, you'll go from paying around $540 each month in interest to closer to $1,080. All of a sudden, locking in at 8.5 percent for five years of steady interest payments around $700 a month seems like a really nice, safe option. A longer term, fixed rate mortgage allows you to put a dent in your principal before facing the possibility of an increase in monthly payments.

Fixed rate mortgages are offered with a variety of options, so make sure you talk to several lenders to see who offers you the most competitive interest rates and terms.

Ask about mortgage products like a *variable rate mortgage*. This is a closed mortgage (usually set up as a five-year term, and fully open after the third anniversary) where the interest rate fluctuates with the market. Because these mortgages are usually open after the third anniversary, the borrower pays no penalty if they want to pay off some or all of the mortgage after three years. If the borrower thinks that rates are going to rise, most variable rate mortgages allow the borrower to lock into a fixed rate (usually a three-year term or longer) without penalty. These mortgages are a good bet if the borrower thinks that interest rates are going to remain stable or decrease in the future.

Also, find out about escape options. If you pay out this mortgage early (before the third anniversary), what penalty will be charged?

You may want to consider a *convertible mortgage*. Convertible mortgages are typically six-month or one-year fixed terms where the interest rate is fixed but you may lock into a longer term (typically a three-year term or longer) at any time without penalty.

Each lender will have subtle differences on how much extra money you may put against the principal (pre-payment options), with different payment schedules offered, and most importantly, they will give you a discount on the posted rates if and when you convert into a longer, fixed rate. Do your research before you commit to a mortgage — you have lots of options out there.

The way your lender adds up the interest you owe has a big impact on the amount of interest you pay over the life of the mortgage. If interest is *compounded* or added to your balance owing every day, you will pay more over the lifetime of the mortgage than if interest is compounded semi-annually. Most mortgages are compounded semi-annually, but your lender may offer you other options.

Blended payments

Mortgages are set up so you get a huge chunk of cash to buy your home and then you repay the money in regularly scheduled payments. In effect, each mortgage payment you make is split: One portion goes toward paying off the principal and the other portion goes toward paying off the interest. Hence, *blended payments*.

Every time your lender compounds the interest that you owe on your loan, your monthly blended payment changes. As you pay down your principal, the actual amount of your payment does not change but the portion of the payment that goes toward the principal increases and the amount that goes toward interest slowly decreases.

If your mortgage is $100,000 (with an 8 percent interest rate compounded semi-annually) to be paid over a period of 25 years, your monthly payments will be approximately $772. Table 3-2 illustrates this.

Table 3-2	Breakdown of Blended Payments		
Time Line	*Your Monthly Payment of $772*		
	Principal	*Interest*	*Balance Principal*
1 month	$105	$667	$99,895
6 months	$109	$663	$99,358
1 year	$113	$659	$98,691
5 years	$156	$616	$92,274
10 years	$232	$540	$80,763
20 years	$515	$257	$38,065

You can see that as you pay down the principal, the distribution of your payments changes. Gradually you begin paying more money toward the principal than toward the interest you owe to your lender.

The more frequently you make mortgage payments, the faster you pay down your principal, which means the more quickly you eliminate your mortgage, and the less interest you pay. Payment schedules can be arranged monthly, semi-monthly, biweekly (every two weeks), or weekly. Arrange with your lender to make payments as often as you can reasonably manage. If you can make weekly payments rather than monthly ones, you'll save thousands of dollars over the lifetime of the loan. Table 3-3 illustrates how making more frequent payments can really whittle down the time it takes to repay a mortgage.

Table 3-3	Mortgage Payment Frequency Comparison	
Calculations for a 25-year $200,000 mortgage at 8 percent interest, compounded semi-annually		
Payment Options	*Monthly Payments*	*Years to Repay Mortgage*
Monthly	$1,526	25
Biweekly	$763	20
Weekly	$382	19.8

Amortization period

The *amortization period* of your mortgage is the length of time on which the calculation of your monthly payments is based. The advantage of a longer amortization is that the monthly payments are smaller and therefore more manageable. The disadvantage is that the longer the amortization, the longer you carry a principal and therefore the more you pay in interest. And interest really adds up. You can see in Table 3-4 that the total interest on a 25-year amortization is almost double what you'd pay for a 15-year amortization.

Table 3-4	Amortization Payment Comparison		
Calculations for a $150,000 mortgage at 8.5 percent, compounded semi-annually			
Amortization	*Monthly Payments*	*Total Paid*	*Total Interest*
15 years	$1,464	$265,000	$115,000
20 years	$1,288	$310,000	$160,000
25 years	$1,193	$360,000	$210,000

Mortgage term

A *mortgage term* is the specific length of time you and your lender agree the mortgage will be subject to certain negotiated conditions, such as a certain interest rate. Terms range from 6 months to 10 years, but occasionally a lender will offer a 15- or 25-year term.

At the end of the term, you generally have the option to pay off your mortgage in full, or to renegotiate terms and conditions. If interest rates are ridiculously high, you will probably want to negotiate a shorter term, then arrange a longer term once rates are more favourable. If interest rates are deliciously low, lock in for the longest term you can negotiate. At the end of your mortgage term, you can also transfer your mortgage to another lender who may offer you a better rate, at no cost to you.

Attention first-time buyers!

If you're a first-time buyer (or haven't owned a home in the last five years), you can take advantage of the federal government's Home Buyers' Plan. You can borrow up to $20,000 per person from your RRSP without penalty to put toward a down payment. The money you withdraw must have been in your RRSP for at least 90 days, and, beginning two years after the date of the withdrawal, you must pay at least 1/15 of that amount back every year over the next 15 years. You don't pay income tax on it, unless you don't repay the RRSP loan in that time. Talk to your lender or lawyer for more information.

Your mortgage mission

Your mission, if you choose to accept it, is to get the best mortgage for your personal situation, while paying the least amount in interest. Use these strategies to keep your interest payments low:

- **Make as large a down payment as you comfortably can.** The larger your down payment, the smaller your loan (*principal*), and the less interest you'll have to pay.

- **Arrange to pay back the loan as quickly as possible.** The longer the *amortization period,* the life of the loan, the more interest you will pay.

- **Commit to making weekly or biweekly payments.** This will allow you to pay off the principal more quickly and therefore pay less interest on it.

- **Make extra payments whenever you can.** For example, when you get a cash bonus at work, win the lottery, inherit billions, or patent the software that will dawn a new era of bug-free programming, immediately put money toward your mortgage.

Even if you can't take advantage of these tricks, you don't have to bid your dream home goodbye. If you've done the research — and the math — you're sure to find a mortgage that fits.

Mortgage-a-rama: All the Nifty Options

Depending on how much of a down payment you can make, you will be eligible for either a conventional or a high-ratio mortgage. If you can bankroll a conventional mortgage, then you have at least 25 percent of the money needed to buy a new home. If your savings amount to between 5 and 24 percent of the home's price, then you can only qualify for a high-ratio mortgage. Either way, you still have a number of mortgage options to choose from.

Before you sign on the proverbial dotted line, you need to know your mortgage payment options. There are open mortgages, closed mortgages, and mortgages that offer something in between. Whichever option you choose affects how much money you pay over the lifetime of the loan and the flexibility of the terms. Some mortgages allow you to pay off your principal in lump sums as you wish and prepay your principal without any penalties. Other mortgages allow you to prepay only once a year on the anniversary date of the mortgage, or there may be no possibility of prepayment at all.

> ✔ **Open mortgages are flexible.** If you have an *open mortgage*, you can pay it off in full or in part at any time with no penalty. By chipping away at your principal early, you can save crazy amounts of money in interest. Of course, every penny you save in interest is a penny that doesn't get into your lender's hot little hands. That's why the average fixed interest rate quoted for an open mortgage is 0.4 to 0.6 percent higher than a closed mortgage for the same term (a specified period of time). The majority of open mortgages with a fixed interest rate are only available for a short term. Most variable-rate mortgages have a fixed five-year term, but may be open after three years, and as you can see in Table 3-1, variable rate mortgages are usually offered at a lower rate.

An open mortgage is a good choice if you're going to move again soon, if interest rates are expected to plummet, or if you're expecting a huge cash windfall once oil is discovered in the scrubland you bought near Medicine Hat. This kind of mortgage is good for the short term when rates are high, and it can usually be converted to a closed mortgage any time.

> ✔ **Closed mortgages are more stable.** The advantage of signing on to a closed mortgage for a *term*, or specified period of time, is that you will typically get lower interest rates and you will be able to budget for fixed, regular payments. The downside is that if you need to move before your term is up, or if you have extra cash, such as an income tax refund, which you'd like to put towards paying off a large portion of your principal, you may pay a penalty for this privilege. Most closed mortgages will give the borrower the ability to prepay ten to 20 percent of the outstanding balance without penalty, often on the anniversary date of the mortgage. In some cases, there may be restrictive conditions that prevent you from getting out of the mortgage altogether — even if you sell your home. Read the fine print before you sign!

Different financial institutions offer a range of mortgages involving different degrees of flexibility for prepayment. Even most closed mortgages have some prepayment options. You can make specified maximum prepayments, usually between 10 and 20 percent, once a year either on any payment date or on the anniversary date of the mortgage, and in some cases you can increase each payment. You're charged a penalty if you pay down more.

Portable mortgages

If your mortgage is *portable* you can take it with you to your new house. When you get ready to move, you'll be glad you asked about this option, especially if you negotiated great terms or if interest rates have gone up since you locked in to your current mortgage. Even if you're buying a more expensive house, it's still to your advantage. For example, if you have a $200,000 mortgage at 6 percent interest, and you're in the third year of a five-year term, you can take the mortgage with you to the $375,000 house you want to buy. You will need an additional $50,000 loan to be added to your principal. If the going rate on new loans is 8.5 percent interest for a three-year mortgage to match the remaining three years of your five-year term, you'll need to negotiate a blended rate on the new amount. The blended mortgage payment will be composed of two parts: your initial payment toward your $200,000 mortgage plus the second payment toward the additional $50,000 mortgage. Remember that your payment will be the result of "blending" two mortgage rates, and of course, your monthly payment itself will consist of interest and principal components.

Both conventional mortgages and high-ratio mortgages can be portable. However, if you have a portable high-ratio mortgage, the one element you can't transfer to a new property is the CMHC insurance premium required on all high-ratio mortgages. That insurance is property-specific, so you'll have to pay it again at your new digs.

Assumable mortgages

When you're buying a house, in addition to contacting financial institutions about mortgages, you may want to ask the sellers if they would allow you to take over their mortgage as part of the price you pay for the house. This option is quick and it saves you the usual costs of mortgage arrangements like appraisals and legal fees. It may also save you money in interest payments if the seller's mortgage rate is lower than what is currently available on the market. Do check the remaining term on the mortgage and discuss this option with your real estate agent or your real estate lawyer.

Having an *assumable mortgage* on your home means that when you want to sell it, you can have a qualified buyer assume the mortgage. This is a great incentive if you have good terms and conditions and it saves the buyer time finding financing and money setting it up. Most mortgages are assumable as long as the buyer can qualify for the mortgage amount.

You can still expect to go through some financial examination even if you're assuming the seller's mortgage. The lender will want to ensure that you meet the mortgage requirements. See "The information game: what your lender wants from you" later in this chapter for more on supplying personal and financial information to your lender.

Vendor (seller) take back mortgages (VTB)

In some cases, if the sellers are anxious to move, if the market is really sluggish, or if they're looking for a good investment once they get their equity out of the house, sellers may offer to lend you the money for your mortgage. This is called a *Vendor Take Back Mortgage*. The sellers may offer you lower rates than big financial institutions will, and they won't require the appraisals, inspections, survey fees, and financing fees you would expect to pay a traditional lender. You will, however, want to have your lawyer draw up the papers to guarantee that everything is in order. Some people will sell buyers a mortgage and then pass it on to a mortgage broker to handle instead of dealing with it personally.

Builder/developer interest rate buy down

If you're in the market for a new home, you may find builders and developers willing to offer mortgages with an *interest rate buy down*. This may take the form of a vendor take back mortgage where the builder/developer will lend you the money, or more commonly, the builder may buy down the interest rate of the mortgage you are getting from a bank — usually by 2 or 3 percent. This explains those newspaper ads for projects and subdivisions for sale with 3 percent mortgages.

The goal of the interest rate buy down is to sell real estate. The buy down will help a buyer who is having trouble qualifying for a mortgage at current rates, or allow a buyer to qualify for a larger mortgage and therefore buy a more expensive property in the development. Keep in mind, however, that these mortgages are typically not renewable. This means that once the term is up, your mortgage rate, and therefore your monthly payments, is likely to climb significantly.

Once that mortgage term is up, you need to negotiate new terms, and find a new lender — usually a bank. Naturally, your lender will do an appraisal of your property. You're expecting this. What you're perhaps not expecting is that your new lender may appraise your one- or two-year-old house at several thousand dollars less than the price you paid for it. Here's why this happens: Builders want to offer reduced interest rates as an incentive to buyers. However, they're still protecting their bottom lines, so to compensate for offering lower interest, they incorporate the cost of the *buy down* into the price of the house itself. This means you pay a larger principal on the builder's inflated price of the house.

The solution? Arrange a mortgage with a financial institution and ask the builder or developer to buy down the interest with your lender. This way, you can take advantage of the deal on the interest rate and you still have the option to renew your mortgage with your lender at the end of the term. Another option is to take your mortgage at market rates and ask the builder to lower the selling price accordingly.

WARNING!

"Can I have a mortgage with that, please?" Like car dealers, sellers can really sweeten the deal by helping you put the financing in place — an option that could save you a lot of money. This is the case with the last three mortgage options addressed: assumable mortgages, vendor take back mortgages, and builder/developer interest rate buy down. But buyer beware: Read the fine print and consult with your agent before accepting any seller's mortgage offer — it might just be too good to be true.

Mortgage Insurance

As you already know, mortgages are a big deal. If you have a high-ratio mortgage, your lender will require *mortgage loan insurance* from the Canada Mortgage and Housing Corporation (CMHC). A private company, GE Capital Mortgage Insurance, also offers mortgage insurance at the same rates as the CMHC, but offers a couple of competitive differences. For example, GE Capital may consider up to 50 percent of the rent from an unauthorized suite as income, while the CMHC will not consider any revenue from an unauthorized suite. Mortgage insurance covers your lender in case you default on your payments. You may also choose to purchase *mortgage life insurance*. This way, if something happens to you, your mortgage payments will be made by the insurance company and not be a burden on your family (see "Mortgage Life Insurance" on the next page).

High-ratio mortgage insurance

If you have a down payment of less than 25 percent of the purchase price of your house, then you're eligible for a high-ratio mortgage. However, lenders will require that you have mortgage insurance so their risk is protected. The high-ratio insurance is arranged by the lender.

How to qualify for high-ratio mortgage insurance

Many buyers have high-ratio mortgage insurance coverage through the Canada Mortgage and Housing Corporation. (See Appendix C for a list of provincial CMHC offices across Canada.) The only alternative is GE Capital Mortgage Insurance, and both institutions have four standard eligibility requirements:

- The home you're buying will be your principal residence.

- The home you're buying is in Canada.

- Your Gross Debt Service Ratio is not more than approximately 30 percent. In other words, the total you spend on housing (including principal and interest, property taxes, heating, and 50 percent of condo fees) is not more than approximately 30 percent of your gross (pre-tax) household income. (See Chapter 2 for help in determining your Gross Debt Service.)

- Your Total Debt Service Ratio, including any car loans, student loans, and credit card debt, is not more than 40 percent of your gross (pre-tax) household income. (See Chapter 2 for details on calculating your Total Debt Service.)

Investors buying an investment property that will not be their principal residence can also get a high-ratio mortgage, but the insurance premium will be higher, up to 5 percent of the mortgage amount.

What high-ratio mortgage insurance will cost you

The premium for high-ratio mortgage insurance is typically 0.5 to 3.75 percent of the price you pay for your new home. CMHC also charges a $75 application fee provided that you include a valid appraisal with your application. If you are buying a house that is listed on the Multiple Listing Service (MLS) system (see Chapter 17 for information on MLS listings) the CMHC fee will be $165, but no appraisal will be necessary. If the house you are buying is not an MLS listing, you will be charged the $75 application fee plus $165 for the appraisal. (See Chapter 5 for advice on hiring an appraiser.)

Mortgage life insurance

Mortgage life insurance guarantees your mortgage will be paid in full if you die. Some lenders offer this insurance and will add the premium to your mortgage payments. It's still a good idea to shop around through an insurance broker for the best rates, though. You may want to get insurance coverage for all parties responsible for the mortgage (for example, if your home is in your name and your spouse's, both of you should be insured).

The lender may offer insurance where they will pay off the balance of your mortgage upon your death. This is commonly referred to as *declining balance insurance*. However, you may also want to consider *regular term insurance*. The premiums should be comparable to declining balance insurance, but this policy covers you for the full amount of your mortgage should you pass away — not just the outstanding balance.

Who Ya Gonna Call?

Mortgages are a good business. That's why so many institutions besides banks have got in on the show. This is good for you because if you don't find the terms and conditions you want in one place, you can shop around. And once you've decided whom you want to do business with, then you can haggle for the options you want.

You do not need to have an account with an institution to qualify for a mortgage there. And there is no reason to limit yourself to banks and trust companies in your mortgage hunt. Credit unions, caisses populaires, and pension funds also supply mortgages and many don't require that you be a member in order to be eligible. You can also look to insurance companies, finance companies, and private lenders.

Mortgage brokers can also be a great resource. Mortgage brokers are not affiliated with any particular institution; they can match you with the lender who gives the best terms and rates for your situation. In addition to banks, trust companies, pension funds, and private lenders, mortgage brokers can access real estate syndicates and foreign banks. The lender typically pays mortgage brokers a finder's fee (a percentage of your mortgage). However, if your credit history is particularly spotty you may be asked to pay a fee to the mortgage broker and/or lender.

The information game: What your lender wants from you

Once you've become intimate with your financial life (we show you how in Chapter 2) and the world of mortgages, it's time to cozy up to your lender — often known as "the bank." Basically, your lender needs two things from you — detailed personal information and paperwork. Don't take the probing questions personally. Everyone goes through the same process, whether it's Elizabeth R, Queen of England, or Gaia Sandalfoot, just off the commune.

Tell us about yourself

Prospective lenders will want to know all about you. They'll ask about your financial status and employment as well as your personal information and history. Expect questions like these:

> ✔ **What is your age, marital status, number of dependants? Where do you work? What is your position? How long have you been with the company? What is your employment history?** Unless you're self-employed, you will probably need a letter from your employer confirming your position with the company. If you are self-employed, you should bring your tax assessments (not your tax returns) from the last two years to confirm your earnings.

✔ **What is your gross (pre-tax) family income?** You may need proof of income like a T-4 slip or, if you're self-employed, personal income tax returns. You will also be asked to show proof of other sources of income from pensions and rental property.

✔ **What do you currently spend on housing? If you're a homeowner, what is the current market value of your house?** You may have to provide copies of your rental lease agreement for the apartment or suite you're renting or a copy of your current mortgage.

✔ **Do you have funds for a down payment?** The lender wants to ensure that your down payment is your own money (and not a loan), so you will probably have to show, through bank records, that your down payment was accumulative or in your bank account for at least three months. If the down payment is a gift from dear old Aunt Bibi, then you'll need a letter from her confirming that the money is not a loan. You'll also be required to demonstrate that the money has been deposited to your account. You also may have to provide current banking information.

✔ **What assets do you have and what is the value of each one?** You can include vehicles, properties, and investments.

✔ **What liabilities do you have?** You can include credit card balances, car loans, student loans, and lines of credit.

Lenders will also ask your consent to do a credit check. A credit check may give you a good or bad credit rating depending on your financial history. We recommend you contact a credit-reporting agency, such as Equifax Canada or your local credit bureau, to obtain a copy of your credit report. Examine it in detail. If you find inaccurate or outdated information in the report, you can have those items corrected or removed to make your credit rating as glowing as it can possibly be. See Appendix C for contact information regarding Equifax Canada, not to mention (but we'll mention it again) many other useful resources dealing with home buying and selling.

Let's have it in writing please: The paperwork

Most banks can pre-approve your mortgage over the phone. You may have to fax them the required paperwork, and in return, they will fax you a written confirmation outlining the terms of your mortgage pre-approval. Often you will not meet your banker until you receive the sellers' acceptance of your offer to purchase their home, and you're ready to seal the deal by finalizing all the financing.

Getting all the papers together for a mortgage is just the beginning of a long paper shuffle you will be doing until you finally get the keys to your new home. Be prepared with the following documents when you meet with your lender:

✔ Copy of a recent appraisal for the home you're buying (if requested — the bank may already have ordered it for you)

✔ Copy of the property listing

✔ Copy of the Agreement of Purchase and Sale (for a resale house)

✔ Plans and cost estimates if you're buying a new house (construction loans only)

✔ Certificate for well water and septic system (if applicable)

✔ Condominium financial statements (if applicable)

✔ Survey certificate

Changing places: Questioning your lender

Just because you're the one requesting money doesn't mean you can't ask questions. Lenders profit from your business, so don't be afraid to bring up your concerns. You should expect to be answered directly in a courteous manner and you should reply to your lender's questions in kind. Keep a list and have paper with you to use in meetings or on the telephone so you can be sure to cover all the bases.

Stay cool and calm as you chat with prospective lenders. Remember, you're shopping for a mortgage, not begging for one. Keep this list handy to be sure you ask the right questions:

✔ **What is your name, title, and phone number?** Start with the basics.

✔ **Is all my information kept confidential?** A reputable mortgage lender will not share your information indiscriminately.

✔ **What mortgage types and terms do you have available? Do you have any that are specifically designed for my situation?** Many major banks have special offers for first-time homebuyers, for example.

✔ **What are your current mortgage rates?** Compare the rate offered on closed mortgages to the rate offered for open mortgages. An open mortgage gives you more flexibility and can save you money, but usually has a higher interest rate than a closed mortgage, as explained earlier in this chapter.

✔ **How are you making your mortgages competitive with other lending institutions? Are any discounts or cash-back options available?** Some lenders lower their interest rate a bit if you ask nicely or show them lower rates from the competition; other lenders offer you a percentage off your mortgage up front — usually between 1 to 3 percent as a cash-back program — to help you with your closing costs.

✔ **What mortgage fees do you charge? Is there a mortgage application fee?** Make sure you know what kind of costs your lender expects you to cover.

✔ **Do you pre-approve mortgages? Is there a fee for this?** Most institutions do not charge a pre-approval application fee.

✔ **How long will it take to process my loan request? Once it is approved, how long should I allow before I close the deal?** When you set your closing dates for the purchase of a new home, the schedule for your transfer of funds is crucial. Know what to expect.

✔ **How is the interest compounded?** Most lenders compound interest semi-annually (every six months). Ask if your lender offers any other compounding options that may save you money.

✔ **Can I convert from a variable to a fixed rate mortgage?** As explained earlier in this chapter, if you choose a variable rate mortgage (VRM) you're vulnerable to fluctuations in the current interest rate. When interest rates rise you pay higher mortgage payments; when rates fall you pay less. You want the option to convert your VRM to a fixed rate mortgage if interest begins to climb significantly.

✔ **What are my payment options?** As detailed earlier in this chapter, to save yourself a lot of money in the long run, you should make payments as often as you can — weekly is best.

✔ **Can I pay off the mortgage early? Is there a penalty for this? Can I pay down some of the principal without penalty? How much a year?** You also want to have the option to make an extra lump sum payment toward your mortgage principal, at least once or twice a year to help you save on the interest.

✔ **Is mortgage life insurance available with your mortgages? Will it cover both my partner and me?** You want to protect your family members in case something happens to you. But check the cost. A separate insurer may offer lower insurance premiums for the same coverage.

✔ **If my credit rating is not acceptable at this point, what can I do to improve it? Or what options do I have?** Be prepared: Any lender who offers mortgages will check your credit rating.

Chapter 4

Finding Your Kind of Home

· ·

In This Chapter

▶ The right fit — what type of home is for you?

▶ Dealing with neighbours

▶ Earning a little extra: Basement suites, duplexes, and triplexes

▶ Considering condominiums

▶ Joining a co-op

· ·

*Y*our choice of home reflects your personality and your lifestyle. Although you may think there are relatively few basic housing options, many homes on the market are a mixture of two or more types. The variety available is impressive, so it's a good idea to know what you're looking for in advance.

In this chapter we help you out by listing some common advantages and disadvantages of the different home types. It's up to you to think long and hard about your individual situation and what makes sense for you. If you're the type of person who likes to hop in the shower at 6:00 a.m., crank up the stereo, and sing at the top of your lungs, you can probably eliminate an apartment-style condominium as an option. But on the other hand, if you would rather cut off your own toes than rake leaves or shovel snow, owning a condo with a year-round maintenance crew may be right up your alley.

Houses: So Many Choices . . .

Most people have a strong preference for either apartment-style condominiums or houses. Chances are, you already know which is more to your taste (if not, start thinking about it right now). Even if you've decided you want a house to call home, there are additional considerations. Do you want a new house? A resale house? A duplex? A detached house?

Ask yourself what's most important to you when it comes to your living space. Decide which kinds of homes are acceptable before you start looking seriously, and tell your agent what your priorities are and which types of houses will best suit your needs and tastes.

Location may determine what you can afford — for example, a semi-detached half-duplex in the best part of town or a detached home in a good but not great part of town. Set your priorities and determine what you really want. Chapter 6 guides you through this decision-making process.

Pros and cons of buying a brand new home

Say you've decided that you must have everything fresh and new in order to be happy with your home-buying purchase. There are two ways to buy new: buy a vacant lot and build your house yourself or buy a new home that's already been finished by a builder or developer. Either situation has some major advantages and disadvantages.

Good reasons to buy new

If you're in the market for a new home as opposed to a resale house, you probably have a pretty clear idea of why. Here are the key advantages of buying a new house.

- ✔ **Safety standards:** Your house will meet the most recent standards in safety and energy-efficiency — saving you money in the long run. Your home will probably also be more technologically up-to-date, which means you don't have to do any major rewiring to get the Internet via cable, or run phone lines from the bedroom to the basement.

- ✔ **Choice of materials:** You get to see the builder's specs, so you know exactly what you're getting — construction materials, operating systems, and so on.

- ✔ **New Home Warranty Program:** You may be eligible for a new home-owner's comprehensive warranty that covers defects in materials and construction, and may also cover building code violations and major structural defects. You may be eligible for the *New Home Warranty Program* (NHWP) in your province. You'll find more information on the NHWP in Chapter 11.

- ✔ **Newness:** There is no previous wear and tear on the structural components, operational systems, or appliances, assuming, of course, you don't buy used appliances for your new home.

✔ **Tax savings:** You may not have to pay the land transfer tax (also called the property transfer tax) that applies in many provinces when property changes ownership (see Chapter 2 for more information on this closing cost). If you are building your home yourself, you may pay the land transfer tax on the value of the land and not on the value of the finished house. Provinces with a land transfer tax are: British Columbia, Manitoba, Ontario, Quebec, New Brunswick, and Nova Scotia. Your agent or lawyer can advise you about land transfer taxes in your particular province.

✔ **Modern construction:** Improvements in home-building techniques and technology over the years may mean you're getting better-quality construction. You also get a home designed with contemporary needs in mind (in other words, you get big closets!).

When your new home is finished, the builder will take you on one last tour before you take possession of the house. This allows you to see for yourself that everything contracted has been done properly. But keep in mind that this tour in no way replaces a professional inspection. See Chapter 11 for more information on inspections.

Difficulties of buying new

If you're buying in a newly developed neighbourhood, chances are it will not look exactly like the promotional material. Even a new house in an established neighbourhood may not look exactly like the artist's rendering that first caught your eye. You may encounter several other potential drawbacks of buying a new home:

✔ **Lack of services:** The surrounding neighbourhood may not yet be equipped with accessible public transportation, schools, groceries, shopping, or other amenities which are standard in an established area.

✔ **Distance:** New subdivisions and lots are generally found outside of densely populated regions, so you may not be able to build or buy a new house in the urban area of your choice.

✔ **Uncertainty about your neighbours:** You won't know in advance what the neighbours are like. Will they be organizing all-night street dances every time there's a full moon? This uncertainty may be particularly true in an apartment building if a number of the suites are sold to investors who will rent them out.

✔ **Taxes:** Property taxes may be higher in a newly developed area that requires roads, schools, sewers, and so on. Also, you likely have to pay 7 percent GST on the purchase of a new home (see Chapter 2 for more information on GST on new houses).

✔ **Fixed prices:** If you're buying in a development, the price of the homes is usually not negotiable and you may have to go through the developer's agent.

> ✔ **Timing:** You may end up constantly scanning the news about the latest construction strike because it has an impact on the finishing date of your home.
>
> ✔ **Construction inconvenience:** You may have to put up with noise and dust created by the continual construction in the area.
>
> ✔ **Undeveloped landscape:** You may move into your home and find that you're surrounded by mud fields and a giant dirt heap with no sidewalks or lawn anywhere in sight. With time you can, of course, add your own landscaping, but lush greenery will take awhile to create.

You can minimize the stress of added expenses by anticipating that they will crop up and by doing your research. Make sure you fully understand all the costs associated with building — get a *detailed* breakdown of all estimated costs from your builder so you know exactly what is covered and what is optional or extra. The contract to build a house will include a lengthy specification list that can run 10 to 15 pages. Everything down to the towel racks should be outlined. If you're doing the building yourself, make up your own specification list.

As for delays in the building process, there's not really much you can do if the porcelain tiles or sleek German faucets don't arrive on time. And if Mother Nature decides she doesn't want you to move in until 2012, you'll just have to wait. Have a contingency plan in the event that your new home is not fit for habitation on time.

Building it yourself

So you've been watching those specials on the Home and Garden channel and you think you're ready to build your dream house with your own two hands? Hang on there, Miss Do-It-Yourself, you should keep a few things in mind before you hit the hardware store to pick up your personalized toolbelt. Specific considerations — both positive and negative — for the "build-it-yourself" case include:

> ✔ **Making it exactly what you want:** You get to choose and/or design the actual structure and components of your home — the building materials, the position on the lot, and so many other features. In a nutshell, you get what you want.
>
> ✔ **Scheduling and planning risks:** Delays and extra expenses are practically guaranteed. As with renovating, building almost always costs more than you think it will initially and it almost always takes longer than you first estimate.

Keep a "reserve fund" or be sure that you can access further funds should the need arise — you don't want to create delays by not having the money to complete the building once it's begun. We suggest padding your building budget by an extra 10 to 15 percent just in case.

Country living in a new home

If you're planning to build a fabulous ranch house so far away from civilization that you forget the rest of the world exists, keep these extra considerations in mind:

- **Electricity and phones:** Bringing in phone and hydro lines may cost you extra. (Nowadays, alternative energy sources are available that may be more amenable to country life, such as wind-powered generators. The popularity of this renewable and emission-free method has been rising steadily in recent years, and it is capable of powering a house equipped with all the usual energy-efficient appliances.)

- **Water:** Water quality may be an issue, and you may have to spring for a proper filtration system.

- **Extra taxes:** If you are in a relatively isolated and unincorporated area, services such as road maintenance and schools may be supported by a small population base, requiring a higher per capita tax burden to maintain even a minimal level of services.

- **Garbage:** As with any home in the boondocks, new or resale, garbage and recycling pickup may be unavailable.

- **Snow removal:** You may need to organize and pay for snow removal yourself, or with others who share your road.

- **Sewage and plumbing:** Building a septic system or hooking up to a sewage line can be extremely expensive and may require substantial preliminary work (researching the water table and underground water flows). In Chapter 7 we cover all the details to ensure your septic system is in acceptable condition.

Resale houses

Suppose you don't feel like dealing with the hassle of building a new home, and new houses or subdivisions don't appeal to you. Fortunately, there are plenty of resale houses on the market. (Whether these are in your favourite region is another question.) You can expect some of the following perks from buying one of these pre-existing beauties.

- **Convenience:** The neighbourhood amenities, like public transportation, schools, parks, shopping, groceries, and so on will already be established.

- **Luxuries:** Extras that would put a serious strain on your wallet to build or buy new (such as a swimming pool, satellite dish, hot tub, custom cabinetry, or a finished basement) may come with the house.

- ✔ **Character:** Older homes may have unique or antique-quality features that give them character and add to the potential resale value.

- ✔ **Tax savings:** You don't pay GST on the purchase of a resale home (unless substantial renovations were done, in effect making the house "count" as new).

- ✔ **Landscaping:** Lawns and gardens will probably be well established.

- ✔ **Immediate readiness:** You can move into a resale home right away in most cases. Things like light fixtures and carpeting are already installed, and usually what you see is what you get. With a good inspection, there should be few surprises once you move in. In a new home, what you picture in your mind may not be the reality when building is complete.

Every rose has its thorn, too — sometimes more than one. Balancing off the advantages listed above, you may have to deal with some of the following difficulties:

- ✔ **Less energy efficiency:** Older houses are usually less energy-efficient, utilities may cost more, or upgrades may be needed in the not-too-distant future.

- ✔ **Repairs needed:** Previous wear and tear on the house may make maintenance more expensive.

- ✔ **Décor challenges:** A used home may not feel like your own until you redecorate.

- ✔ **Space constraints:** Older homes are often smaller than newer ones: hallways, rooms, and closets can sometimes feel like they were meant for Smurfs rather than the average-sized Canadian; many basements will not have even 6-foot-high ceilings.

- ✔ **Modern updates needed:** Minor renovations or repairs may be necessary to accommodate your lifestyle, or to meet new safety or building codes.

- ✔ **Structural concerns:** You have no say in the layout or what building materials are used, so you may not be entirely satisfied with the structure of the home.

- ✔ **Tax:** Land transfer tax may apply on the purchase, depending on the province. Talk to your agent or lawyer about this.

Ready to move in or willing to fix it up: the right resale home for you

Like most significant questions, the answer to whether buying a fixer-upper is a good idea is "that depends." Most resale homes can be put into one of three categories: move-in condition, "handyman special," or adequate condition (meaning somewhere in-between).

Ready to move in

Houses in move-in condition are exactly that — ready for you to drag the furniture up the front steps and settle in. A house in move-in condition may have been repaired or renovated to bring it up to tip-top shape. Buyers pay more for a premium house — but many prefer a lower price and the chance to do upgrades their way, rather than a higher price and lots of sparkling new designer cabinetry that's totally at odds with their taste. There is nothing worse than a house with a new $20,000 custom kitchen tiled from floor to ceiling in colours you can't stand.

Needs care and attention

A handyman special is a house that is cheaper because it needs some work — anything involving a plumbing tune-up to a major overhaul might fall into this category.

A handyman special is potentially a bargain if and *only* if the defects are fixable — and fixable within a reasonable budget. If the defects include close proximity to a known brothel, there's nothing you can do to bring up the property value, so don't even consider it. But if the only problems are those you can actually do something about — without having to pawn a few organs — then feel free to think about it seriously.

Let's assume that the defects are fixable and it would be possible to increase the property value. If you're an electrician, plumber, or carpenter, for example, involving yourself in this sort of venture might be worthwhile — *if* you have the time. But, whatever tasks you don't have the skill, expertise, or time to manage yourself, you will have to pay someone else to handle. That means you will be financially responsible for materials, labour, tax, and other expenses. That can get very expensive, very quickly.

For first-time homebuyers, who generally have enough trouble finding money for the down payment, it's not advisable to invest in a house that needs a lot of work. But don't let this discourage you from buying one of the cheaper houses on the block — that's *always* a smart move, since the value will be affected positively by the more expensive neighbouring houses.

Many people buy houses that badly need renovation to fix them up and then sell for a profit. If you plan to sell the house in the future, be careful — if your upgrades result in the house becoming the most expensive on your street, you won't recoup the money you put into renovating.

Ask your agent, or investigate on your own, the price range of houses in your vicinity. If your $200,000 house is the cheapest on the block, and the most expensive house is $560,000, you may be in a good position to renovate and sell for a profit. But if you pay $200,000, do major renovations, and then ask for $400,000 — while every other house on the block is valued around $275,000 — you simply won't be able to sell unless you drop the price. If you are not using an agent, an appraiser will use comparable current listings and recent sales to help you determine market value in your area.

Never spend more on renovations than the difference between the value of your home and the value of other houses around it. For example, if the house you're thinking about buying is worth $225,000, and it's the cheapest on the block by $75,000, don't plan to spend more than $75,000 on renovations. (Really, you shouldn't plan to spend more than $15,000 to $30,000 if you want to make a reasonable profit on the resale.) Get detailed estimates of how much your intended renovations will cost — then compare the money you'll put into your home (buying costs + renovation costs) to the neighbouring home values. Alternatively, you can figure out how much you could spend on renovations without going over the average value of a home in your area, and then find out what you can get for that much money. Will that be enough to turn the house into the dream palace you intended? If not, don't buy it. If you're buying with the intention of reselling, will it be enough to upgrade so that the new selling price will make you a profit? If not, don't buy it.

Your average resale home

Most resale houses will fall into the category of adequate condition — houses that are in good condition structurally and are certainly liveable, but will need to be recarpeted, repainted, or redecorated to become *your* home. Don't be afraid to tackle cosmetic changes — in fact, expect it. Although making structural, plumbing, or electrical repairs to your new home would be cause for worry, basic finishing changes are par for the course. Putting a fresh coat of paint here and there, or refinishing the hardwood floors is most often a worthwhile expense. If you're uncertain what everything will cost, make your offer subject to receiving and approving a contractor's or architect's estimate before committing to the purchase.

Your Neighbours: How Close Is Too Close?

Whether you're buying new or resale, you need to think about your neighbours and how much room you'd like in between your home and theirs. There are varying degrees of "attachment" — the four most common are the following:

- **Single-family detached:** A *single-family detached* house sits by itself on its own lot. Ownership includes the entire structure and the lot. The owner or owners are responsible for all repairs and maintenance, property taxes, and associated costs.

- **Semi-detached:** *Semi-detached* houses are joined by a shared wall, but the structure as a whole (i.e., both units) is independent of other houses on the street. Ownership includes your half of the structure and land, and you're responsible for all the costs and work associated with that half.

- **Link houses or carriage houses:** *Link houses* or *carriage houses* share a garage — usually separated into two garages that share a common wall — that provides a joint access route to the backyard. Often these houses share a basement wall so that they seem detached to passers-by. Ownership and responsibilities are similar to semi-detached houses.

- **Rowhouses or townhouses:** *Rowhouses* or *townhouses* share a common wall on one or both sides. You may have full ownership of a townhouse, although in some cases, townhouses are condominiums. It is not uncommon for a group of independently owned townhouses to have a housing association that will collect dues and handle some of the maintenance for the whole row.

- **Apartment units or condos:** *Apartment units*, also known as *condos*, are in low-rise or high-rise buildings that usually offer a secure entrance, elevators, and shared common areas — and lots of neighbours. We'll talk more about condos later in this chapter.

Obviously, the closer your house is to your neighbours, the more exposed you are to potential noise and disturbances. Remember, sound does not travel in only one direction. Your neighbours' teenagers may drive you insane with loud music and frequent parties, but what sounds from your house drive them crazy? If your two dogs spend their days howling for you to come back from work, preventing the writer next door from completing her screenplay, you have a problem. If you can show your neighbours consideration, they will probably show you the same respect.

Also, if you buy a home built close to your neighbours, the yard is generally quite small — this can be a good or a bad thing, depending on how you feel about yard work. You will also limit your options to expand your living space. Detached houses are easier to renovate.

Money-Making as a Homeowner

Not all properties are purchased as a principal residence. Investors buy properties with the intention of renting them out, with the tenants paying off the owners' mortgage so that in the long run the owner may have a clear title property. Investors will need a higher down payment to ensure the rent covers the expenses (property taxes, maintenance, and insurance, for example) and banks offer investors a number of mortgage options depending on the investors' track record and other holdings.

Many homebuyers may need the revenue from a basement suite to help them afford the house of their dreams. Local bylaws and regulations regarding basement suites vary across Canada and you should check with the local authorities before buying a house with one. Check with your bank if you will be relying on the revenue from a basement suite. Some banks will consider the rent from a basement suite as income, even if the basement suite is illegal.

A property with two legal suites is called a duplex, and three suites is a triplex. Duplexes are homes that are split into two units, often one above the other, where one of the units is intended as the owner's residence, the other as a rental unit. Duplexes are usually detached houses, but can occasionally be townhouses as well. The owner of the duplex is responsible for all expenses and maintenance associated with the structure and lot (minus, of course, whatever costs are picked up by the tenants). If the owner intends to live in one of the units, financing the purchase of a duplex should be similar to the purchase of a single home, although some banks may require a higher down payment (and high-ratio CMHC insurance may not be available) for a duplex or triplex. Banks will consider the rent from legal suites (and sometimes from unauthorized suites) as income, which will help the buyer qualify for a mortgage they could not otherwise afford.

Obviously, the advantage of owning a duplex is that it will provide additional income via your tenants' rent. Buying a duplex can be a good long-term investment too — the income generated by the rental unit can increase the resale value of the property. The potential profit from renting will depend on location. Before you buy a duplex, you need to know what average rents are in the area.

It's also possible to buy a *half-duplex* where each half of a building is owner-occupied. Half-duplexes can be side by side, top and bottom, or front to back, to form a two-unit apartment building with many of the maintenance costs split between the two owners.

Talk to a lawyer about the legalities of buying a rental property. If the rental suite currently has tenants, you need to know where you stand. Confirm what your rights are according to the Landlord and Tenants' Act in your province. Find out about the maximum legal rent for a suite in the duplex. Make sure the home has been registered as a duplex, since this will tell you whether it's legal to rent out part of the house. Just because the previous owner rented out the basement doesn't mean it was allowed. The Blue Pages in the phone book will list the phone number for the provincial Tenancy Branch, which can answer any questions about tenant and landlord rights and the paperwork necessary to comply with the provincial legislation.

Buying a duplex does not often go as swimmingly as planned. Most people don't realize how much work, or how expensive, it is to be a landlord. Don't take the responsibility lightly. If your tenant's toilet springs a leak, you have to look after it, or if they're late with the rent, you have to deal with the financial strain.

Your financial advisor can tell you how owning a rental property will affect your income taxes — both now and when you sell. If you claim part of a home's rental income as personal income and write off part of your home expenses, this may affect your claim to principal residence tax exemption should you realize a profit when you sell the house. (See Chapter 14 for details on the tax benefits of the principal residence exemption.)

Condominiums

You love being surrounded by others; you love having the gym a short elevator ride away; you love the security of a 24-hour doorman; you love the view from the 27th floor; and you love not having to worry about yard work. You're a condo dweller through and through.

A common misconception is that condominium complexes are all high-rise blocks with little character or individuality. "Condominium" refers *only* to a type of ownership, *not* to a type of architecture. Condo owners have sole ownership of their individual units (which could be townhouses), and they share ownership of common areas with other unit owners.

Weighing the ups and downs of condo living

Whether you buy into a new *condominium corporation* (the organization responsible for the condominium's upkeep) or an established one, there are several advantages to condo living:

- ✔ **Greater security:** Many condominium residences have a 24-hour concierge to screen visitors to the building. In a modern condominium complex, you can expect security cameras and coded passes for access to the building and garage.

- ✔ **Low maintenance:** You have less outside maintenance to do — no house painting in the blistering summer sun for you! In most cases, yard work is also a thing of the past for a new condo owner.

- ✔ **Amenities:** Much like a university residence, a condominium may feature on-site amenities such as a convenience store, gym, laundry facilities, and sometimes even a putting green!

- ✔ **Sense of community:** Ideally, you'll find a condominium has an interactive community of people living within it. Although you may not get along with everyone at the condo meetings, there's a good chance you'll discover a supportive group of residents who make you feel at home.

But before you start rubbing your hands together anticipating your carefree lifestyle as a condominium owner, let us bring to light a few of the downsides as well:

- ✔ **Less autonomy:** You can't always do exactly what you like — you may not be able to hang bright curtains in your windows, blast the radio on your balcony, or accept the little kitten your friend brings for your birthday.

- ✔ **Unpleasant restrictions:** You may have to accept inflexible rules or disagreeable decisions made by your condo corporation. You may be forced to compromise on rules governing conduct of condo owners or issues regarding the building structure or facilities (for example, if everyone in your condo complex except you votes in favour of erecting a 20-foot-tall gold statue in the lobby, you're stuck paying for your share of the cost regardless).

- ✔ **Proximity to neighbours:** Your home will be very close to your neighbours, and you may not get along with them — but you still share a business and managerial role with them in the condominium corporation.

- ✔ **Maintenance concerns:** You must depend on the condominium corporation to handle building repairs and to be financially responsible with your maintenance fees.

- ✔ **Financial risk:** You share responsibility for large, unexpected repair bills — for example, if your Vancouver condo springs an ominous leak.

The condominium corporation

When you buy a condo you're buying a share of the condominium corporation. As a unit owner and shareholder, you have some say in how the condominium corporation, sometimes called the *condo corporation*, conducts itself. The corporation has a board of directors that is elected by the shareholders/owners. Usually, ownership of one unit equals one vote.

The condo corporation is the organization that's responsible for funding many of the improvements or repairs of the structure or surrounding land. The *Condominium Certificate* lays out exactly which expenses are the responsibility of the corporation, which fall to individual owners, and which will be shared by all unit owners and how those shared costs will be proportioned (it will also lay out the bylaws that govern conduct of unit owners and how the corporation is run). The certificate will tell you what your monthly condo fees will be for shared expenses, what your individual unit costs will be, and what the financial status of the corporation is — especially regarding the *reserve fund*. A reserve fund is money put away by the corporation for any repairs or upgrades that become necessary. Usually, a portion of your monthly condo fee goes into this fund. It is crucial that your corporation has a well-maintained reserve fund.

Although the board of directors may be composed of condominium unit owners, it's quite common for a board to hire professional property managers to act under their supervision. The corporation has a legal obligation to hold regular meetings that all unit owners can attend. It's your right to have information about how the corporation is run, but it's also your responsibility to take an active role in this process.

You have the right to ask the developer for a copy of the *proposed Condominium Certificate*. (If there is *no* proposed Condominium Certificate, get out as fast as you can!) Have this document reviewed by a lawyer before agreeing to purchase a unit.

New versus established condos

There is always some uncertainty about the stability of a new corporation — you cannot be sure that you will have the best property managers or a competent board of directors. If the corporation is mismanaged or, worse, has insufficient funds, you're in serious trouble should your condo building require repairs, renovations, or upgrades. In this situation, unit owners may be forced to foot the entire bill and the resale value of the unit may be drastically reduced.

Buying from an established condo corporation is the safest financial course. You will have access to minutes of the building meetings to see how the corporation has responded in the past when repairs were necessary or emergencies arose. You can find out how well the reserve fund has been maintained, how well the governing body has responded to owners' requests for upgrades, and if condo fees have increased or are about to increase because of planned renovations. An established condo corporation has a track record you can look to for assurance that the property managers have unit owners' best interests at heart. Most of this information will be provided by the listing agent if you show serious interest in the condo. You may have to make an offer "subject to you approving the buildings records etc." to get everything you need. That means peace of mind that you're making a sound investment.

The downside to buying an older condo is that fixtures and appliances may be reaching the end of their lifespans. For example, if the toilet or ceiling fan breaks down, you'll probably have to pay for the repair or replacement.

Rules to live by

In addition to the financial details of ownership, the Condominium Certificate lays out the bylaws that are the code of conduct for residents. It stipulates how many units can be rented and whether pets are allowed, among other things. For either a new or established development, pay close attention to these bylaws. But as with any rules, the bylaws are only good insofar as they are enforced. This is where the established complexes gain the advantage.

With a new complex, you have to assume that the proposed rules (if there are any) will be enforced. Your province's legislation regarding condominiums should form the basis of the bylaws. When you decide to buy a new condominium you have no way of knowing who will buy in that complex and how the rules will change in accordance with the other residents' tastes and demands. On the other hand, the proposed bylaws may not change after you move in, but they may not be enforced by the corporation or, more importantly, by the other residents.

If a big selling point with you is the proposed bylaw stating that there will be "quiet hours" after 10:00 p.m., you have no guarantee that this will be enforced. If some residents ignore the rule, and other residents don't seem to care, you may simply have to put up with noise all night long. Even if residents get up in arms over the ill-conduct of a few, complaints may fall on deaf ears — you can't be sure the governing body will be receptive. It is possible in all provinces to get rid of a problem tenant, but it is very difficult to remove a problem owner.

In a well-established complex, many uncertainties disappear. You can go to the complex and talk to the present owners. We suggest you make several visits to any new home you're considering buying. You can ask the selling agent for some of the owners' telephone numbers so you can talk to the people living in the complex. Find out how any complaints have been received and handled, what rules are enforced, how often or drastically the bylaws have been changed, how many people rent out their units, and so on. Furthermore, you can find out in advance, to some degree, whether you will get along with your neighbours. All this adds up to a better understanding of the lifestyle in the complex and how many compromises you will have to make while living there.

Choosing between a new or established development is a question of how much risk you're willing to take. Disaster is not inevitable should you buy in a new complex, but is more likely than if you were to buy in an established complex — assuming you've done your research. You should also look into what warranty the developer is offering (see the point about New Home Warranty Programs above), and if possible find some of the builder's other developments and see if warranties have been honoured willingly in other projects. The moral of the story is to get out your magnifying glass, put on your shoes, get out there, and investigate!

Visit the condo complex more than once when you're doing your research. Go at different times of day and night to get a real feel for the atmosphere. An agent will have you drop by at the best time for showcasing the unit, so you may end up with an inflated opinion.

Lofty aspirations

Lofts have become quite popular among city-dwellers. A *loft* is just a specific style of condominium (assuming we're talking about lofts you buy, not lofts you rent) and the same general pros, cons, and considerations apply. The difference between what is marketed as a loft and what is marketed as a condo has to do with architectural style and, potentially, how "finished" the living space will be when you purchase it.

Lofts have open floorplans and typically high ceilings, often with exposed pipes and beams, and large windows that let in plenty of natural light. Many are in older buildings that have been converted into residential units — if you're looking at a converted building, make certain that the structure is sound, safe, and reasonably efficient. Some "hard" lofts have no walls at all, other "soft" lofts have 3 or 4 walls. Clearly, if you're at all opposed to sound travelling from one end of your living space clear across to the other, a loft is not for you. Whether loft living is for you greatly depends on your lifestyle and taste.

Lofts can come equipped with as many features and facilities as traditional condominium complexes. Although you usually don't buy condos that come unequipped, you can purchase "raw" lofts that are devoid of appliances and sometimes even toilets and sinks. A raw loft does give you the freedom to choose materials, appliances, and finish the space to best suit your lifestyle and taste, but it also means that extra work, time, hassle, and money have to go into your living space before you can actually start living there.

If you're thinking about a loft as an investment property, you should keep in mind that their popularity is quite recent and may not stand the test of time. If loft living goes out of fashion as quickly as it came in, you may find it's a difficult property to unload.

Living Co-Operatively

There are two different kinds of co-ops: *market co-ops* and *non-market (subsidized) co-ops*. While the units in a market co-op are for sale, those in a non-market co-op are for rent only and cannot be sold. In this book we focus on market co-ops. Co-operative housing is often thought of as synonymous with "low-income" housing, but this simply isn't the case.

Co-operative living is something of a compromise between house living and condo living. It retains the community "feel" of a condo complex but with greater control over living space. In a market co-operative, owners do not own the unit itself, rather they jointly own, with the other members of the co-op, the *co-operative corporation*. This is the corporation that owns the structures and land that form the co-op. The owners are assigned shares in the company based on the size of their unit — these shares are the owner's "equity" in their unit.

As a shareholder in a co-op corporation, you're entitled to occupy one of its units. The lease you have on the unit is different from a rental lease — it gives you the legal and exclusive right to occupy that unit (so long as all the stated obligations to the co-op corporation are met) and it gives you the right to participate in governance of the co-op. Take note: Whereas in a condo complex you have the option to participate, in a co-op you're *expected* to put in the time and effort required to take your share of responsibility for governance of the community. In fact, in a market co-op you must be approved by the board of directors (made up of other elected owners) before buying the unit. When you buy into a condo, you approve the building. When you buy into a co-op, the building approves you.

It may be tricky, but not impossible, to find a bank that will finance the purchase of a co-op unit. The equity in the suite is the assigned shares in the corporation, and many banks will not accept these shares as collateral for a mortgage. Therefore, co-ops are both harder to buy, and harder to sell. They will generally appreciate as the market moves up (or depreciate as it slides down), but because any potential buyer may have difficulty securing a mortgage, co-ops tend to have a lower market value than an equivalent freehold condo.

You may be inclined toward buying a co-op rather than a condominium because:

- ✔ **You're not just buying, you're joining:** In contrast to condominium corporations, many non-market co-ops are non-profit organizations.

- ✔ **You have lower costs:** Monthly fees are typically less in a co-op compared to those of a condo (and monthly fees are set by a vote of the co-op members).

- ✔ **You perform less maintenance than with a house:** As with a condo, some maintenance and yard work will not be your responsibility.

- ✔ **Your opinion counts:** Your views will probably have greater weight in a smaller co-operative community than a larger one.

- ✔ **You have some influence over who lives there:** As a co-op member, you have a say in who is allowed to purchase shares in the co-op corporation (and therefore who your neighbours will be) if you sit on the Board of Directors.

Some serious disadvantages to co-operative living should also be considered:

- **Member approval controls the community:** Selling the right to your unit requires that your buyer be approved by the co-op community.

- **Limited choice of areas:** You may not be able to find a co-op in the neighbourhood you want.

- **Financial arrangements:** It is often more difficult to get financial backing for the purchase of a co-op, and mortgage rates are often higher.

- **Community commitments:** It takes time and effort to be a participating member of the co-op community.

- **Participation in upkeep of the co-op:** Some maintenance and yard work *will* be your responsibility.

- **Regulations:** There are often similar codes of conduct for members of a co-op as there are for condo owners, and these may be restrictive.

- **Group finances:** If another member of the co-op goes broke, you may be affected.

Part II
Discovering Your Perfect Home

In this part . . .

Close your eyes (okay, don't really close your eyes 'til you've finished reading the rest of these instructions), lean back, put your feet up, and picture your ideal home. Maybe it's a century-old Victorian manor with turrets and a coach house. Maybe it's a modernist square, with miles of skylights and orderly gardens. Maybe it's a condo with a view of the park, a huge balcony, on-site tennis court, and bowling alley. Got a good picture of it? Excellent. Take a mental snapshot — that's probably the only way you're going to see that home.

Yes, most of us have to settle a bit. But if you're old enough to buy a house, you're probably familiar with the fine art of compromise by now. This section will help you prioritize what you *need*, what you *want*, and what you'd be really lucky to find. Once you've figured that out, you'll find advice on where to look and what to look for, as well as tips on discriminating between real and imagined benefits, obvious and not-so-obvious drawbacks.

Chapter 5

Home-Buying Help

*Y*ou're taking a really big step when you decide to purchase a house. Fortunately, there are lots of experienced people around to help. Do yourself a favour and pick a good team. Don't be afraid to ask a lot of questions and shop around until you find professionals you have confidence in and you can relate to. In this chapter, we'll help you locate the three key players on your home-buying team: your real estate agent, your appraiser, and your lawycr.

What Is the Agent's Role?

Lots of real estate agents will want to work with you. Make sure you find one you want to work with. You will rely on your agent for information and advice about your specific situation. Your agent deals with the sellers, negotiates for you, and advises you throughout the process. Try to find someone who speaks your language . . . literally and figuratively.

Buying a house is like a mission to deliver a package to someone in a strange city. Not an impossible task, but it can be a bit daunting if you're not used to driving into the city, finding your way around, locating the destination, delivering the package, and completing the transaction. If you get to pick one person to help you through, you will want someone who (a) has done this tonnes of times already; (b) knows the city well and can choose the best route for the circumstances; (c) knows what to do and who to call if things get dicey; (d) knows all the dead-end streets, parking restrictions, and hidden potholes; and (e) has back-up from a James Bond–style action hero who puts everything right when disaster strikes, and can fulfill the mission just in time for the credits to roll and all the good guys to live happily ever after.

When you apply this scenario to buying a home, your helper is your real estate agent, and the action hero is the agent's broker (we'll explain brokers a little later in this section). In brief, what you are looking for in an agent is someone who has the following:

- **Knowledge:** Your agent must be familiar with the neighbourhoods you like and the style and price range of house you are looking for.

- **Experience:** Your agent should be someone who has worked with clients like you before, who knows how to help you buy the house you want for a fair price and who can steer around problems before they come up.

- **Time:** Your agent must be willing to spend time to give you the support and direction you need . . . when you need it.

- **Contacts:** Your agent should have colleagues and advisors to call in when you need financial advice or assistance, legal work, appraisals, etc.

- **Ethics:** Your agent should always have your best interests in mind.

- **Established broker/office manager:** Your agent relies on the back-up of a respected and well-connected broker who is often also the office manager. If a serious problem arises, you'll rely on this indispensable person too.

Understanding your relationship with your agent and the broker/manager

I know, you thought you had your work cut out for you just understanding the relationships you already have in your life. Well, the relationships among you, your agent, and the agent's broker can be no less confusing. But help is on the way! In this section we take you through the ins and outs of what an agent and a broker do, and then talk a bit about the different types of agents out there.

- **Real estate agent (also sometimes referred to as salesperson or sales associate):** Subcontracted by broker to work on behalf of buyer or seller or, very rarely, both.

- **Broker or broker/nominee:** Legal "agent" who works on behalf of buyer or seller or both; usually serves as office manager overseeing daily operations.

When you decide to work with a real estate agent, you are effectively engaging the services of the agent's broker as well, regardless of whether you meet that individual. The broker is the person you can turn to if things go terribly, terribly wrong and your agent can't manage the situation. A skilled broker is able to call in favours if bureaucratic roadblocks or procedural questions arise or if your home purchase spirals into one of the rare legal disputes that can happen when closing a real estate deal. As we mentioned above, the broker is the action hero with all the tools and influential friends to stay one step ahead of the game and save the day.

Note: Some real estate agents also have the qualifications to legally call themselves brokers, but they tend to use the more commonly understood term of *agent* or even *salesperson*. In many provinces, a broker's licence (called an agent's licence in B.C.) requires additional training and testing and a licence designation beyond that of a salesperson. With this extra education, an individual can own a brokerage or run an office (be the "nominee" for the office) and ensure that the salespeople and all of the office's trust accounts adhere to the requirements of the provincial Real Estate Act.

A broker or brokerage company, and by extension a real estate agent, may be a seller's agent, or a buyer's agent. In some cases, real estate agents working for the same broker will represent both the seller and the buyer in a deal. Although each party has its own real estate agent, since both agents work for the same broker or legal agent, the situation is referred to as *dual agency*. The agent that you are working with to find a home may show you a property that is listed with his or her office. If you buy that property, you will have to agree to enter into a limited dual agency agreement. Agency relationships are discussed here and in Chapter 16.

Another term you will encounter is *Realtor*. This is a trademark of the Canadian Real Estate Association (CREA). Only brokers and real estate agents who are CREA members may use this term to describe themselves professionally. Extensive training and continuing education are required. Realtors also follow a very strict Code of Ethics, and Standards of Business Practice, designed to protect *your* best interests.

The rules and regulations governing agency relationships vary a bit from province to province. Ask your local real estate board or your provincial real estate councils for specifics. In general, agency relationships break down as follows.

Seller's agent

When real estate agents are *seller's agents* they owe full loyalty to the seller and must give them all information and take every action to obtain the highest price and best conditions of sale for the sellers. Don't expect the seller's agent to tip you off to the fact that a seller is anxious to move and would probably accept $10,000 less than the asking price. And if you meet a seller's agent at an open house, be discreet. If you say that you're going to put in a bid on the home at $10,000 less than the asking price, but you're willing to pay full price in order to get into the neighbourhood, the seller's agent is legally obliged to disclose that information to the seller. Remember the one point in your favour: The seller's agent also has a legal obligation to tell you, the buyer, if he knows of any serious problems with the home being sold. Expect honest, complete answers to your inquiries.

Buyer's agent

Surprise, surprise — a *buyer's agent* works in the best interest of the buyer. Even though your buying agent's commission is paid out of the seller's proceeds from the sale, her legal and ethical duties are to you. Your buying agent should keep your personal and financial information confidential. If the sellers let slip that they are going through a messy divorce and want to sell the house as soon as possible, your buying agent will share this information with you. Likewise, if your agent finds out the sellers are willing to accept a lower price. Your buying agent helps you determine how much you can spend on a new home and how much is reasonable to offer on the homes you are considering. A buyer's agent negotiates the best deal possible on the buyer's behalf, ideally the lowest price and best conditions for you, the buyer.

Dual agency

If both the buyer's and the seller's agents work for the same broker or brokerage company, this is called *dual agency*. One company is brokering a deal between two parties, and it legally represents both sides. This situation can open up a number of conflict-of-interest concerns.

To head off any problems, the broker is legally obliged to tell you and the seller she is representing you both. Ask the broker to explain clearly what the implications are for the sale negotiations. You will be asked to accept the dual agency situation in writing. If you're unsure what to do, contact your local real estate board for clarification. Although both agents may work out of different offices and not know each other, if they work for the same company they must also acknowledge in writing that they are in a dual agency situation.

Choosing an agent

When you choose a real estate agent, look for someone who will work hard for you. Someone who asks questions to clarify what you need and what you want is miles ahead of someone who tries to *tell* you the same information.

The best agent will be curious about you, your family, your finances, and your future plans. Someone who asks questions and listens to your answers will serve you far better than someone who takes charge and tells you what you want. Your agent should respect your time and independence; a good agent will provide you with all the information you need, and give you room to make your own decisions. The best client/agent relationship results when the agent and buyer have similar temperaments in terms of enthusiasm, sense of humour, and energy level.

Select an agent who works primarily in the community or area where you want to live. Real estate agents have in-depth knowledge of neighbourhoods, selling prices, schools, property taxes and utility rates, local amenities, and civic issues.

Choose a full-time agent over one who works part-time. The real estate market changes constantly and part-time agents just won't be able to keep up with new listings and market activity. A full-time agent not only stays more in touch with the market, but is also more familiar with the paperwork involved.

Be sure your agent is familiar with the use of the Multiple Listing Service (MLS). Most agents have access to MLS. This is a database of all currently listed properties which makes it easy for agents to run a search for properties that fall into your price range and offer the amenities you are looking for.

Taking referrals into account

If possible, use an agent recommended by a friend, relative, business associate, or someone else you trust. If the agent provided good service to that person, chances are that you'll get good service too.

Speaking to a head broker at a major real estate company may be extremely helpful. Even if you're moving cross-country, chances are the broker will have a list of contacts for agents working in particular areas, as well as agents who deal with particular types of properties. Search the Internet too: www.mls.ca is an excellent site that is linked to all real estate boards across Canada and can help you get a feel for prices and neighbourhoods anywhere in the country. Through this site, you may also find an agent active in an area you may want to check out.

Once you have the names of a few agents, arrange to meet with them. Ask each of them to bring a record of all the houses they've listed and sold in the past year. This way you can verify what kind of homes, neighbourhoods, and price ranges are most familiar to each agent. You will also figure out quickly whether you get along with the agent. Remember that an agent with good people skills will not only be nicer to work with, he will represent you well to sellers and will be an effective negotiator when the time comes to make an offer.

Asking the right questions, making the right choices

You can ask these questions when you're interviewing prospective agents:

- ✔ **How long have you been an agent? Do you work full time?** The longer your agent has been in the business, the more you benefit from the wide range of experience.

- ✔ **What professional designation do you have? Are you continuing your education?** A dedicated professional strives to update skills and knowledge. To stay current, your agent should have completed at least one course in the previous year.

- ✔ **Who do you represent?** Some agents work on behalf of buyers and some prefer to work on behalf of sellers.

✔ **How many clients do you have right now, and will you have the time to work with me?** A good agent has an established client list and will be working with a number of buyers and sellers at any time.

✔ **Do you have access to the Multiple Listing Service (MLS)?** Knowledge of the Multiple Listing Service is an essential tool in the home search process.

✔ **How many agents work in your office? Are you working in an active and vibrant office that is up-to-date on market activity and is aware of new listings as they come onto the market?**

✔ **Does your office have an active and attentive manager/broker?** In case of emergency, you need to know you have someone to turn to if you and your agent need help with a particularly complicated or unusual circumstance.

✔ **Will any responsibilities in my home search be delegated to someone else?** You want to know that you're going to receive the agent's personal attention.

✔ **What neighbourhoods/types of homes do you specialize in?** You probably already know the kinds of properties you're interested in and you want your agent to be an expert in that particular field.

✔ **What price range do you deal in primarily?** You know the budget you're working with and you need an agent who's skilled at working within that money range.

✔ **How many people have you helped buy a home in the past year?** You want an active agent who's successful in the current real estate market.

✔ **How many people have you helped sell a home in the past year**? It never hurts to know the stats on your agent, but the best agent for you doesn't necessarily have the hugest number of sales.

✔ **Can you refer me to real estate lawyers, mortgage brokers, inspectors, or appraisers if I need their services?** Any agent with some experience will have a few contacts that you can capitalize on.

✔ **Do you have a list of client testimonials that I could look at?** You should read over what other former clients have to say about your agent. Over-whelmingly positive personal opinions can really open your eyes to an agent's best qualities.

✔ **Could I phone some of your clients from the past year to talk about their experience?** If your agent doesn't have testimonials for you to read, you should ask some former clients about their experiences.

Suppose you haven't chosen an agent and you go to an open house and absolutely love the house, what do you do? Remember the agent holding the open house works for the seller. If you are comfortable with that agent, you can ask her to represent you, and enter into a limited dual agency agreement.

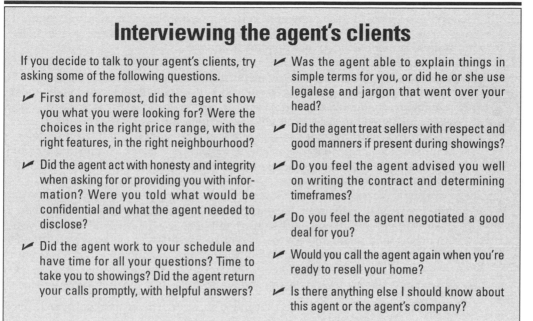

Interviewing the agent's clients

If you decide to talk to your agent's clients, try asking some of the following questions.

✔ First and foremost, did the agent show you what you were looking for? Were the choices in the right price range, with the right features, in the right neighbourhood?

✔ Did the agent act with honesty and integrity when asking for or providing you with information? Were you told what would be confidential and what the agent needed to disclose?

✔ Did the agent work to your schedule and have time for all your questions? Time to take you to showings? Did the agent return your calls promptly, with helpful answers?

✔ Was the agent able to explain things in simple terms for you, or did he or she use legalese and jargon that went over your head?

✔ Did the agent treat sellers with respect and good manners if present during showings?

✔ Do you feel the agent advised you well on writing the contract and determining timeframes?

✔ Do you feel the agent negotiated a good deal for you?

✔ Would you call the agent again when you're ready to resell your home?

✔ Is there anything else I should know about this agent or the agent's company?

However, if you are not comfortable with the agent or the concept of a dual agency relationship, you can scramble and find another agent to work with you as your buying agent. You do not have to work with the agent holding the open house unless you want to.

It doesn't matter who you talk to — the agent, your Uncle Wayne, who referred you to the agent, the senior broker where the agent works, or the agent's most recent clients — don't be shy, and don't let things slip because you don't want to offend anyone. No question is too silly and all questions are relevant. After all, you are trusting your real estate agent to help you make the biggest single investment of your life.

Making your agent work for you

Explain your home-buying requirements to your agent. Bring along your list of household and neighbourhood priorities (see Chapter 6). Once the agent knows your needs, tastes, and budget, the fun really starts — you go on tour. Your agent will show you around various homes and neighbourhoods until you decide you've found the one you want. When you're ready, your agent will present your offer to the sellers. In most cases, your real estate agent will help you negotiate the sale terms and conditions and close the deal for you. To facilitate the whole sale process your agent should give you referrals (if you need them) to other professionals, including real estate lawyers, appraisers, financial advisors, lenders, contractors, and inspectors.

A good agent will be adaptable and creative in order to meet your needs. If you can't visit a house in person, you may be able to arrange for an online "virtual" tour, or if you're planning a cross-country move, your agent may be able to provide a video tour of some homes.

Your agent helps you best if you are straightforward. If you decide to work with more than one agent, let them both know and tell them why. Since most agents are connected to the MLS system they will all be trying to show you the same listed houses that fit your price, location, and style specifications. The more agents you work with in one area, the more likely you are to get poor service. It's probably better to work with one agent whom you trust and who has the time to help you and the personality to make it work than with several semi-committed agents.

Most real estate agents are hard-working, responsible professionals who do everything they can on your behalf. It will probably be really obvious to you if your agent doesn't fall into this category, but just in case, we've compiled this handy list of warning signs that point to poor agents:

- ✔ They never point out any problems with the houses they show you.
- ✔ They swear up and down that the foundation isn't crumbling, even though your two-year-old has kicked in the corner.
- ✔ They only show you houses that are being listed by their company.
- ✔ They only show you mansions when you are in the market for a semi-detached.
- ✔ They make you feel pressured or bullied.
- ✔ If your real estate agent is (a) too busy, (b) too pushy, (c) too clueless,

END THE RELATIONSHIP!!!

You're in the driver's seat — your agent is supposed to be guiding you into a great deal, not over the edge of a cliff. If you signed a brochure (an acknowledgement of the buyer-agency relationship, not a contract) it doesn't bind you to that agent forever. Call the local and provincial real estate board for advice on your particular situation. If you signed a buyer's contract with the agent that stipulated that you would pay a finder's fee to the agent if he finds you a house (as opposed to the usual sharing of commission paid by the seller), make sure that contract has a termination date or a release clause if you want to terminate that agreement.

Don't commit to anything that you don't feel comfortable with. You want to buy a house, and you want the process to be as pleasant and hassle-free as possible.

Why You Need an Appraiser

Car buyers have used car guides to help them determine whether a certain car make and model is a good deal. Homebuyers access this resource in the form of people called *appraisers*. As a buyer, you want an appraisal done to confirm that the offer you have made is fair market value. Your lender decides what kind of mortgage you are entitled to based on the appraised value of the home you're buying. The lender is using your new house for collateral for the mortgage, and the bank will want an appraisal to make sure the offer you have on the house is fair market value.

Your mortgage lender will probably insist that their appraiser conduct the assessment of the home you're buying. If this is the case, you have no say in the choice of the appraiser. But chances are the lender's appraiser is both qualified and experienced. After all, a financial institution depends on the appraiser's expertise to decide whether to lend out hundreds of thousands of dollars.

What is an appraisal?

An *appraisal* is an evaluation of a home's worth. When you pay a professional for an appraisal of your house, you get an unbiased, informed assessment. The appraiser looks at the property and makes an assessment based on the home's size, features, amenities, condition, and recent sales of comparable homes in the neighbourhood.

Appraisal reports must contain the purpose of the appraisal, the legal description or identification of the property examined, a listing of *encumbrances* (any financial charges owing against the property), and an analysis of the best use of the property.

The most common method of appraisal is the *CMA*, which is short for *Comparative Market Analysis* (although sometimes it stands for *Competitive Market Analysis* or *Current Market Analysis*). To determine a property's CMA, the appraiser compares the home you're considering buying to other homes in the same neighbourhood that are comparable in size, features, and amenities.

Two less common methods for determining a home's worth are *replacement cost* or *rental income approach*. The *replacement cost* appraisal approach involves figuring out how much it would cost to rebuild exactly the home in exactly that spot. But because building costs are not always square with market value (for example, a house across the street from a nuclear power plant is not going to sell for what it would cost to rebuild), the replacement cost approach is less common. But using a replacement cost approach may be more useful if you're trying to appraise a home in a rural area where there are no other neighbourhood homes to provide a comparison. A *rental income* approach is only useful if the home under consideration has rental units. The *rental income* approach makes a comparative evaluation, like a CMA as outlined above, but it also takes into account the extra income that will be generated by the rental units within a home.

In most circumstances, a comparative market analysis (CMA) is the best way to evaluate what you should actually consider paying for a home. Before you make an offer on a home, your agent should prepare an overview of the market for you . . . essentially a CMA to help you determine fair market value. If you are not using an agent, then an appraiser is necessary.

What will the appraiser look for?

The appraiser scours the house and the neighbourhood. In particular, appraisers look at the following:

- ✔ **Size, age, and condition of the house:** Does the home need repairs now or in the near future? Have upgrades, refinishing, or renovation work been put into the home recently? (This part of the appraisal tends to focus on kitchens and bathrooms.)

- ✔ **Operating systems:** Do the heating, air conditioning, plumbing, and electrical systems all function properly?

- ✔ **Amenities:** What kind of luxury features does the home possess, such as a pool, wine cellar, hot tub, solarium, or four-car garage?

- ✔ **Neighbourhood characteristics and immediate surroundings:** What does the yard back onto? Which way do the windows face? Are schools, shopping, and transit services nearby? Is the home within what's considered a safe neighbourhood?

- ✔ **Special or unique features of the home:** Is it a designated heritage home, or is it situated on a ravine lot with a stunning view?

Appraisers are only required to do a visual inspection, but they may probe further. This means the appraisal process can vary in length, from a quick walk-through to a few hours' inspection. If you are requesting a *very* small mortgage or have great assets and collateral securing your mortgage, the appraiser may even do a *drive-by appraisal*, a quick confirmation that the home is still standing and appears to be of fair value.

Don't expect to be given the final assessment as the appraiser walks out the door. After going through the house, the appraiser needs to research comparable housing prices. This means you will probably have to wait a few days for the results of the assessment, and it may be a week if the last home sale in the neighbourhood was 48 years ago.

If you are looking at buying a condo, you should be warned that an appraiser may not be aware of the status of the condominium corporation and so may not take this into account. Make sure you ask the appraiser if this has been factored into the assessment — maybe the current owners are asking $50,000 less than the appraised value because they want to unload their leaky condo before a huge repair bill comes in. Make sure the appraiser has as much information as possible (everything you know, they should know!) to determine an accurate reflection of market value.

If your $350,000 offer has been accepted and *then* your bank's appraiser determines the home is worth only $325,000, the bank may not give you the mortgage you need, especially if you are asking for a high-ratio mortgage (meaning you have less than a 25 percent down payment). If you run into this financing difficulty, you can try to do some serious negotiating with the buyers to lower the home's price. Or, if you have pre-approval for the $350,000 mortgage, you may need to cough up a larger down payment to reduce the risk your lender is taking by giving you a mortgage. On the other hand, if the appraisal is for $370,000, give yourself a pat on the back — you're getting a great deal! (For more on mortgages see Chapter 3.)

Bear in mind that if your lender conducts the appraisal, you likely won't receive a copy. Ask to see the appraisal, though, because chances are you will pay the fee for it. (More on appraisal fees later in this section.) If you're concerned about the value of the home you want to buy, you can add a *"subject to appraisal"* clause to your purchase offer. This means that your offer is subject to the buyer receiving and approving the appraisal for the subject property on or before a specified date. This condition is for the sole benefit of the buyer.

Adding this subject to appraisal clause to your home purchase offer gives you some protection from paying too much for the home you're planning to buy. If you're unhappy with the appraised value you can reconsider your offer. If you suspect that the lender's appraisal radically undervalues the home, talk with your real estate agent. Perhaps the appraiser has deducted a commission from the appraised value of the home. It's also entirely possible that the appraiser simply isn't familiar with the area where the home is located. Express your concerns to your lender — you should be able to obtain information on the appraiser's background and experience. If it's apparent that the appraiser simply doesn't know your market well, you may be able to have a reappraisal conducted at no cost.

What should I look for in an appraiser?

Certification is what you look for in an appraiser, plain and simple. An independent appraiser should have an AACI (Accredited Appraiser Canadian Institute) or CRA (Canadian Residential Appraiser) designation. Make sure you ask to see your appraiser's credentials.

Reputation is also key — it's always best to work with someone you can trust. Ask any friends who've bought homes recently for their suggestions or contact the *Appraisal Institute of Canada* (www.aicanada.org) for a list of certified independent appraisers in your area.

How much should I expect to pay?

You can expect to pay anywhere from $200 to $500 for an appraiser's services. You may be able to work out an agreement with your mortgage lender to pick up the appraisal cost. Ask your agent about writing a condition into your offer to purchase. (See Chapter 9 for details on adding conditions to your offer.) The price of an appraisal varies depending on how difficult a job it is for the appraiser. If there have been many recent sales in your neighbourhood and the home doesn't have scores of out-of-the-ordinary features, it will be a straightforward assessment and a cheaper assessment.

How a Lawyer Fits into the Picture

A good lawyer or notary is like an insurance policy: if you ever need one, you'll really be happy you got it. You will definitely need a lawyer or notary to *close* the transaction, that is, to handle the final mortgage paperwork and title transfer. The best way to protect yourself and your rights is to show all contractual documents to your legal professional before signing them.

What a real estate lawyer does for you

Once you have signed the offer, your lawyer or notary handles the final mortgage and closing paperwork. Your lawyer furnishes the following important services:

- **Title search:** checks that the sellers of the home are the registered owners of the property; checks that any claims registered against the property (any debts or liens for example) are cleared before the title is transferred to you.

- **Conveyancing:** prepares and reviews all documents needed to transfer the ownership of the new home and ensures you get valid title (the deed) to the property.

- **Application of title insurance:** gets insurance that protects you and the lender in the event of any problems with the title or zoning of the property.

- **Survey review:** confirms the survey is accurate and valid.

✔ **Assessment of builder commitments:** reviews the specification lists and contractual obligations if you're purchasing a newly built home to ensure that the builder provides everything you're entitled to receive.

✔ **Inspection review:** checks for a complete inspection if you are purchasing a new house, and makes sure that your new house has a valid occupancy permit from the local city or municipality.

✔ **Tax investigation:** checks if any municipal taxes are owing if you're buying a resale home, or determines if you or your builder is responsible for paying GST if you're buying a newly built home.

✔ **Land transfer tax:** calculates amount of the land transfer tax that you must pay (if applicable in your province).

✔ **Fees payable to seller:** tallies the *adjustments* (the amounts you owe the seller to compensate for pre-paid utility bills, property taxes, and other service fees paid in advance).

✔ **Mortgage paperwork:** draws up your mortgage documentation if the bank allows your lawyer to do this, which is usually the case (there are rare cases where the bank will want their lawyer to draft the mortgage documents).

The *Contract of Purchase and Sale* (sometimes called the *Agreement of Purchase and Sale*) is the legal document you use to make an offer to purchase a home, and you need to be sure it's drawn up correctly. (See Chapter 9 for more information on the Contract of Purchase and Sale and adding conditions or "subject to" clauses.) If your real estate agent has many years of experience drawing up home purchase offers, you may feel confident she can write an offer and present it to the sellers without a lawyer's scrutiny. Don't take chances. Ask your agent to add a subject clause to the offer that gives your lawyer a chance to review the agreement of purchase and sale after the sellers have accepted your offer, but before all the conditions of sale (the "subject to" clauses) are removed. You will likely have to stipulate a short 24- or 48-hour time period for the legal review or the seller's agent will object to this condition.

Remember that the agreement of purchase and sale is a legally binding contract. A lawyer may be able to give you valuable input before you sign your agreement. Damage control is often less effective, and more costly and time-consuming than prevention. Yes, everyone makes mistakes. But if it's your *lawyer's* mistake, at least your lawyer is insured, which in turn protects you.

If you're buying a newly built home, you'll use your builder's agreement of purchase and sale, and it will be quite different from the standard form found in your province or region. No two builders' contracts are alike; they tend to be lengthy documents and often contain details that favour the builder. Have your lawyer or notary advise you which clauses to remove before you sign, and which to clarify with the builder/seller.

Where to find a lawyer or notary

The corporate lawyer who you went to public school with in grade 3 is probably not the best legal counsel to use when you're buying a home. Look for someone who specializes in real estate law. In most of Canada this will be a lawyer; in Quebec, you will hire a notary. Friends, neighbours, or relatives who have recently bought or sold a home are a good source of recommendations. Your real estate agent or broker will also have contacts among local lawyers or notaries and should be able to give you the names of several real estate specialists to choose from.

Find someone who speaks your language. As you interview lawyers and notaries, pay attention to how open they are to your questions and how clear their answers are. If they make their fee structures sound complicated, they may not be able to adequately explain the ins and outs of your agreement of purchase and sale or other legal documents involved in the purchase of your home. Choose a lawyer you can understand and who has the patience to explain terms adequately.

Don't base your final choice of lawyer or notary only on *price*. More experienced lawyers will often charge higher rates but get more done in less time, saving you money in the long run. Also, keep in mind that you are hiring a lawyer to give you peace of mind. A competent lawyer or notary should be able to explain every step of the transaction to you in clear and simple language regardless of whether the firm occupies a flashy corporate office tower or a modest street-level suite.

Before you hire a real estate lawyer, make sure you know a bit about what you're getting into. Consider the following sections as guidelines for the questions you ask.

Local real estate experience

Laws regarding rent control, condominium conversion, and zoning are regional. A local real estate lawyer or notary will be up-to-date on all regional laws and probably have good connections with the enforcing bodies. These two questions are key:

- ✔ How many years have you specialized in real estate law?
- ✔ How long have you worked in this region or city?

Fees and disbursements

We're sure you already know that a lawyer's fees can be positively heart-stopping. Since you can't skip the cost of a lawyer (though your heart's probably skipped several beats by now!), you'd better know how much you should budget to cover legal expenses. Start by making these inquiries — and write down the answers:

- How do you structure your fees?
- Do you provide free estimates of cost?
- If I opt for a flat fee, what services are included?
- Under what foreseeable circumstances might I require additional services?
- When and how will you let me know if the fees go above the amount estimated?
- How much would you recommend I budget for disbursements?
- What taxes are applicable to the fees?

When you're searching for a lawyer, ask the ones you interview for references. Take the names and telephone numbers of some recent clients (if possible). If you found lawyers' or notaries' names using the phone book or a professional association, asking for references is especially important. Call the lawyer's references and see what they have to say.

Hello, I'm calling regarding . . .

For those of you who feel nervous about speaking to complete strangers as you're checking references, keep this list handy. Try asking a lawyer's former clients the following:

- Were you satisfied with your lawyer's services?
- Did you find any surprises in the final bill for your lawyer's services and disbursements?

- Did you feel your lawyer adequately explained to you the implications of all the decisions you made and documents you signed?
- Is there anything else about this professional or the services provided that I should know?

Chapter 6

Prioritizing Your Needs

In This Chapter

▶ Knowing what you want in a home
▶ Ranking the features you need in a new home
▶ Choosing a neighbourhood
▶ Staying flexible

*B*efore you start going to open houses or call an agent to take you out looking at homes, decide what you're actually looking for. There are three criteria to consider: what you *want*, what you *need*, and what you *can afford*.

If you looked at our financial advice in Chapter 2, you probably already know the price of the home you can afford. (If not, we recommend you take a look.) The trick is to fit the home you need and want into your financial plans. You have to prioritize, and be prepared to leave at least some (and potentially most) of what you *want* by the wayside, without sacrificing much of what you really *need*. This chapter will help you organize your thoughts so you can make a home purchase that has the right features and location for you.

What's Right for You Now

We all want the perfect home. White picket fence, manicured lawn, and tennis court. Or maybe your dream home has a 1,000-square-foot deck complete with hot tub, built-in barbecue, and surround sound party speakers. If you're self-employed, maybe a suitable home office space is at the top of your list. Or maybe you're tired of mowing in July and shovelling in January, so your ideal space is an apartment-style condo in the heart of downtown Lunenburg.

Whatever your current dreams, chances are your life will be different 20 years from now, with new priorities. You may not need that office space as much as another parking space, now that your spouse has *finally* learned to drive. But you can't really predict 20 years down the road, so stop worrying about having sextuplets and focus on what you think is probable in the next few years.

Your foreseeable future

One of the first things you need to decide is how long you expect to stay. Your requirements will be very different if you plan to live out your days in your new home than if you're looking to turn around and sell it for a (hopefully) quick profit. But since the quick resale is a risky — and usually unprofitable — idea, let's assume you're settling in for at least the next five years. In addition to what you think you need now, consider the potential for change in your future. While you can't plan for everything that could possibly happen in the next ten years, your next few years should be visible. If you're "just married" and starting out, think about the possibility of having children somewhere down the line. It may be *way* down the line, but will it be before you're ready to move again? If so, build those twinkle-in-your-eye kids into the plans. If you're heading toward retirement, on the other hand, think about the difficulties you may encounter as you get older. Will you still be able to climb the stairs to the third-floor master bedroom in ten years? Is there room for the grandkids to come and visit? Is that a good thing? There's a lot to keep in mind when you start to prioritize your needs. Make one list of your current priorities, and another one of your expected future needs. Consider both lists as you shop for your home.

Saving space for change

Is the number one reason for needing more space in a home (a) your partner's addiction to neighbourhood garage sales, or (b) expanding family? As you've probably guessed, it's family — children especially, but also mother-in-laws, cousins who come for a "visit," pets (is a small two-bedroom townhome really going to handle your three sheep dogs?), and your live-in nanny. If you want to ensure that none of these people ever live with you, then keep it small. Just remember that "ever" is a long time. If you admit to the possibility of sharing your space at some point, looking for a home with an extra room, or a basement or attic that can be converted when the time comes, is a good idea. In the meantime, of course, you can use that space as a home theatre, or build that Elvis room we describe in Chapter 1. Remember, if some flexibility — whether in the form of another bedroom or a basement full of potential — isn't built into your home, you may find yourself moving again faster than you think, and certainly faster than you'd like.

Knowing What You Want

So many elements make up a home that often it's hard to decide which ones are most important to us. You may take many things for granted when you have them (like huge closets!) but don't forget to make a record of those (sometimes) small items that make all the difference in your satisfaction with where you live. Remember to think seasonally, too. It's hard to remember in July that you need enough backyard space for a homemade ice rink, but come December when your four-year-old daughter needs to practice her speed skating six times a day, what are you going to do?

Part of knowing what you want is knowing what you don't want. *I don't want to mow grass* is a good start, for example. Or, *I don't want a basement where my shoulders hit the ceiling.* There are things we don't like about our current home and other people's homes, whether it's the lack of water pressure, the windows not opening wide enough, or the lack of street parking. By identifying your pet peeves, you can narrow down what you're looking for.

You can't always get what you want

Prioritizing the features that you absolutely can't live without in a home alongside those that might sound nice but that, at the end of the day, you don't really need, will stand you in good stead when your agent starts showing you houses. When push comes to shove, you'll be willing (and able!) to compromise. And, you just might find that you get what you need.

Franco, who de-stresses through cooking, has always dreamed of having a big kitchen with lots of countertop space. When discussing homes with his agent, he mentioned his price range, his ideal neighbourhood, the number of bedrooms he needed and emphasized that he really wanted a big kitchen — that was his priority. His agent found him a nice house in the neighbourhood with a newly renovated kitchen, but Franco was a little disappointed that the house didn't come with a washer or dryer or central air. His agent found him another home with a great kitchen, a washer, dryer, and central air, but it had a small backyard, and Franco had visions of summer dinner parties outside.

After the third house, which had an unfinished basement (which Franco definitely did not want), his agent had him list the ten items he wanted in a home, and ten items he definitely didn't want. Looking at the first few homes helped Franco focus on what was really important besides a big kitchen, and after a bit of thought, Franco gave his agent the two lists. Armed with these two lists, Franco's agent showed him some more homes, and Franco began to feel that they were definitely making progress toward finding the right place. Eventually, his agent showed him a home with a renovated kitchen, six appliances including a freezer, a big backyard, a finished basement, and new windows. Even without central air, Franco bought the home, having decided that central air was less important than he originally thought.

In an ideal world

We all know what we'd like in our ideal home. The features of your dream home provide a good starting point for your search; most of us judge potential homes with our standards of perfection in mind.

Try to keep your mind focused on your home-buying needs. You shouldn't let your emotions overrule practicalities. (See Chapter 8 for the dangers of falling in love.) Even though you really want the home with the incredibly landscaped backyard, reminding yourself that the rest of the house just doesn't meet your basic needs will help you to overlook the cosmetics.

If you're a first-time buyer, remember you are just that — buying for the first time. Chances are, you'll sell your home in five to ten years, and trade up to a bigger one. So don't worry if you can't buy your absolute dream home in the perfect neighbourhood right now. Instead of trying to buy a home with seven bedrooms for the 12 kids you plan to raise, realize that you can live comfortably right now with a four-bedroom home with a fenced-in backyard at a reasonable price. You may not like the idea of buying a smaller "starter home," but it puts you in a better position to buy a bigger home down the road without sacrificing vacations, evenings out, and hockey lessons to your mortgage. What you can afford will probably never match your ideal, but with a little bit of flexibility, you can find a home that suits you until child number eight comes along.

Making the list

Since you're probably going to be making compromises, it's important to keep focused on your basic needs, and not give them up too quickly, while being aware of where you can be flexible. Here are some of the things you'll need to consider:

- ✔ **Location:** Perhaps the most obvious factor . . . where do you want to live? Once you have been pre-approved for a mortgage, you now have a good idea what you can afford, which may determine where you will end up living. But within your price range, you will have a lot of options based on the type of home you are looking for.

- ✔ **Type of home:** What type of home would best suit your needs? If you have a habit of falling down the stairs and breaking your toes, you might think about buying a bungalow or an apartment-style condo. Or, perhaps you were thinking about a detached home, what with the "talented" family of violinists and all. (If you're curious about what different types of homes there are out there, have a look at Chapter 4.) If your tastes run to modern architecture, you won't want to look at century-old Victorian-style homes.

✔ **Exterior:** What do you need outside? Is there enough room for the Great Dane to do laps? Do you need fencing around your yard to keep the kids in? Do you need a sunny yard to garden in, or are you more of a herbicidal maniac? Like to throw summer parties? Then you'll probably want that sunny yard bricked in or covered with a large deck. Or maybe you need a lot of pavement on which to park your three cars, two motorcycles, and RV.

✔ **Kitchen:** What do you need in a kitchen? If you have a big family, you probably want an eat-in area and an automatic dishwasher. If you're a professional cook, counter space and large appliances may be your priority. The presence of appliances may not be the deciding factor, but room to install them is.

✔ **Bathrooms:** How many do you need? If you're looking for anything with more than one storey, bathroom location is important, too. Is there one on the ground floor, or do you have to send your guests up to the one between your kids' rooms? If you like to take long, relaxing bubble baths on Sundays, you won't be interested in a home with only stand-up showers.

✔ **Bedrooms:** How many bedrooms are you looking for? Do you need an extra one for a home office or frequent house guests? If you're just starting out and you may be having children in the not-so-distant future, count them in when calculating your needs. If your children are finally off to college and moving out, you may want fewer bedrooms.

✔ **Other considerations:** How small is *too* small for your bedroom? For your kitchen? Will stairs be a problem for anyone in your household, now or in the future? Do you need a finished basement for your home office, your home theatre, or your kids' playroom?

Use Table 6-1 to organize the features you need or want in a new home. Complete the chart by considering what is absolutely essential to your needs, and what you would really like to have (but that you *could* live without).

For example, Karl and Matilda Grooberman have one child, but hope to have another one in a year or two. Karl is self-employed and needs a home office. He fills out the following chart, and when he gets to "number of bedrooms," he enters three under "essential needs" (master bedroom, Junior's room, office/future nursery), and five under "nice to have" (master bedroom, Junior's room, office, future nursery, plus a spare room for guests or child #3). On the other hand, Aunt Edna likes to visit — for a month at a time — so maybe you'll make that a four.

For some items in the chart, like a dishwasher or a fireplace, it's a simple yes/no proposition. A fireplace might be "nice to have," but is it really "essential"? You decide.

Choosing features in a home isn't all sunshine and roses. You may think you want a corner lot with a big yard, but have you bargained for the snow shovelling, leaf raking, and lawn mowing that goes with it? How about the settling foundation and structural decay of your dream Victorian mansion? We're not saying you should change your mind about what you want, but when you set your priorities, think about the drawbacks of maintenance and repair that go along with the benefits of home owning.

Table 6-1	Home Priority List	
	Essential Need	*Nice to Have*
Type of Home		
Detached, semi, etc.	_____	_____
Victorian, modern, etc.	_____	_____
Number of storeys	_____	_____
Interior		
Size (m^2 or ft^2)	_____	_____
Number of rooms	_____	_____
Living Room		
Size (m^2 or ft^2)	_____	_____
Open concept/separate dining room	_____	_____
Fireplace	_____	_____
Flooring	_____	_____
Ceiling height	_____	_____
Kitchen		
Size (m^2 or ft^2)	_____	_____
Condition	_____	_____
Eat-in area	_____	_____
Fridge	_____	_____
Stove (gas?)	_____	_____
Dishwasher	_____	_____
Large kitchen cupboards	_____	_____
Accessible kitchen cupboards	_____	_____
Countertops	_____	_____
Flooring	_____	_____
Bedrooms		
Number	_____	_____
Walkout to balcony	_____	_____
Closet in each room	_____	_____
Flooring	_____	_____

	Essential Need	Nice to Have
Main Bedroom		
Size (m² or ft²)	_____	_____
Ensuite bathroom	_____	_____
Walk-in closet, south-facing window, fireplace, or other special feature	_____	_____
Flooring	_____	_____
Bathroom		
Number of bathrooms	_____	_____
Size (m² or ft²)	_____	_____
Location(s)	_____	_____
Shower/tub/Jacuzzi	_____	_____
Flooring	_____	_____
Sunroom/Den/Home Office		
Size (m² or ft²)	_____	_____
Location	_____	_____
Flooring	_____	_____
Family Room		
Size (m² or ft²)	_____	_____
Location	_____	_____
Flooring	_____	_____
Hallways		
Width (m or ft.)	_____	_____
Linen closet	_____	_____
Coat closet near main entrance	_____	_____
Flooring	_____	_____
Basement		
Size (m² or ft²)	_____	_____
Finished	_____	_____
Basement/in-law apartment	_____	_____
Washer/dryer	_____	_____
Freezer	_____	_____
Heating (oil, gas, etc.)	_____	_____
Flooring	_____	_____

(continued)

Table 6-1 *(continued)*

	Essential Need	Nice to Have
Other		
CAC (central air conditioning)	_____	_____
Central vacuum	_____	_____
Finished attic	_____	_____
Property will accommodate expansion	_____	_____
Water view	_____	_____
Security system	_____	_____
New windows	_____	_____
Sliding glass doors	_____	_____
Natural light	_____	_____
Exterior		
Frontage (size and direction facing)	_____	_____
Brick/siding/wood	_____	_____
Roofing material (slate, cedar shake, asphalt shingles)	_____	_____
Parking		
Garage	_____	_____
Carport	_____	_____
Space	_____	_____
Private/shared driveway	_____	_____
Street parking	_____	_____
Yard		
Size of lot (m^2 or ft^2)	_____	_____
Shed		_____
Deck/patio/porches	_____	_____
Fence enclosure	_____	_____
Swimming pool	_____	_____
Established landscaping	_____	_____
Landscaping/garden space	_____	_____
Sunlight	_____	_____

Can you afford to be picky? You should be picky if you don't like where the washroom is, or the stairs in the middle of the living room. Don't be picky if you don't like the doorknobs. Even central air you can install later for less than, say, tearing down a wall or two to open up the dining room. Make concessions on small things you can fix or change yourself later.

What's Close to Home

When identifying your home needs, you focus on both the home's interior and exterior elements. However, the neighbourhood your home is located within is a very significant concern. You may be able to renovate a bathroom in your house, but you can't just move the bus stop in front of your sidewalk or force the fire department to move several blocks away.

Consider the specific location of your desired home, as well as the general area. Living three streets away from train tracks may be fine for you, but being across the street from them is absolutely unthinkable. Or maybe you like a certain neighbourhood, but don't want to live on the busy main drag.

What about local amenities — those pesky little details like a grocery store, movie theatre, or pharmacy? If you drive everywhere then perhaps you don't need amenities close by. On the other hand, if you don't have a car it may be important to have some of these places within walking distance, and you want to be close to public transportation services.

A neighbourhood isn't only a particular location, it's a type of environment. Look at the characteristics of the areas you like best. Do you like a dense community with people and activity? Or does a secluded location appeal to you? Do you like to see Christmas decorations up in the middle of November, or would you rather not see any at all? Do you want plenty of trees, playgrounds, and parks? Or are sleek high-rise condominium towers near the theatre district more your style?

Think about your family's needs. If your family is athletic, you may want to be near a community centre or a soccer field. If you have children, check out the local schools and find the boundaries (if any) for the *catchment areas*. A catchment area is the geographical area that outlines the boundaries of the neighbourhood that qualify for admission to a certain school. Maps of school catchment areas are available from local school boards. If you want junior to go to that special French immersion academy, you'd better make sure the location of the house you're considering allows him to attend that school.

You and your favourite hangouts

Okay, they may not be your *favourite* hangouts, but they are where you spend most of your days: the office for you, and schools for the little ones. How far away are you willing to live from where you work? Don't forget that there's added expense if you're moving farther away (more gas, more wear and tear on your vehicle) as well as more stress (longer travel time, more traffic). If you work the night shift and you don't have a car, does public transportation run in the neighbourhood all night long? If you love a particular area and would have less stress in general by living there, the extra distance you travel may not trouble you.

Try to do a test drive or transit ride from your potential neighbourhood to your workplace during rush hour. How long does it take you? How is the traffic on the new route or the service of the bus or subway? Your initial reaction to the commute will tell you whether you're making a good move.

If you're a parent, think about transportation challenges for the kids too. Can you let the little ones walk to school or will they need to take a bus or get a drive from you? Is there a nursery or daycare conveniently near to your commuting route?

Neighbourhood concerns

If you buy a home at a bargain price because there are train tracks through the backyard, chances are you'll have to list it at a lower price when it comes time to sell.

You may find that your relatively quiet community turns into an unbearable street party every time there's an important soccer game (i.e., at least once a week). Make sure your potential neighbourhood suits your needs during the day, in the evenings, and on weekends. Find out what you can't see just by looking.

- ✔ **Safety:** Consult the local police stations and community papers for statistics on neighbourhood crime.

- ✔ **Emergency services:** Check for the proximity of fire stations, police, and hospitals. Not only will you feel safer if these are close by, but they can help reduce your insurance costs by reducing the risk of burglaries or total destruction in a fire.

- ✔ **Local information:** Check community newspapers to assess how much of a community the neighbourhood really is, and to discover important information on major construction and housing or commercial developments, as well as any potential rezoning in the area.

✔ **Owner statistics:** Ask around to try and determine the ratio of owners to renters in the neighbourhood. More owners means more commitment to keeping the neighbourhood clean, safe, and happy.

✔ **Education facilities:** Visit the local schools. Find out if most of the children in the area attend the local schools, and if not, why. Conversely, it's a good sign if many students come to school from out of the area.

✔ **Commercial activity:** Visit the local eateries and businesses. If new ones are moving in and businesses are thriving, it's a sign that the community is growing and property values may have gone up by the time you get around to reselling your new home.

✔ **Major construction:** Keep your eyes open for street construction, transportation expansion, or shopping malls and community centres being built — all are signs of a growing community.

✔ **Public transit services:** Find out how accessible public transportation is in your area. Easy access increases the value of homes for resale, even if you don't need to use it yourself.

✔ **Community affairs:** Attend a neighbourhood meeting. This will give you an idea of how involved residents are in local affairs, as well as what their local concerns are.

✔ **Overall contentment:** Talk to the people in the area to find out how happy — or unhappy — they are. You will most likely feel the same way once you move in.

Signs that a neighbourhood is improving

What if you find that perfect neighbourhood, but a few quick inquiries tell you that it's out of your price range? Well, you'll probably have to start neighbourhood-hunting again, but now that you know what you're looking for, it should be an easier process. Check out the fringes of your dream area for gems that are close to, but not smack in the middle of, your preferred community. You may be able to find a home in the path of that community's expansion. Or, find yourself a neighbourhood that seems to be up-and-coming. Here are some things to look for when trying to find that diamond in the rough:

✔ **Home improvements:** Look at houses in the fringe areas for signs of renovations, improvements. When homeowners spend money to improve their homes, it shows that they are happy enough with the neighbourhood to invest in it.

✔ **Real estate activity:** Look for "sold" signs on homes: It means that there are many buyers wanting to live in the area, or a number of sellers who want to leave. Perhaps you'll find several retirees living there who are anxious to make a permanent move to their condos in Florida.

✔ **Commercial postings:** Look for signs that shops and restaurants are developing. A healthy area attracts the investment of new business owners.

✔ **Major public developments:** New transportation sites can be a stimulus for business and development, new zonings can indicate the government's interest in investing in the area. New parks and schools can indicate the growth of families in the area.

✔ **Attractive exteriors:** Look for well-maintained homes and well-groomed gardens and yards. You can see if the owners care about their homes by the image the neighbourhood projects.

What's going on outside your home is as important as what's going on inside. Use Table 6-2 the same way you used Table 6-1 (Home Priority List) — to help you form an idea of what qualities in a neighbourhood and community matter to you.

Table 6-2 Neighbourhood and Location Priorities List			
	Essential	*Nice*	*Not Applicable*
Close To:			
Work	_____	_____	_____
Partner's work	_____	_____	_____
Schools	_____	_____	_____
Place of worship	_____	_____	_____
Parks, playground	_____	_____	_____
Daycare	_____	_____	_____
Shopping	_____	_____	_____
Public transportation	_____	_____	_____
Major roads, highways	_____	_____	_____
Fire station	_____	_____	_____
Police	_____	_____	_____
Hospital	_____	_____	_____
Doctor/Dentist	_____	_____	_____
Public library	_____	_____	_____
Cultural centres (e.g., theatre)	_____	_____	_____
Restaurants	_____	_____	_____
Rec/health centre	_____	_____	_____
Public swimming pool	_____	_____	_____
Ice rink, baseball diamond	_____	_____	_____
Airport	_____	_____	_____
Other	_____	_____	_____

Away From:

Noise	_____	_____	_____
Traffic, major roads	_____	_____	_____
Train tracks	_____	_____	_____
Airport	_____	_____	_____
Other	_____	_____	_____

General Location Features:

Established neighbourhood	_____	_____	_____
High property values	_____	_____	_____
Neighbourhood Watch/ neighbours concerned about neighbourhood issues	_____	_____	_____
Good snow removal	_____	_____	_____
Good garbage/ recycling pickup	_____	_____	_____
Quiet street	_____	_____	_____
Picturesque view	_____	_____	_____
Other	_____	_____	_____

Nothing Is Perfect

While home hunting, you'll find that many houses match some but not all your requirements. Or that a house will match all your interior criteria, but won't have parking, or won't be in the ideal neighbourhood. Don't be too narrow in your requirements; remember the difference between what you absolutely need and what you just want to have. The art of buying real estate is making as few compromises as possible while being realistic in your expectations.

Each home is different, and each will have its pros and cons. The home you want may not be in the price range you can presently afford. You may simply not be able to afford Montreal's Westmount area, though you're dying to live there . . . or you may sacrifice your dream home to live in your dream neighbourhood. Theoretically, you can always change your home if it isn't perfect, but there isn't much you can do about the neighbourhood. Keep an open mind when searching for a new home, and make comparisons to help you narrow your list of priorities.

Be flexible. Trust your agent's professionalism — she's likely seen many buyers with similar desires and circumstances. Take her advice and look at the homes she suggests even if you have reservations. Your agent may find a house that's great for you, but that you can't picture until you actually take a tour of it. Your agent may understand what you want even if you can't express it.

Chapter 7

Home Shopping

In This Chapter

▶ Uncovering homes for sale

▶ Understanding exactly what you're getting in a new home

▶ Comparing the homes you see and picking a winner

*W*hen you begin your home search adventure you have to replace the dream home in your mind with the one you can realistically buy. (Unless of course you've won the lottery or just inherited a cash windfall, in which case you can probably buy exactly what you like.) But how do you find the right home to fit your budget and your basic needs? You could sit back and leave it to your agent, but most of us would like to be more involved in the process. In this chapter we give you home-hunting tips and suggest ways for you to evaluate the advertised listings and home tours you take so that you can make well-informed buying decisions.

Finding That Perfect Home

If you already have a list of priorities that clearly outlines the features you need and want in a home, and you've done some neighbourhood research (see Chapters 5 and 6), you probably have a good idea what and where you want to buy. Now you can focus your attention on the real estate market.

Use your agent

Be open to the expert guidance your real estate agent has to offer. If you hired an agent, let that person match you with a new home. Agents spend hours every day looking at homes and they have years of real estate experience. A good agent who's in touch with the market may even know about sale properties before they're officially put on the market. (See Chapter 5 for advice on finding an agent.)

Give your agent as much information as you can about what you're looking for, but be open to his or her advice. If you feel your agent's not listening to you or not providing you with good service, talk about the situation. If you're not able to clear up the problem, you may need to find a different agent.

If you only want to live on one particular block, or in one specific apartment building, you can ask your agent to send out letters to people living there to see if they're considering moving. You may be able to find a property before it hits the market.

Neighbourhood watch

Frequent the neighbourhoods you're interested in. Look for new "for sale" signs and jot down the address, listing agent's name and phone number, or private seller's number. Talk to your agent about booking a time to see the home, or make your own appointment if you don't have an agent. Spending some time in the area gives you a better impression of the number of homes for sale, and your chances of finding a home there. If there appears to be little turnover, you may have to target your search in a different location. Make a note of any streets in the area that you definitely do *not* want to live on (such as the street where backyards face the abandoned sugar refinery) so that you and your agent don't waste time booking appointments to see homes on that street.

MLS listings

The *Multiple Listing Service* (MLS) is a very useful home search tool. The MLS database contains listings of all homes for sale that are represented by a selling agent. A typical MLS listing gives you a great deal of detail about a given home, including the number and size of rooms, lot size, interior dimensions (square metres or square feet), approximate property taxes, and additional information — details such as "renovated kitchen" or "professionally landscaped."

Recently, it's become very simple to access MLS listings through the Internet. A few simple clicks and you can find out about homes for sale in many cities across Canada. The Canadian Real Estate Association's MLS Web site at www.mls.ca links to local Real Estate Board Web sites across the country. Using this online resource you can access information similar to what an agent receives through the MLS database. (Some of the MLS listings' details are only available to Realtors, so use your agent to get the full story on any homes that interest you.) You can also check out www.realtor.com and www.homeseekers.com to search through MLS listings.

Figure 7-1 shows a sample home listing. Note that a listing contains many important details, which can save you, the buyer, many wasted trips to see inappropriate homes. The distance to schools and transit is given, as is information about plumbing, heating, and sewers.

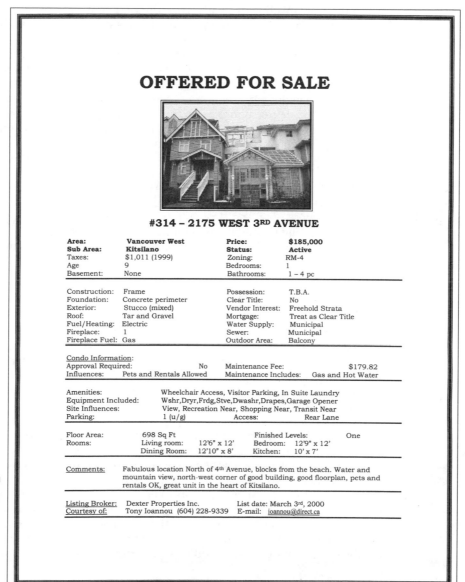

OFFERED FOR SALE

#314 – 2175 WEST 3RD AVENUE

Area:	**Vancouver West**	**Price:**	**$185,000**
Sub Area:	**Kitsilano**	**Status:**	**Active**
Taxes:	$1,011 (1999)	Zoning:	RM-4
Age	9	Bedrooms:	1
Basement:	None	Bathrooms:	1 – 4 pc

Construction:	Frame	Possession:	T.B.A.
Foundation:	Concrete perimeter	Clear Title:	No
Exterior:	Stucco (mixed)	Vendor Interest:	Freehold Strata
Roof:	Tar and Gravel	Mortgage:	Treat as Clear Title
Fuel/Heating:	Electric	Water Supply:	Municipal
Fireplace:	1	Sewer:	Municipal
Fireplace Fuel:	Gas	Outdoor Area:	Balcony

Condo Information:

Approval Required:	No	Maintenance Fee:	$179.82
Influences:	Pets and Rentals Allowed	Maintenance Includes:	Gas and Hot Water

Amenities:	Wheelchair Access, Visitor Parking, In Suite Laundry
Equipment Included:	Wshr,Dryr,Frdg,Stve,Dwashr,Drapes,Garage Opener
Site Influences:	View, Recreation Near, Shopping Near, Transit Near
Parking:	1 (u/g) Access: Rear Lane

Floor Area:	698 Sq Ft	Finished Levels:	One
Rooms:	Living room: 12'6" x 12'	Bedroom:	12'9" x 12'
	Dining Room: 12'10" x 8'	Kitchen:	10' x 7'

Comments: Fabulous location North of 4th Avenue, blocks from the beach. Water and mountain view, north-west corner of good building, good floorplan, pets and rentals OK, great unit in the heart of Kitsilano.

Listing Broker:	Dexter Properties Inc. List date: March 3rd, 2000
Courtesy of:	Tony Ioannou (604) 228-9339 E-mail: ioannou@direct.ca

Figure 7-1: This sample listing resembles a typical MLS listing.

Internet

Don't have much time to go driving through neighbourhoods looking for "for sale" signs? One of the fastest, most efficient home search tools is the Internet. Many agents, brokers, and the real estate companies they work for have posted their own Web sites to advertise their current listings. You can also find for-sale-by-owner sites that promote homes being sold privately.

Not only can you access information about homes for sale, but you can also view colour photographs of the properties, and these are a vast improvement over the grainy black and white images in newspaper ads. Some high-tech Web sites even include "virtual tours," with streaming movies of a home's interior, or a 360-degree photograph that you can click on with your mouse and view as though you were standing in the centre of the room and turning around. You may be just clicks away from finding the right home. Check our suggestions in Appendix C for a list of real estate resources on the Web.

The Internet is especially helpful if you are moving a long distance. You can acquire valuable local information through municipal Web sites, such as www.ottawa.com, www.incalgary.com, and others. Researching neighbourhoods, local public transit, schools, community centres, shopping malls, and recreation facilities can all be done from the comfort of your desktop.

Word of mouth

The more people who know you're buying, the more people will suggest properties to you. Friends may have friends in the area who are thinking of selling. If you talk to people in the neighbourhood you're considering, you may get leads from strangers, too. Neighbours may know who's outgrowing their home or who's retiring to Florida next winter. Don't underestimate the value of word-of-mouth networking.

Don't get so caught up in getting a bargain that you lose sight of what you're buying. If your cousin's neighbour's daughter-in-law's brother is trying to sell a home to you, make sure it's the house you want before you even think about shaking his hand. Don't forget you're trying to buy a home, not make a deal. Never ever engage in oral agreements even if the price seems right. (See Chapter 9.) You need a written agreement and the opportunity to do some in-depth investigation before you negotiate the price and terms of sale. An objective assessment of the property value and a professional home inspection must be carried out to ensure you make the right purchase decision.

Read the news

Most cities have free weekly real estate magazines and newspapers that can usually be picked up at real estate offices, street boxes, and convenience stores. These weeklies contain a selection of local residential listings. However, they often promote various real estate agents as much as they promote the listings. In most cases, the real estate weeklies do not present all the homes on the market; they print just the listings of the companies that advertise within them. Some of the weeklies will also rotate ads so that a house will appear every second week. In some areas two or three real estate weeklies are published, and you would have to read them all to see everything on the market. Be aware that the printed listings are several days old by the time you see them, which may hurt your chances of buying any of the listed homes within the magazine or paper.

The classified sections of local newspapers also have real estate information worth examining — you should watch for open houses. Often the advertisements have keywords to clue you in on the property. "Reduced" or "motivated seller" may be good bargains. Terms like "TLC needed," "fixer-upper," or "handyman special" send strong cautionary signals.

Open houses

Often sellers host open houses when they first put their homes on the market, giving you a great opportunity to check them out. You can talk to the seller's agent in person. Find out why the sellers want to sell, and how motivated they are to sell. If you don't like the idea of having other people looking at the home the same time as you, remember you can always make an appointment to see the home again privately. Pay attention to what other potential buyers have to say; they may notice something about the home that you've missed, or done some productive snooping where you were too shy to look. Listen to their potential plans for the home; they may give you some good ideas.

Don't misrepresent yourself to the seller's agent. If you're working with an agent of your own, be up front about it when talking to the seller's agent at the open house. When an agent spends time and effort on your behalf and then finds out you're working with someone else, you can expect an angry reaction. Don't jeopardize your situation by being dishonest; you may face difficult sale negotiations if the seller's agent is unhappy with you.

In a hot real estate market, you'll find that many properties sell without ever hosting an open house. A home may be listed on MLS and a few days later the selling agent holds an open house to give other agents an opportunity to view the home, but a public open house just isn't necessary.

Sizing It Up: Do You Like the House?

The first thing you think about when you view a home is what it looks like from the outside, or what is known as its "curb appeal." Do you find it inviting? Can you picture yourself on the lawn? Do you know just where to put your prize rosebushes?

Style is an important factor too. You may find it difficult to choose what you like from the many styles of home architecture available. Perhaps you'll "just know" what's your favourite when you see the house you love. Your gut instincts play a big part in choosing a home. You may just feel that everything comes together perfectly in a certain home — good neighbourhood, close to schools and parks, big yard (but not too big), great floorplan, attractive exterior, ample parking — the whole package.

Consider buying a home the same as making an investment. Think about the resale value of the home you're buying, and what kind of profit you will make on your investment. Someday, for some reason, you will want to sell your home, and hopefully get more than you paid. Factor in the potential that someone else will be buying the home from you eventually, and look for features that will stand the test of time. If the wiring in the Georgian house you're looking at is fine now, think about whether it will still be fine in 5 years, or 20, and consider that you may need to invest in repairs before you can sell again. Will your finances handle it then? Are you prepared to replace the chimney when it crumbles? Always keep the long-term outlook in mind.

The more homes you see, the easier it will be to compare them and focus on what you're looking for. If you can, stick to the 20-house rule: look at at least 20 homes, including open houses as well as appointments set up with your agent, before you decide to make an offer. You may think that this is extreme, but the first set of homes will probably wow you with just their cosmetic charms; after 20 wows, you will have become more critical than "I really like the colour of that bathroom." Keep in mind that if you want a very specific neighbourhood, it may take years for 20 houses to come on the market. You may be faced with a "3-house rule" instead.

When looking at homes, it makes a great deal of sense to book appointments one after the other: It's efficient, and it's easier to compare homes when they're fresh in your mind. But try to look at only five or six homes at a time, and take careful note of each home's features. (Later in this chapter we discuss making organized records for the homes you view.) Many homes also have feature sheets that present detailed information about the home and include a picture. Remember to pick up feature sheets wherever you can to help your recall when you're trying to make decisions later.

Look at homes more than once; don't feel you have to make a decision about a home when you first step into it. Unless you're looking in an incredibly strong seller's market, you should make more than one visit to a home you're seriously interested in, preferably during different times of the day and of the week.

As competitive as you may be, don't buy the most expensive home in the neighbourhood. Because home values are influenced by the value of the other surrounding residences, the most expensive homes on the block will have a smaller appreciation than others. After all, if most homes on the street are selling for $225,000, people will probably think twice before making an offer on the home that's listed at $450,000, regardless of how nice it is. Buying the lowest priced house in the best neighbourhood is a strategy worth considering.

I Still Haven't Found What I'm Looking For

If you've looked at what seems like a million homes, and you haven't seen any you like, discuss your concerns with your agent. It's possible that there has been some miscommunication somewhere and the two of you are working at cross-purposes. Review your priority list (see Chapter 6) together and talk about why you haven't liked any of the homes you've seen so far.

The problem may be that you have too fixed an idea of what is essential and you need to be more flexible. We can't help but say it again: The home of your dreams may not exist. What you're looking for is a home that's as close as you can get to your ideal, but you're going to have to compromise. Your agent will probably let you know if you're being too picky and may re-direct your attention to some homes you've already seen. Once you've rethought your priorities, you may have new appreciation for some homes' advantages. Your agent should also keep you informed if one of the houses you found somewhat interesting has had a price reduction. Suddenly the house that wasn't quite right can become much more appealing given a $25,000 price reduction.

If you sense your agent doesn't understand what you really want, you may need to find a new agent. Shop around for someone you click with, someone who might better understand your needs and priorities. If however, you have very, very specific criteria, be prepared to wait a long time to find your home. Or you may have to relax your requirements a little bit, and find a patient agent who understands the importance of your specifications.

Knowing What You're Getting: All Systems Go

Although you definitely need a professional home inspector to tell you if all the systems in your potential home, such as heating and electricity, are in good condition (see Chapter 8), you may be wondering what all these different systems are about anyway. Knowing the kinds of systems you're buying will help determine what your future home expenses will be, as well as warn you about potentially costly problems you may not notice. Besides, what is a GFCI outlet anyway, and why is it recommended? You should understand what the difference is between a 60-amp service and a 100-amp service before you get an inspector involved.

Many people rent or lease the hot water tank in their home instead of owning it outright. Ask the seller (or seller's agent) what the status of the hot water tank is; if it's a rental it may cost you about $10 a month to continue renting. Also find out how the hot water is heated. Like the home itself, you will find it more costly if the water tank is heated by electricity, which will probably be the case if your heating system also runs on electricity, or on oil. (Electric heat takes much longer to warm a tank of water than gas or oil-fired heating does.) One final thing: Check the water tank's capacity — you don't want to run out of hot water every time you shower. On the plus side, a rented hot water tank can easily be exchanged for one with a larger capacity.

Heating systems

Although you get an estimate of what your heating costs will be from your seller's previous bills, it makes sense to know what kind of system you're getting. A poorly maintained furnace with overused filters and clogged ducts will be more expensive to run than a serviced one, regardless of its heating source.

Forced air

A forced air furnace is the most common type of furnace. Fuelled by *natural gas* or *oil* to heat the air, the furnace then pushes warm air up through the house. A properly maintained forced air furnace can be very efficient and economical, but there are different levels of efficiency. Older, conventional furnaces rely on the "hot air rises naturally" idea, which can result in cold basements and warm third floors. This may necessitate ceiling fans on the third floor to circulate the heated air.

Newer, high-efficiency furnaces are, as the name suggests, more efficient than older forced air models and cheaper to run, but they can be relatively expensive to install. In the long run, you can recoup the installation expense through savings on heating bills. High-efficiency furnaces are also very compact; they take up much less space than the older-style forced air furnaces. Many homes can be heated with a high-efficiency furnace that's no bigger than a hot water tank. Any home that already has a high-efficiency furnace installed has at least one solid feature going for it. A forced air furnace can last between 10 and 25 years, and can cost about $2,000 or more to buy, depending on the level of efficiency you want.

Hot water

Hot water heating uses radiators, hot water baseboards, or in-floor hot water radiant grids to heat a house or condominium. The hot water is usually heated through a natural gas, electric, or oil-fired boiler. A hot water system heats very well, and is controlled through thermostats that control zone valves throughout the system. In older systems, it may be impossible to control the temperature of individual rooms because one thermostat controls the whole house. Also, the valve on above-floor hot water radiators has a tendency to rust.

A standard gas boiler for a hot water heating system may cost around $3,000 and should last anywhere from 15 to 50 years, depending on what type it is. The benefit of hot water heat is there's no dust blown around by a forced air furnace, a great benefit for people with allergies. The hot water system is quieter than forced air and the heat is more level — you don't get a blast of warm air whenever the furnace kicks in.

If you want to install central air conditioning in a home that has a hot water heating system, you may find it very expensive since you'll have to install new ductwork as well.

Baseboards

Using baseboards means that there is no ductwork to fill your walls, and each heating unit has its own thermostat, so different rooms of the home can be kept at different temperatures. Hot water baseboards can usually be controlled by a valve on the baseboard, and electric baseboards are controlled by a thermostat dedicated to that baseboard.

Electric

Due to rising energy costs, electric heating can be very expensive to run (though in some places it may still be cheaper than oil or gas). Heating your home electrically can be done two ways: through baseboards, or using a main furnace or hot water boiler (see above). Because there is no need for a chimney with electric systems, the efficiency tends to be better, though some people complain that electric systems just don't heat well.

If your property (a new condominium, for example) was designed for electric heat and your property is well insulated, you may find electric heating to be economical and efficient. However, if you're converting a drafty old house to electric heat, your heating bills will be sky high. Avoid buying any property where electric heat has been installed if the structure was not designed with this kind of system in mind.

Oil

Well, your home won't blow up. That's all one oil furnace owner had to say when we asked her about the advantages of oil furnaces. Oil furnaces were commonplace before the 1970s, but have declined in popularity because they're more expensive than natural gas, and require an oil tank that sits in your backyard or takes up room in already overcrowded basements. Some complaints about oil heating include having stinky oil odours in your home, and dirty walls near the tank. If you find a home with an oil tank in the backyard, have it inspected thoroughly before you purchase the house. Despite the move toward forced air heating systems, many homes still have oil furnaces, which suggests that they are remarkably reliable.

Supporters of oil heating argue that modern oil furnaces can be the best and cheapest way to heat your home, especially if natural gas lines are not available in your area. With proper maintenance, an oil furnace (you should have it serviced every year) can be quite efficient, though oil has to be delivered in truckloads to your home. Oil can be used to fire a forced air or hot water heating system. An oil-fired furnace can be replaced with a natural gas furnace if gas lines are available in your neighbourhood.

In many parts of the country, there are incentive plans to convert from oil-fired heating to a more economical natural gas–fired furnace.

If you discover a home in which the furnace was converted, you may also find an abandoned oil tank buried in the backyard. If this buried tank is empty, it's possible the oil escaped, and has contaminated the surrounding soil. You certainly don't want toxic waste in your backyard. Be sure you check if the house ever had an oil heating system, and if so, make sure the oil tank has been properly removed. When you do your home inspection, this is a good time to search for abandoned oil tanks.

Natural gas

Natural gas is generally more economical than other types of fuel. The catch: You can only have it installed where there are pipelines. The beautiful thing about natural gas is that other appliances that require heat can be bought to run on natural gas, and they tend to be cheaper to run. Many people swear by gas stoves; others love the economical benefits of gas clothes dryers. In very rare cases, homes with natural gas heating may have a problem with carbon monoxide, but with proper maintenance (you should have your furnace serviced every year) and carbon monoxide detectors in your home, this shouldn't be an issue. Natural gas can fire a forced air furnace or a hot water heating system.

Heat pumps

Heat pumps work like air conditioners, but as the name suggests, they provide heat as well as cool air. Like a refrigerator, a heat pump compresses and decompresses gases to create or use heat through electricity. Because a heat pump can use more energy than it will produce if the outside temperature is less than 10°C, it works best in conjunction with a central furnace. Again, there are differing degrees of efficiency for heat pumps, they're very expensive to install (sometimes three times the price of a gas or oil furnace), and they require a larger duct system. Heat pumps are also expensive to maintain, and require yearly service. However, with a heat pump in your home, you don't have to worry about installing a separate cooling system.

Electrical systems

From lighting to cooking, electricity runs most of the important household services you use on a daily basis. You need a reliable and safe electrical system in your home. Stay aware of these two important points regarding a home's electrical system.

Service amps

Electricity comes in two common sizes: 60 amps and 100 amps. Sixty-amp service is an older electrical standard, usually found in homes with a bit of history. While there isn't anything inherently wrong with 60-amp service, the bells should still sound off in any buyer's mind. Sixty-amp service poses two big problems: first, you may be hard pressed to find an insurer willing to cover the property, and second, if you ever had dreams of central air conditioning, a dishwasher, or an electric hot water heater, forget them.

Sixty-amp service can't usually handle the demands of anything beyond the usual small appliances, and pushing those limits can increase the risk of fire (which explains our first point). Remember, too, that 60-amp homes were wired before the advent of the power-hungry electric dryer and microwave. Think twice before buying a home with 60-amp service, because sooner or later you'll likely have to upgrade to a minimum 100-amp service. If you want to proceed, be aware that it can cost $750 to $1,500 to bring a house up to 100-amp service, and adjust your offer accordingly.

Older homes may have knob and tube wiring, which also should be upgraded if you are upgrading the house to 100-amp service. This will, however, require rewiring most of the house, another expensive proposition depending on the size of the house.

GFCI

GFCI stands for *Ground Fault Circuit Interrupter*. You've probably seen them in a hotel bathroom: you know, the outlet with the little red button and the little black button. GFCI is designed for places where water (a very good conductor of electricity) might cause an electric shock and possibly seriously injure a person. GFCI receptacles should be placed in all wet environments, including kitchens, bathrooms, wet bars, laundry rooms, and outdoor outlets. Inexpensive safety measures, GFCI outlets should be installed if the home you buy doesn't already have them.

UFFI

No, we're not talking about Martians, it's insulation we're addressing here. *UFFI*, or *Urea Formaldehyde Foam Insulation*, was a popular insulation in the mid-1970s. Unfortunately, when the UFFI foam ingredients were not mixed properly, the resulting insulation released quantities of formaldehyde gas in homes, causing long-term adverse effects for some people. UFFI was banned in Canada in 1980. However, UFFI may still be in some homes today: the government gave out three times more grants for manufacturing UFFI insulation than the number of rebates that have been applied for to replace it.

If the UFFI in a home was installed properly, it should not break down or pose a risk to you. The Canada Mortgage and Housing Corporation (CMHC) will now insure UFFI-equipped homes. As a safeguard, you may still want to include a clause in your offer to purchase contract, stating that the seller warrants that the home is not insulated with UFFI. Most sellers will be able to disclose that, to the best of their knowledge, they *are* or *are not* aware of any UFFI in their home.

Septic tanks

Many rural areas are not serviced by the local municipality's waste management system, and even some urban sites rely on private septic systems to dispose of wastewater. Instead of wastewater flowing through a city sewer system to a treatment site, the septic tank with a leaching bed (also known as weeping tiles or a tile bed) treats the water before it goes back into the soil. The average septic tank requires a space of about 10 square feet. Your septic tank should be at least 5 feet from your home and 55 feet from sources of water. The leaching bed should be 100 feet from sources of water. Sludge collected in the tank should be pumped out every four years. Table 7-1 shows you how big your septic tank should be, depending on the size of your house.

Table 7-1	Recommended Septic Tank Capacity
Home Size	*Capacity Recommended*
1 or 2 bedroom house	750 gallons
3 bedroom house	1,000 gallons
4 bedroom house	1,200 gallons

The problem with septic systems is that they're not very well regulated by the provincial or federal governments, and so there is no standard that sellers need to comply with. You can get a certificate for the septic system from the home's municipality, but it only verifies the location of the tank and the leaching bed, not its condition.

Don't assume that every rural home has a septic system; ask the seller exactly what kind of waste system is in place. There is a possibility that the house could have a holding tank instead. Unlike a septic system, which processes sewage on-site and needs pumping every few years, a holding tank must be pumped every few months. If the home has a holding tank, speak with the seller about the cost of maintaining it.

If you buy a home with a septic system, you should get a plan (either from the owner or the municipality) that shows where the septic tank and leaching bed are located in relation to the house and water sources. Ask about the tank's capacity and when the tank was pumped out last. To ensure the tank was indeed emptied when the seller claims, ask for a receipt of the cleaning, which will confirm the date.

The *drainfield* is the area in the yard directly over the septic system. The drainfield should consist of at least 4 feet of native soil between the system and the surface of the yard. When looking at this area, watch for the following problems:

- ✔ **Trees or shrubs on the drainfield, rather than grass.** The root systems of trees and shrubs could interfere with the septic system.

- ✔ **Pavement, a parked car, a patio, or a building of any kind, such as a garden shed.** This puts undue downward pressure on the septic system, which can crush pipes and prevent the system from working properly.

- ✔ **Patches of lush growth, or overly moist soil over the drainfield.** This may be a sign that sewage is not being processed properly.

- ✔ **A bad smell around the yard.** This may be a sign that sewage is surfacing, which could pose a major health hazard.

Don't expect a home with a septic system to switch over to a sewer system in the near future, unless there are firm plans for the municipality to do so. Sewer systems are expensive to install, and usually, the government will decide it's not worth it. A septic system, however, should last about 30 years depending on maintenance.

Well water

Similar to septic systems, a private source of water is used in a home where there are no municipal water lines to supply the residence. The minimum water storage tank you should consider is 10 gallons. The main problems with well water are that it can become contaminated and therefore undrinkable, and if the well dries up you have to do some serious digging.

If you buy a home with well water, ensure that you get a certificate from the seller that guarantees the water to be drinkable. In some provinces, the seller is obliged to have the water certified by the government before the home goes up for sale. Water is generally tested for bacteria, hardness, and other harmful chemicals; the well water should be tested annually for these.

If water becomes contaminated, the municipality sometimes has no choice but to extend a water line up to the area, so there is a possibility of your water source changing from private to municipal. Your property taxes may increase if water services are extended to your property.

Stacking Them Up — How the Homes Compare

To help you organize your thoughts as you look at various homes, use the comparison chart in Table 7-2 to record information about the homes you see. Make a copy of the chart and take it with you when you go to an open house or private home tour. Recording all the details makes it easier for you to keep track of the potential benefits or drawbacks you observe about each home.

Table 7-2	Home Comparisons			
	Home 1	Home 2	Home 3	Home 4
General Info				
Address				
Type/style of home				
Dimensions (m^2 or ft^2)				
Age of home				
Size of lot (m^2 or ft^2)				
Facilities (applicable to condominiums)				
Asking price				
Property taxes				
Fees (applicable to condominiums)				
Financial reserve fund (applicable to condominiums)				
Overall condition				
Exterior				
Frontage				
Siding				
Condition				
Eaves				
Roof				
Material				
Age				
Parking				
Driveway				

(continued)

Table 7-2 (continued)

	Home 1	Home 2	Home 3	Home 4
Garage				
Number of parking spots (applicable to condominiums)				
Yard				
Condition				
Size				
Landscaping				
Porch				
Deck/patio				
Shed				
Fencing				
Swimming pool				
Special features				
Utilities				
Heating				
Type				
Average annual cost				
Electrical service				
Amps				
Type/age of wiring				
Water				
Municipal/well				
Hot water tank				
Sewers/septic				

	Home 1	Home 2	Home 3	Home 4
Central air conditioning				
Living Room				
Size				
Condition				
Flooring				
Windows				
Dining Room				
Size				
Condition				
Flooring				
Windows				
Kitchen				
Size				
Condition				
Eat-in area				
Flooring				
Windows				
Appliances				
Stove/oven				
Electric/gas				
Condition				
Fridge				
Freezer				
Age/condition				
Washer				
Dryer				

(continued)

Table 7-2 (continued)

	Home 1	Home 2	Home 3	Home 4
Dishwasher				
Freezer				
Microwave				
Attic				
Condition				
Insulated				
Bathrooms				
Number of bathrooms				
Size				
Ground floor bathroom				
Basement				
Finished				
Size				
Flooring				
Windows				
Separate entrance				
Bedrooms				
Number of bedrooms				
Main bedroom				
Size				
Condition				
Flooring				
Closet				
Ensuite bathroom				
Other features				

	Home 1	Home 2	Home 3	Home 4
Bedroom 2				
Size				
Condition				
Closet				
Bedroom 3				
Size				
Condition				
Closet				
Family Room				
Size				
Condition				
Sun Room/Office/Den				
Size				
Condition				
Other Features				
Central vacuum				
Light fixtures				
Fireplace				
Coat closet				
Linen closet				
Security system				
Soundproofing (applicable to condominiums or townhouses)				
Balcony				

(continued)

Table 7-2 (continued)

	Home 1	Home 2	Home 3	Home 4
High ceilings				
Kitchen pantry				
Jacuzzi/hot tub				
Sliding glass doors				
Neighbourhood				
Overall				
Police/fire station nearby				
Public transportation available				
Parks				
Schools				
Shopping				
Distance from workplace				
Traffic				
Nuisances				
Other Comments				

Chapter 8

This Home Is Great! (Except For . . .)

. . . .

In This Chapter

▶ Fools rush in — homebuyers beware!

▶ Fix-it-upper or money pit — don't kid yourself

▶ Sherlock Holmes investigates — clues to look for in potential homes

. . . .

Your dream home may turn into a nightmare if you don't take the time to make sure it's in acceptable condition before you buy. Approach home buying with a cool head. You're probably not going to find the *perfect* home (if you do, fantastic!), so try to see the *potential* in homes you're looking at. You may discover a home that, with only a bit of work, can become exactly what you want. Because some things can be remedied for a minimal amount (think replacing the stove) while others can take thousands of dollars (think replacing the foundation), knowing the difference will save you time, money, and stress later. In this chapter we help you sift through the kinds of homes that are "unfixable" to uncover a diamond-in-the-rough — a home that you can realistically buy and convert into your own shining gem.

Don't Fall in Love

Most people find home buying a very emotional experience. After all, you're not just making a purchase, you're choosing a new lifestyle and environment, for at least a few years. Although you must like the home you purchase, you can easily fall in love with a place for the wrong reasons. Don't overlook a home's faults or underestimate its problems simply because the kitchen's to-die-for, or the view from the master bedroom is spectacular. And don't just dismiss a home because you detest the neon pink paint job in the bathroom — there might be a wonderful home there waiting to be redecorated.

Minor details can turn into major headaches

Our friends Bartek and Usha found a beautiful house with all the right features except a private parking spot. Situated across the street from a park with a baseball diamond and an indoor ice rink, the home was surrounded by lots of trees. Both Usha and Bartek drove to work, and although they really needed parking spaces for their cars, they had fallen in love with the view so they bought the house, figuring permit street parking wouldn't be that bad. Unfortunately, once they moved in, they realized that they could never get parking in front of the house because of the dozens of parents driving children to baseball and hockey on evenings and weekends. They then planned to make room for a parking spot in their front yard, but the location of the fire hydrant prevented it. Often the nearest parking spot Bartek and Usha could find was several streets away — incredibly inconvenient when they went grocery shopping. And although they loved entertaining, many of their friends stopped dropping by because there was never any parking.

The right location is essential to your home-buying happiness. If you're thinking of buying, look at the home more than once. Every neighbourhood has its own activity periods. Visit the area at different times (evening, during the day, weekends) to assess the traffic and noise. Take a walk around. Do you see neighbours outside? Children? Yappy dogs? Decide whether you're comfortable with the environment that surrounds the home.

Reality Check: Can You Fix the Home's Problems?

Part of the evaluation process when looking at homes involves telling yourself, "I can always fix that after I move in." If you're a professional contractor with time on your hands, more power to you. But if you're an average Joe or Joanna, you may be biting off more than you can chew. Some things that need "fixing" are pretty easy to take care of: painting over an ugly wall, or stripping off 20-year-old wallpaper, for example.

But some fixes are just too big to take on, especially if they need to be done immediately after sinking your savings into the purchase of your new home. And remember the sad truth about home renovations: They will almost always require more time and money than you anticipate. To be on the safe side, add 10 to 20 percent to your renovation cost estimate to cover unexpected difficulties.

Household cosmetics

Although you may be the king or queen of high fashion, Mrs. Olafson, whose 75-year-old bungalow is up for sale, may not share your aesthetic tastes. Making cosmetic changes to personalize your home is not a big deal, and you can undertake the expense gradually. It won't kill you to live in a salmon pink stucco-clad home for a few months until you can afford to repaint the exterior.

Many sellers paint their homes in neutral colours to make it easier for potential buyers to visualize the home as they would want it. Of course, not everyone is fond of beige or taupe, so you may encounter a home that requires you to look beyond the shiny turquoise lacquer on its kitchen walls. Then again, if all the appliances, cupboards, and countertops are in shades you find horrifying, you may have a problem.

A putting-green lawn in a home's front yard can always be landscaped so that *you* never have to mow. Squeaky planks can usually be fixed with a nail or two (unless you, like many of us, have a hammer phobia). If you're a handy person, you probably won't worry about the sticky closet door. If you're really a do-it-yourselfer, you can rip out that ugly '70s shag carpet and refinish the hardwood underneath — just make sure that there *is* hardwood underneath, and that it's in good condition. Remember that if the hardwood has been refinished once, it may not be possible to refinish the floor a second time — you could end up replacing it.

Things you can't change

Accept that you can't change some things about a home, no matter how much you may want to do so. If there's no room for parking, you can't make space that isn't there. You can't make a semi-detached home as soundproof as a fully detached home. If you have to walk through the living room (or worse, a bedroom) to get to the stairs or the bathroom, you've got a problem. You can solve some floorplan problems through renovations, but if you need to tear down walls or relocate your staircase (likely putting you out of the house during renovations and ransacking your child's college fund), you might want to find a home that doesn't require the rebuild.

Location matters are largely out of your control. Unless you put up a mural or demolish the home next door, your large bay window in the dining room is always going to face that large brick wall. The cemetery attached to the backyard isn't likely to move any time soon (and you really wouldn't want its residents to get up and leave, would you?).

Knowing when it's not worth it

Some problems will probably be just too big for you to handle. We're not referring to the long-term renovations you may think of doing later, such as adding a second floor to a bungalow or upgrading the bathroom. We're talking about the kinds of problems you have to deal with immediately — things that take a lot of time and cost a lot of money, usually more than your original estimates.

Our friends Radek and Maya found a wonderful, spacious, completely renovated *legal duplex* (a property with a legal second suite for extra revenue) for a really good price. There was only one catch: The foundation was rotting, a condition discovered by the inspector. The happy couple loved the home so much that they thought they could just have it repaired and take the cost out of the price they paid for the home. But because the home was hedged in by the house next door, the estimated cost to fix it was $50,000, plus they'd have to jack it up to do the work. This meant that neither tenants nor owner could live in the home during this time. The cost of the repair, plus the cost of finding somewhere else to live while it was being done (in addition to putting up the tenants) outweighed the good things about the home, and Radek and Maya abandoned the idea of buying.

If you decide to purchase a fixer-upper of a home, check out your financing options. Most banks will extend lines of credit to ambitious types like yourself. Talk to your mortgage lender.

There are many repairs that are tempting to try, but you have to be realistic. Things like moving a bathroom or kitchen are not impossible to do, but the cost can be enormous, since it may involve relocating pipes and completely changing the roofline of the home.

Make sure you're legal

If you're considering buying a home with a rental unit, do your homework. Most sellers do *not* warrant their home's apartments as legal, which means if you move in and immediately rent the suite, you're putting yourself at legal risk. If anything is unsafe or improperly done, you — the new owner — are legally responsible. Take care calculating how much time and money will go into making that apartment legal. In many cases, basement apartments aren't at all legal, so make sure you check with your lawyer or your local bylaw office before you buy. Municipal zoning may not allow a secondary, legal suite no matter how well it is built. Don't forget the increased cost of insurance that an apartment requires!

In case you've never done any major repairs to a home, Table 8-1 will give you an idea of the costs involved. So take a look if you're thinking: Hey, we can just add a door from the outside to the basement!

Table 8-1	Rough Estimates for Home Repairs and Renovations
Item	*Approximate Cost*
Bathroom renovation	at least $6,000
Furnace — gas, forced air (mid-efficiency)	$2,000–$2,800
Central air conditioning, with existing ducts	$1,500–$3,000
Doors	
Aluminum storm door	$350
Metal insulated door	$750
Exterior basement door	$6,000–$10,000 (including cutting through concrete foundation and new exterior stairs)

Check It Out: Investigating Your Prospective New Home

After you take a few tours of a home and its surrounding neighbourhood and you decide you're ready to buy, it's time to take things a bit more seriously. Advise the listing agent that you really want to go through the house carefully before making an offer, and that this will *not* be a quick five-minute viewing. Although we recommend you check the interior and exterior of any home you're buying, remember that your own once-over is no replacement for a professional home inspection done by a certified building inspector (professional inspections are covered in Chapter 11).

If you're flexible about timing, you might want to consider buying a home in the winter. Not only do the homes in some areas tend to be cheaper in winter, but you can also get a better sense of how the home copes with the cold. Is the furnace capable of keeping the home sufficiently warm? At what cost? Check the home for drafts: Are some areas of the home much colder than others? One common place for drafts is electrical outlets that haven't been sufficiently insulated. Is there snow on the roof of the home? If all the other homes have snow, and the one you're looking at doesn't, the attic is probably not properly insulated, and escaping heat is melting the snow. How well do the eaves work? Chances are, if there are huge icicles hanging at one point in the eaves, they need work. Another great time to check out a home is after a big rainstorm. You may be able to see whether the roof or foundation has leaks that need repair.

Consider all of the following items when you make a serious inspection:

- ✔ **Foundation:** Check for trees, especially willows, near the foundation: Roots can get into sewers and damage your pipes. Inspect cement cracks for roots. Also, see how far the foundation walls come up — the higher the cement walls for the foundation are, the better protected your foundation is from water damage. The land should slope away from the house to provide proper water runoff.

If there is poured cement sloping between detached houses, this can be an indication that the residents attempted to prevent water from seeping in. Sometimes this helps, sometimes it doesn't. Have a careful look at the foundation and basement inside. A good home inspector will be able to determine how successful any past repairs were.

- ✔ **Eaves:** Check the condition of the eaves; look for blockages or places where things may overflow. Where the drainpipe ends, check to make sure the runoff is going away from the house.

Nobody likes to stand outside in stormy weather, but this might be the best time to examine the eaves of a house and to judge their capacity to handle heavy rain or snow. Focus on the areas where the eaves overflow. Does rain build up in a particular area? Building inspectors may be the only people who like heavy rain — every house looks good on a sunny day. When it rains, though, you can see problems with a home that may not otherwise be evident.

- ✔ **Basement:** Look in the ceiling corners for water damage. Use your nose: Does the basement smell musty? Tap any exposed wood foundation; if it's hollow, you have a problem. A dehumidifier in the basement might point to a water problem, and you should check it out. In areas where cold is definitely a problem in winter (say, Ottawa), follow the exposed water pipes as much as possible. Are they all insulated? Are there drafts around where you know the pipes run? Ask if the owners have had problems with freezing pipes.

- ✔ **Electricity and wiring:** Make sure there is at least 100-amp service. Older homes were built with 60-amp services, which just can't handle the demands of an electronic and technologically advanced generation (see Chapter 7 for more on electricity). Insurance companies may not even be willing to insure you until you improve the electrical service, which can cost anywhere from $500 to $1,500 or more to upgrade. Watch out for lots of extension cords too; it probably means there aren't enough electrical outlets in the home. In older homes, be on the lookout for funny wiring or funny phone or cable lines due to former rooming-house situations. Are there enough phone jacks for your five teenagers? Check the dryer and stove outlets, if possible, and flick all the light switches on and off; sometimes light switches are also attached to outlets, rather than lights.

- **Water pressure:** Turn on the shower or tub and the sink and then flush the toilet. You don't want to be surprised by a sudden loss of hot or cold water while you're taking a shower! Taste the water; it's an added expense if you're always going to be buying bottled because the tap water tastes or smells bad.

- **Effects of water damage:** Always look inside a home at the corners and ceilings for signs of water damage. Make sure you check the closet ceilings, too; chances are whoever fixed the roof and repainted the bedroom ceiling didn't do the closet. If you discover water damage, ask the seller what repairs have been made to address the problem.

- **Evidence of pests:** Look for ant traps, mouse traps, roach motels, or other signs of infestations of any kind. These may be temporary or one-time-only problems, but then again, they may not . . .

- **Windows:** Check the screens, window locks, and the glass. Are they single or double-paned? How secure are the basement windows? If they're an older style, they may not be as energy-efficient or as safe as you'd like.

- **Attic:** Is it insulated? Heating costs can skyrocket if it isn't, or you'll have the added expense of adding the insulation yourself.

Make full use of your senses when looking at homes — they can tell you a lot about the atmosphere, and alert you to potential problems. What do you smell, hear, and feel when you approach the house? When you enter different floors and rooms?

Don't be afraid to snoop

Remember not to ignore nooks and crannies when you're inspecting a home. Look inside closets and cupboards for drafts or signs of water damage. Many new homeowners run into problems later that they didn't notice — but should have — when they inspected the home. A common complaint is that the closets are considerably smaller than they remember, or there are no medicine cabinets in the bathrooms.

Out of shyness or courtesy, you may skip over some details when you're touring a new home — we're Canadian, after all: Intrusiveness isn't our style (we'd like to think so, anyway). But that's no excuse — you really need to know what you're getting into, so don't be afraid to look through everything! The sellers should be prepared for a thorough inspection, so you probably won't encounter mounds of dirty laundry or an avalanche of sports equipment when you open the closets. Open the cupboards too and check the back of them for drafts or cracks; open the fridge and see how cool it is; look under the carpet if you're thinking of pulling it up and exposing the hardwood underneath.

Measure the doorways: can you get your washer and dryer down to the basement? Will your great-grandmother's armoire fit through the door?

Ask questions!

If the seller's agent is at the home when you make your inspection visit, don't hesitate to ask lots of questions. Prepare a list and write down the answers. You don't want to rack your brains later trying to remember what the agent said the average hydro bill was. Ask for a *Vendor's Property Information Statement (VPIS)*, which provides a *vendor's* (seller's) disclosure of the home's condition. If the seller is not forthcoming with a copy of the Property Disclosure Statement, make sure your offer is subject to your receiving, reading, and approving it. Has the home been pre-inspected by a building inspector? Ask about the owners, why are they selling, what's new about the home, what are the neighbours like, what problems are they aware of — the list is endless.

Even if the selling agent can't answer your questions on the spot, you can expect the agent to get back to you. The more you know about the home, the better position you're in when you go to the bargaining table — and the fewer surprises you'll have when you move in.

Has the home been looked after?

Like a car, a home requires preventive maintenance. You want a home that has been taken care of by its previous owners, because past neglect can translate into huge problems later. This applies to condominium buildings as well as detached houses. If you can, try to find out about the owners and whether they looked after their home. A big warning sign is absentee owners. If the owners just rent out the home, and don't actually live there, it's probably not as well maintained as it should be. Here are some indications that the present owners are maintaining the home properly:

- **Fire safety:** There are working smoke detectors and carbon monoxide detectors in the necessary spots in the home.
- **Roofing:** The roof is no more than ten years old.
- **Windows:** The windows are well sealed.
- **Foundation:** There are no cracks in the exterior foundation.
- **Exterior:** The yard(s) is in good condition.
- **Bathrooms:** The area around the tub or shower has no signs of water damage or mould.
- **Appliances:** Major appliances like the fridge and stove are well maintained and in good working order.
- **Electrical system:** Ground Fault Connection Interrupter (GFCI) outlets are installed in all the necessary areas.

Part III
Getting the House You Want

The 5th Wave   By Rich Tennant

"Here's to the new owners of our house - may you have better luck with the plumbing, electricity, and foundation than we did!"

In this part . . .

Yes, we know it's boring and complicated, but paperwork is a huge part of buying a home, so you'd better read this section. Offers, contracts, surveys, closings . . . it's all here for the learning. Then there is the active process of negotiating the terms and conditions you want and closing the deal — when and how you want.

Chapter 9

Let's Make a Deal

. . . .

In This Chapter

▶ Writing it all down — making your offer to purchase

▶ Setting out terms and conditions

▶ Going through your Contract of Purchase and Sale

▶ Negotiating your way to the best deal

. . . .

*I*t's finally here — that Mecca you've been searching for — your ideal gem of a home. Your goal is to successfully negotiate a deal to buy the wondrous abode. Look in this chapter for advice on making an offer to purchase a home and how to write the best possible terms into your sale contract. We explain what the conditions ("subject to" clauses) in your agreement mean — and why you want them, anyway.

Soon enough you can go back to loafing around watching TV, or tooling around on your bike, or driving your kids all over town, or whatever it is you used to fill your time with back before you decided to buy a new home. Here's what you need to know to make your purchase and get yourself the home you want.

Making an Offer

Before you can call any home yours, you have to make an offer to purchase it from the sellers, and they must agree to accept your offer. The offer must be made in writing. Just saying, "Hey, I'll give you millions of dollars for your house" won't hold up in court (and if you have a habit of exaggerating, thank goodness for that!). The sellers won't take you seriously enough to consider your offer unless it's on paper. Your agent will have all the necessary paperwork required to make an offer. If you don't have an agent, your lawyer will be able to draft the contract for you. Known as a "Contract of Purchase and Sale," an "Agreement of Purchase and Sale," or an "Interim Agreement" in some provinces, it includes basic terms and phrases that protect both the buyer and the seller.

We provide an example of the *Ontario Real Estate Association's* (OREA's) standard contract later in this chapter, to give you an idea what to expect. You will find slightly different forms offered by the provincial real estate associations across Canada. Although you complete the entire contract form, the document is only considered an "offer" to purchase a home up until you and the seller come to full agreement on the contract's terms and conditions, and you both meet those conditions acceptably.

In an active seller's market, there may be a couple of groups looking at the same house. If you find yourself in this situation, be prepared to be in competition with another buyer, and possibly be in a bidding contest. Negotiating strategies — or battle plans — concerning "bidding wars" are discussed in more detail in Chapter 21. When there is more than one offer, you should make *your* offer as attractive as possible to the seller, with as few conditions as possible. Occasionally you will be informed after you have drafted your offer that another offer is being prepared. At this time you may want to re-write your offer or change a couple of terms to make it as attractive as possible in light of the competing offer. You should rely on your agent's advice but remember you have a budget that you have to stay within, and you should not pay over what you comfortably think the house is worth.

Adding conditions

Tailor any standard contract to match your specific offer. In your contract, you may want to specify that the sellers leave the "'Elvis room" as is, but that they can remove the stove and the fridge. Your offer can be as specific as you need it to be — but remember the sellers have the option to reject any part or all your offer if they think you're making unreasonable demands or conditions. (We discuss negotiating strategy a little further ahead in this chapter.)

You can make your offer *unconditional*, meaning that you do not require the seller to do anything except agree to the purchase price and deposit. However, we advise that you make your offer subject to some conditions — these will give you some protection from making a bad purchase (we discuss conditions in more detail later in the chapter). Finalizing your sale depends on you and the seller meeting whatever conditions (or "subject to" clauses) that are written in your offer. For instance, you may make a condition that the sale be "subject to" your receipt and approval of a professional building inspection of the home. The sellers may reply to your offer with a counteroffer, making a condition that the sale go through "subject to" their ability to find another home to buy in the next 60 days. If, after reasonable efforts are taken, one or more of the conditions cannot be met, you can walk away from the deal and get your deposit back.

When each of your conditions and the seller's conditions has been met, you acknowledge it in writing. Typically, you and the seller sign a *waiver* stating that the conditions have been met satisfactorily for both parties. The waiver, in effect, removes or withdraws the conditions from your sale contract. Once you and the seller have signed off on the fulfillment of all the written conditions of sale, you're just about ready to move in.

Don't engage in oral agreements. Put it in writing. If an oral agreement comes up in conversation — "Hey, those are great drapes, would you consider leaving them?" — remember to write it into the contract. Then and only then can that condition become binding. Your offer to purchase a home becomes a binding contract when the seller signs the Contract of Purchase and Sale that contains all your terms and conditions.

Money isn't everything

So you've found a house you want; now it's time to ask for it. There are a few things to consider that will help you make a fair and successful offer.

Making a winning offer, believe it or not, has a lot to do with people sense. Take some time to evaluate the possible motivations of your seller. Has the house been on the market for a while? What are the circumstances surrounding the decision to sell? Is the owner buying another house? Has there been a divorce? Are the owners looking to get out soon or do they have the time to wait for their best price?

At the same time, have a very clear idea of what is essential to you as a buyer. Certain things you think you can't live without may become easy sacrifices to the great god of compromise if you really fall in love with a home.

You can sweeten the deal you offer by accommodating the sellers' timeframe if they're in a rush to move, or if they need some leeway while they find a new home. You may also agree that they can take all the appliances and the drapes. If you are absolutely not willing to go above your offer price or negotiate other terms, be prepared to walk away from the deal. Advise your agent that you won't be begging, and have him advise the sellers you are firm with your offer.

Preparation — know your limits

To get to the happy stage of a binding contract you have to know what you really want and what methods of negotiation will help you to get your new home. Do your research and establish your priorities. Take a look at Table 6-1 in Chapter 6 where you rate the features you need and want in a new home to help you put things in perspective. Remember, your home-buying needs are non-negotiable. Your wants should be listed in order of importance. Beside each want, indicate the price limit you're willing to pay. Make a list of your "I can't live without this" items and your "I can take it or leave it" items.

You will be under stress, so just accept it. Stress is a natural reaction to a major change. Try to stay calm and put your well-considered thoughts on paper to save you from making panic decisions.

Get your mortgage pre-approved

If by this stage, you haven't gone to the bank to get your mortgage pre-approved, then put this book down and head straight there (well, take the book with you, you'll probably be standing in line for a while). Pre-approval is a great tactic in the hunt for your dream home — it shows the sellers how serious you are, and more importantly, it shows you can pay them (see Chapter 2 for more information on having your mortgage pre-approved). Indicate to the sellers that you have a pre-approved mortgage. If five offers come in for the home you want after an open house, those that come from people with pre-approved mortgages will move to the top of the pile.

Get to know the local market

Make sure your offer falls in the right price range. Check out neighbouring homes for sale to compare prices. Figure out what to expect. Just as you know you shouldn't be paying five dollars for an orange, you should also know the approximate value of the homes that interest you.

Your real estate agent should provide you with area property statistics, including a list of selling prices versus asking prices of homes recently sold in your prospective neighbourhood. Contrast the original asking prices and the selling prices. The length of time homes spend on the market indicates how much demand there is for homes in the area. If the market is slow for selling, then you may be able to offer a price slightly under the market value. But if the market's full of eager buyers, you need to be able to compete. Cyclical factors also apply: For example, the market is usually much slower in the winter months, as fewer people move in the cold. Urban centres that have low vacancy rates may be an exception to this rule.

Your goal in making an offer is to work toward the lowest reasonable price without aggravating the seller. This is no small feat and you need to know your stuff. Your offer carries more weight if it matches average selling prices for similar homes and is confirmed by an appraiser's assessment, or your agent's evaluation of the market. This objective approach helps keep the sellers from getting emotional and digging in their heels. Develop a strategy with your agent for presenting your offer to the sellers. Be prepared to point out pertinent sales and comparable houses presently on the market to show your offer is a fair and attractive one.

Keep in mind that statistics are only a starting point; homes are not created equally. The property next door or houses that look similar from the outside will not be an exact value match for the one you want. In the end, only you know what you are willing to pay, and only you know how far you are willing to stretch your dollars.

Reading and Writing the Contract of Purchase and Sale

The Contract of Purchase and Sale sets the groundwork for negotiation, so it should specify the parties involved, the property, as well as the elements on your "want list." Standard forms exist (though they vary slightly from region to region), and most people freely cross out the terms that don't apply and add in their own. You and your agent will modify the contract to reflect your requirements and add conditions and requirements that are in your best interest. See Figure 9-1 for a standard Contract of Purchase and Sale for use in the province of Ontario. Because much of the contract's legalese can be daunting, we've described the main parts of the contract in plain language. Also, your lawyer or agent will be more than happy to go through it with you and answer any questions you might have.

Go through any contract you sign very carefully. Determine your needs and wants for each item. Write them down if it helps. The common advice for every decision also applies here: Be realistic. If you don't want to go above your offer price, be flexible on other terms.

Who's who and what's what in your contract

The terminology and organization of contracts may vary from region to region, but five elements are basic to every Contract of Purchase and Sale:

- **Vendor:** The *vendor* is the seller (or sellers). The seller's full legal name, exactly as it is shown on the current title deed to the house, is written into the contract.

- **Purchaser:** The *purchaser* is you, the buyer. Write in your legal name, exactly as it is shown on your personal identification documents, and exactly as it should be shown on the deed. If you and a partner are making a joint purchase, add both full names. Joint purchases can take two forms: *joint tenancy* and *tenancy in common*. The differences between the two, as outlined in Chapter 10, are significant. "Joint tenancy" allows for the "right of survivorship" from one spouse to the other when one dies. "Tenancy in common" allows for one spouse's interest in the house to go to that spouse's heirs, not automatically to the other spouse.

OREA
Ontario
Real Estate
Association

AGREEMENT OF PURCHASE AND SALE
(FOR USE IN THE PROVINCE OF ONTARIO)

REALTOR®

PURCHASER, ..., agrees to purchase from
(Full legal names of all Purchasers)

VENDOR, ..., the following
(Full legal names of all Vendors)

REAL PROPERTY:
Address .... fronting on the .... side of ....

in the ....

and having a frontage of .... more or less by a depth of .... more or less and legally described as

....(the "property").
(Legal description of land including easements not described elsewhere)

PURCHASE PRICE: .... Dollars (CDN$ ....)

DEPOSIT:
Purchaser submits (..) .... Dollars (CDN$ ....)
(Herewith/Upon acceptance)

cash or negotiable cheque payable to .... to be held in trust pending completion or
other termination of this Agreement and to be credited toward the Purchase Price on completion. Purchaser agrees to pay the balance as follows:

SCHEDULE(S) .... attached hereto form(s) part of this Agreement.

1. **CHATTELS INCLUDED:** ....

2. **FIXTURES EXCLUDED:** ....

3. **RENTAL ITEMS:** The following equipment is rented and **not** included in the Purchase Price. The Purchaser agrees to assume the rental contract(s), if assumable:

4. **IRREVOCABILITY:** This Offer shall be irrevocable by .... until .... p.m. on the .... day of .... ,20........,
   (Vendor/Purchaser)
   after which time, if not accepted, this Offer shall be null and void and the deposit shall be returned to the Purchaser in full without interest.

5. **COMPLETION DATE:** This Agreement shall be completed by no later than 6:00 p.m.on the .... day of .... ,20........
   Upon completion, vacant possession of the property shall be given to the Purchaser unless otherwise provided for in this Agreement.

6. **NOTICES:** Vendor hereby appoints the Listing Broker as Agent for the purpose of giving and receiving notices pursuant to this Agreement. **Only if the Co-operating Broker represents the interests of the Purchaser in this transaction,** the Purchaser hereby appoints the Co-operating Broker as Agent for the purpose of giving and receiving notices pursuant to this Agreement. Any notice relating hereto or provided for herein shall be in writing. This offer, any counter offer, notice of acceptance thereof, or any notice shall be deemed given and received, when hand delivered to the address for service provided in the Acknowledgement below, or where a facsimile number is provided herein, when transmitted electronically to that facsimile number.
   FAX No. .... (For delivery of notices to Vendor) FAX No. .... (For delivery of notices to Purchaser)

7. **GST:** If this transaction is subject to Goods and Services Tax (G.S.T.), then such tax shall be .... the Purchase Price.
   (included in/in addition to)
   If this transaction is not subject to G.S.T., Vendor agrees to certify on or before closing, that the transaction is not subject to G.S.T.

8. **TITLE SEARCH:** Purchaser shall be allowed until 6:00 p.m. on the .... day of .... ,20........, (Requisition Date) to examine the title to the property at his own expense and until the earlier of: (i) thirty days from the later of the Requisition Date or the date on which the conditions in this Agreement are fulfilled or otherwise waived or; (ii) five days prior to completion, to satisfy himself that there are no outstanding work orders or deficiency notices affecting the property, that its present use (..) may be lawfully continued and that the principal building may be insured against risk of fire. Vendor hereby consents to the municipality or other governmental agencies releasing to Purchaser details of all outstanding work orders affecting the property, and Vendor agrees to execute and deliver such further authorizations in this regard as Purchaser may reasonably require.

9. **FUTURE USE:** Vendor and Purchaser agree that there is no representation or warranty of any kind that the future intended use of the property by Purchaser is or will be lawful except as may be specifically provided for in this Agreement.

10. **TITLE:** Provided that the title to the property is good and free from all registered restrictions, charges, liens, and encumbrances except as otherwise specifically provided in this Agreement and save and except for (a) any registered restrictions or covenants that run with the land providing that such are complied with; (b) any registered municipal agreements and registered agreements with publicly regulated utilities providing such have been complied with, or security has been posted to ensure compliance and completion, as evidenced by a letter from the relevant municipality or regulated utility; (c) any minor easements for the supply of domestic utility or telephone services to the property or adjacent properties; and (d) any easements for drainage, storm or sanitary sewers, public utility lines, telephone lines, cable television lines or other services which do not materially affect the present use of the property. If within the specified times referred to in paragraph 8 any valid objection to title or to any outstanding work order or deficiency notice, or to the fact the said present use may not lawfully be continued, or that the principal building may not be insured against risk of fire is made in writing to Vendor and which Vendor is unable or unwilling to remove, remedy or satisfy or obtain insurance save and except against risk of fire in favour of the Purchaser and any mortgagee, (with all related costs at the expense of the Vendor), and which Purchaser will not waive, this Agreement notwithstanding any intermediate acts or negotiations in respect of such objections, shall be at an end and all monies paid shall be returned without interest or deduction and Vendor, Listing Broker and Co-operating Broker shall not be liable for any costs or damages. Save as to any valid objection so made by such day and except for any objection going to the root of the title, Purchaser shall be conclusively deemed to have accepted Vendor's title to the property.

11. **CLOSING ARRANGEMENTS:** Where each of the Vendor and Purchaser retain a lawyer to complete the Agreement of Purchase and Sale of the property, and where the transaction will be completed by electronic registration pursuant to Part III of the Land Registration Reform Act, R.S.O. 1990, Chapter L4, and any amendments thereto, the Vendor and Purchaser acknowledge and agree that the exchange of documents and the release thereof to the Vendor and Purchaser may, at the lawyers' discretion; (a) not occur contemporaneously with the registration of the transfer/deed (and other registerable documentation), and (b) be subject to conditions whereby the lawyer receiving documents and/or money will be required to hold them in trust and not release them except in accordance with the terms of a written agreement between the lawyers.

OREA Standard Form: Do not alter when printing or reproducing the standard pre-set portion.

Form No. 101   01/00

Figure 9-1:
A Contract
of Purchase
and Sale
from
Ontario.

12. **DOCUMENTS AND DISCHARGE**: Purchaser shall not call for the production of any title deed, abstract, survey or other evidence of title to the property except such as are in the possession or control of Vendor. If requested by Purchaser, Vendor will deliver any sketch or survey of the property within Vendor's control to Purchaser as soon as possible and prior to the Requisition Date. If a discharge of any Charge/Mortgage held by a corporation incorporated pursuant to the Trust And Loan Companies Act (Canada), Chartered Bank, Trust Company, Credit Union, Caisse Populaire or Insurance Company and which is not to be assumed by Purchaser on completion, is not available in registrable form on completion, Purchaser agrees to accept Vendor's lawyer's personal undertaking to obtain, out of the closing funds, a discharge in registrable form and to register same on title within a reasonable period of time after completion, provided that on or before completion Vendor shall provide to Purchaser a mortgage statement prepared by the mortgagee setting out the balance required to obtain the discharge, together with a direction executed by Vendor directing payment to the mortgagee of the amount required to obtain the discharge out of the balance due on completion.

13. **INSPECTION**: Purchaser acknowledges having had the opportunity to inspect the property and understands that upon acceptance of this Offer there shall be a binding agreement of purchase and sale between Purchaser and Vendor.

14. **INSURANCE**: All buildings on the property and all other things being purchased shall be and remain until completion at the risk of Vendor. Pending completion, Vendor shall hold all insurance policies, if any, and the proceeds thereof in trust for the parties as their interests may appear and in the event of substantial damage, Purchaser may either terminate this Agreement and have all monies paid returned without interest or deduction or else take the proceeds of any insurance and complete the purchase. No insurance shall be transferred on completion. If Vendor is taking back a Charge/Mortgage, or Purchaser is assuming a Charge/Mortgage, Purchaser shall supply Vendor with reasonable evidence of adequate insurance to protect Vendor's or other mortgagee's interest on completion.

15. **PLANNING ACT**: This Agreement shall be effective to create an interest in the property only if Vendor complies with the subdivision control provisions of the Planning Act by completion and Vendor covenants to proceed diligently at his expense to obtain any necessary consent by completion.

16. **DOCUMENT PREPARATION**: The Transfer/Deed shall, save for the Land Transfer Tax Affidavit, be prepared in registrable form at the expense of Vendor, and any Charge/Mortgage to be given back by the Purchaser to Vendor at the expense of the Purchaser. If requested by Purchaser, Vendor covenants that the Transfer/Deed to be delivered on completion shall contain the statements contemplated by Section 50 (22) of the Planning Act, R.S.O. 1990.

17. **RESIDENCY**: Purchaser shall be credited towards the Purchase Price with the amount, if any, necessary for Purchaser to pay to the Minister of National Revenue to satisfy Purchaser's liability in respect of tax payable by Vendor under the non-residency provisions of the Income Tax Act by reason of this sale. Purchaser shall not claim such credit if Vendor delivers on completion the prescribed certificate or a statutory declaration that Vendor is not then a non-resident of Canada.

18. **ADJUSTMENTS**: Any rents, mortgage interest, realty taxes including local improvement rates and unmetered public or private utility charges and unmetered cost of fuel, as applicable, shall be apportioned and allowed to the day of completion, the day of completion itself to be apportioned to Purchaser.

19. **TIME LIMITS**: Time shall in all respects be of the essence hereof provided that the time for doing or completing of any matter provided for herein may be extended or abridged by an agreement in writing signed by Vendor and Purchaser or by their respective lawyers who may be specifically authorized in that regard.

20. **TENDER**: Any tender of documents or money hereunder may be made upon Vendor or Purchaser or their respective lawyers on the day set for completion. Money may be tendered by bank draft or cheque certified by a Chartered Bank, Trust Company, Province of Ontario Savings Office, Credit Union or Caisse Populaire.

21. **FAMILY LAW ACT**: Vendor warrants that spousal consent is not necessary to this transaction under the provisions of the Family Law Act, R.S.O. 1990 unless Vendor's spouse has executed the consent hereinafter provided.

22. **UFFI**: Vendor represents and warrants to Purchaser that during the time Vendor has owned the property, Vendor has not caused any building on the property to be insulated with insulation containing ureaformaldehyde, and that to the best of Vendor's knowledge no building on the property contains or has ever contained insulation that contains ureaformaldehyde. This warranty shall survive and not merge on the completion of this transaction, and if the building is part of a multiple unit building, this warranty shall only apply to that part of the building which is the subject of this transaction.

23. **CONSUMER REPORTS: The Purchaser is hereby notified that a consumer report containing credit and/or personal information may be referred to in connection with this transaction.**

24. **AGENCY**: It is understood that the brokers involved in the transaction represent the parties as set out in the Confirmation of Representation below.

25. **AGREEMENT IN WRITING**: If there is conflict or discrepancy between any provision added to this Agreement (including any Schedule attached hereto) and any provision in the standard pre-set portion hereof, the added provision shall supersede the standard pre-set provision to the extent of such conflict or discrepancy. This Agreement including any Schedule attached hereto, shall constitute the entire Agreement between Purchaser and Vendor. There is no representation, warranty, collateral agreement or condition, which affects this Agreement other than as expressed herein. This Agreement shall be read with all changes of gender or number required by the context.

26. **SUCCESSORS AND ASSIGNS**: The heirs, executors, administrators, successors and assigns of the undersigned are bound by the terms herein.

DATED at.. this.................................. day of .... ,20........

SIGNED, SEALED AND DELIVERED in the presence of: IN WITNESS whereof I have hereunto set my hand and seal:

_____   _____   ● DATE................

(Witness)   (Purchaser)   (Seal)

_____   _____   ● DATE................

(Witness)   (Purchaser)   (Seal)

I, the Undersigned Vendor, agree to the above Offer. I hereby irrevocably instruct my lawyer to pay directly to the Listing Broker the unpaid balance of the commission together with applicable Goods and Services Tax (and any other taxes as may hereafter be applicable), from the proceeds of the sale prior to any payment to the undersigned on completion, as advised by the Listing Broker to my lawyer.

DATED at.. this.................................. day of .... ,20........

SIGNED, SEALED AND DELIVERED in the presence of: IN WITNESS whereof I have hereunto set my hand and seal:

_____   _____   ● DATE................

(Witness)   (Vendor)   (Seal)

_____   _____   ● DATE................

(Witness)   (Vendor)   (Seal)

SPOUSAL CONSENT: The Undersigned Spouse of the Vendor hereby consents to the disposition evidenced herein pursuant to the provisions of the Family Law Act, R.S.O.1990, and hereby agrees with the Purchaser that he/she will execute all necessary or incidental documents to give full force and effect to the sale evidenced herein.

_____   _____   ● DATE................

(Witness)   (Spouse)   (Seal)

CONFIRMATION OF EXECUTION: Notwithstanding anything contained herein to the contrary, I confirm this Agreement with all changes both typed and written was finally executed by all parties at....................... a.m./p.m. this................ day of.. ,20.........

_____

(Signature of Vendor or Purchaser)

CONFIRMATION OF REPRESENTATION

I hereby acknowledge and confirm the Listing Broker represents the interests of the

.... in this transaction.

(Vendor/Vendor and the Purchaser)

_____

Signature of Listing Broker or authorized representative

Name of Listing Broker: ....

(.........)..................................   (.........)..................................

Tel No.   FAX No.

I hereby acknowledge and confirm the Co-operating Broker represents the interests

of the .... in this transaction.

(Vendor/Purchaser)

_____

Signature of Co-operating Broker or authorized representative

Name of Co-operating Broker: ....

(.........)..................................   (.........)..................................

Tel No.   FAX No.

ACKNOWLEDGEMENT

I acknowledge receipt of my signed copy of this accepted Agreement of Purchase and Sale and I authorize the Agent to forward a copy to my lawyer.

_____ DATE................

(Vendor)

_____ DATE................

(Vendor)

Address for Service:..

.... Tel. No.(.........)..................

Vendor's Lawyer ....

Address ....

(.........)..................   (.........)..................

Tel. No.   FAX No.

I acknowledge receipt of my signed copy of this accepted Agreement of Purchase and Sale and I authorize the Agent to forward a copy to my lawyer.

_____ DATE................

(Purchaser)

_____ DATE................

(Purchaser)

Address for Service:..

.... Tel. No.(.........)..................

Purchaser's Lawyer ....

Address ....

(.........)..................   (.........)..................

Tel. No.   FAX No.

FOR OFFICE USE ONLY   **COMMISSION TRUST AGREEMENT**

To: Co-operating Broker shown on the foregoing Agreement of Purchase and Sale:

In consideration for the Co-operating Broker procuring the foregoing Agreement of Purchase and Sale, I hereby declare that all moneys received or receivable by me in connection with the Transaction as contemplated in the MLS Rules and Regulations of my Real Estate Board shall be receivable and held in trust. This agreement shall constitute a Commission Trust Agreement as defined in the MLS Rules and shall be subject to and governed by the MLS Rules pertaining to Commission Trust.

DATED as of the date and time of the acceptance of the foregoing Agreement of Purchase and Sale.   Acknowledged by:

_____   _____

Signature of Listing Broker or authorized representative   Signature of Co-operating Broker or authorized representative

✓ **Subject property:** *Subject property* refers to the street address and an exact legal description of the property you are buying. This may also include the lot size, a general description of the home (semi-detached, single family dwelling with a mutual drive, or other), the specific lot and plan number, and any *easements*. An easement is a specified area of a property that is acquired by another property owner for his or her benefit. For example, your neighbour's driveway may cross the corner of your property. Since it's his driveway, even though it's technically on your property, he has the right to use that part of your property to park his car. This right is registered on your title.

✓ **Purchase price:** The *purchase price* is the price you're initially willing to pay. This price will probably change throughout the negotiation; it's typical to see it go up and down repeatedly. When setting your offer price, keep in mind the additional expenses you'll be incurring, such as land transfer tax, realty taxes, fuel and water rates, legal fees, and insurance costs (these expenses, known as closing costs, are described in Chapter 2). Also allow yourself room to negotiate up. If it's a seller's market (there are more people looking to buy than there are homes for sale), you may want to make a higher initial offer right off. We discuss negotiating the price more later on in this chapter.

✓ **Deposit:** Your *deposit* is not only part of your down payment, but it is also an indication to the seller of your interest in the house and a symbol that you are negotiating in good faith. The initial deposit may be relatively low, but the total deposit may be much more. Five to 10 percent of the purchase price is often considered a fair amount for a total deposit, but there are no hard and fast rules. Refer to Chapter 2 for a full discussion regarding deposits.

List the amount of the deposit that is accompanying your offer and specify that it will be applied to the purchase price of the house on the closing (or completion) of the sale. Normally it will be held in trust by your agent in a trust account until the completion of the sale. You may want to write in that any interest that accrues while the funds are in trust accrue to the buyer, and will be paid after completion of the sale. Note that if you back out of an offer once it has been accepted and all the terms and conditions have been met, you will most likely have to forfeit your deposit to the vendor and will likely open yourself up to other legal action. If you want to try and get out of the deal, you should consult a lawyer and be prepared for bad news.

All about terms and conditions ("subject to" clauses)

Most contracts have a blank space where you can write in the specific terms and conditions of your offer. This is where you build as much safety into your offer as you need. Conditions are typically worded as "subject to" clauses (I will buy the house, *subject to* financing, subject to inspection, subject to selling my current house, or some other condition). Basically you are saying, in legal terms, I will buy your house if particular conditions are met, such as:

- ✔ **Subject to financing:** You will buy the home if you're able to arrange a suitable mortgage. (Note that some buyers specify the maximum interest rate, the payment schedule, and the monthly payment amount they can consider.)

- ✔ **Subject to selling my present home:** You will buy the seller's home if you can sell the home you currently own (within a set period of time, such as 60 to 90 days).

- ✔ **Subject to the home's repair:** You will purchase the home if the seller fixes the leaky roof or other substandard feature.

- ✔ **Subject to legal review:** You will purchase the home provided that your lawyer reviews and approves the contract (usually within a specified amount of time, such as 24 to 48 hours).

- ✔ **Subject to inspection:** You will buy the home if it passes a professional building inspection.

- ✔ **Subject to survey:** You will purchase the home if a land survey is conducted or a legal, up-to-date land survey is provided, showing that the home does not violate any easements or rights-of-way.

Specific requirements can also be written in the same area as your conditions, such as the stated requirement that the seller agrees to remove the abandoned car from the garage prior to the completion date. There may not be enough space on the contract to add all of your terms and conditions. They can be written up on *schedule forms*, which are attached to the main body of the contract. Schedule forms (or addenda, or appendices in some provinces) are extra forms that allow you to write as many terms and conditions as are necessary on additional pages that form part of the contract. Make sure that all of the schedules you attach are listed on the contract. Keep in mind that when you start negotiating, you may end up adding or removing conditions, and so might the seller. For example, if the vendor will not fix the roof, then you may agree to remove that condition, but try to deduct the estimated cost of that repair from your offered price.

Don't overdo the conditions. It's definitely a good idea to write a thorough, detailed offer. But make sure you keep your conditions from piling up. Be reasonable. Don't write into your offer that you have the right to inspect the property five times before the closing date — one or two times should suffice.

Once you and the seller sign off on all the terms and conditions of your purchase offer, your conditions will (hopefully!) be met and you can then add the paperwork (addendums or waivers, if necessary) to confirm, for example, that the roof has been repaired, that you have secured a mortgage, that you have sold your current house, and so on. Once all the conditions are removed, you enter into a binding agreement to purchase.

Scheduling the deal

Timing of the sale — which includes scheduling the *completion date*, the *possession date*, and the *adjustment date*, defined below — is handled differently in different parts of Canada. Your agent will be able to tell you what to expect and help negotiate dates that will work for you.

As a basic guideline, be aware of the following important deadlines:

- **Irrevocability/Time allowed for acceptance:** *Irrevocability,* or *the time allowed for acceptance,* is a deadline written into your terms and conditions — for example, 48 hours — for the seller to respond to the offer, or counteroffer. If you hear nothing after 48 hours, it means the seller has refused your offer. You can, however, make another offer after that point. You may also withdraw your offer any time up until it is accepted.

- **Viewed date:** The *viewed date*, a specific date on which you viewed the house, confirms that the property and everything included in the sale will be in the same condition that they were in when you toured the home and observed them on that particular date. The viewed date is written into the contract.

- **Completion date:** The *completion date* (also known as the closing date) is the date when the money (via certified cheque, bank draft, cash, or lawyer's/notary's trust cheque) will be delivered. Note that the seller is entitled to his or her proceeds *on* the completion date. Therefore, all bank waiting periods should have been cleared in order to make the money readily available to the seller. To avoid difficulties, you should deposit the money or hand over a cheque at least two days before the completion date. Because of the legal transfer of funds, the completion date is also the date by which all documents need to be registered, signed, and acknowledged as legally binding.

- **Possession date:** The *possession date* is when the property is vacant for you to move in. You will not be able to move in to (take possession of) the property before the seller has received your payment. Usually, possession takes effect at noon on the day specified in the contract. In some provinces, however, you may take possession on the completion date.

- **Adjustment date:** On the *adjustment date,* you, the buyer, assume all tax rates, local improvement assessments, and utility charges related to your new property. Any bills that have been prepaid will be pro-rated and your portion will be charged to you. The adjustment date is usually the same as the possession date.

Many Contracts of Purchase and Sale are signed without absolutely definite closing and possession dates in mind. Unless you're adamant that you must close on February 29 or on your astrologically chosen day, letting the sellers know that you would like to close in approximately 30 or 60 days (or however many you're thinking) is recommended to give the sellers some flexibility. You and the sellers will probably agree on some arbitrary date to write into the contract — to change at a later date, if necessary. Once your offer is accepted, though, it's a good idea to agree on a final set of dates early on, so you can to start to finalize things with your lawyer, lender, and home insurance agent. Your real estate agent or lawyer can draw up an amendment or waiver to your contract to change the date if both parties agree to the change.

In some provinces, such as British Columbia, the closing date and the possession dates are two separate dates, allowing for the money the buyer gives to the seller to be processed before the buyer gets possession of the home. (There is a clause in the contract that states that "the property and all included items will be substantially the same condition at Possession Date as when viewed by the Buyer on [the viewed date].") In other provinces, such as Ontario, possession and completion day are usually the same, so that you have possession of the home as soon as you are legally responsible for it. Because you use a certified cheque, the seller doesn't worry about the cheque bouncing. If your possession and completion dates are the same, you may find yourself waiting impatiently while your lawyer goes down to City Hall or the Land Titles Office with the seller's lawyer to change the title to your name — you probably won't get the keys until mid-afternoon of the closing day. So don't hire your movers for 9 a.m. on the day of closing, because they'll just spend hours waiting around to get into your new home.

 When not to close: Don't close on a Friday if possible, or at the end of the month. These are busy days at the land titles office and you don't want a problem to hold up the closing until the following Monday. You'll find more details on timing the closing in Chapter 12.

Should it stay or should it go?

The following three clauses let you and the buyer agree on what items of the house will stay for you to enjoy, and what items leave with the seller's moving truck:

- **Chattels:** *Chattels* are items that are not structurally part of the house, but that you want to be included in the sale. Commonly purchased chattels include major appliances such as the fridge and stove, but you can include those drapes the sellers said they'd leave, or the unique works of art that make the Elvis room so magical.

- **Fixtures:** *Fixtures* are things that are affixed to the house, such as light fixtures, overhead fans, and built-in bookcases. Unless otherwise noted, fixtures are included in the purchase price of the home. If there's a crystal chandelier in the dining room that makes your jaw drop, be prepared for the seller to stipulate that it be excluded from the sale. If you don't want to let the chandelier go, be prepared to raise your offer to make sure it becomes yours.

- **Rental items:** *Rental items* are things that the sellers rented, like hot water heaters or propane tanks and security systems. They are not included in the house's purchase price unless you and the seller agree that they are. The contract should note that the buyer will assume the lease and all lease obligations for the propane tanks or security system. If the seller has not provided copies of the rental or lease documents prior to you making your offer, make your offer subject to you receiving and approving the lease agreements as necessary.

Make sure that the seller doesn't bash the head off that Elvis bust you love before you move in, or steal the most valuable crystal teardrops from the chandelier. When you're writing up your contract's conditions, include a phrase like "the property and all included items will be in substantially the same condition as when viewed by the buyer at the date of inspection."

Signing it all away

The signatures of both parties — all sellers and all buyers — are usually required on each page of the contract. These signatures should be witnessed where necessary. In some provinces, it may be sufficient to initial some of the pages. Your agent or lawyer will tell you where to sign and where to initial. If any changes are made during the negotiations, the buyer and the seller must initial the change to show that it's been accepted.

The sellers must indicate their country of residency in the contract, somewhere near their signature. If the sellers are residents of Canada, there is no problem. However, if the sellers are not Canadian residents, your lawyer will want to make arrangements to ensure the sellers have paid all taxes due (or alternatively, that taxes due are withheld from the proceeds of the sale). Otherwise, there is a possibility that the Canada Customs and Revenue Agency (formerly known as Revenue Canada) could come knocking on your door looking for taxes payable from the long-gone sellers. Make sure the residency box or line is completed on the contract.

The Art of Negotiation

Unless you and the seller turn out to be twins who were separated at birth, it's likely that some of your terms will not be agreeable to the seller. In this case, the seller may send your offer back with a few suggestions for changes. This is known as a *counteroffer*. Most often, the main sticking point in such negotiations is the purchase price. Don't be surprised if you find yourself in a back and forth session with the seller, as each of you writes in and crosses out prices and terms, with each change being initialed.

Keep it short and sweet and on the up and up

It is possible that you find not only the dream home, but the dream sellers — and your negotiation period is quite painless. Here are several things you can do to make your negotiations go as smoothly as possible:

- **Make concessions — on the little things:** Often, just a little concession from you indicates to the seller that you are a reasonable person. Concede on the small items. If the sellers want to take the curtains you like, but are willing to cover the roof repair costs, then you can certainly find your own curtains. If, however, they refuse to entertain your requests for a full building inspection, then it's time to think about polishing up those walking shoes.

- **Be appreciative and polite at all times:** Always keep in mind that you are looking at someone's personal property. The sellers are giving up their home, and want to be assured that it will be well cared for by respectful people. If you think that they have bad taste and that you could furnish the place to look much better, keep it to yourself. You are not there to share your opinion on the sellers' velvet art collection — you're buying their house. Think of how you'd feel if someone barged into your house and insulted your prized set of vintage beanbag chairs. It will help you to keep your tongue in check.

- **Don't get too personal:** Sure, you want the sellers to like you. They probably want you to like them. And friendliness is essential in business relations. But this is, first and foremost, a business relationship. The less personal you get, the less chance there is of giving in where you may not want to. Everyone has a personal stake in the selling or buying of a house, but intimate stories of births and deaths connected to it might be a little too much information.

✓ **Be honest with your agent:** You don't want your agent guessing what is important to you. Communicate your needs and wants just as clearly as you outlined them on paper for yourself. Make a copy for your agent. This way, you and your agent are a united team, and there will be less need for frequent conferencing. Remember that an agent is just that: your agent, the person who represents your interests. As such, he or she needs to be fully aware of your priorities.

✓ **Don't be afraid to walk away:** Remember that sombrero in Acapulco that you really wanted? Remember how you refused to pay such a ridiculous price and stalked off down the beach? Remember that the vendor followed you and offered you your prize at half the original asking price (which was still too high)? You must, at some point, be willing to walk away from the negotiating table — or beach shack — if you recognize that a compromise just can't be reached.

Deal breakers: An almost-tragic tale

While buying a home is a business transaction, important personal matters are also on the line. For many, a home means stability and comfort: Your home is where you raise your family or come to unwind, and that's why this simple purchase of goods can become complicated. You may have things in your mind that are *deal breakers* — those things on which you will not compromise. And these, of course, are different for everyone.

When Angela and Myriam put an offer in on Ziggy and Martha's house, they went in prepared to negotiate: expecting both sides would give a little and everyone would walk away getting more or less what they wanted. But what they didn't realize was Ziggy wanted to sell; Martha didn't. Martha was a walking deal breaker. Ziggy put the house onto the market, but she wasn't letting it go without a fight. She would not budge on price. She would not leave

her appliances or her garden gnomes. She would not negotiate.

Angela and Myriam really liked the house. It was in great shape, nicely renovated, it backed on a big park, and the location was perfect. They didn't even mind about the garden gnomes. But it drove them crazy that they couldn't even get one lousy little concession out of Martha. Everybody knows that listing prices are higher than selling prices! Everybody knows that extras get thrown in! What was going on here?

Ready to walk away from the deal, Angela and Myriam sat down with their real estate agent and Ziggy and Martha's agent and said they just couldn't buy the house unless the sellers budged a little. After some serious soul searching, Martha agreed to leave the washer and dryer . . . she had contemplated getting new ones anyway. This gesture of goodwill sealed the deal.

Many contracts specify that the buyer has a final walk-through before the sale's closing (or completion) date. Suppose that the seller has accepted your offer and you have a binding unconditional contract of purchase and sale. What happens if you arrive to take your walk-through, and the house is in a far different condition than when you first saw it? Call your lawyer. You may not be able to fold the deal and walk away, but your lawyer *may* be able to negotiate a holdback from the seller until the house is returned to the condition specified in the contract. Be very specific in your offer about how you expect to receive the home upon closing.

Avoid lowballing

When you start thinking about an offering price, avoid these two mistakes: The first is offering too high a price for the house. The second, much more common mistake is called *lowballing*: offering a price much lower than the home's fair market value.

Put yourself in the seller's shoes. You've worked hard for months, fixing up your house inside and out and cleaning it from stem to stern, and then you receive a purchase offer with a ludicrously low price. This is what you'll likely think of a lowball offer:

- ✔ **This buyer must be extremely stupid.** This guy's insulting my intelligence — his offer is ridiculous.

- ✔ **This buyer has just flown in from Timbuktu.** Has this dimwit done no research at all into house prices in the neighbourhood?

- ✔ **This buyer must think I'm desperate to get out and that I'll accept any offer.** Maybe he's heard rumours about my impending divorce. Maybe he's done some digging and has found out that my company's relocating. Either way, he's a slimeball.

Here's an example of how lowballing can get you into real trouble. Say that a home is listed at $299,000 and all similar homes in the neighbourhood have sold for between $275,000 and $285,000. You'll know this by looking at how much homes in the area have sold for, as we explain earlier in the chapter. If you make your first offer at $240,000 — a classic lowball offer — you risk annoying the seller, who may counter back at $298,500, or simply not counter at all. Suddenly everyone's stress level goes up. Say you come back at $245,000. The seller thinks you're not serious and breaks off negotiations. If you ever do reach an agreement, it will be a long and difficult process that was instigated by your low initial offer. A purchase offer that starts with lowballing — and continues with a frustrating and unrealistic bargaining strategy — will end up wasting everyone's time.

If instead you make your first offer for that home around $265,000, you have some room to move up, and you're letting the seller know you are serious. The seller is then required to move off his asking price to get the ball rolling. If the seller comes back at $290,000, there's a possibility you can find the middle ground, at a price that's fair to both parties.

Everyone wants to get a great deal, but you have to be realistic and analyze all the data you and your agent have collected — with a rational eye and with the goal of achieving an accepted offer you can live with. If you are comfortable with your bargaining strategy and with the results it generates, you will not suffer from "buyer's remorse."

Agreeing to Terms

Your offer to purchase is considered accepted once it has been signed and sent by one party, then signed and sent back by the other with no further changes. This constitutes approval of all the terms listed, and becomes an accepted offer. Congratulations! You've almost bought a home!

Your contract is still subject to whatever conditions you or the seller may have placed on it. If you inserted a condition requiring the home to pass a building inspection and your inspector finds that the home has a leaky roof, if the seller refuses to fix it (or to reduce the price of the home accordingly) you can cancel the contract and get your deposit back. If your lawyer does a title search on the home (see Chapter 5) and finds a problem (for example, the sellers aren't really the legal owners), you can get out of the contract by not removing the "subject to approving the title search" condition from the contract.

Usually, the terms and conditions are met, and your lawyer or real estate agent draws up waivers so that you and the seller can sign off on the satisfaction of each condition, thereby removing it from the contract. However, if you agree to *rescind* a condition without the specific requirements of the condition being met — for example, if the seller refuses to pay for the updated land survey that you stipulated in the offer and you agree to foot the bill — an *amendment* (also called a *waiver*) will be drawn up to that effect acknowledging that you are removing the condition without the seller having fulfilled it and furthermore acknowledging that you will fulfill the condition yourself (i.e., pay for the survey). More on surveys in Chapter 11.

If any agreed-on changes need to be made to the contract at this point (you and the seller have agreed to change the moving date, for example), your lawyer or agent can draw up a document, called an "Amendment to the Contract," to cover the change. All waivers and amendments must be signed by you (and the seller if necessary) to make them legally binding documents. Once all the conditions have been waived, *then* it's time to get those champagne glasses out!

If you walk away from a purchase offer that your seller has accepted *after* all the conditions have been removed from the Contract of Purchase and Sale, you not only risk losing your deposit, but if the seller is forced to sell to a lower bidder, you may be sued for the difference in price, and the seller may have other legal remedies, too. Clearly, this is to be avoided at all costs.

Once you and the seller have agreed to all the terms and have met and removed all the conditions contained in your contract, you can really congratulate yourself — you've just bought a home. You should have legible copies of all the documentation and any attached addendums or schedules, plus copies of the title search, survey certificate, and any other documents that were necessary to reach a deal. Your agent will provide you with these copies, and the agent's office will forward copies to the lawyers (or notaries) acting for both parties. (See Chapter 5 for details on hiring the services of a real estate lawyer, sometimes known as a "conveyancing lawyer.")

The final package that is your contract should include a number of separate documents:

- The Contract of Purchase and Sale
- Any schedules or addendums that have been negotiated
- A copy of the survey
- A copy of the title search
- A copy of the condominium certificate if you're buying a condo

Chapter 10

Signing On to a New Life

· ·

· ·

So you've just handed over your deposit — your first cheque with five figures (more of those to come!) — and shaken hands with your seller. Whew! That was a lot of work, but you and the seller agreed on the conditions of the Contract of Purchase and Sale and the seller accepted your offer. But just because the offer's signed doesn't mean you can sit back and relax just yet. There's a lawyer to see, an insurance company to call, a mortgage to finalize. . . . Though it may seem a little tedious, all this "official stuff" is vital to your purchase of a home.

Taking Care of the Paperwork

Don't be fooled — there's always *more* paperwork, even after you feel you've got carpal tunnel syndrome from signing documents and cheques. In order to take care of the paperwork, however, you will need help from your carefully selected team of home-buying professionals. So make those calls, schedule appointments, and get things rolling.

Professionals whom you want to see include:

✔ Lawyer

✔ Lender

✔ Home insurance agent

✔ Surveyor

✔ Inspector

This chapter deals with the fine print your lawyer sifts through when closing your deal (don't worry, you'll find no legalese here) and then takes you through the process of getting a mortgage signed off. To finish, we give you the run-down on the different types of home insurance available to safeguard your new investment. We discuss professional surveys, inspections, and warranties in Chapter 11.

Removing conditions

The main reason why you have to see so many people is to take care of the conditions you've written into your offer to purchase. In order for the contract to be binding, every condition — any clauses that you wrote into the Contract of Purchase and Sale — must be met. If your offer to purchase is "subject to financing," "subject to approval by lawyer," or "subject to roof repair" these conditions must be fulfilled. (You'll find more on conditions, or "subject to" clauses, in Chapter 9.)

In most provinces, you sign waivers to confirm that you or the seller has met each of the necessary conditions. Be sure that every condition the seller is responsible for, like fixing the roof, is done and done properly before you sign off. Make sure all conditions have been met by the prescribed subject removal date. Once all the conditions have been removed, the contract or agreement of purchase and sale is binding. The waivers, or subject removal documents, are prepared by the buyer's agent or the buyer's lawyer if no agent is used.

Paying your lawyer a visit

We recommend you choose a lawyer early in the game so once you're ready to sign the deal you know exactly who's going to review the paperwork. (Chapter 5 includes tips on how to choose your legal counsel.) If you know your lawyer's ready and waiting for your business, take the Contract of Purchase and Sale to her once the sellers have accepted your offer.

Ask your lawyer to do the following:

- ✔ Review your Contract of Purchase and Sale with you.
- ✔ Examine the conditions of sale and the subjects.
- ✔ Discuss the completion (closing) date and the anticipated subject (conditions) removals.
- ✔ Answer any questions or concerns you may have.

Your lawyer needs to know how you and your partner (if you have one) have agreed to hold title. If you are buying a house alone then you will have, of course, *sole ownership*. With co-ownership, however, you have two options:

- ✔ **Joint tenancy:** The most important feature of *joint tenancy* is "right of survivorship." If your spouse or partner dies, title to the home will be transferred over to you automatically.

- ✔ **Tenancy in common**: Unless *joint tenancy* is specifically chosen, all co-ownership situations (whether spouses, family, or friends) are deemed to be *tenancy in common*. Under *tenancy in common*, each owner's share of the home's worth is passed on to that person's heirs. Tenants in common can have unequal interest in a property (for example, two-thirds versus one-third), and can specify who will inherit their interest in the property on their death.

Your lawyer acts not only as a legal guide for your contract, but also oversees the entire process of transferring the property from the sellers to you. Your lawyer will interact with many of the professionals you're seeing, so make sure she has all their contact info. Your lawyer will:

- ✔ Arrange with your lender to transfer money from your mortgage to the seller. In most cases, your lawyer also drafts your mortgage document, double-checking that all the terms and conditions of your mortgage are properly met.

- ✔ Contact your insurance agent to verify for the lender that your home insurance is in place on the closing date. (Most lenders won't finalize your mortgage until you have home insurance.)

- ✔ Calculate the amount of money you owe the seller due to prepaid utilities and taxes (these are known as "adjustments"). Often, your lawyer will also transfer the utilities to your name. (More on adjustments later in the chapter.)

- ✔ Review the survey with you, noting any oddities that may be a concern.

- ✔ Check out the background of the property to ensure that it is legally owned by the sellers (called a "title search") and that there are no debts or claims against it (called "liens").

- ✔ Arrange with the seller's lawyer to transfer the deed from the seller to you on the closing date. The balance of the purchase price — the agreed price, minus the deposit, plus any adjustments — and the keys will also be exchanged. Review the condominium certificate with your lawyer, if you're buying a condo. Condominium certificates are also discussed in Chapter 4.

Give it due process

The time frame for your lawyer's duties will vary, depending on how many days you have until closing. One little piece of advice: Trust in the process. You may have a lot of questions and concerns, but don't panic if the lawyer says she'll do her thing, and will see you again in a month and a half. She'll let you know when she needs anything from you, whether it's a signature, the survey, or your agent's number. Waiting for the day that home is yours isn't easy — especially if you're waiting 90 days to move out of your tiny bedroom in your parents' home — but you have many more things to do before you close, so stop worrying that something might go wrong because you haven't talked to your lawyer in a couple of days.

Since condominiums are regulated provincially, there are different documents, regulations, and procedures in every province. What we refer to generally as the condominium certificate may comprise more than one document and may go by a variety of aliases in different provinces, including, but not limited to: Estoppel Certificate, Status Certificate, Information Certificate, and Declaration Document. Ask your real estate agent which documentation applies in your situation.

At the end of all this, your lawyer draws up a *statement of adjustments*, which is a summary of the financial transactions between you, your lawyer, your lender, and the seller. Items on the statement will include:

- The purchase price of the home (owed to the seller)
- Adjustments owed to the seller
- Your deposit
- The mortgage money from your lender
- GST or land transfer tax, if applicable (to be paid through the lawyer)
- Your lawyer's fees, including disbursements (costs the lawyer has taken for you: for example, couriers, photocopying) and GST

You will then get a final sum of the money you owe, which should essentially be your down payment (minus deposit), plus your lawyer's total fees and applicable taxes. This must be given to your lawyer by the closing date.

Getting that mortgage

Most mortgages won't be finalized until after the seller has accepted your offer. Hopefully, you got your mortgage pre-approved before you started home hunting (see Chapter 2). Once your offer is accepted, all you have to do is go back to your lender with the details about the home and sign lots of paper. Taking the MLS listing or feature sheet is a good idea because it should have all the information about your home that your lender will need. Many lenders will also require an appraisal; they may have their own appraisers to do the job, but the appraiser or the listing agent will make an appointment with the seller (see Chapter 5 for more information about appraisals). If you're buying in a rural area, you also have to present certificates from the government that verify the location of your well and septic tank.

Some mortgages are more flexible than others in terms of missing payments, doubling up payments, and the like (as detailed in Chapter 3), so review your specific mortgage with your lender to remember what you can and can't do.

You may be a little too short on cash once you've bought the home, paid the lawyer, redecorated, and purchased that antique armoire, so many lenders are happy to also provide a line of credit to keep you afloat for the first months. Once your lender finalizes and approves your mortgage, your lawyer will receive a cheque in trust to be given over to the seller's lawyer on closing day. Before the lender will give over all this money, however, you will have to verify that you have home insurance covering the home from the day of possession.

Insuring Your Home

"Mortgage" is just a fancy term for one whopping loan. And your collateral for this loan is your home — so it needs to be protected from anything or anyone that might cause damage (this includes *you*). Suppose one groggy morning you nod off while supervising the bacon and drop your newspaper onto the burner. Within minutes, your kitchen is a sea of flames and you can't remember where the heck that fire extinguisher went. Anything can happen in that pre-coffee stupor. In short — insurance is an absolute must. (Don't confuse this with *mortgage life insurance*, which we discuss in Chapter 3.) There are different items to protect and different ways you can protect your home, so talk to your insurance broker and make sure you get the coverage you need.

What to protect

There are two parts to home insurance: *property coverage* and *liability coverage*. Property coverage protects both your dwelling and its contents; liability coverage protects *you*. Although most policies cover all three aspects (your dwelling, your dwelling's contents, and you), you can tailor your insurance to fit the coverage you need. For example, if you are renting your home, you may simply need your dwelling protected and not its contents.

Protecting your dwelling

A dwelling is considered to be the home's structure and all permanent attached components. This can include different elements depending on the specific policy you have, so confirm what is covered with your insurance provider, especially if you get a different type of insurance for your contents than for your dwelling. The insurance provider will most likely insure you for the amount of money it will take to rebuild your house, rather than the price you paid for it.

You should be aware that your policy likely covers the replacement cost of your home *exactly as it was*. Suppose a horrible fire burned your 75-year-old house to the ground. When building codes and regulations are changed, they generally exempt existing homes. Now suppose that current building regulations do not allow houses to be built in the same way, with the same materials, or even in the same place on your lot (suppose current regulations no longer allow waterfront homes to be so close to the shoreline)! If new building standards require an upgrade when you rebuild, the extra cost will most likely *not* be covered by your insurance policy. Ask your insurance agent about a rider (an add-on policy that lets you specify additional items to be covered) or extended coverage, if you have any concerns.

Protecting your contents

Homeowners need to insure both the permanent structures (the dwelling) *and* the contents of their homes. In contrast, condo buildings are generally insured by the condominium corporation, so most condo owners need only worry about ensuring the contents of their homes. If you are a condo owner, you need to find out exactly where the condo corporation's policy ends and yours should begin. Sometimes the corporation's policy will only cover the bare walls, leaving you to provide coverage for fixtures like kitchen cabinets. There are two forms of content insurance:

✔ **Actual cash value:** when you make a claim (assuming it is approved) you will receive cash for the current value of the item. This is *not* the value of buying the same item new, but rather the cost of buying the item minus the depreciation in value due to age, wear, or obsolescence.

✔ **Replacement cost:** the lost or damaged item is covered for the cost of replacing the item with one of comparable quality. Obviously, since a replacement cost policy costs your insurance provider more than a depreciated-value cash payout, this kind of coverage comes with a heftier price tag.

Protecting yourself

Liability insurance protects you in the event that you, or your property, damage either someone else's property or someone else's person. This type of coverage covers you anywhere in the world. So, if while staying at a lovely B & B in the Welsh countryside, you knock over a lamp and burn down the building, liability insurance will cover any damage, medical, or legal fees that become your responsibility. It also covers you if a tree on your property falls onto your neighbour's car. How much coverage you require is up to you. If you buy a new home with a swimming pool at the edge of a sea cliff and you know the neighbour's kids will be hanging around your place, you may want more liability coverage than if you buy a basic bungalow.

How you're protected

There are two general ways that you can be covered by insurance. Both policies work on an *exclusion principle*: Either the insurance provider will cover an event only if it's specifically named in your policy (standard), or the provider will cover all events *with the exception* of those specifically named in your policy (all-risks). Because an all-risks approach covers many more situations (such as your dog causing significant water damage by knocking over your 100-gallon fish tank), all-risks policies are more expensive.

✔ **Standard (or basic):** *Standard* policies generally cover most "acts of God" damage, such as fire, lightning, wind or hail, theft, vandalism, and other incidents that are inherently beyond your control. Standard policies work on a *named perils* basis. A *peril* is what insurance companies call potentially damaging events, like the ones just mentioned. To work on a "named peril" basis means that an event is only covered if it is specifically named in your policy.

✔ **All-risks:** *All-risks* coverage typically involves some *exclusions* — specific events named in the policy contract that will not be covered under the policy. Exclusions might include faulty workmanship, wear due to regular use, or damage that would have been prevented with proper maintenance. Any event not specifically listed in your policy is covered, so if things just "happen" to you, consider getting an all-risks policy.

While the term "standard" is also applied to dwelling and content coverage at a standard level, insurers usually use the term "comprehensive" to describe insurance that protects both your dwelling and your contents on an all-risks policy. (Be aware that even under a comprehensive policy there will be limits imposed on the value of your claims for some items of personal property.) Homeowners wanting to protect both their dwelling and their contents don't necessarily have to protect both parts with the same kind of policy. They can also get protection known as *broad coverage*. Broad coverage works partly on an all-risks basis and partly on a named perils basis. A broad policy covers "all risks," meaning anything that might cause loss or damage to your *dwelling*. A broad policy covers named perils when it comes to the *contents* of your home.

Read your policy carefully! Make sure you understand exactly what is covered and what is not. Insurance providers can differ greatly on their coverage of certain types of damage — coverage for water damage, in particular, ranges all across the board. Note the deductibles for various categories.

There are no ballpark figures we can offer here on what home insurance costs. Your *premiums* (annual fees) depend on a large number of individual factors. For example, home size, modernity, and features, as well as neighbourhood, proximity to fire stations and hydrants, type of coverage, coverage provider, and your track record can all play a part in determining your premiums. The value of your home will also come into play, but that is not necessarily the same as its sticker price. The important price for an insurance provider is not how much you paid for your home, or what its current market value is, but how much it would cost to rebuild it. This amount may not be equivalent to what you paid for your house.

Extending your coverage

If there are particular items you want covered, or particular events you are worried about, you can introduce *riders* to your insurance. Riders are add-on policies that allow you to customize (as much as possible) your policy by specifying that particular additional items or perils are covered. However, your insurance provider has to agree to provide coverage for these items or events, which is not a given, and they will adjust your premiums — upwards! — to take account of the extended coverage. You can also choose *endorsements*, which are similar in purpose to riders, but are simply add-in statements or amendments to your current policy, as opposed to whole additional policies. Again, the more you ask to be covered, the more expensive your premium typically will be, but if you want your $10,000 painting fully protected, your peace of mind will be worth a rider or endorsement. Ask your insurer about the various extended coverage packages they offer.

Home office owners beware

Home insurance is not business insurance. If you run a small business out of your home, have a home office, or have property in your home that you use for business purposes, chances are this property is *not* covered by your home insurance policy. Furthermore, should a client be injured while visiting your home office, your liability insurance may not cover the accident. Many insurance providers offer home business packages as either riders or endorsements. If you use your home for business purposes at all, ask specifically what is covered and what is not under your home insurance policy.

In this information age, your home office's data may be more valuable than the computer you use to access it. Although you may be reimbursed for hardware, and perhaps software under some policies, you will not be reimbursed for lost data. Similarly, if your Web site inspires a liability claim against you, your insurance may not protect you. Find out before you upload that sensitive classified document! Ask your insurance provider exactly what is and isn't covered.

Getting the best deal

Once you know what sort of policy you want, and the particular riders and endorsements that suit your needs, you can start comparing prices. There are three steps you can take to make sure you're getting the best deal:

1. **First and foremost, shop around.** Different insurance providers offer a variety of packages and prices. The cheapest is not always your best option — ensure that the insurance you're buying meets your requirements as closely as possible.

2. **Ask all the providers you investigate about special discounts.** For example, some insurance providers may give discounts to non-smokers, or to houses that have good safety and security systems.

3. **Find out what the reduction in your premiums will be if you increase your deductible.** The *deductible* is the amount that you, the policyholder, have to pay toward replacement costs. For example, if your $2,000 stereo is stolen, *you* pay the $500 deductible and your insurance company pays the remaining $1,500 to replace the system. You can usually save a lot of money in the long-run by reducing your deductible. Standard minimum deductibles are anywhere from $200 to $500, but if you increase it to $1,000, you should be able to reduce your premiums significantly.

Are you covered?

If you take nothing else away from this section, take this single piece of advice — assume nothing, question everything. Make sure you ask *at least* the following questions when you investigate different insurance providers:

✔ Whom does the policy cover?

✔ Exactly what property is covered (e. g., does it include the backyard shed)?

✔ What perils/items are included and what perils/items are excluded?

✔ What discounts do you offer?

✔ What are my responsibilities as a policyholder? Under what conditions are you allowed to terminate my coverage?

✔ Are riders or endorsements available? How will they affect my premiums? How will they affect my responsibilities as a policyholder?

✔ What is the procedure for making a claim?

✔ How and when can I contact a representative with questions about my policy or a claim (e.g., is there a 24-hour toll-free hotline for policyholders)?

✔ How long does it usually take to process claims? What is the maximum time limit, upon your approval of my claim, for providing me with due compensation?

Picking up the tab on less expensive accidents or damages, even if they are covered by your policy, can save you money over the long haul. The fewer claims you make, the less your premiums increase. If you make numerous small claims, you can even risk being branded a "potential risk," and not only will your premiums increase, but insurance providers could reject you in the future.

Last but not least, make sure your home insurance kicks in the very same day you take legal ownership of the property — whether or not you've actually moved in. But, if you're building your home, you should be aware that damage or loss during the building process is often not covered by home insurance policies. Once again, and we can't repeat it enough, ask providers exactly what is covered and what is not.

Chapter 11

Closing Time: Inspections, Surveys, and Warranties

● ●

In This Chapter

▶ Getting what you pay for: professional home inspections

▶ Staking out your territory: land surveys

▶ Insuring your newly built home: new home warranties

▶ Walking through your home

● ●

*T*he next two chapters cover the "before" and "after" picture of closing the deal on your new home. We tell you what to expect from your inspection, land survey, and new home warranty (if you're buying a newly built home) — all-important parts of closing that shouldn't be overlooked. We tell you why this is. Chapter 12 takes a look at closing-day events and moving tips. Then you celebrate!

The Ins and Outs of Inspections

We can't stress this enough: Make sure your offer is subject to an inspection. We'll spare you the dreadful horror stories we've heard and simply say that it's wise to have a professional inspector examine the home. Some sellers have inspections done before they put their homes on the market (a pre-inspection), but as a buyer you should have your own professional home inspection done. Occasionally lenders require an inspection before approving a mortgage, so unless you're Mr. or Mrs. Moneybuckets and have the cash in your back pocket, getting financing may be your main motivation for getting an inspection. The same goes for condominiums. In the Vancouver market, for example, a lender may request a copy of an inspection report if she's unsure about a particular building's soundness, before giving final approval for the mortgage.

Include a *"subject to inspection"* clause in your Contract of Purchase and Sale to purchase any home. (See Chapter 9 for more information on "subject to" clauses.) In effect, a "subject to inspection" clause acts as a safety mechanism:

It releases a buyer from the obligation to purchase a home if an inspector finds major faults in the building.

Once the seller accepts your offer, have the house inspected as soon as possible. If there are any problems, you'll want as much time as possible to resolve them and make decisions. Even if the home is sound, the inspector will be able to share a lot of good information about your new house with you and tip you off to anything that you'll want to keep an eye on.

Your inspector will look at the structural elements of the home, including the basement, the roof, and the heating, plumbing, and electrical systems. She usually goes systematically through the home and gives you a full, written report when she's finished. A good inspector will also make recommendations on what should be improved (for example, install GFCI outlets and a vent in the bathroom, or add a banister to the basement stairs).

If any problems are uncovered — and this can be anything from a leaky faucet to a leaky basement — it's decision time. One option is to *collapse* (cancel) your offer, since the condition of a positive inspection was not met. Your other option is to write in a new condition that will require the seller to fix the leaky basement and any other problem areas. You are now renegotiating the contract, and adding new conditions requires consent from both the seller and the buyer (see Chapter 9 for more on the negotiating process). If the seller refuses to accept a new conditional clause, your next option is to propose a price reduction to cover the costs you will incur to fix the problem. If you and the seller can't reach an agreement, you can collapse the offer and look for another house. Keep in mind that the seller is under no obligation to renegotiate. In fact, she may have priced the house acknowledging there was work to be done, and in her mind she has already discounted the price to cover the repairs.

Inspection costs can vary greatly if you're buying a very large or unusual property. In most cases, however, you'll find inspectors charge a fee in the range of $250 to $500. A typical building inspection will take two to three hours. On completion, you should receive a full, written inspection report that's signed and dated by the inspector.

Inspecting a newly built home

Even if you're buying a newly built home, you should have an inspection done before you accept the home. You can make this part of your "pre-completion" inspection, before the completion of the sale. In new construction contracts, there is usually a provision for a pre-completion *deficiency inspection* of the property. You can write into your contract that a professional building inspector will accompany you when you are doing your deficiency inspection. Before you agree to the terms of the sale contract, talk to your lawyer to ensure that you are entitled to a deficiency inspection.

If you don't know enough about construction to recognize potential problems or faulty work, you should bring along a professional home inspector. After the visual inspection is completed, you will be asked to sign a *Certificate of Completion* (sometimes also referred to as a *Certificate of Completion and Possession*), stating that everything you paid for is complete. You can have the certificate drawn up by your lawyer and a representative of the builder, although many New Home Warranty Program–registered builders will already have professionally prepared documents for this purpose. Any apparent omissions or defects discovered during your inspection should be noted on the Certificate of Completion, since this certificate is registered at your local NHWP office. Filing the certificate is necessary for your warranty coverage to commence. More on New Home Warranty Programs later in this chapter.

Your inspector should double-check that the materials the builders used are the same as what you requested or expected, that new appliances are properly installed, and that fittings and equipment are located as specified. Look at many of the same things you would investigate if you bought a resale home: Make sure the *gradient*, the angles of the land around the foundation, will direct water away from the house and look for any signs of leaking in the basement and from the roof. Check the metal flashings around windows and the chimney to make sure they are properly caulked, and check to make sure all the toilets flush properly. You wouldn't believe what gets thrown down the toilet during the construction process! Look into whether your province has a New Home Warranty Program (see Appendix C).

The inspection

A professional inspector knows what to look for to ensure that a resale home is up to snuff — that it meets modern requirements and has a sound structure. An average inspection should take two to three hours, depending on the size of the home. A good inspector will have you accompany him and will encourage lots of questions. Sometimes the inspector will start when you're not in the home — there's not much for you to do when the inspector is poking through the attic. You should definitely be present for the last hour or two of the inspection so that the inspector can go over the good, the bad, and the ugly with you.

An inspection is a visual walk-through to report on the elements of the home. It's not meant to be a picky this-door-knob-won't-turn-fully kind of examination, but an overall report of whether the home is sound. Of course, there are no guarantees, since a home may have problems even the inspector can't find. If the sewer system (which belongs to the city) under your new house is about to collapse, causing the bottom to literally fall out of your home, there's no way an inspector can anticipate that.

What you see isn't always what you get

Say you make an offer on a beautiful detached two-storey house in Toronto's Little Italy. Elsie and Peter, the older couple who've lived there for 45 years, have lovingly maintained the home. You arrange an inspection to cover one of the conditions of the sale. You and your spouse are both present when the inspector does a routine check behind a three-prong electrical outlet, and he discovers that it still has the old two-wire, ungrounded system. Building code requires that every three-prong outlet be connected to a grounded system. When you look behind an electrical outlet, you should see three conductor wires: a black "hot" wire, a white neutral wire, and a green ground wire. Elsie and Peter's outlets only have a hot wire and a neutral wire. The "grounded" outlets weren't grounded at all.

Peter and Elsie, the owners, are devastated. They had paid thousands of dollars to have the house rewired with a grounded system. It turns out that the contractor had only changed the two-prong outlets to three-prong outlets, nothing more. Behind the walls, the original, ungrounded system remains. When you go back to the negotiating table, you can ask for a significant price cut to cover the costs of getting the house properly rewired. But Peter and Elsie are still horrified that the contractor has duped them, and they can't bring themselves to cut the price on their house, which represents the bulk of their retirement fund.

At this point, you could break off negotiations, by choosing not to remove the subject to inspection clause, thereby collapsing your offer. Or you could go with your agent's suggestion to keep the deal alive: the original electrician should be contacted and forced to deliver the grounded electrical system he was hired to install in the first place. You can remedy a few unpleasant surprises that are discovered during a home inspection, but you need to uncover the problems in order to address them.

The inspector completes most of the inspection report while touring the property, so the report is usually organized into locations starting with the site itself, and working through the exterior and interior of the house. See Appendix B for a good example of a full home inspection report. Your inspection report should cover all categories of concern relevant to each part of the house and property, including structural, exterior, interior, plumbing, electrical, and heating and ventilation components. Here's a rough list of the kinds of problems an inspection report will alert you to:

Home exterior

Your inspector will examine the following exterior components of the house:

- ✔ **Roof surface:** The roof should be in at least *visibly* good condition. An unacceptably aged roof surface will be obvious, but in the early stages roof degeneration can be quite subtle, and virtually invisible to the untrained eye. A roof surface in poor condition can mean water leakage, poor insulation, and in extreme cases even lead to roof collapse.

- ✔ **Eaves:** The eaves should be in good condition, with no holes and minimal rust. Eaves in poor condition mean rain and snow will not drain appropriately and this can cause serious difficulties if water accumulates on your roof or near your home's foundation.

- ✔ **Chimney(s):** The chimney(s) should be free from cracks or loose sections in the masonry, and should have a chimney cap. Chimneys in poor shape could cause ventilation problems.

- ✔ **Chimney flue(s):** The chimney flue is the exhaust vent over the fireplace. An unused fireplace can quickly have its flue blocked by debris or even a bird nest or two. Flues that are not in good condition may signal a malfunctioning or improperly maintained chimney.

- ✔ **Windows:** The windows should not show any signs of wood or water damage. Damaged windows will be sure indications of water and air penetration into the interior of the home.

- ✔ **Siding/exterior walls:** Whether brick or siding, the house's exterior walls should be free of cracks, gaps, or signs of water damage. These will be possible indications of damage to *interior* materials, rotting, or moulds inside walls. Watch out!

- ✔ **Gradient:** The gradient, or slope of the ground, should be properly angled away from the home. An incorrect gradient will allow water drainage into the basement or foundation, causing water damage, rotting, or even fungus growth.

- ✔ **Foundation:** The house's foundation should be free of cracks, bulges, or deformities. These abnormalities could indicate an extremely serious structural problem. Also, termite tubes or other signs of infestation will manifest themselves in this area.

- ✔ **Septic system/cesspool:** Septic tanks and cesspools should be tested for possible leaching. You can request a dye test if the inspector does not plan to run one.

Basic home interior

This is what you can expect your inspector to check for on the inside:

- ✔ **Flooding/leaks:** The inspector will note these and other visible signs of water damage inside the home. The inspector will also be able to tell you if any waterproofing measures, a *sump-pump*, or other additions have been installed. A sump pump is an electric pump installed in a recess in the basement (or occasionally outside the house) that will kick into action if the level of water in the drainage system starts to rise. The pump will mechanically aid the gravitational flow of the water away from the house. Waterproofing a home is extremely expensive, and this makes it important for buyers to be aware of measures already in place.

✔ **Insulation/ventilation:** This becomes problematic if the home leaks or doesn't allow moisture to evaporate, putting pretty much all of the major structural components at risk. Excessive moisture can cause rotting, rust, electrical shorts, and fungal growth. Furthermore, good insulation and ventilation will keep heating and cooling costs to a minimum.

✔ **Other unsafe components:** This is largely dependent on the age of the house. For example, paint may be old enough to contain lead; there may be missing railings on staircases; or there could be urea formaldehyde foam insulation (UFFI) throughout the home. (See Chapter 7 for information on UFFI.) Building materials change over the years and so do safety standards. A qualified inspector will have up-to-date information and will recognize potentially dangerous components.

Interior systems/mechanics

Your inspector examines these systems:

✔ **Plumbing:** Plumbing systems and pipes may no longer be up to scratch. The inspector will be on the lookout for rust and leaking or water stains that warrant further examination. Checking water pressure and the condition of drains and pipes are also part of the job.

✔ **Heating:** Heating systems may be outdated or inefficient. For example, the valve that controls the flow of hot water into radiators can rust away, leaving you with no way to turn down the heat in that individual unit. Other problems might be unsafe exhaust venting or chimneys that are blocked. The inspector looks for all of these problems, as well as for indications that the furnace, including the motor and burners, is functioning properly.

✔ **Electrical:** Electrical systems may be potential fire hazards or simply not dependable. Wiring always warrants extra attention. Your inspector should check any exposed wiring and its condition. If your home or condominium was built in the 1970s, it may have aluminum wiring that is not reliable. In aluminum wires, electricity actually flows away from the screws used to hold the wiring in place at the back of an electrical outlet. Air pockets form between the wires and the screws, letting electricity arc between them, ultimately burning the wire away and deadening the outlet. Your inspector checks for signs of unreliable wiring, and also for problems such as reverse polarity outlets and two-prong convenience outlets.

Once you get the inspector's full report, you'll be able to evaluate whether the home in question is as good as it looks. The inspection report should list any substandard or failing elements, and the inspector should make suggestions regarding necessary repairs and how those jobs should be prioritized. Your inspector should also be able to furnish some rough estimates of the repair costs.

B.C.'s leaky condo crisis affects more than just condos

One of the first things they teach budding architects is "Water is your worst enemy." Homeowners in British Columbia's coastal climate learned this lesson the hard way. After the building explosion from the mid-1980s to the late 1990s, it was clear that something was very, very wrong. Buildings were leaking all over the lower Mainland and Vancouver Island, and protective tarps became a standard part of the streetscape. Condos were singled out as the problem at first, but it quickly became clear that *building envelope problems*, structural flaws that permit water to penetrate a building, don't affect condos exclusively.

In 1998, the B.C. government passed the Homeowner Protection Act and opened the Homeowner Protection Office (HPO) to license builders, enforce new home warranty regulations, conduct research and education, and administer financial assistance programs to owners of leaky homes. Builders in B.C. now need to be licensed through HPO in order to get a permit to build any detached house or condominium project. If you're buying a house in B.C.'s lower Mainland or on Vancouver Island, do some investigating: If it's a fairly new resale home, is the warranty still valid? If it's a brand new home, make sure that the builder is licensed with the HPO.

Contact the Homeowner Protection Office (HPO) at:

P.O. Box 11132 Royal Centre
2270-1055 West Georgia Street
Vancouver, B.C. V6E 3P3
Toll-Free: 1-800-407-7757

E-mail: buildingbc@hpo.bc.ca
Web site: www.hpo.bc.ca

A good inspector won't offer to do home repairs for you — it would be a huge conflict of interest. Your inspector should not recommend contractors to do the repairs unless they are very specialized repairs that require highly skilled trades. Your inspector is hired to investigate your home — not to give work to his buddies in the building trades. On the other hand, if the inspector gives you a choice of several recommended contractors, he's probably not just advertising for his friends.

Choosing a good inspector

Find a licensed inspector with a good reputation and membership in the *Canadian Association of Home Inspectors* (CAHI). The CAHI maintains minimum standards for home inspectors regarding education and professional conduct. If you know any people who have recently bought (or possibly sold) their home, ask if they had an inspection and if they were happy with the inspector.

If not, there are a number of resources to try. Ask your real estate agent, friends, relatives, or people in the neighbourhood if they can recommend some good inspectors, or call your provincial or regional association of home inspectors. (See Appendix C for a list of the CAHI offices across the country.) Your local CAHI office can provide the names of home inspectors in good standing who work in your neighbourhood. If you still haven't found anyone, check the Internet (some real estate board sites have links to real estate lawyers, inspectors, or appraisers) and as a last resort look in the phone book (although this is the "eeny meeny miney moe" method). Check to see if the people you call are members of an association of home inspectors, have an office you can visit (rather than a cell phone number), and have a current business licence.

You Are the Owner of All You Survey

Once upon a time, kings and queens built their castles on hills because they could rule over all they could see. In today's smaller kingdoms, you can rule over all you survey. It's a surprising fact that many of Canada's homebuyers don't bother to get an updated land survey before closing the deal — especially when you consider that your lender will probably want to see a copy before agreeing to finance the purchase, and your lawyer will draw up your deed using information from the survey. The sellers may have a survey of the property and the bank may accept a recent survey, but if there is any uncertainty, a new survey will be required. No surveys are required for condominiums.

Land surveys are also known as Building Location Certificates, Mortgage Certificates, Surveyor's Certificates, Real Property Reports, Plot Plans, and Certificates of Non-Encroachment.

Why you need a survey

A land survey is a legal map of a property's boundaries. In the best-case scenario, the seller will have provided you with an up-to-date survey that's perfectly legal — in other words, one that's copyrighted and valid only if the original is signed and sealed. If the survey the seller hands you is old, unsealed, or otherwise fishy in any way, get your own done. When it's performed by a professional who is familiar with your region, a land survey clarifies the following issues:

✔ It informs you of zoning, building, or land commission restraints. This means that you'll be able to know whether that swimming pool you plan to build (not to mention the solarium that the previous owner built) is legal.

Parking problems

Toronto is famous for its lack of parking, so Bert and Ernie decided they really needed parking when they went to buy a home. They found a wonderful home that didn't have parking, but were encouraged by the other homes on the street, most of which either had front-yard parking or garages accessible by a laneway. The sellers had a survey from when they bought the home ten years ago, and Bert and Ernie didn't notice anything different about it: The deck and shed hadn't changed. They decided, against their lawyer's recommendation, that this survey was fine.

Once they bought the home, however, Bert and Ernie were appalled to find that a Toronto bylaw prohibits the installation of front-yard parking in their neighbourhood, a bylaw enacted after the survey was done. Street parking was hard to come by, so instead of putting in a garden in their backyard, they decided to put a parking spot in there.

Due to the size of their backyard, Bert and Ernie ended up with a small open parking spot, and the survey revealed they would not be able to build a garage because it would encroach on their neighbour's property. The survey may not have shown the change in parking bylaws, but it would have shown the poor parking arrangement available in the backyard.

✔ It gives you certified, accurate measurements of the property and the house, garden shed, garage, and any other buildings on it.

✔ It lets you know of environmental or contamination problems on your site, such as whether your well draws on runoff from a nearby major road, or whether the site is in an area proven to contain dangerous levels of lead in the soil.

✔ It states who may review the survey. A land survey, contrary to popular belief, is not a public document.

If there is no up-to-date survey available, be sure to write "subject to survey" into your offer — this will allow enough time for a proper and thorough survey to be done. A slipshod, cheap, hurried survey won't do you any good if a boundary dispute comes up, or if you decide to subdivide, build an addition, or re-mortgage.

Finding a professional surveyor

Like finding a good doctor or mechanic, the first step in the hunt for a professional surveyor is to ask around. Ask your potential new neighbours, as well as the previous owners of the home, for the companies they used.

They may provide you with an excellent surveyor who is familiar with your locality — and all the environmental, archeological, and regulatory quirks that might go along with it. Your agent, banker, or lawyer may be able to recommend a surveyor.

Failing this approach, hit the Yellow Pages. You may also be able to surf the Net for a good surveyor. Many provincial land surveyors' associations have Web sites, complete with member lists and other helpful information. Look for long-established companies, or those that are members of your provincial land surveyors association. Call three of them, describing the job you need done, and be ready to supply them with a legal description of the property as well as the civic address. Record how each company proposes to do the job and approximately how much they would charge to do it. Finally, ask to see samples of their work. Compare the companies' methods, estimates, and samples, and you'll find the surveyor who is right for you.

Does This Come with a Warranty?

A $30 clock radio comes with a warranty, but what about your house? If you're buying a newly built home, you may be covered by something called a *New Home Warranty*. But it's nothing like the piece of paper that came with your new coffee maker. A New Home Warranty is actually a type of third-party insurance. And it may or may not come with your home, depending on whether or not your builder has bought into a plan.

Complicated? Well, yes. Basically, a New Home Warranty is insurance for your builder while the home is being built. Then, once the *Certificate of Completion* has been transferred over to you, it becomes a kind of consumer warranty. Unlike homeowner's insurance (which you'll also need and which we discuss in Chapter 10), the builder rather than the homebuyer buys the policy. Of course, just because you don't buy it doesn't mean you won't end up paying for it: The builder will likely tack the cost of the warranty on to the purchase price.

Legislation concerning New Home Warranties varies across the country, and not all provinces require them. In other words, not all homes come with them, and not all homes are covered in the same way. You'll have to ask your builder whether your home is protected by one. Your builder should be able to provide you with a registration, enrollment, or membership number for the warranty plan. That way, you can check with the issuer of the warranty to ensure that everything is in order.

If you do have a warranty for your house, keep it. Keep all documentation and policy information, registration confirmation, and contact numbers somewhere safe, where you can access them if you ever need to.

Note that in order to be covered under a province's *New Home Warranty Program* (NHWP), you may have to pay a registration fee. Pay attention to the timing and schedule of the warranty. Some coverage is only good for one year after you take possession of the house, and coverage of different problems may expire at different times. If you do have any problems or questions, you should call your provincial NHWP office. They can answer your questions and give you a list of builders that are registered with them as members of the NHWP. Some provincial NHWP offices provide ratings of the local registered builders based on track record for both creating and solving problems. Others supply you with a list of criteria that builders have to meet in order to be registered members. Either way, you get the security of knowing you're choosing a builder that has been evaluated on a regular basis and meets high standards for quality and service. The New Home Warranty Program should be listed in your local phone book, or, your provincial government's Consumer Affairs Ministry can direct you to the warranty program specific to your province.

What's covered

So what does your New Home Warranty cover? The details vary across the country. Most include protection for some (but not necessarily all) the following, with different items covered for different lengths of time:

- Settling cracks in drywall (usually for the first year or two),
- Defects in workmanship and materials,
- Water penetration,
- Violations of building and safety codes,
- Structural defects, and
- Down payment protection.

Timelines on the coverage also vary from sea to shining sea, so you'll have to check your specific policy for the details. It's important to know what you are covered for as well as what you're *not* covered for.

With a warranty, you're in the driver's seat

A warranty can come in handy when things go wrong. If your "unobstructed view of the lake" is seen through a gaping hole in the wall, you'll want to have that certificate to turn to. In the best of worlds, you let your builder know of the problem and she builds you a new bay window where you can relax and enjoy the vista. In the worst of worlds, he or she might argue that the hole isn't really a hole, but a great alternative to a cat door. Without another person there to arbitrate — except for the courts — things can get ugly pretty quickly.

In the event that you and your builder disagree over needed repairs, or what exactly qualifies as a defect, a New Home Warranty can come in handy. Because a New Home Warranty is backed up by a third party, someone else can step in to settle disputes, keeping both your interests and the builder's interests in mind.

You might want to think twice about your purchase if your builder isn't making a warranty part of the bargain. If you're buying a condo, make sure that you get a warranty for the unit and that the condominium board has a separate warranty that covers the common elements.

Put it in writing

Verbal agreements don't usually hold much clout. If you notice any defects and wish to make a claim, you *must* put the complaint in writing to your builder and keep a copy for your records. You should also send a copy to the issuer of the warranty to keep on file in case of a dispute. Photographs are also a good way to document problems. Many builders will give you a form to fill out; otherwise, organize your concerns room-by-room and include as much detail as possible about the nature of the problem. These documents should always include the plan number, lot number, and address of the residence in question. Oh, and of course, you have to file before the end of the warranty period.

When things go awry

Your warranty should outline a "reasonable time frame" in which builders should fix any problems that have been brought to their attention. "Reasonable," unfortunately, can mean a lot of things. One plan, for instance, gives builders up to a year to rectify defects. So if the light fixture in your bathroom doesn't work, you might be sitting in the dark for a long, long time. Getting your brother to re-wire might not be a good idea: Most plans won't automatically reimburse you if you go ahead and get someone else to do the work, and some repairs might void the warranty altogether.

Pre-Closing Walk-Through

Taking a pre-closing walk-through is more common in some parts of Canada than in others. Your agent will arrange a time that is suitable for you and the seller, and will accompany you on the walk-through; an hour should be sufficient. You should try to schedule your final walk-through around 24 hours before your scheduled closing date. The less time you leave between your final check and the actual closing assures that you will definitely take possession of the home in exactly the condition you want. Hopefully, the home will be empty of all the seller's possessions, so it's easier to imagine where you'll put the grand piano, but chances are the home will be waiting for a final packing.

This is a perfect time to take measurements for curtains and blinds, carpets, and large pieces of furniture. You might also want to bring in paint chips or wallpaper samples — or your decorator — if you plan to change the decor.

When you take your final pre-closing walk-through, check that all the chattels are in place — that everything that the sellers agreed to leave with the house is still there. Things like the fridge and stove are commonly indicated as chattel in a Contract of Purchase and Sale. Besides confirming that the home contains all the chattels agreed on contractually, your pre-closing walk-through gives you a chance to check that everything you *expected* would stay with the house is still there. Some people, for reasons yet to be determined, take fixtures with them: They cut off phone jacks, remove light switch panels, towel racks, cupboard doors, toilet roll dispensers, and sometimes fridges. If you find out early, you can discuss new problems with your lawyer, before your final exchange with the sellers.

If the sellers are at home, you can ask them all kinds of questions about the quirks of the home and neighbourhood. In addition to the neighbourhood gossip, you can find out when garbage day is, when the roses will bloom, how to keep the raccoons out the garbage, and the standard temperature the home and furnace likes. At this point, the sellers will probably be more predisposed to tell you about the not-so-great things: how the next-door neighbour likes to hog two parking spaces with her Continental, how the outlet for the washing machine is linked to the basement light (so that if you turn off the light when you go upstairs, the washing machine will stop), and how the neighbourhood tomcat thinks of your front porch as his territory and marks it as such. Although these things might deflate your enthusiasm toward your new home, it's better to know about them in advance.

Chapter 12

Closing Time: Closing Events and Moving Day

*W*hat happens on closing day depends on what you do *before* closing day. Stripped to its bare bones, the *closing day*, sometimes called *completion day*, is when you must have the papers signed (usually, you'll do this a day or two before), pay for your new home, and transfer the title. If your real estate team is well organized, you may just have to sit by the phone and wait for your lawyer or agent to call to congratulate you that your new home is now registered in your name and you can come get the keys. All the professionals on your team, your real estate agent, your lawyer, and your lender, will be able to give you an idea of what remains to be done on the closing day and which elements will involve you.

You probably don't need us to remind you to read all documents and raise any concerns you have *before* you sign.

What You Sign

How does closing work? First of all you have to read, clarify, and sign the following:

> ✔ **Mortgage:** Also called a *Deed of Trust*, this includes all the details of the mortgage agreement and, typically, allows that the lender can take possession of your property if you default on the loan.

✔ **Mortgage note:** Also known as a "commitment letter," this guarantees you will pay your mortgage and lays out the terms of the loan, when and how it must be paid, any penalties that may apply, etc.

✔ **Affidavits:** Depending on the laws of your province or the requirements of your lender, you may sign several of these. Your lawyer will explain the implications of each. For example, often you will be asked to confirm that your property will be your primary residence.

✔ **Down payment cheque:** To seal the deal, you will have to sign away a very large amount.

✔ **Title:** The transfer of title (registration of change of ownership) is done at the land title office. The seller must sign a warranty deed stating that no new loans have been taken out against it and it is clear for the new owners. This deed must be notarized by a lawyer or notary and registered at the land titles office.

What you pay

We explain closing costs in Chapter 2, but here is a reminder of the costs you'll be expected to pay on that day.

✔ **Down payment:** You pay the portion not covered by deposit that accompanied the offer

✔ **Mortgage costs:** You may pay some or all of the following: application fee (usually waived), assumption fee, processing fee, prepaid interest, mortgage insurance, CMHC insurance, application fee, and the GST on the insurance if you have a high-ratio mortgage, etc.

✔ **Insurance:** You pay for fire and liability insurance on your property. It's necessary to purchase this before closing.

✔ **Lawyer's fee:** You usually pay between $400 and $600. Discuss this with your lawyer early in the process.

✔ **Lawyer's disbursements:** You usually pay between $400 and $600. This not only covers the cost of more complicated procedures your lawyer performs on your behalf, such as the title search, it also covers miscellaneous everyday tasks like courier fees and photocopies.

✔ **Adjustments:** You pay money due to the seller for prepaid taxes and utilities.

✔ **Land transfer taxes:** You pay provincial tax on a home purchase, ranging from 0.5 percent to 4 percent. Check with your lawyer, banker, or agent to see if these taxes are charged in your province.

> ✔ **GST:** You pay GST on a newly built home as well as on a home that has been substantially renovated. You may be eligible for a rebate if the home costs less than $450,000. Note that you will also be charged GST on the services of your lawyer.

If you ever thought it would be really fun to open a suitcase and start unloading packets of bills like they do in the movies, this might just be the one transaction where you could fulfill that fantasy. Most people, however, settle for paying their closing costs with a simple, pocket-size certified cheque or bank draft.

In addition to paying the rest of the down payment (some will be covered by the deposit you made with your offer), you will also have to pay lawyer's fees and *disbursements* (expenses your lawyer incurred on your behalf, such as courier charges, photocopying), taxes, etc. Your lender will provide the mortgage money to your lawyer, who will forward the full amount owed to the seller's lawyer. Once the exchange is complete, the two lawyers (or agents acting on behalf of your lawyer) go to the local land titles office, and formally change the title and transfer the deed.

In some cases, the *possession date*, the day you get the keys, is the same as the completion or closing date. If so, the seller's lawyer or agent will give your lawyer or agent the keys when the title is transferred and they will bring them back to you. Never count on getting your keys very early in the day!

Give yourself enough time to collect all your funds into one account. If you are wiring substantial amounts of money from investments or from a partner's account, you may need a couple of days to process the transfers. Ask your lawyer for a chance to review all the closing charges at least one business day before closing. Keep funds ready in case it totals more than you expected and keep credit card balances low so you can access additional funds quickly if necessary. Most lawyers will let you know well in advance how much money you will need.

A Moving Experience

Hopefully you had a good party when you got possession — because your life is about to turn upside down. Moving ranks as one of the top ten most stressful events in a person's life. Why? Well, technically, moving means transporting all your worldly possessions from one place to another. What it really means is moving your life. From finding a new school for your children to figuring out where the best place is to get pizza in the middle of the night, moving involves more than packing tape and a loaded van. Moving your stuff may take as little as a few hours. Moving your life will take a lot longer.

Moving day versus closing day

Although it may seem like the logical choice, moving day shouldn't necessarily be closing day. The actual closing involves many different players, can take a long time, and doesn't always go as planned. What if you've got movers sitting on your front porch at dawn, clocking time on closing day?

It gets worse. If the land titles office happens to be busy on the date you planned to close, the title may not even be transferred by day's end, and you will have to wait to take possession. This doesn't happen all that often, but when it does, it tends to be on a Friday. A lot of people close their houses on Friday, thinking they can move in on Saturday. This makes for a very busy land titles office. If the office closes before your house does, you'll be stuck waiting around until Monday before the deal is done.

It might be wise not to plan to have your closing day coincide with moving day, especially if it's at the end of the week, or at the beginning or end of a month, when city clerks are busiest. Schedule your closing day well before your moving day, so you're ready for anything.

Timing is everything

When you move can have as much of an impact on your wallet as what you move and how you move it. You can sometimes save a lot of money by choosing your moving date strategically.

Keep in mind that, like hotels, rental and moving companies often have "off-season" rates geared to times when demand is at its lowest. Pricing rates generally revolve around renters' patterns. For instance, a truck rental company may charge you less if you're not moving within the first or last week of a month.

People also want to move when it's most convenient. Generally, this means that rates get hiked for Thursday to Sunday, since most people want to move sometime around the weekend. Consumer demand also drops dramatically during snow season. After all, what dummy would want to move in the middle of a snowstorm? (Answer: a dummy who wants to save money!) Accordingly, May to September is high time for moving, while October to April could land you a deal. You should be able to negotiate a discount if you:

- Move during an off-peak time (October to April).
- Choose a day that falls early in the week (Monday to Wednesday).
- Pick a date that falls outside of the roving-renter period (first and last week of each month).

Less is more

Jim and Sue had been living together in a one-bedroom rental ever since university. Their furniture was a curious amalgam of hand-me-downs, most of which had seen better days back in the late seventies. The orange and brown colour scheme wasn't dreamy, but the couple had decided to wait until they moved into their first home before investing in "real" furniture. When the day came to move, however, the moving truck was filled with their outdated collection of clunky chesterfields and armchairs. They had forgotten that these pieces didn't fit into their new life and didn't have to come along for the ride.

One big way to save on moving costs — and hassle — is to only move what you'd really like to keep. Not only will you save the cost of moving these articles, you'll also save the chore of packing and unpacking them. You can also *make* some money by holding a garage sale and selling what you don't want to take along. Or you can do a good deed and give what you don't want to local charities like the Sally Ann or Goodwill that can turn your giveaways into social programs.

Moving your life

Be prepared for the long haul. When you start trying to take care of all the little details, you'll realize that your life is a lot more complicated than you thought it was. If you're moving to a new city, for instance, medical, dental, and even veterinary records for every member of your household will have to be sent on. You'll also want to track down a qualified provider for each of these services. A simple task like redirecting your magazine subscriptions can require a month's notice or more, even if you're just moving down the block. Your lawyer will probably take care of some of these details, including electric and gas utility hook-ups and water and property taxes. The rest is up to you.

If you are being relocated, and you are moving at least 40 km closer to your new school or job, your moving and selling expenses will be tax deductible. This includes the cost of shipping and storing your belongings and up to 15 days' temporary accommodation near either your current or future home. Contact Canada Customs and Revenue Agency for details, any eligibility requirements, and the necessary claim forms or visit their Web site using the search words "moving" and "principal residence."

Even though moving may be the furthest thing from your mind as you run around finding an inspector and otherwise arranging for your grand purchase, the more organized you are about moving, the less stress you'll have as the closing date approaches (besides, you want to save all that worrying for real problems that may arise). The best way to tackle the workload is to create a list of tasks that need to get done and a calendar that sets deadlines for accomplishing them. The list below will give you a head start, but keep in mind that every situation is unique. We suggest carrying around a notebook where you can jot down extra "to-do's" as you think of them.

Moving your stuff

Before you start rooting through your home, keep in mind that one person's trash is another's treasure. If you can, have everyone in your household participate in the weeding process. That way, you won't end up accidentally discarding a beloved object. Children need to be part of this process so they will understand why old favourite sweaters have suddenly disappeared. You may want to encourage small children to keep a "memento" like a prized teddy bear. Soon they will have to adjust to a strange, new environment and may find themselves hankering for an old friend.

Keep the following tips in mind as you go through your belongings:

- ✔ Get rid of anything you've outgrown, especially bulky items like that old pair of skis with size-five boots and bindings.

- ✔ Be honest with yourself about what you use and what you don't use. If your sweater shaver hasn't seen the light in over five years, it might be time to get rid of it — no matter what you paid for it originally. Same goes for the carrot juicer that's gone untouched ever since you moved on from your macrobiotic diet.

- ✔ Look at your new home's floor plans to evaluate what will fit in and what won't. You may discover that you're not truly wedded to the loveseat Sparky the cat has been using as a scratching post for the last five years. Or that your grandmother's old kitchen table doesn't look good in your new stainless steel kitchen.

- ✔ Get rid of clutter. Take a serious look at your attic, basement, closets, and other storage spaces. You might be surprised (or scared) by what you find there.

- ✔ Use the two-year rule. Unless it's a vintage piece, if you haven't worn something within the last two years, part with it. Leg warmers and acid-washed jeans went out of style a *long* time ago.

- ✔ Don't forget the garden shed and garage. These places are chock full of items you *can't* take with you, including inflammable, explosive, or other hazardous materials.

You may also want to start thinking about your storehouse of food. Generally, it's not worth the hassle to transport food, especially perishables like cheese and meat that could spoil en route. If you've got hundreds of dollars worth of ham hocks in a deep-freezer, you'll want to be sure to eat them before moving day. You may well find that you have two months worth of food in the home — and it all has to disappear by the time the last box is loaded into the van. In fact, it's probably a good idea to plan on eating take-out the night before moving day — or better yet, go to a restaurant and celebrate.

Packing it all in

Let's admit it: Packing is a loathsome chore. It always takes longer than you think it will, and you'll always need more packing supplies than you planned on. That said, there are ways to make packing — and unpacking — a lot less painful.

If you can, give yourself plenty of time to pack. Otherwise, you'll end up throwing things haphazardly into boxes or, worse, not packing them at all. Count on packing being a big job, not a last-minute chore. Trust us: You're sure to find that you had more stuff than you thought you did.

Essential supplies are:

- ✔ **Boxes.** Big boxes, little boxes, picture boxes, and bike boxes. Boxes are far easier to pack into a van than irregular shapes, and will save you and your movers space and time. Use new materials, even though you might be tempted to pick up some discards at your local grocer. These may not be clean or sturdy enough for the job.

- ✔ **Tissue paper or old newsprint and bubble wrap.** Lots of it. Tissue paper is ideal for wrapping small objects, like coffee mugs, to prevent breakage. Although newspaper may seem like a good, cheap, and environmentally friendly alternative, it blackens whatever's wrapped inside. A friend of ours packed her china in last week's news, only to find out she had to re-wash all her dishes at the other end.

- ✔ **Packing tape with a tape dispenser and extra rolls.** This puts the final seal on every box. Jake, who works in the shipping department at a local bookstore, recommends a criss-cross pattern around the box for added strength.

- ✔ **Big markers.** Indicate the destination and an abbreviated list of the contents of each box.

Before the packing begins, photocopy the floor plans of your new home, clearly marking each room with labels like Bedroom A, Bedroom B, Bathroom A, Bathroom B, and so on. Give everyone a copy, and arm your crew with markers. Then, pack the boxes by room, labelling each box appropriately once it's full. You might also want to micro-label, indicating which kitchen cupboard or dresser drawer the contents belong to. The movers will (or at least, they should) use these labels as directions, putting each box in its rightful place. If you keep a running list of the boxes and what's inside, you'll have a full inventory by the time the job is complete. When it comes time to unpack, everything will magically end up where it belongs. You won't have to move heavy boxes from room to room, nor will you have to guess what's in each one. This is a simple trick that will save you a lot of headaches.

Pack with care. Once you're all packed up, you'll have very little control over what happens to your boxes en route: They may get jostled around in the truck, stacked one on top of the other, or (worse still!) accidentally dropped. Packing in bubble wrap or tissue paper cradles your belongings. Towels and other linens can also double as padding. Large appliances, like refrigerators, often require special handling before and after a move. And a computer may need to readjust to its surroundings for a day before being plugged in. Read your owner's manual, contact the manufacturer, or speak to your movers for instructions.

Beware the random packer. If your partner or child is helping you, make sure they understand your system. Deciding you need to redo their work will probably create tension you would all be better off without!

The moving timeline

Trust us, you want to be as organized as possible as you work toward your move. Use this moving timeline as a reference while you pack, make calls, wrangle with your movers, and generally tear your hair out.

Two months and counting

Hey, it's never too early to get things rolling! Did we mention now is a good time to start packing?

> ✔ Start saving! Moving is a huge expense. If you start budgeting in advance for movers, insurance, supplies, utility transfers, child (and pet) care, and the bevy of incidental costs, your wallet won't be so hard hit when the bills come in. Remember, too, to factor in the costs after you arrive: Painting, housekeeping, and carpentry work should all be taken into account.

✔ Begin the pick-and-choose process: Decide what you want to take with you and what you want to leave behind. Plan to sell any discards — at a garage sale, for instance, or through the classifieds — at least a month and a half in advance.

✔ Start scouting out your new neighbourhood. Speak to the principal of your children's new school to take care of transfer details and learn important dates. While you're there, find a neighbourhood restaurant where you can feast after the big move. You won't be in any mood to cook.

One month to moving day

It's amazing the number of people who apparently care that you're moving. Here's what to do to keep them in the know. Oh yeah, keep filling those boxes.

✔ Ask your doctor, dentist, and veterinarian for referrals, and arrange for the transfer of records.

✔ Contact the phone company. While you'll technically have a lot of leeway in hooking up your phone service — it usually only takes a few days — getting in touch with the phone company in advance is a good idea. That way, you'll have your new number handy to give out along with your new address.

✔ Contact the subscription office of any magazines you subscribe to and inform them of your new address, letting them know which issue should be delivered to the new location. If you receive any catalogues that you'd like to continue to receive, don't forget to let the mail-order company know of your change of address.

✔ Visit your local post office at least two weeks in advance to request a redirection of mail service. For a period of six months, any mail that is sent to you at your old residence will be redirected to your new address, and you'll pay only $30 for the convenience.

✔ Start packing non-essential items (like trinkets and knick-knacks, off-season sports equipment, books). This really eases the packing load as the big day gets nearer.

One week

Now the countdown's really begun. Take deep breaths. Keep packing.

✔ Pick up any dry cleaning, shoe repairs, or other items left with local businesses. Return any outstanding library books (and that glue gun you borrowed from your neighbour three months ago).

✔ Call a locksmith to arrange to have your locks changed after you have possession of the house.

✔ Get boxes if you need more and start packing. You'll find tips to make the process easier in the section "Packing it all in" earlier in this chapter.

✔ Get rid of your kids! Having children and pets underfoot can slow down movers and increase the chances of an accident. If possible, make arrangements to send young children to a best friend's for a sleepover on the evening before moving day. You should also board pets for the few days around the move. (The last thing you want to do is hold up the moving process because Sparky the cat escaped and is nowhere to be found.)

The day before

You may feel like a character on *Survivor* at this point. Look at all those boxes!

✔ Stock up on snack food and bottled water to keep you going through moving day. Consider preparing some sandwiches, too.

✔ Buy paper plates and plastic cutlery and cups to use until you can unearth the real things.

✔ Deliver Sparky to the kennel or to a generous friend so that the fur doesn't fly on moving day. At the same time, drive the kids over to a best friend's house for their sleepover.

✔ Confirm your movers.

✔ Designate a box or bag for items that will be thrown in at the last minute, including bedding and pillows.

The big day

This is it — the day you've been working toward for the past two months. You probably wish you could just go away somewhere and leave it to the movers. Bad idea. We suggest you stick around — 'til the bitter end.

✔ Be there when the trucks arrive so you're available to give instructions to the movers and to point out any items that need special handling.

✔ Stay out of the way. A good moving team works like clockwork: They have a coordinated way of moving as a group and an efficient method for packing a truck. Although you might think carrying boxes out to the truck will speed things up and save you money, lending a hand may actually impede progress.

 ✔ Count the boxes as they are loaded onto the truck to make sure everything makes it on board.

 ✔ Do a final check around the house once everything is loaded. Look inside cupboards, closets, and the garage.

 ✔ Collect your children and pets after the move is complete.

After the move

That is, after you've slept. You should consider the following:

 ✔ Different provinces have different regulations regarding change of address notification. In Ontario, for instance, you're obliged to change your driver's licence and health card within ten days of moving. Some provinces provide automatic kiosks where you can make the change yourself — which might save you the time and frustration of standing in a long line.

 ✔ If you're a first-time homeowner, stock up on some of the basics before you need them: a mop, stepladder, drill, hammer, screwdriver set, wrench, snow shovel, rake, hedge clippers, garden hose, outdoor broom, lightbulbs. . . . You get the idea. Otherwise, you'll end up going to the local hardware shop every other day for a month. If you're planning a housewarming party, make the most of your friends' generosity and ask them to bring an item on your "stuff needed" list. If you are planning a painting party, make sure your friends bring brushes, sandpaper, and paint. When Marcus first moved into his new home, his friends put together a cooler full of stuff they thought he would need, including duct tape, band aids, a flashlight, and slippers.

Getting Possessed, We Mean, Getting Possession

When you have the keys in your hand, at the open door of your new home — *now* you can celebrate! Grab your partner by the hand, spin down the hallway, and waltz around your new kitchen. Your friends really will think you're possessed. The drapes, appliances, and any other chattels that were specified in the contract should be right where you last saw them. But really, this is the fun part: The home is legally, officially, and absolutely yours, so do what you will. Enjoy.

Try not to second-guess yourself. Chances are, after you've bought your home, you'll start seeing "For Sale" signs on all sorts of other dream homes. You'll begin to wonder, Should we have waited longer to buy? Did we make a hasty decision? Was this the right choice for us? This is normal. We'll call it Consumer Regret After Purchase syndrome (CRAP!). It happens after every major purchase. That's why sellers of big-ticket items, like cars, keep advertising their products well after the big selling period is over. They want to remind any customers going through CRAP syndrome how smart, sexy, and sensible they were to have bought such a great product.

Don't regret your choice. Lots of hard work, careful consideration, and late night debate went into your purchase. The grass may look greener on some of the newly listed homes, but up close you'd see all the yellow marks left by the previous owner's dog. Remember what you learned throughout your search: The outside of a house gives no reliable indication if its interior.

Accept that every new place you move to will cause you to feel a bit unsettled at first. Often this will pass as you come to put up your own pictures, get your furniture where you want it, put your favourite sheets on your bed. It will take some adjustment time before you can move about the house in the dark without bumping into anything.

You have been in decision mode for so long that you may just be in shock once you are sitting comfortably in your living room with no more papers to sign or bank hours to contemplate. So your mind starts to wander and you start to think that maybe you should have tried harder for that house with the Chinese garden. After all, the crooked floors weren't SO bad. . . .

So instead of spending your energy on drooling after the Jones's cozy cottage next door, spend it on making your new house into your very own home. You want roses? Start planting! You want to create an arbour effect in the foyer? Get out the lattice! Welcome home.

Part IV
Deciding to Sell

The 5th Wave   By Rich Tennant

I JUST THOUGHT IT WAS TIME TO SELL. THE LACES KEPT COMING UNTIED, THERE'S A LEAK IN THE HEEL, AND IT NEEDS ALL NEW ODOR-EATERS.

FOR SALE BY OWNER

In this part . . .

Decisions, decisions, decisions. . . . Should you stay or should you go? Should you buy, then sell, or vice versa? Can you afford to move? Can you find something better or more suitable than what you have?

If you're thinking about putting your home on the market, this is the section for you. Just like buyers using the first section, you won't find pat answers to these questions here, but you *will* find help on how to answer them yourself.

Chapter 13

To Sell or to Stay

· ·

In This Chapter

▶ Determining your wants and needs

▶ Identifying good reasons to stay put

▶ Identifying good reasons to sell

▶ Timing the sale

· ·

*F*ew decisions have a bigger impact on your life — at every level — than deciding to sell your house. In fact, moving is one of the three most stressful life events (after death and divorce). A major change is scary, but as our lives develop, change may be necessary and even welcome. How much change you're ready for is up to you. You may decide you don't really need to move — you need to tear down some walls and finally renovate that bathroom.

In this chapter, we explain how to sort your priorities so you can be sure that you really do want to sell your home and you know what you want to gain from the sale. Taking the time to consider how selling your home affects your life helps you avoid costly and unnecessary mistakes, and ensures that you'll be satisfied with your choices. Thinking it through and deciding what you really need gives you incredible peace of mind.

Making the Big Decision

Your house shapes your lifestyle. The amount you spend on housing determines how much money you can save for things like vacations, your retirement, or your kids' education. The location of your home dictates how much time you spend getting to work, school, and shopping — and how much money you spend on transportation, groceries, utilities, taxes, and maintenance. Your home also affects your social life and leisure time. Are you close to friends and relatives? Can you entertain easily at home or meet conveniently? Can you go for walks in the nearby park or putter in the garden when you need some time to yourself?

It's time to take stock of what you have and what you need. Don't try to keep track of all the reasons you want to sell in your head. Sit down and get everything out on paper (if it's been ages since you've written anything by hand, use your computer and just print it off).

Not all of your reasons to move carry equal weight. Once you've made your list of likes, dislikes, needs, and wants, start thinking about what your priorities are and which factors are most important. When you feel you've got a handle on the issues, organize your list according to your priorities.

Organize your likes and dislikes for your current home, as well as your needs and wants for your future home, into three categories: property, location, and finances. We'll use these categories to discuss weighing out your decision to stay or sell.

Home sweet home: Your property

What makes your house a great place to live? Consider aesthetics like style, decor, and view, as well as practicalities like an eat-in kitchen, a two-car garage, and plenty of natural light. What's lacking in your living space? Do you find yourself coveting your neighbour's stunning stone fireplace, big backyard, sunny solarium, and well-stocked wet-bar? Does the open loft with a rope railing that once appealed to your minimalist sensibilities now terrify you as a parent?

Often we change homes because our needs change. Room for a patio and garden might be an absolute must when you're retiring and finally have daylight time to spend outside. Perhaps your home office has to expand beyond the corner under the stairs.

Make a list with two columns, one for all the benefits of your current home and the other for all your dislikes concerning your living situation. Then make a second two-column list of the items that you and your family may need now or in the future, and all the things you don't absolutely *need* but would still give an arm and a leg for.

How significant a change do you need to make? Look at your lists and think about whether your home can grow with your needs. If you build the sunroom that you've always wanted, or finish the attic to add an extra bedroom, keeping the home you have makes sense. But it may not be worth adding one extra bedroom if you're planning to have three more children. Be realistic about how much renovation your home can accommodate.

Location, location, location: Your neighbourhood

Look at the logistics: Is your home located in a good area that suits your needs and tastes? Location is the seller's mantra and it was probably a big factor when you chose your current house. Consider what sets your neighbourhood apart. Are the streets nice, safe, and quiet? Are good schools, public transit, and shopping in the area? Are there job opportunities for you and your family members? Is your extended family nearby?

Just as your housing needs may change over the years, so too may your priorities concerning location. Maybe you don't want to live next to your favourite dance club anymore, but you would like to be next to your favourite bingo hall. In addition to the basic physical features of your location, don't forget the intangibles. The personality of your neighbourhood may be a big factor in your happiness or dissatisfaction with where you live. Over the years, communities change as people move in and out of neighbourhoods.

Remember why you moved to your neighbourhood in the first place. Ask yourself if those reasons are still valid. Are the people still as friendly as when you first moved in? Is the crime rate still low? Are the surrounding woodlands still unspoiled? Is the air quality good? Do your neighbours still show incredible enthusiasm for Hallowe'en festivities? Make sure your list of likes and dislikes concerning your current home includes mention of the surroundings.

Don't overlook commuting time when you consider the merits of your location. Although you may stand to earn a lot of money by selling your house in a premium location and moving farther out, it may not be worth it once the new hour-and-a-half commute takes its toll on you and your family. And with the rapidly rising cost of gasoline, the extra 45 minutes on the road ends up costing a mint.

You might want to sell your home because you want to make a *big* change in location. From the big city to the suburbs, from the West Coast to the East — even though the grass may be greener or the salmon tastier on the other side, you may find the climate really isn't for you. See Chapter 6 for advice on researching new neighbourhoods.

Dollars and sense: Your finances

Think about your budget. You know whether you're straining to meet financial obligations or whether you've got a nice fat nest egg in the bank. In addition to paying the mortgage on your home, you also pay for utilities, insurance, taxes, repairs, and basic maintenance (you can use the budget worksheet in Chapter 2 for a detailed examination of your current financial picture).

If you're looking to reduce these expenses, then downsizing to a smaller, less expensive home or area may be the smartest thing to do. However, if you're a prosperous business owner who was once a struggling entrepreneur, you may be ready to leave the cramped starter home behind and spend some money to get yourself a big house with a two-car garage and heated indoor swimming pool. Include your financial outlook in your list of pros and cons about the home you have now. Is it too costly? Or is it very affordable, but simply not big enough for you, your spouse, the twins, and Alfie, your St. Bernard?

Don't forget that it costs time and *money* to sell your house. The transaction costs of selling a house and buying another can easily total 3 to 7 percent of the price at which you sell your property. In addition to the 3 to 7 percent you'll likely spend in selling costs, be aware that unless you have paid off your mortgage, interest payments and discharge fees take up an even larger percentage of the money you have invested in your home.

Get a good idea of what the market offers in your price range. If you are considering selling your $250,000 townhouse to invest in a $500,000 detached house, go to open houses and compare whether the houses in that price range have all the features that you expect. You may discover that the benefits of buying a house in that price range aren't as great as you think.

The amount of money you have tied up in your house takes away from what you have for other financial goals. Determine the minimum you'd like to have to set aside for holidays, your retirement, and your children's education. *Then* decide how much you have to spend on your next home. See Chapter 14 for more details about the financial aspects of selling your home.

Good Reasons to Stay Put

Examine your lists of likes, dislikes, needs, wants, and priorities (we provide guidelines for such a list in Chapter 6). Pay particular attention to the physical features you want or need in a home and your financial status and goals. Both of these considerations may be reasons for you to stay in your current home.

✔ **Renovating is a viable option:** If you're after more space, a new look, modernization, or greater efficiency, renovating your home might be the wisest course of action. If you live in a great neighbourhood, consider building an addition. Renovations may be a steal compared to the transaction costs of selling, and they may also add to the resale value of your house. See Chapter 19 for more details on which home renovation projects add the most value when you do decide to sell your house.

If you want to move because your house needs some costly repairs, investigate your options carefully. You may end up paying for the repairs anyway when your house doesn't sell because of them, or when the buyers insist on deducting the repair cost from the price they will pay for the house. Buyers always overestimate the cost of repairs in order to protect themselves from the worst-case scenario.

Consider taking out a *home equity loan* to cover the costs of renovations. Home equity loans, also known as *second mortgages*, and *home equity lines of credit*, give you access to the equity you have in your home. See Chapter 15 for more on home equity loans.

✔ **Your finances are shaky:** If you are already having trouble living within your means, it may be wise to delay buying your dream home until you've paid off your credit cards and devised a realistic plan to reach your financial goals. Even if you are thinking about moving to a less-expensive house, keep in mind that you will incur plenty of one-time expenses when you sell your house, buy a new one, and move. This means you have to be looking for accommodation in a range several thousand dollars below what you initially thought you could afford. If you can possibly get your debts under control while staying in your current home, your financial and emotional state will be that much better off.

Nothing is more stressful than trying to move when you are strapped for cash, except perhaps trying to move when you are strapped for cash *and* time.

Good Reasons to Sell

Even if you love your home, there are times when it just won't be able to adapt to your ever-changing needs. Because you can't always build what you need or make the neighbourhood exactly how and where you'd like it, it's often best to find a new place to call home. If any of the following conditions describe your situation, you're probably ready to sell.

✔ **The location of your home is unsuitable.** If you have a job offer in a great location with good long-term employment potential, or if you are ready to retire and look forward to the security and low maintenance of a retirement community, selling your house makes a lot of sense. (And if you're relocating for professional reasons, you may get a tax break on all your moving expenses — see Chapter 12 for more details.)

✔ **Your house is too small or too big.** If you and your family need more space and you don't want to renovate, or you can't get a building permit to put an extension on the back of the house, moving is probably your best bet. On the flip side, if the last of your six kids has finally moved out of your seven-bedroom home, it may be time to downsize — before any of them decide to move back!

✔ **Life throws you a curve ball.** After a traumatic event like a divorce or the death of a family member, you may simply want to leave bad memories behind. Take the time to review your financial situation and personal goals so you make a move that is right for you.

✔ **Life is fine — but the neighbourhood isn't.** Maybe your life hasn't changed a bit, but somehow the neighbourhood has changed around you in ways you're not happy about. If you find yourself with the best house on the street — or the worst — it's a good time to move. If every other bungalow in your formerly sleepy neighbourhood has been replaced by a monster home, next time a real estate agent calls you, it's time to say, "Yes, as a matter of fact, I am interested in selling!"

Timing: Sell First and Then Buy, or Vice Versa?

Not a gambler? Even for people who enjoy moving from home to home, timing the move is really tricky. On the one hand, you could find yourself with no house, having sold your home and not found a new one of the appropriate size, style, or location. On the other hand, you could find yourself with no money as you carry two houses. You can avoid these pitfalls by basing your timing decisions on current real estate market trends, and your own needs and priorities.

Riding the real estate cycle

Real estate goes through cycles. It's a *seller's market* when there are a lot of buyers and not many homes available. This is also called a *hot market* because homes tend to sell more quickly and for a higher price. In a hot market, you might nail down the house you want — the tough part in this case — and then sell your house.

It's a *buyer's market* or a *slow market* when there are more homes listed for sale than there are buyers shopping for new homes. Prices tend to be lower and homes take longer to sell in a buyer's market. If the market is slow but there are lots of houses you can see yourself happy in, sell your house first — the hard part in a slow market — and then pick your next house from among your favourites.

Although trying to sell your home in a buyer's market means you may have to drop your asking price, chances are the next house you buy will also be at a reduced price, since market conditions tend to be similar within a particular city or region. Unfortunately, if you're moving cross-country, you can't count on being so lucky.

Real estate also goes through predictable highs and lows over the course of a year. Spring is usually a peak transaction time anywhere in the country. If you need to sell your house quickly during a slower time of year, drop your price a bit below actual market value. On the other hand, if you want to get the best price possible, put your house on the market at the beginning of the peak season. Market activity varies with geography too, so talk to a local agent to find out what the trends are in your area. Price is an important marketing tool, so you want to get it right the first time. Chapter 14 gives you the lowdown on pricing do's and don'ts.

Meeting your needs

Your needs form another important variable in the buying and selling equation. Do you need to sell your home quickly? Do you want a certain price, and if so, are you willing to wait for it? Do you want to be in your next home by a particular date?

If you want to get your kids moved into a new house before the beginning of the school year, you may decide to buy that perfect house in the new neighbourhood before you have sold your current house. The way to avoid hanging on to two houses is to price your current home to sell. For example, if you have to sell and are facing the prospect of owning two homes in six weeks' time (carrying both would probably cost you an extra $2,000 to $3,000 per month), drop your asking price by a couple of thousand dollars. Accepting an offer — albeit below your original asking price — meets two important needs: your kids start the new school year off on the right track and you only have one home to carry — much more manageable. Examine your financial situation and determine your personal priorities early. But as a rule, it is almost always better to sell before you buy. In Chapter 15, we take a more detailed look at the financial consequences of both scenarios.

How much can you get for your house?

If you're going to sell your home, naturally you want to recoup the money you spent buying it and fixing it up, and you're thinking about how much money you *need* in order to buy your next home. Unfortunately, these factors don't determine the resale value of your home.

The cold, hard truth is that *buyers* determine the actual market value for your house through what they offer to *pay* for it. If all the similar houses in your neighbourhood sell in a certain price range, buyers will likely offer a similar price for your home. Surveying the asking prices and recent sale prices of comparable homes in your neighbourhood gives you a basic idea of what price you can expect to get (we show you how in Chapter 14). In effect, timing is everything — being aware of the real estate market's trends makes you better prepared to get the price you really want or need.

If you are working with a real estate agent or broker, ask for a *Comparative Market Analysis* (CMA), a report used to determine a home's market value. Your home is "ranked" next to similar homes in your neighbourhood based on details like size, condition, desirable features, and listing and sale prices. If you are selling on your own, you would be wise to get a professional appraisal to determine the actual market value of your home. See Chapter 14 for more on Comparative Market Analyses.

Although it's not exactly a scientific approach, try talking to your neighbours to get an idea what your home is worth. We're willing to bet that everyone on your street will also give you opinions on how much more your house could sell for with its renovated kitchen or the new hardwood floors.

Your house gets the most exposure to the buying market in its first few weeks of listing. The closer your house is priced to its actual market value, the more quickly it will sell. If you price your home too high and scare off buyers in the beginning, you may end up having to sell for less than your home is worth. See Chapter 15 for all the details on home appraisals and pricing your house accordingly.

What can you spend on your next house?

Figuring out how much you can afford on your next house is a long but relatively simple equation. It involves solely the basic math of addition and subtraction. You need to total your cash in-flow and out-flow, then subtract the expenses from the income. The tricky part is taking inventory of all your sources of income and expenditure, and the exact amounts associated with each. Chapter 14 takes you through the cost assessments and calculations step by step.

Careful calculations help you be realistic about what you can afford. Once you know how much you can spend, you need to investigate whether it really will get you the kind of house you want, while maintaining your standard of living, and allowing you to save for long-term financial goals.

Never assume *anything* when investigating what you will get for your money. The perfect home may not be in the perfect neighbourhood. The perfect neighbourhood may only have listings in your price range for properties half the size you need. You may have to make sacrifices to make improvements, so you need to know what your priorities are. Even if you can make a decent profit on the sale of your current home, there's no guarantee you'll be better off if you sell.

The safety net: conditional subject-to-sale offers

One way to synchronize buying and selling is to find a house you like, make an offer conditional on the sale of your current house, and once the conditional offer is accepted, *then* put your house on the market. If the condition (selling your house) is not met by the expiry date in the clause, then the offer you made becomes null and void.

By writing a *subject to sale* condition into your purchase offer, you don't have to buy the house you want until you've sold the house you are living in — giving you the peace of mind and the financial security that comes with not owning two homes *and* not being homeless.

You should know that a *subject to sale* conditional offer is less attractive to a home seller and therefore puts the buyer in a weak negotiating position. Since most sellers don't want to delay the sale of their home, they often are willing to accept a "clean" offer for less money. If the seller receives such an offer and is considering it, they will usually invoke the *time clause*, the amount of time the first buyer has to either remove all the conditions from their offer — including the *subject to sale* condition — or withdraw their offer altogether. Now it's time to hustle. If you really want that house, you need to remove your *subject to sale* clause and firm up your offer, even though the competitive offer may be several thousand dollars less. Some sellers won't even look at offers made subject to the sale of the buyers' current house, as they don't believe the buyers are serious. Ask your real estate agent how conditional offers are received in your local market.

Here's how it works. You write into your offer a *subject to sale* clause that essentially states, "This offer is subject to the sale of the buyers' current residence located at [address], on or before [expiry date of clause]. However, if another acceptable offer is received, the sellers will notify the buyers in writing and give the buyers 48 hours (24 or 72 hours is also common) to remove the *subject to sale* condition as well as all other conditions from the offer or the offer will be considered null and void." The *expiry date* of the clause indicates the amount of time you have to sell your house from the time the offer is accepted and therefore to remove the condition and make your offer firm, or withdraw your offer if the condition was not met. This date is usually negotiated to fall between four and six weeks after the offer is accepted and it can be extended if both parties agree.

Don't confuse the expiry date of the clause with the completion date of the offer itself. The *completion date* specifies the date you will close the deal if all the specified conditions are met. It is the day you become the legal owner of the property.

The *time clause*, which is negotiable, identifies how long you have to remove the subject to sale condition or withdraw your offer should the seller receive another acceptable offer before the expiry date on your clause. You see, even after the sellers accept your conditional purchase offer, they will still actively market their home, looking for a "clean offer" — an offer without conditions. If the seller receives another acceptable offer, they will *invoke the time clause* and notify you in writing that you have 24/48/72 hours (or whatever was written into the clause) to make a decision. At this point you can remove the conditions and commit to buying the house — whether or not you have sold your own — or you can withdraw the offer.

If you've really found your dream home and your conditional offer has been accepted, you don't want your *subject to sale* clause to expire or the time clause to be invoked before you sell your current property. You must price your house to sell, which means being very realistic about its market value. The closer your house is listed to market value, the more quickly you will receive good offers.

For most people, it makes sense to put your house on the market *while* you look for your next home. This gives you a good sense of what buyers are willing to pay for your house, and saves you from inflating the amount you think you can spend on your next home. If offers come rushing in, you can always accept the best, subject to the purchase of your next house.

Some buyers won't accept a seller's proposed counteroffer (conditional on the sellers' purchase of their next house). If you find yourself in this position, you have to decide what you're willing to risk. If you sell before you've found a new home, you risk becoming homeless — at least temporarily. On the other hand, if you reject the buyer's offer because you can't include the condition of buying your next house, you may wait a long time before receiving another one, depending on the market conditions, and whether your home's priced at its actual market value.

If you have a lot of money, you could just buy your dream home and *then* put your current house on the market. Through *bridge financing* you can use the equity in your first property to finance the purchase of the next. (See Chapter 15 to find out more about bridge financing.) It's the riskiest option financially, but it guarantees you the house you absolutely want.

Buying time with the closing dates

Getting the paperwork right is the next step in making a smooth transition. Once you've found a buyer for your current home and a new house to move into, you'll need to schedule each *closing date,* the day you transfer ownership of a property and finalize the sale. Ideally, both the sale of your current home and the purchase of your new one should close one right after the other.

This affords you the most security financially — and emotionally. If it simply can't be done, the next best option is to try to extend the closing date on your purchase so that it follows the closing date of your home's sale. See Chapter 21 for details on negotiating deadlines that will work for you.

Try to avoid the last day of the month or year as a closing date. These times are particularly busy for the agencies that will be registering and filing paperwork for the transfer of ownership, termination of insurance, and the like, not to mention movers.

Chapter 14

The Price of Selling

*Y*ou may be thinking, "Great! I'm selling my house, there's a big cheque coming in, I'm gonna be swimming in cash!" Although it's true that there *will* be a big cheque at some point, there are some costs tied to selling your house that you ought to keep in mind. The idea is to provide for these costs in advance, since most of them must be paid before that cheque gets cashed. Careful and informed planning can help ensure that the process of selling your house goes smoothly.

Pricing Your House to Sell

It's common sense that if you price something too high, it won't sell. This is especially true for big-ticket items like houses. Potential buyers are skittish to begin with, having to make such a big decision. If your price tag is too high, you'll scare them off right away. The key is finding the balance between reeling in the buyers at the start and getting your home's true value in the end (after negotiation, of course).

How much is your home worth?

The best way to find out how much your home is worth is to ask a professional. You can hire a professional appraiser to give you an *appraisal*, or you can ask your real estate agent to give you a *Comparative Market Analysis* (CMA), sometimes also referred to as a *Current Market Analysis* or a *Competitive Market Analysis*. A sample CMA is shown in Figure 14-1.

As far as assessing the market value of your house, appraisals and CMAs are the same. Both professionals consider all the factors influencing the worth of your property (such as location, square footage, general condition of the home, and amenities). They research the recent sale prices and current asking prices of similar homes in your area, compare the finer details, and adjust up or down to determine your home's *fair market value* (FMV). Say your home has an attached double garage, then it may be worth a little bit more than someone else's down the street that, like yours, is a three-bedroom two-storey with four baths and a finished basement, but comes with only a carport.

COMPARATIVE MARKET ANALYSIS

COMPARABLE HOMES RECENTLY SOLD

Address	Age	Lot Size	Floor Area	Bdrms	Bthrms	Bsmt	Listed Date & Price	Selling Date & Price	Ass. Value ('99)
312 Main St.	55	33 x 120	2000	3	3	Full	Dec./99 $430,000	Feb. 20/00 $425,000	$419,987
2525 Ontario St.	48	33 x 120	1956	3	2	Part	Nov./99 $425,000	March 3/00 $410,000	$405,700
4323 E. 21st	51	33 x 120	1830	3	2	Full	Sept/99 $420,500	Feb 5/00 $405,000	$410,050

COMPARABLE HOMES FOR SALE NOW

Address	Age	Lot Size	Floor Area	Bdrms	Bthrms	Bsmt	Listed Date & Price	Ass. Value ('99)
3737 E. 25th	63	33 x 112	1860	3	3	Full	Dec. 15/99 $409,000	$386,510
461 Main	47	33 x 122	1750	3	2	Full	Jan 19/00 $419,000	$392,100
518 Manitoba	45	33 x 120	1905	4	2	Part	Jan 25/00 $439,000	$398,000
2431 Main	55	35 x 115	2000	3	3	Full	Feb 5/00 $440,000	$405,205

YOUR HOME

Address	Age	Lot Size	Floor Area	Bdrms	Bthrms	Bsmt	Recommended List Range	Recommended Sale Range
495 Main	51	33 x 120	1850	3	2	Full	$439,000/$449,000	$425,000/$435,000

MARKET VALUE DEFINED: … the price expected when a reasonable time is allowed to find a purchaser when both seller and prospective buyer are fully informed.

LISTING PRICE: … the price asked for a property, as set by the vendor. The vendor is urged to take into account information supplied and market conditions.

Sales Representative: _Shelbon Napper_ _____

Figure 14-1: Your real estate agent should give you a comparative market analysis that looks something like this. It will let you see what similar houses in your neigh-bourhood are selling for, so you can determine your home's fair market value (FMV).

Most real estate agents will prepare a CMA for you free of charge. You will always have to pay an appraiser. If you're selling without an agent, you should definitely hire an independent appraiser. The legal system, as well as most financial institutions, only recognizes the estimates of certified professional appraisals. (You can read more about appraisals for sellers in Chapter 18.)

Your buyer can put a *clause* (a condition) into the offer stipulating that it is subject to the home's sale price being confirmed by an independent appraisal. If you don't obtain an accurate estimate of your home's value in the early stages of selling, you may have to renegotiate your home's sale price with your buyer later. Worse, if your buyer's appraisal reveals they have offered more than your home is worth, your buyer might retract the offer, or your buyer's mortgage lender might refuse to finance the purchase.

The three most common pricing mistakes

We know it's your home and you can ask whatever price you like for it, but we're here to tell you to proceed with caution. Your selling price heavily influences your likelihood of selling success; it can determine whether your home is snapped up by eager buyers or languishes in the classifieds for months. Here are three pricing mistakes that sellers often make.

Trying to make a hefty profit

The reasoning for setting a high price goes something like this: "If someone buys it for the high price, great, I made some money. If I have to drop the price a little to sell, then I haven't really lost anything because I still got a fair price." The problem is, it doesn't work that way. Your home gets the most attention for the first few weeks it's on the market. If you set the price too high, you run the risk of alienating buyers who may have paid a fair price. If your home isn't fairly priced for those crucial first few weeks, it may become stigmatized by the time you do lower the price. Buyers see your listing and think, "If it's been on the market for this long and they have to keep lowering the price, there must be *something* wrong with it."

Furthermore, if the initial asking price is too high, the buyer won't feel that there is competition for the home — and this means they won't be in any hurry to make an offer, let alone close the sale. Either way, by the time you do lower the asking price, agents (and their buyers) have lost interest in your home and you may have to sell for less than your home is worth in order to sell at all.

Setting the sale price based on your needs

Many sellers have a new location (or even a new house) in mind and know how much money they need to make on the sale of their current home in order to purchase a new one. Other sellers may be planning to "trade down" as a way to make money they can then invest for retirement. Frankly, buyers don't care about your needs. Buyers have their own needs to worry about, one of which is getting a good deal on a new house. If you keep the sale price too high because you "need the money," you simply won't be able to sell your home.

Setting the sale price based on how much you have "put into" your home

Thirty thousand dollars' worth of renovations does not necessarily equal an extra thirty thousand dollars on the sale price of your home. Some improvements to your home will increase its value, others will not (for example, kitchens and bathrooms are often the best places for renovations that add to the resale value of a home). Cosmetic improvements, such as fresh paint, are always good investments. Although they will not increase the value of your home by a significant margin, basic home touch-ups are relatively cheap and extremely important for making a good first impression on buyers. A good agent will know what counts and what doesn't, and so will most builders — you can also see Chapter 15 to find out which renovations are most valuable for sellers.

Estimating the Costs of Selling

On the surface, the economics of selling your home seem pretty simple. You sell your home and, hopefully, you make enough money to cover the payments on another one. If the sale price of your current home is greater than what you pay for your new home, "I save money" appears to be the logical conclusion. Unfortunately, a few steps in the middle of the process may shrink your profits from the sale. With proper planning, you can accurately estimate the proceeds of the sale to find out for sure. This section takes you through the expenses you are responsible for as the seller.

Agent's commission

Unless you have time and energy to burn, chances are you'll hire an agent to help with the sale of your home. Your agent receives a commission when you sell — usually a percentage of the sale price — as does your buyer's agent. And guess what, you are responsible for both! A typical total commission expense might be between 4 percent and 6 percent of the selling price, but rates are negotiable. If you decide to sell privately, you will probably still deal with buyers who are using an agent, so you may get stuck with some commission fees no matter what.

Legal fees

The sale of a home requires complex legal documentation. You may need a lawyer to draw up or check over all paperwork and documents. Depending on the amount of work to be done, your legal fees will vary. Talk to several lawyers to get an idea of how much your case might cost, but budget at least $500–$1,000, including *conveyance* (the transfer of the title to the property), and more if you need documents to be drafted by the lawyer.

Repairs or renovations

Most homes will *not* require major renovations to ensure a sale. If you've kept your home in good shape or if your home is relatively new, you may need to do only minor repairs. First impressions go a long way — no matter how new your home is, pay attention to cosmetic details (chipped paint, leaky faucets, loose doorknobs, etc.). Your home has to look good to sell.

Your buyer will have a building inspector evaluate your home (for plumbing and structural problems, etc.) to find out what improvements (if any!) are necessary. Whatever repairs are needed may be deducted from the selling price, likely with a margin of error that will benefit your buyer. In some circumstances you may wish to have your home inspected first if you suspect there is a serious problem, or if you live in an area where properties, often condos, are commonly listed as having a "positive inspection" available to potential buyers. Other people use their inspections as a marketing tool to demonstrate how "good" their homes are and thereby to get top dollar for them. If you're selling a condominium and the building has a *positive engineering report*, you have an excellent selling point — use it. A glowing inspection report from a reputable agency provides an incentive to potential buyers. However, if the inspection reveals any serious liabilities, you are legally obligated to disclose that information to potential buyers.

There is no right answer to whether or not you should absorb the cost of the building inspection. You may be wasting your money since the buyers will probably have their own inspection done anyway, but you could see some benefits at the negotiating table. Talk to your agent (if you have one) and take a look at Chapter 18 for more information about inspections for sellers. If you choose to have your home inspected, remember to include the inspection fees when totalling the cost of repairs and renovations.

Discharge of your mortgage

If you don't have a mortgage, give yourself a pat on the back and skip ahead to the next point; otherwise, read on! Most lenders have a few options available for handling your mortgage when you sell, depending on the specifics of your current mortgage agreement. You may be allowed to take your mortgage with you to your new home, you may be able to let the buyer assume it, or you may be able to pay it off early. (We cover all the options in Chapter 15.)

Lenders often charge legal and/or penalty fees when you choose one of these options. Check your mortgage agreement to see what is permitted and talk to your lender to find out what fees you might incur. Fees are sometimes negotiable. If you have been a loyal client of your lender for many years, you may be able to "talk down" a prepayment penalty. Whatever arrangements you make with your lender, be sure to get a copy *in writing*.

Property taxes and prepaid utilities

The day you usually pay your property taxes is not likely to coincide with the day you sell your home (if Fate loves you that much, skip ahead to the next point). In the sale contract, there will be an *adjustment date* (the day the buyer assumes all responsibility for paying property taxes, and so on). Usually the adjustment date is the same day as the *possession date*, or the day you hand the buyer the keys. In effect, your buyer may owe you a refund on a portion of your annual property tax (or you may owe the buyer some money if you don't prepay your property taxes). Likewise, any prepaid utilities, condo fees, or assessments need to be reviewed. Your lawyer can work out exactly how much is owed to whom and adjust the taxes as part of the conveyance or statement of adjustment. (The *statement of adjustment* shows the net result for the vendor [seller] or purchaser of the home, taking into account the purchase price, deposit, real estate commissions, legal fees, property purchase tax, property taxes, and all other adjustments.)

Moving costs

Obviously, how much it costs to move depends on how much stuff you are moving, how far you are moving it, and what moving company you hire. Other factors may enter into the tally, including the time of year and any "special care" items you may be moving (such as your baby grand piano). Do your research. Find out exactly how much stuff you've accumulated over the years and how much it's really going to cost to get it to your new home.

An extra few hours assessing the contents of your basement and garage, plus a phone call or four, are a lot less hassle than under-budgeting your moving costs by several thousand dollars, or finding out too late that your one-bedroom home has three bedrooms' worth of memorabilia (two-thirds of which will not fit into the moving truck).

Survey fees

Some banks require a survey in order to approve a mortgage on a house. (There are no surveys required for condos.) Usually, this cost is absorbed by the buyer (as you probably already know), but it's not uncommon for sellers to have an existing survey certificate from when they purchased the house. If no alterations or additions have been made to the property, it may still be acceptable to the bank. The fee for having a survey done depends on the size and particularities of your property (be warned, it could cost up to $1,000).

Appraisal fees

You need to know the value of your home before you set the selling price. If you're not using an agent, you may want to hire a professional appraiser for an expert opinion of how much your home is worth. (Your buyers will still have a second appraisal done — their mortgage lender may require it, or they may simply want to be certain they are getting a good deal.) If you are using a reputable and experienced agent, you may not bother with a pre-listing appraisal. (For more information on appraisals, see Chapter 18.)

Don't confuse an inspection with an appraisal. An inspection reveals any major structural or systems-related problems with your home that will need to be fixed before you sell; an appraisal investigates what the market value of your home is. The appraiser may take into account if there are any of those problems that the inspector looks for, but he or she is really only interested in the dollar value on the bottom line.

Location-specific expenses

Some geographic regions come with their own unique set of housing issues. As a seller, you may be responsible for extra costs associated with your particular region.

Believe it or not, there are termite hot spots in Canada. If you know you live in a hot spot, you may want to have a termite inspection performed. Insects and other pest problems are not part of a standard home inspection. If you live in a region notorious for pest infestations, you may have to pay for a separate inspection. It is possible in some cases to get a termite warranty. If you have one, and keep it active, it may cover the cost of the inspection.

As a rural dweller, you may want to have the well water tested or a modern filtration system installed. As a resident of Nova Scotia, you may want to have the results of a recent ground test for radon handy for showings. Maybe you live on a fault line or maybe you live on a flood plain. Wherever you live, be aware of the extra expenses you will incur due to your location (and see Chapter 22 for more on regional concerns).

GST

Regardless of whether the sale of your home is GST exempt (see "Some Good News about Taxes" later in this chapter), this tax applies to most services you will use in selling your home. So expect that real estate agents, lawyers, appraisers, building inspectors, surveyors, and anyone else you hire to help sell your home will charge GST on top of their service fees.

Selling your home is an expensive endeavour. Unfortunately, money is not the only currency associated with selling. You're also going to spend time — lots of it. We can't supply you with the numbers in discussing all of the expenses you will encounter when selling your home, you need to figure them out for yourself. This is because each situation is different and each requires investigation, which will eat up many hours. The old saying that "time is money" certainly applies when it comes to selling your home. Many aspects of home selling can't be done on your own, and there are many other tasks that you must take on yourself. Anything you pass off to someone else will cost you money, anything you don't will cost you time.

Doing the Math

Now that you have an idea how much selling your home will cost, you can estimate how much money you will make (let's assume the best) on the sale of your home.

If you have investigated the market value of your home and each of the costs above, then you've already done the hard part. Just fill in Table 14-1 to determine the net proceeds you'll realize from selling your home. Start with your home's estimated sale price and substract whichever associated costs apply. What you're left with are the net proceeds from the sale.

Table 14-1	Calculating the Net Proceeds
Item	*Amount*
Estimated sale price	_____
– Agent's commission	_____
– Legal fees	_____
– Repairs or renovations	_____
– Discharge of your mortgage	_____
– Property taxes and prepaid utilities +/–	_____
– Moving costs	_____
– Survey fees (if applicable)	_____
– Appraisal fees (if applicable)	_____
– Location-specific expenses (if applicable) (termite inspection, well water inspection)	_____
– GST (if not already included)	_____
Net proceeds from sale =	_____

Some Good News about Taxes

The money you make on the sale of your home (remember, we're assuming the best) and the money you spend moving to your new home may be tax deductible (it's true!). Here's how it works.

Principal residence exemption

If you have lived in your home the entire time you have owned it, *all* proceeds of the sale are tax exempt — this is known as the *Principal Residence Exemption*. If this is true for you, skip ahead to the next section. If, however, you bought a residential lot and waited a while to build on it, or if you rented your house out for a few years while you hunted truffles in the French country-side, or for some other reason your home was not your principal residence for a period of time while you owned it, read on.

If the final sale price is less than what you paid originally for your home, that money is non-taxable. Isn't that generous? You too get to skip ahead to the next section. However, if the sale price is greater than what you paid for your home in the first place, a portion of that money may be taxable. You should talk to your accountant about the particulars of your situation, but the approach outlined here gives you a good idea of how much of the proceeds you will be taxed on.

Consider the case of Chris and Pat. In 1984, Chris and Pat bought a beautiful lot in the then sparsely inhabited West Collins Bay area of B.C. They spent three years renting while they built their dream home, which was finally completed in 1987. Chris and Pat lived happily in their new home as the nearby city quickly expanded, and they eventually decided to sell and move farther away in 1995. Owing to the large influx of new residents in their area, housing prices had skyrocketed. The happy couple managed to sell their home for $437,000, more than double the $185,000 they had initially paid for its construction between 1984 and 1987. Chris and Pat figured out their taxable gain on the sale when they filed their tax returns for 1995 using the *Principal Residence Exemption formula*:

> 8 years as principal residence (1987–1994) + 1 year (the current taxation year) = 9 years
>
> 9 years ÷ 11 years that they owned the property (1984–1995) = 0.82
>
> 0.82 × proceeds of sale (calculated as the net proceeds from the sale of their home minus the amount they originally paid for it). Therefore, 0.82 × ($437,000 – $185,000) = $206,640

Therefore, $206.640 is not taxable!!

So, if $206.640 of the proceeds of the sale are not taxable, that means that Chris and Pat owe tax on just $45,360 ($437,000 – $185,000) – $206.64, which is the difference between the proceeds of the sale and the non-taxable portion of the sale as calculated using the Principal Residence Exemption formula.

The portion of the proceeds that is taxable is considered a "capital gain," and is reported on Chris and Pat's income tax returns. Some capital gains are tax-deductible, but these deductions are restricted to the sale or disposal of small business shares and qualifying farmland.

If you owned your principal residence since before 1982 there is a slightly more complex formula you need to use — due to a change in the taxation policy in 1981. The procedure for long-time homeowners is the same, only you have to calculate the exempt portion twice, under the hypothetical assumption that you sold your home on December 31st, 1981, at it's FMV for that year and reacquired it on January 1st, 1982.

Moving tax credits

If you are an employee relocating for a new job (or being transferred), if you are self-employed and relocating for professional reasons, or if you are moving to become a full-time post-secondary student, your moving and selling expenses are tax deductible! This includes all of the selling costs listed above, except repairs or renovations, and your personal travel costs including food and lodging. It also includes the cost of shipping and storing your belongings, and up to 15 days of temporary room and board near either your current home or your new home. Even legal fees and transfer taxes (affectionately known as "the welcome tax") incurred on the purchase of your new home count as moving expenses. The only catch is that your new home has to be at least 40 km closer to your new school or place of business (so if you're moving from one part of the city to another, it probably doesn't count).

As with any tax breaks, there are some eligibility restrictions — contact the Canada Customs and Revenue Agency for details and claim forms (or visit their Web site at www.ccra-adrc.gc.ca (use the search terms "moving" and "principal residence"). Or, ask your accountant or financial advisor for assistance.

Chapter 15

Balancing Selling and Buying

. . . .

In This Chapter

▶ Investigating financing options for mortgage holders

▶ Exploring the options involved in trading up and trading down

▶ Timing your buying and selling properly

▶ Deciding not to sell

. . . .

Congratulations, your finances can handle the sale! So now it's time to sit back and let the buyers come, right? Not so fast. You've got a few more details to work out — like where your next home will be and how you're going to pay for it. After all, you can buy a house without selling one, but not vice versa.

Remember all the work and hassle that went into buying your current home? Well, the bad news is: You have to go through the hassle of selling *and* buying now. The good news is: Buying is easier the second (or third, or fourth) time around. If this is your second sell, you've already become acquainted with the fine points of coordinating the sale of your house with the purchase of another — probably the hard way. For you lucky first-time sellers, this chapter will help you figure out how to balance selling with buying *before* you get into trouble.

What to Do with Your Current Mortgage

What happens to your current mortgage if you decide to sell your home? You have three choices:

  ✔ You can pay off your mortgage.

  ✔ You can let your buyer take your mortgage along with your home.

  ✔ You can take your mortgage with you to your new home.

When your parents were buying their first house they probably had to beg and pray for a mortgage. Times have changed. Today's mortgage market is buyer-driven. Instead of crawling into the bank on your hands and knees and pleading for your mortgage, you can stand tall and ask potential lenders, "What can *you* do for *me*?" Here are a couple of items the lender may offer you:

- A ½ to 1 full percentage point reduction off the current interest rate if you're looking for a new *first* mortgage on a property (it doesn't matter how many mortgages you've had in the past on other properties — only the home you are looking to buy is in question here).

- A legal package that allows you to use the lender's lawyers, at a discount, for the *conveyance* of the title and preparation of the mortgage documents. The "conveyance" of title is the transfer of ownership, and the registration of the new owners, and registering the mortgage, at the appropriate land titles office (See Chapter 20 for more information on conveyancing.)

You may find even more competitive terms offered in the near future, as our southern neighbours get set to invade the Canadian mortgage market. Before you make any final decisions, *shop around and negotiate*. Money is a commodity, and some lenders will charge you a higher price to use their money than others will.

Paying off your mortgage early

If you've owned your home for a long time, you may have built up substantial *equity*. Equity is the difference between the value of your property and the outstanding debts against it — for example, if your home is worth $250,000 and you have paid off all but $12,000 of your mortgage, you have accumulated $238,000 worth of equity in your home. If you have only a small portion of your mortgage to pay off, you might consider *discharging* it (paying it off early).

Most lenders offer financing plans to help you discharge your mortgage faster while avoiding high penalty fees. A financing plan may allow you to do one of the following to help discharge your mortgage more quickly:

- Increase the amount of your mortgage payments.

- Make mortgage payments more often.

- Exercise "prepayment" options (*prepayment* means that you can pay a certain amount of the principal each month or each year in addition to your regular payments, or a percentage of the principal can be paid down each time you renew your mortgage terms).

Using any of the above options decreases your mortgage's *amortization period* (the length of time it takes to pay off your mortgage). (We discuss mortgages in detail in Chapter 3.)

If you're a long-range planner and you're considering selling your home in the next five years, talk to your lender to see about renegotiating your terms. You may be able to modify your payment schedule or negotiate a mortgage renewal that permits you to discharge your mortgage as soon as possible, without paying a *penalty fee* (you pay this fee to your lender as compensation for paying off your mortgage early). However, if you want to put your house on the market tomorrow or next week, paying off your mortgage with a lump-sum amount, including the applicable penalty fee, may be your best option.

If you want to pay off your mortgage with a single cheque you will likely pay a penalty fee. The amount of a penalty fee is usually equal to either three months' interest or an *interest rate differential*. If interest rates have gone down since you signed on to your mortgage, your lender stands to lose a portion of the interest money when you pay off the loan early. For example, if you're making payments on your existing mortgage at a 10 percent interest rate and the current rate is now 7 percent, your lender will charge you for the 3 percent difference. Because the lender can only charge the current 7 percent rate on any loans it currently negotiates, the rate differential penalty accounts for the reduced profit your lender will make on new loans, as compared to your original loan. Interest rate differentials usually amount to a higher penalty than if your lender charges you a penalty equal to three months' interest.

Some financial institutions negotiate the mortgage penalty fees if your buyer also takes out a mortgage with them, or if you use the same lender as your next mortgagee. Whatever arrangement you make with your lender, get a copy *in writing*.

Letting your buyer take over your mortgage

If you're trying to sweeten the deal for a potential buyer, and your mortgage rate is lower than the current rate, consider taking advantage of the "assumability" option. Basically, you allow your buyer to assume your mortgage at its existing rate when he purchases your home. Assumability is often restricted to fixed rate mortgages. (See Chapter 3 for a discussion of fixed rate and other types of mortgages.)

It's rare to assume a seller's mortgage, however. Generally, if circumstances make your mortgage look attractive to a buyer, it's probably a mortgage you want to hang on to, rather than approaching a lender for a new mortgage at the higher current interest rate. The only scenario that truly warrants considering the assumability option occurs when you've got a great mortgage and your highest priority is selling *fast* (and you can afford not to take that great mortgage with you).

Here's how the assumability option works. Your buyer must meet your lender's credit requirements before your lender approves the mortgage transfer from you to your buyer. There may also be fees (which could be hefty) for the legal work and paper shuffling required. Fortunately, because most lenders now require your buyer to meet their credit and income standards, you no longer risk taking financial responsibility if your buyer fails to pay the mortgage, as was the case in the past in some provinces.

If your buyer assumes your mortgage, you benefit in three ways:

- An assumable mortgage is a marketing tool; it may be just the enticement a buyer needs — the lure of a lower interest rate.

- Because your lender is already familiar with your home, the home appraisal requirement may be waived and this saves you a few hundred dollars.

- If the buyer assumes your mortgage, you're no longer responsible for the discharge penalty fees, which saves you even more money.

Do not take it for granted that you will be absolved of all responsibility if the new owner defaults on mortgage payments! Make absolutely sure to indemnify yourself — get it *in writing* — that you have no further financial obligations with regard to the mortgage once your buyer assumes it.

Taking your mortgage with you to your new home

Some mortgage agreements have a *portability* option that allows you to apply your current mortgage to a new home if you decide to sell. "Porting" your mortgage may be your best alternative if there's too much still owing on your mortgage for you to consider paying it off immediately, and if your existing mortgage rate is lower than the current rate.

Often, only fixed rate mortgages are portable. If your new home requires extra financing, you can usually borrow additional funds at the current rate — your new mortgage rate will be a blend of your mortgage's existing interest rate and the current interest rate. For example, if you have three years left on a five-year mortgage term, you may be able to borrow the extra money at the current three-year rate. (So the additional $20,000 you borrow to finance your new home will fit into your existing mortgage at the current three-year rate.) The additional mortgage you just took out to finance your new home has the same expiry date as your original mortgage. When the time comes to renew them, you renew them as one mortgage.

Should you keep the mortgage you already have?

If you're wondering about the benefits of porting your existing mortgage to a new home, you can check out the financial consequences online. Surf the Internet — find a Canadian online mortgage calculator (try www.canada mortgages.com or www.imoney.com) and pretend you're going to port your existing mortgage and borrow a bit more at the current rate. The calculator will determine your new blended interest rate, and tell you what your payments will be. You can simply multiply your monthly payments by the number of months in the mortgage term to get the total amount that you will pay if you port your mortgage.

Use the mortgage calculator a second time to figure out the total amount you would pay on a new mortgage at whatever the current interest rate happens to be. If the total amount payable for a new mortgage is less than you would pay by keeping your current mortgage with a new blended interest rate, then you stand to make a savings if you pay off the current mortgage rather than porting it to your new home. Just be sure that the savings you will make with the new mortgage are greater than the penalty fee you'll be charged for paying off your current mortgage early.

Porting mortgages has become quite common due to the low interest rates of recent years, but choosing what's best for you always depends on your unique financial situation and how much risk you are willing to take. If you've taken to following the rise and fall of mortgage rates religiously in the past few years, you may feel confident in allowing your buyer to assume your current mortgage so that you can take out a new variable-rate or short-term open mortgage on your new home. (See Chapter 3 for details on variable rates and open and closed mortgages.) If you can stand the headache of renegotiating your mortgage every six months, you'll probably end up saving money in the long run.

If you're not a risk-taker and can't be bothered to scour the financial section of the newspaper every morning for the latest trends in mortgage rates, it's worth the bit of extra money you may pay to port your fixed rate mortgage, just for the peace of mind.

Trading Up: Your Options

What's a trading-up situation? When your grand plans for the future involve investing in a home bigger and better than the tiny one-bedroom condo you currently own, you're in a trading-up position. Like any other homeseller with a mortgage, you have three kinds of financing options (discharge it, let your buyer assume it, or port it). Which one is best for someone in your shoes? The most economical option will depend on the current state of the mortgage market.

✔ **If the current interest rate is equal to or lower than the rate on your existing mortgage:** You may want to discharge your current mortgage and take out a new one with the same lender. Because lenders usually offer a one-half- to one-point discount off the current mortgage rate to keep your business, you're guaranteed to get a lower rate. But bear in mind the cost of prepayment penalties for discharging that we discuss earlier in this chapter.

Don't sacrifice important options for that extra one-half- to one-point discount on your mortgage rate. For example, if your current mortgage allows you to prepay as much as you want every six months, you may end up saving *more* by sticking with your current mortgage and paying it off faster — even though it has a higher interest rate.

The mortgage market is highly competitive these days, and this makes discharging an existing mortgage favourable for many sellers. Lenders want your business, and they'll bend over backwards to get it. With all the tools available on the Internet, it isn't difficult to figure out if you'll save money — even if you're charged a penalty fee for paying off your mortgage early.

✔ **If the current mortgage interest rate is higher than your existing rate:** You may want to port your mortgage and borrow a little extra at the higher rate — your new rate will then be a blend of the two rates. As a previous *mortgager* (someone who's taken out a mortgage) you may have some extra bargaining power. Your existing mortgage lender may cut you a deal on a new mortgage in light of your loyalty and good credit history. Or a new lender may sweeten the pot by offering you better terms to lure your business away from your existing lender.

If you're thinking about porting your mortgage, talk to your lender about any fees or restrictions that might apply to your case. If you know you're going to be taking out a new mortgage, shop around for the best deal, and get pre-approval. Most major lenders now offer online pre-approval services.

✔ **In times of drastic changes — if interest rates skyrocket or house prices drop catastrophically:** You may want to let your buyer assume your mortgage to make your house as attractive as possible to potential buyers. However, in most cases, letting a buyer assume your mortgage is probably not going to be in your best interest. If you're trading up, you're not on an extremely tight sale deadline. You can afford to wait for a buyer who is willing to pay a fair price, so there's no need to sell at a loss or give up a great mortgage rate. That flexibility makes the assumable option unfavourable. But if your back is to the wall and you need to move fast, you may be willing to give up a great mortgage rate to facilitate a quick sale. Even if you need to sell quickly, it could be more economical to lower the asking price than to give up a great mortgage rate.

Trading-up fire sale?

Slashing your home's sale price could mean the difference between making a fast sale or no sale at all in times of high interest rates that continue to rise. By dropping your home's sale price, you could end up saving more in the long run.

Calculate the total amount you'd end up paying for a new mortgage at a higher rate. Compare that with what you'd pay if you kept your current mortgage and borrowed extra at the current rate (resulting in a blended rate). There could be a huge difference between the two totals — suppose it's $40,000. Now wouldn't it be better to drop the sale price $15,000 and save that extra $25,000 for a new car or a month-long second honeymoon in Paris?

Trading Down: Your Options

The kids have all moved out, it's too quiet, and you have more space than you need. Besides, you can always use some extra money for those approaching retirement years. It might be nice to turn Sally's bedroom into the other half of your home office — but maybe now is the time to trade in your home for something smaller and less expensive.

Consult Chapter 14 to find out how you determine the net proceeds of your home's sale. Decide how much you want to spend on your next home, and if you can afford it after paying the costs of selling your home, go ahead and sell. Depending on your plans for retirement (and your health), you may want to rent instead of buying your next home. If (now that you've *really* thought about it) you can't imagine living anywhere else, or you're not sure you'll be able to find something suitable in your price range, you might consider taking out a *reverse mortgage* (we explain reverse mortgages in the next section).

A home is a tax-free investment. By using the money you made on the sale of your previous home to purchase another one, you are putting your money into an investment that will (hopefully!) grow tax-free. If you decide to rent from the time of your home sale onward, any interest subsequently made on the money you received from the sale of your previous home will likely be taxable (assuming it's invested outside of an RRSP) — and could potentially bring you into a higher tax bracket! Real estate appreciation is tax-free growth, but it is *slow* growth, in contrast to mutual funds or stocks that generate taxable income but appreciate *quickly*. When deciding whether to buy or rent, think what your investment decisions will mean for your taxes.

Trading-down dilemma: to buy or rent your next home?

Renting does allow greater flexibility than simply trading down. If you think that it won't be long after selling your home that you might need to move to a nursing home or some other residence where personal assistance and medical attention are close at hand, you may want to rent for that short time. If you're in perfect health, renting may allow you to spend your retirement years living a few months here and a few months there — experiencing life in all those little towns you always wanted to visit but didn't have the time to while you were working.

If you're no longer interested in, or capable of, dealing with the responsibilities of home ownership and you don't mind letting a landlord call some of the shots, renting may be a viable option. Keep in mind, however, that many of the freedoms afforded by renting are also available to condo owners. Condo upkeep is a shared responsibility plus you have a smaller likelihood of break-ins should you decide to spend a few winter months somewhere sunny.

Renting involves three big pitfalls you should be aware of: You will be vulnerable to rent inflation, you will have to deal with a landlord, and each time you move there is a chance that the owner of your new home will not be compassionate and fair. If you have many independent years ahead of you and would prefer to settle in one place, buying may be the safest course.

Reversing Your Mortgage

If you need extra income to help maintain your current standard of living after you retire, or if you need extra income for personal care expenses, you may want a *reverse mortgage*. A reverse mortgage is an agreement between you and a lender that allows you to "tap into" the equity built up in your home. You can do this in a few different ways: Your lender may give you a lump-sum payment, send you monthly payments, offer a line of credit, or some combination of these options.

There are some standard restrictions on who can enter into a reverse mortgage agreement — usually, you must be at least 62 years old and have no outstanding debts against your home. However, you do not need to meet credit or income requirements to be eligible for a reverse mortgage. In Canada, reverse mortgages are offered through the *Canadian Home Income Plan*. (See Appendix C for their contact information or consult their Web site at www.reversemortgage.org/canadian.htm).

The amount of money that you can access ranges from 10 to 48 percent of the value of your home. The total funds you can access is determined by:

> ✓ The value of your home
>
> ✓ Your age
>
> ✓ Current interest rates
>
> ✓ The type of reverse mortgage you choose

Unlike a conventional mortgage, a reverse mortgage does not have to be repaid right away — repayment starts when your home ceases to be your principal residence (a home is no longer considered a principal residence if the borrower moves elsewhere, dies, or sells the home). When you do begin to repay the mortgage, you are responsible for the borrowed principal plus interest and any other legal or administrative fees associated with the agreement.

The amount that you must repay for a reverse mortgage *cannot* exceed the value of your home, and you *cannot* be forced to sell your home to repay the mortgage if you still reside there. When lenders determine the amount a borrower can receive, they're betting that the home will not depreciate significantly and that the borrower will not reside there so long that pay-out exceeds the value of the home.

Repayment can be made by you, your family, or your estate, and need not involve the sale of your home. If you do decide to sell your home, whatever profit you make over the market value of your home is yours (or your family's, or estate's) to keep. Should the sale generate less than the market value of your home, it is usually the responsibility of a third party, such as an insurance provider, to make up the difference.

Although not many homeowners have taken out reverse mortgages, their popularity is growing. If you feel it's important to pass down your home to children or grandchildren, you may not want to experiment with a reverse mortgage. Although pay-back does not require the sale of your home, unless you have a home's worth of money stashed away, you may not have any other resources available.

To Sell Before I Buy, or Buy Before I Sell?

You do not always have a choice whether you'll buy first then sell, or sell first then buy. Carrying the costs of two homes, or having to move out without having a place to go to may cause panic. Do not despair — you are not the first to face these scenarios, and there are options.

Selling before you buy

Selling your current home before you buy your next one certainly does eliminate some of the financial uncertainty. At least you know you have enough money to buy another home. If dear Auntie Edna would love to take in you and your six children for five months while you search for a new home, then don't worry about selling first (and consider yourself lucky for having such generous relatives). But, if you don't have anywhere to stay in the time between selling and buying, you might be in dire straits both emotionally and financially.

If you are trading up, you may be counting on all the money you made on the sale of your home to go toward the purchase of a new one. Renting a space large enough for an entire family can cost thousands of dollars per month, and renting for several months will put a significant dent in your buying power. And then there's the stress that goes along with residing in limbo for extended periods of time, not to mention the hassle of having to search for a new home when you've just started at a new job or a new school in an unfamiliar community. If you're trading down, the proceeds of sale may be enough to cover the cost of renting for a few months. You need to work out the financial implications *beforehand*.

Whether you decide to sell before you buy or buy before you sell, *do not underestimate how long it will take to find a new home.*

Buying before you sell and bridge financing

So you've found the most amazing new home — it's only 20 minutes south of your new job, it's surrounded by parkland to the west, there's a gym, a huge grocery store, and a local fruit and vegetable market to the north, and the best theatre, restaurants, and shopping in town to the east. It's even in your price range. You know that if you wait to make an offer someone else will snatch it up, but you haven't sold your current home yet, you still owe $125,000 on it, and you don't have a spare $50,000 to make the down payment. What can you do?

Rest assured you are not the first homeseller who has been caught in the middle of buying and selling. Mortgage lenders have developed a plan for precisely this situation — it's called *bridge financing.* With bridge financing, your lender lets you borrow the money you need to bridge the gap between buying a new home and selling your old one. It usually involves a personal fixed rate loan, often one lump sum that can be repaid in one lump sum at maturity or prepaid at any time without penalty. There are no standard maximum or minimum amounts for bridge financing; your lender will decide how much they are willing to give you based on how much they think you will be able to repay. Since you have already worked out the proceeds of sale and your cash flow for before and after the move, you should be able to make an educated guess about how much your lender will be willing to give you.

There is a downside to buying first and then selling if you require bridge financing. (If owning two homes simultaneously won't put a crimp in your style, buy to your heart's content!) The downside to bridge financing is that you are paying interest on a relatively large sum of money for however long it takes to sell your current home and repay the loan. Remember our earlier warning: Do not underestimate how long it will take to sell your home. If market conditions are favourable for sellers in your area, your home may sell in a week. If conditions are not so favourable, it could take many months (or even a few years if the government just tore down the school across the street to build a biohazardous materials–testing facility). What if your home's value takes a nosedive? What if you simply can't sell your home at all? Murphy's Law will govern the sale of your home to some degree. It could generate only some small hassles, but the worst scenario could leave you in the bottomless pit of debt. Buying first in a slow market is extremely dangerous. You should talk to a local real estate agent about the current market conditions in your area specifically as they relate to your home.

Timing it right: The ideal selling and buying scenario

If you must be stuck in either position, selling first is the less risky of the two. Unless you are moving just because you see a home you like better, you have (hopefully) put considerable thought into where and when you will move. Assuming that you've done your homework, you'll know what to expect when shopping for a home in your new area. Even if it takes a little longer than expected to find the perfect one, you know exactly how much you can afford and have the security of knowing that you are in a financial position to buy.

The ideal situation is that you sell your current home and buy a new one *at the same time*. This entails stipulating in your offer on a new home that the offer is conditional on the sale of your previous home. Usually there is a specified time limit — like 30 days — for the condition to be met. (For a more detailed discussion of "subject to" sale clauses, see Chapter 20.) It's not an uncommon practice, but it may make some sellers reluctant to accept your offer.

If it's a seller's market in your neck of the woods and a buyer's market in your new area, you may have enough leeway to make such stipulations. But if you're moving into a seller's market, you may not have this option. Would you accept a conditional offer on your home if you thought you could get an unconditional offer easily? If you are moving into a seller's market, you may be competing with others making offers on the same home. Making a conditional offer may be just enough to tip the balance in someone else's favour. On the other hand, if you think the sellers may be receptive to a conditional offer, it's a great way to buy first without taking a huge financial risk.

Changed Your Mind about Selling?

Selling your home is scary business. After researching your new area, maybe you've realized that you've been taking your current location for granted — it's really not so bad, perhaps staying put and making some renovations is the best plan. (If you have already listed your house and then change your mind, you can always cancel the listing.) If you've come to this conclusion, you have some financing options to help foot the bill.

Home equity loans and homeowner lines of credit

Most major lenders offer home equity loans (also known as second mortgages and home equity lines of credit) for homeowners. These options allow you to access whatever equity you have built up in your home. If you have paid off your mortgage in full, you may be able to borrow up to 70 to 75 percent of the value of your home to put toward renovations. Home equity loans (exactly like mortgages) are often fixed rate loans with long repayment periods. Lines of credit for homeowners usually have variable interest rates and are available as long as you like after only one application.

If you are undertaking large renovations all at one time, a home equity loan might be the best option. If you know exactly how much the renovation will cost and are planning to pay for it all up front, a home equity loan gives you the security of knowing precisely how much your regular payments will be. If you intend to make smaller renovations over many years or if you are unsure how much renovations will cost, a line of credit may be better suited to your needs. After all, you only have to pay interest when, and if, you use the line of credit.

Many financial institutions allow you to combine home equity loans and lines of credit (for example, you may start off with a line of credit borrowing only small amounts over a longer period, and then decide to borrow a large chunk of money for a bigger renovation project at a later date — as a home equity loan). Most financial institutions will allow you to structure your payments to suit your financial situation. Home equity plans are a great advantage to those of you who decide that renovating makes more sense than selling — they allow you to borrow large amounts of money at lower interest rates than regular personal loans or lines of credit.

Refinancing your mortgage

Another option to pay for renovations is *mortgage refinancing*. If it is time to renew your mortgage and interest rates are relatively low, this may be the preferred option. Some lenders will allow you to borrow up to 90 percent of the value of your home, less whatever you still owe on your current mortgage. You borrow at the current interest rate, and your new mortgage rate is a blend of your previous rate and the current rate (weighted according to how much is owed at each rate). Talk to your lender about the products they offer for home renovators to figure out the most economical route.

Part V

Preparing Yourself and Your House to Sell

THE SALESMAN CONVINCED US THAT A SECURITY SYSTEM WOULD REALLY INCREASE OUR HOME'S RESALE VALUE.

In this part . . .

This part contains the most "for sale by owner" information, since it outlines the steps in putting your home on the market, but it contains lots of useful information for everyone. From choosing an agent (if you want one) and a lawyer, to getting an appraisal or inspection, as well as all the contracts, statements, and steps in between, this section gets you from the decision to sell to the point where you're ready to talk to potential buyers.

Chapter 16

Selecting Your Selling Team

. . . .

In This Chapter

▶ Deciding to sell your house yourself

▶ Selecting an agent

▶ Selecting a lawyer

. . . .

*I*f you're a really take-charge kind of person with some time on your hands, you may be considering selling your home privately. Wait just a minute, though! We want you to know what's in store for you in the home-selling process. Read this chapter to be sure you're making the right decisions, whether you want a real estate agent to handle your sale or you're determined to do it yourself. An experienced lawyer who specializes in real estate will ensure everything goes smoothly, whether or not you are using an agent. If you want to sell your home on your own, you will rely on a real estate lawyer to draft and review all your documentation. Either way, make sure you have the right kind of help to secure your home's sale.

Deciding to Sell Your House Yourself

If you decide to sell your home without a real estate agent, your greatest asset is recognizing what you know and what you don't, what you can do yourself and what you should delegate.

Realize that selling a home privately is an extreme sport. In between answering the phone, scheduling appointments, verifying potential buyers' identities, confirming their qualifications with financial institutions, and showing off your home, you need to maintain a perfectly groomed house and lawn. You may also be trying to raise a family and hold down a job at the same time. Your lawyer is indispensable when it comes to arranging a title search, negotiating with buyers, and reviewing legal contracts. Fair warning: This is a time-intensive undertaking.

And the stakes are high. Selling your home is a business transaction and a legal transaction — involving your largest single investment. When it comes to marketing your home, negotiating with sellers and dealing with contracts, you have to make a lot of decisions and do a lot of work that most people rely on their agents to do.

We want you to be realistic and prepared to deal with all the complexities of making a private sale. In this chapter, we help you determine your limits so that you know which aspects of home-selling you can handle and how to find a lawyer or agent to take care of the home-selling processes that you can't (or choose not to).

Saving the commission

The big reason people like the idea of selling their homes privately is the money savings they anticipate. By selling privately, you will not pay a *commission* (percentage of the sale amount that goes to the agent who made the sale). Commissions vary across Canada and from agent to agent, but they tally in the thousands. (For details on commissions see Chapter 14.) In Toronto, for example, where many sellers pay a 5 percent rate of commission, a $250,000 house generates a $15,000 commission for the agent — and don't forget the additional 7 percent Goods and Services Tax payable on the total gross commission.

Selling your home yourself will probably cost less than a tenth of what you will pay if you hire a real estate agent to make the sale. However, if your buyer has an agent, then your savings won't be as great because the buyer's real estate agent is entitled to a commission from the sale.

 If you want to sell your home yourself to save commission dollars on the sale, you have to work hard for them. The closer you can match a real estate agent's professionalism, realistic pricing for the current market, and focus on getting the property sold, the more savings you make.

Working out the costs of selling it yourself

We know you're visualizing what you can do with all that commission money you save by selling your home yourself. Well, take those dollar signs out of your eyes! Here are the expensive and troublesome realities you face if you plan to sell your home privately:

✔ **You may have to lower the asking price for your home.** If a buyer is considering two identical properties with the same asking price, one being sold by the owner, one by an agent, unless you can offer your buyer a better price, chances are he'll take advantage of the expertise and facilitation provided by a real estate agent.

✔ **You incur the cost and hassle of advertising that your home is "for sale."** You will actually have to sell your house before you cash in on your saved commission. In order to reach buyers, you need to drop a significant amount of money on advertising since you won't have access to the Multiple Listing Service (MLS) and all the contacts an agent would provide. Advertising in local and regional newspapers quickly adds up. Visit www.privatelist.com where you can advertise online and get lots of information on selling privately.

✔ **You are responsible for researching and accurately determining the right price for your home.** Pricing your home is very important. (See Chapter 14 regarding comparative market analysis and potential pitfalls when setting the price for your home.) If you hire an appraiser to assess the current market value of your home, expect to pay between $150 and $300 for this service. A real estate agent may offer you a Comparative Market Analysis (CMA) free of charge to try to get your business. A CMA states what your home is worth (its *fair market value* or FMV) based on comparisons to similar homes selling currently in your area. (We compare appraisals and CMAs in Chapter 14.)

✔ **Selling your house on your own is not going to fit neatly into a schedule.** You must be very accessible — by phone, by pager, or online if you're going to sell your home privately. Expect prospective buyers to knock at your door at all times of day and night . . . regardless of how large the words "By Appointment Only" appear on the For Sale sign in front of your house. You will have to accommodate the needs of prospective buyers' schedules in order to show the home, and if you have a family, you also face juggling their schedules. When you sell privately, you don't have the luxury of a real estate agent who organizes and administrates the showings of your home.

✔ **The legalities involved in selling a home are considerable.** You may not be aware of special legal considerations when selling your home and you could risk being held liable by the buyers. An experienced agent is on the lookout for any possible legal issues — after all, her commission and her reputation are at stake if something goes wrong with the sale of your home. And if she by chance overlooks a legality, she has errors and omissions insurance to cover her butt — you don't! (See Chapter 5 regarding an agent's roles and responsibilities.)

✔ **Emotions may cloud your judgment.** You need to be professional and objective during negotiations with your seller. Your personal attachment to the property may prevent you from being an effective negotiator. If you don't have experience at a bargaining table, you're probably not the best person to haggle with a potential buyer's experienced and well-informed real estate agent.

✔ **Real estate agents will see your "private sale" advertisements in the newspaper and they'll be calling you, too.** Like any ambitious business people, real estate agents look to expand their business, and they're in touch with the market. When your house appears available, agents will solicit you, hoping that you're tired of dealing with the headaches of trying to sell your home yourself and will hire them instead.

Setting aside your emotions as a homeowner to be an effective homeseller

In Chapter 19 we talk about making your house look its best to sell more quickly. A big part of that process is putting away the most personal items in your house — your collection of autographed hockey cards, the pipe cleaner crafts your kids have been bringing home since kindergarten, etc. The goal is to de-personalize the house so buyers can immediately imagine themselves living there.

Similarly, you'll want to put away your emotional connections. This house is no longer your home. It is a product you are selling. Try to stay detached and objective. You'll need to give yourself little reminders about this as you do research into the current market value of your home and when you are dealing with buyers face to face.

Not all buyers will like your house and not all will have the nicest manners. Try to take negative comments in stride. At the very least they reveal the prospective buyers are imagining themselves living in the house. Don't get defensive. Since any purchase is a matter of balancing the pros and cons, just make sure you show prospective buyers all the selling features as well. If they hate the broadloom, point out that there are hardwood floors underneath. If they complain it is too far from town, let them know it is only a five-minute walk to the lakeshore and anyway there's a well-stocked convenience store just a kilometre farther down the road.

Learn as much as you can about buyers so you can demonstrate all the benefits your house has to offer them. Also look at every potential buyer as part of your test market. If enough people comment that the house seems dark and gloomy, for example, replace 60-watt light bulbs with 100-watt bulbs. Your house will seem bigger and brighter and more inviting to the next buyers who visit.

Remember, you don't have to like potential buyers, you just have to get along with them well enough to keep them interested in your house, allow as few factors as possible to turn them off, and negotiate a deal.

Although you will want to set aside your emotional connection to the house when you are dealing with buyers, understanding your motivations to sell and the impact it has on your life are important tools in keeping the process moving forward. Develop a plan to get what you need out of the sale and review it regularly to see if anything needs to be changed.

Do you need to get a certain amount out of the sale in order to retire comfortably? Does your market research support this selling price? Do you need to move quickly? Price is the biggest selling feature of a house. What is the lowest price you could live with to expedite the sale? Are enough people hearing about your house? Are there any good advertising venues you haven't tried?

Your goal is to sell your house and get on with your life. If you are determined to sell your home yourself, be honest about what you do know and what you don't know, and be realistic about what you can do and what you can't do. Do your research and hire the necessary experts.

Identifying the Right Real Estate Agent

Most people approach the task of selling their homes as a team sport. Make things easy for yourself by picking the best players to back you up. The most important positions on your selling team are your real estate agent and your real estate lawyer. Choose both individuals with care. In this section, we take you through the ins and outs of finding the best agent. We do the same for lawyers a little later on. Another potential member of your selling team is your real estate agent's broker. See Chapter 5 for more on the relationship between you, your agent, and her broker.

Real estate agents, also known as *salespeople* or *registrants* in some provinces, can use the term *Realtor* provided that they are registered members of their local real estate boards or associations. This means they are licensed professionals and are legally bound to protect and promote your interests as they would their own.

Picking the perfect real estate agent for you is partially luck and partially knowing what to look for. We recommend you interview several candidates before you make a decision.

British Columbia Real Estate Association explanation of relationship between seller and real estate agent

Realtors work within a legal relationship called agency. The agency relationship exists between you, *the principal*, and your *agent*, the company under which the individual salesperson who is representing you, is licensed. The essence of the agency relationship is that the agent has the authority to represent the principal in dealings with others. Here, the relationship between seller and agent, as expressed by the British Columbia Real Estate Association (BCREA):

Agents and their salespeople are legally obligated to protect and promote the interests of their principals as they would their own.

Specifically, the agent has the following duties:

1) To show **undivided loyalty** to the principal by protecting the principal's negotiating position at all times and disclosing all known facts that may affect or influence the principal's decision.

2) **To obey all lawful instructions** of the principal.

3) An obligation to **keep the confidences** of the principal.

4) The responsibility to **exercise reasonable care and skill** in performing all assigned duties.

5) The duty to **account for all money and property** placed in an agent's hands while acting for the principal.

What to look for in your agent

The best real estate agents score high on the list of qualities below. Keep these in mind when you're asking more targeted questions during your interview (we give you a list for that as well, later on in the chapter). Your agent should:

✔ **Be a full-time professional.** When you sell your property, you hand over a sizeable amount of money to your real estate agent — probably anywhere between 3 and 6 percent of the price, and up to 10 percent on recreational properties. A good agent earns a commission by giving you good advice, promoting your property, skillfully closing the deal, and taking care of the details. To do the job right, you need a full-time professional. A big part of selling a house is being in contact with many buyers and understanding what they respond to. Don't settle for anything less than a dedicated, full-time real estate agent.

✔ **Charge a reasonable commission rate.** Find out what commission the agent charges on a sale. Is the agent's commission rate in keeping with the average you have been quoted? A range of commissions is charged across the country and commissions are calculated differently in different areas. In Toronto, a seller may pay a 5 to 6 percent commission. By comparison, in Vancouver, many companies charge a 7 percent commission on the first $100,000 of a sale and 2½ percent on the balance. Recreational properties are usually more difficult to sell than conventional homes, so commissions may be as high as 10 percent of the sale price.

The agent willing to accept the lowest commission isn't necessarily going to do the best job of selling your home. Often a company that charges a lower commission requires the owner to pay for all advertising (including occasionally buying a sign from the agent!), as well as doing all their own showings and even hosting the open houses. Sometimes a company quotes a low commission to secure a listing, and after the house has been on the market for a month or so, recommends that you pay a higher commission for more services. Suddenly the commission looks pretty much like all the other quotes you found. Also make sure that the commission quoted allows for commission to be paid to a buyer's agent. Make sure the total commission quoted is all you will be paying . . . you don't want any surprises.

✔ **Inform you how she handles holdover clauses as they apply to commission.** In some rare cases, you may still owe your agent the commission even if your home doesn't sell while you have it listed with his agency. Your agent can use a *holdover clause* to claim a commission even if your home's sale happens after the listing expires. An average holdover period might last 60 to 90 days from the expiration of the contract. Occasionally, a buyer who made an unacceptable offer on your house while it was listed may approach you again once the listing has expired, this time with an acceptable offer. Depending on the timing of the offer and the wording of the listing contract, you may still have to pay your agent the commission. Check the fine print of the listing contract to see if there is a holdover period, and ask your agent if she has ever enforced the holdover period.

If a real estate agent doesn't negotiate a fair and equitable commission for himself, will he negotiate a good price for your house when dealing with buyers? If you're looking for a good deal overall, the commission might not be the best place to cut corners.

✔ **Quote a reasonable listing price for your home**. Beware the agent who quotes the highest listing price. When you interview real estate agents, ask them what listing price they would assign your house, and ask how they determine this price. You'll quickly sense how knowledgeable the agent is about houses in your neighbourhood, as well as the real estate market in your price range. Take a look at Chapter 14 to find out how you can get a pretty good idea of what's reasonable . . . and why pricing your home too high initially is a big mistake.

Listless and lost

There is, in some parts of the country, a breed of agent referred to as *listers* because of their "list 'em and leave 'em" attitude. These are the agents who will agree to an unreasonably high asking price, just to get your listing. If the market is really hot, then nothing else is done until another agent brings buyers to your door, at which point your *lister* shows up to collect "their" part of the commission. Most of the time, however, your house just languishes on the market, and they ultimately convince you to lower your price . . . to where it should have been to sell your house in the first place.

✔ **Have a good track record.** Ask the agent how many years she's been working as a real estate agent. Ask for references — get the names and numbers of at least three people whose homes she's sold in the past year or two. Call the references your agent provides. If the people you speak to have mixed feelings about the way the sale was handled, find out what went wrong and how, looking back, they would have prevented it. Hindsight is always 20/20. What questions will they ask real estate agents next time they are preparing to sell?

✔ **Have a stellar local record.** If you're selling a starter home in the suburbs, the best real estate agent in the neighbouring city isn't the right choice for you. You want an agent who works full-time in your area. Your agent's networking and connections are, in fact, the most valuable marketing tool available to you. The more local agents (and therefore buyers) that your agent works with, the larger the pool of potential buyers for your home.

Working with your local real estate star, you'll see that the agent knows your neighbourhood inside and out. A well-versed local agent knows what home-buyers are after, and how to showcase your neighbourhood and community. Chances are, the agent has a pretty good idea how to sell your house from the moment she pulls up to the curb.

✔ **Sell houses like yours.** The agent who sold the largest number of local monster homes last month is not the best candidate to sell your starter home. Hire an agent who lists and *sells* lots of other starter homes — someone who's constantly working with people in the market for a home like yours, and who understands which buyers will be interested.

✔ **Make selling your home a priority.** Be alert to signs that the real estate agent won't have time to personally work on marketing your house. Some top-selling agents just have too many listings to personally take care of your property. Their assistants take care of the legwork, attend open houses, schedule showings. You don't want to find out partway through the process that the agent you so carefully selected has delegated your listing to an assistant.

But a busy agent is busy for a reason. If your real estate agent has many listings, that means many phone calls to sell other homes. If your agent is in demand, he's probably a good one.

Similarly, you don't want to list your house with an agent who you'll never see again until the listing is ready to expire and they swing by to renew the contract. If the agent is planning an extended vacation in the near future, don't use that agent! Sometimes selling your house takes longer than you think it will, even when the price is right. For all the work you are doing to keep your property looking its best, you don't want to let buyers slip through your fingers while your agent is cavorting with the locals in Bora-Bora.

✔ **Be Web-proficient.** The Internet is a great tool and is changing how the real estate market works both in Canada and internationally. An agent who has been inspired to be proficient on the Web is an agent who can adapt and innovate along with the times.

✔ **Have specific ideas for marketing your home.** You can even request a written marketing plan from each of the real estate agents you interview. The marketing plan should include the listing price for your home, a list of comparable properties on the market, recommendations for making your home more marketable, plans to advertise and promote the property, and how the agent intends to manage open houses.

✔ **Be enthusiastic about the prospect of working with you to sell your home — from start to finish!**

Getting connected

One dedicated downtown real estate agent we know tirelessly promotes her listings and her business to the 8,000 households in her *farm area*, that is, the downtown neighbourhoods she works in constantly. At peak periods she might have dozens of "For Sale" signs up. Every time she gets a new listing, she advertises it in local papers and features the home in a flyer sent to every home in the area.

As a result of her high profile in the area, she finds a buyer for 45 percent of local homes she lists. She believes it's not the specific listing advertisement that sells the home, it's her contacts. Because so many people call her first when they want to sell or buy in the neighbourhood, she can quickly match sellers and buyers.

We're not suggesting that you track down this agent (or one like her — they're out there) and hire her at all costs. But, keep the agent's profile in the neighbourhood you want to buy into in mind when picking your agent.

Build a list of real estate agents to interview. Once you've decided to sell your house, you'll start to notice "For Sale" signs and "Sold" signs posted on people's lawns. Take a walk around the neighbourhood and write down the names and phone numbers of the agents who have the most signs up. The more "Sold" signs the better. Presto! You have a list of agents who are clearly active in your neighbourhood and skilled at closing deals. Interview them. Talk to people you know who have bought and sold houses recently. Add to your list the names and numbers of local real estate agents who come with good recommendations.

What to ask your agent

Once you've got a healthy list of agents to interview, consider some of the following questions that will quickly narrow it down.

- ✔ Are you a full-time real estate agent?

- ✔ How long have you been in the business?

- ✔ What area do you work in primarily?

- ✔ Do you use the Internet as a sales tool?

- ✔ Do you have a Web site?

- ✔ Do you have access to the real estate portals such as www.realtor.com or www.homeadvisor.msn.com?

- ✔ Do you take colour digital photographs of homes to post online?

- ✔ Do you typically sell houses in any specific price range?

- ✔ What asking price would you recommend for our house?

- ✔ How did you determine the asking price for our house?

- ✔ What specific ideas do you have for marketing our house?

- ✔ Would you be present at all showings of our house?

- ✔ Do you use lock boxes? If so, how do you log visits? (See Chapter 19 for more on lock boxes.)

- ✔ How many local homes in our price range did you sell last year?

- ✔ Can I get the names and numbers of three people whose homes you sold in the past two years?

- ✔ How will you keep me informed once my home goes on the market?

Don't Let Your House Come Back to Haunt You . . . Hire a Good Real Estate Lawyer

In case you're wondering whether you need a real estate lawyer to help with the sale of your home, the answer is yes. Emphatically, YES! There's a reason law school takes *years* to get through — because laws are complex and sophisticated. No matter how smart you are, you need a professional. Period. Your lawyer performs a number of necessary tasks to cement your home's sale, tasks that you don't have the knowledge or resources to accomplish — unless maybe you're a lawyer yourself.

You risk losing hundreds of thousands of dollars if you try to put the sale through yourself and get it wrong. If you can spare hundreds of thousands of dollars and you really want to represent yourself, you can go ahead and gamble — it's legal. But for 99 percent of homesellers, selling their homes without a lawyer's involvement simply isn't worth the risk.

At the very least, you require a lawyer (or a notary public in Quebec) to handle the change of ownership for your home, even if you're selling the home privately. Don't forget, a real estate lawyer has liability insurance as a safeguard in case any problems arise with settling the title for your home.

Picking the right real estate lawyer

Recommendations from friends, family, and business associates give you the best place to start your search for a top-notch real estate lawyer. Often banks work with real estate lawyers, and your local bank manager may be able to give you the names of some of the lawyers they use.

Your provincial law society also has names of local real estate lawyers — get a list of names and telephone numbers so you make further inquiries . . . . When you call the lawyers on your list, ask them to estimate how much work will be required for your particular circumstances, and what are the approximate costs. Also see Appendix C for our suggestions on locating legal counsel across Canada.

Costing out lawyer's fees

When you call your lawyer to make an appointment, ask how much it will cost (as if you need to be reminded), what exact amount you will have to bring into the lawyer's office, and the preferred method of payment. Make sure that you specifically ask for the *"all in"* cost which will include all your legal fees, any applicable taxes and adjustments for property taxes, and other pro-rated fees.

Lawyers charge a flat fee, usually around $300 to $400, but that's not the total cost of their legal services. You also pay disbursements and taxes. *Disbursements* are any fees that your lawyer encounters while working for you. (Disbursement fees can include, for example, courier fees, registration fees, long distance phone calls, reproduction costs for documents, and any other costs your lawyer pays on your behalf.) And of course, you're responsible for the tax on any goods or services provided. An average "all in" cost for the straightforward sale of a residential property with a single mortgage, which can be discharged using the proceeds of sale, might be $500 to $1,000. The cost varies, however, depending on the complexity of your case.

You should also ask what your lawyer's rates are, in the event that something goes wrong and you need extra services. Most of the time, extra services can be obtained on an hourly-rate basis.

Knowing when to contact your lawyer

Most homesellers go to their lawyers *after* they have signed the sale contract. For simple, straightforward sales done through a real estate agent, you can safely wait to see your lawyer until you have your buyer's contract or agreement of purchase and sale in hand. If you're selling privately or if yours is a complicated sale, ideally your lawyer reviews the conditions of sale prior to you signing any agreement of purchase and sale.

If you're selling through an agent, a typical scenario might run something like this: Your agent comes over to your home at 7:00 p.m. with the buyer's offer. The buyers will pay the price you want, but there are a few *conditions* (see Chapter 9 for a discussion of conditions). Your agent thinks the conditions are typical and shouldn't evolve into any problems, but you would like a second opinion from your lawyer. You need to make up your mind quickly and want to jump on that great price. Unfortunately, your lawyer closed up shop at 5:00 p.m. So you write in a clause making the contract or agreement of purchase and sale subject to your lawyer's approval within 24 hours and you go ahead and sign. If you have an experienced and reputable agent, don't expect any problems.

In a private sale, the prudent course is to review the conditions of the offer with your lawyer before signing anything. Because you don't have a real estate agent to review the conditions of the sale agreement, you take a significant risk if you accept the offer unadvised. Most buyers' offers are not made and sealed in a slam-dunk time frame. At a minimum, the "subject to lawyer's review" clause allows you to sign the contract and still have a safety hatch in the event that your lawyer subsequently discovers problems.

Provincial real estate associations across Canada (see the list of contact information in Appendix C) have standard forms for their Contracts of Purchase and Sale, which have been created by lawyers. If your buyer uses one of the appropriate standard provincial forms such as the Ontario Real Estate Association's document (shown in Chapter 9), chances are that your lawyer will not uncover any problems with your buyer's offer.

If you fear your home's sale is going to get complicated, talk to your agent to get an idea of the *likely* conditions before you see any buyers' offers. Your agent can help you compile a list of possible scenarios to present to your lawyer for an expert legal opinion. Armed with the advice of your agent and your lawyer, you're as ready as you'll ever be to evaluate an offer that comes in late on a Saturday night.

Definitely make the offer subject to review by your lawyer if you face either of these situations:

- ✔ Your buyer stipulates conditions that your agent views as strange.

- ✔ You have a rental unit on your property and the tenants will remain once the new owners take possession.

If your lawyer is also your brother, and he's willing to get out of bed at one in the morning to come over and review the offer on the spot — by all means, take advantage of your connections. It's always better to have a professional opinion. But if the timing doesn't allow for a trip to your lawyer's office and you are selling a fully residential property with a real estate agent, you have one mortgage, you are using a standard contract, and there are no unusual encumbrances or conditions, don't be afraid to go ahead and sign — that is, if you're happy with the offer.

Preparing to visit your lawyer

Give your lawyer all the necessary information right off the bat. When you call to make an appointment, ask what documentation you should bring. Your lawyer will probably ask for the following:

- ✔ A legible copy of the accepted offer

- ✔ Latest property tax bill

- ✔ Utility bills for the past year

- ✔ All mortgage information, or your mortgage discharge statement if you no longer have a mortgage, or if you intend to discharge your mortgage with the proceeds of your home's sale

- ✔ Any transfer or conveyance documents from when you purchased the home (if you still have a copy)

- ✔ Documentation for any chattels (any items you agree to leave in the house for the new owners) that are to be included in the sale and that have their own title or lease, such as a leased security system

- ✔ Any additional information relevant to the condition of your property or the title (ownership) of your property

Taking care of business — what your real estate lawyer does for you

Once your real estate lawyer has all the relevant information, things get cracking. The role of your lawyer and the role of your buyer's lawyer are not set in stone. Although there are some tasks commonly relegated to the buyer's or the seller's lawyer, if you would like to arrange with your buyer to do things differently, there's nothing to stop you from doing so. As the seller, your lawyer's traditional role involves the following tasks:

✔ Reviewing the sale contract

✔ Ensuring that the titles and documentation for any chattels that are included in the sale are in order

✔ Reviewing your mortgage information and performing or verifying calculations

✔ Reviewing your property tax bills

✔ Pro-rating to the adjustment date any annual utility costs, condominium fees, and municipality fees

✔ Determining if any refunds are owed to either you or your buyer, and the amount of these refunds. Preparing a statement of adjustments

✔ Preparing the transfer deed

Performing a title search and verifying that there are no encumbrances (or other adverse conditions) against the property are typically the domain of the buyer's lawyer.

Preparing for the worst

When you're buying or selling a house, your will is probably the farthest thing from your mind. However, everyone who owns real estate should have a will, and when you're selling or buying a home is an excellent time to write your will or revise the one you have because:

✔ You are acquiring or disposing of a major asset that may affect the distribution of the assets of your estate.

✔ At conveyance time, you're already using the services of a lawyer or notary public who will necessarily become acquainted with your personal financial situation.

As you shop around for a lawyer or notary public to handle your conveyance, you can negotiate the extra cost of your will into the conveyance package and you should pay less than the "stand alone" cost of the drafting or review of a will.

Chapter 17

Listings and Disclosures

· ·

· ·

*I*f getting ready to sell your house only meant painting the fence and waiting for your agent's call, the process would be a lot less stressful. But like so many other major events in life, selling your home involves lots and lots of papers. In this chapter, we'll tell you what you need to know about this unappealing pile, and before you know it, you'll be breathing easy again.

Listing Contracts

If your home is going to sell, buyers have to know about it. Marketing your home involves listing it either on your own or through an agent. If you are listing through an agent, you will need to fill out and sign a listing contract. The listing contract gives authorization to one or more agencies to sell your home, and specifies how much you will pay for their services. The contract is a legally binding agreement that places obligations on both you and your chosen real estate agency. You have a few options for listing your home.

Selecting your listing type

When choosing the kind of listing that's right for you, consider all the variables. What are the general market conditions? How well are other homes of the same size, price, and location selling? Do you have the time to be searching for buyers on your own? What is your top priority? Once you know what your needs are, and you know the market conditions for homes like yours, you are in a good position to decide on your listing strategy. And when you have a listing strategy squared away, you'll need to know what to expect when it comes to signing the listing contract.

There are three kinds of listings: MLS (or multiple) listings, open listings, and exclusive listings. MLS listings are the most common.

✔ *Multiple Listing Service* **(MLS) listings authorize your selling agent to work with other agencies' salespeople.** An MLS listing markets your home across Canada, reaching a huge network of real estate agents. Your agent is free to co-operate with all other agencies and gives them all full co-operation and access to your home's listing. The MLS system, and the local real estate boards that maintain it, has very specific requirements regarding co-operation between real estate agents. MLS listings are often in the best interest of the seller, as they can give your home maximum exposure to the market. The listing contract and the MLS data indicate what portion of the total commission is payable to the buyer's agent, who brings along a ready and willing buyer for the property.

✔ **An** *open listing* **authorizes one or more agent(s) to sell your home while protecting your right to sell it yourself.** Open listings are rarely if ever used in residential real estate, but are frequently found in commercial real estate where properties or businesses are made available without being actively listed through an agent. The owner may sell the property without an agent or entertain offers that come through any agent. You, the seller, don't have to personally deal with any of the agents who are working on your behalf, and if you find a buyer, you are not obligated to pay any commission fees. Often the buyer will pay the agent a "finder's fee" for locating the property, and the seller does not have to pay commission. (The "finder" agent will have an agency relationship with the buyer, but the seller has no agency representation.)

✔ **An** *exclusive listing* **authorizes an agency to market your home for a specified period of time.** Exclusive listings are rare. Generally, exclusive listing contracts don't allow you to sell your home yourself during the listing period, and often involve a *reduced* commission fee, which is a benefit to you. By bypassing the MLS system, an exclusive listing means your agent's not under any obligation to show your property to other agents. Your listing agent has more control over the marketing of your home. Usually the listing agent co-operates with other real estate agents, but the listing *broker* calls the shots. (See Chapter 5 for an explanation of the role of a real estate broker.) As an exclusive listing, the property does not appear on the MLS system (see Chapter 7 for details of the MLS system) and does not get the exposure provided by the MLS database. Most sellers, however, want the extra exposure and agent co-operation guaranteed by the MLS system.

Most people who really want to sell list their homes via the MLS system, as it gives their homes maximum exposure on the market. Because of this, many buyer's agents do not consider open or exclusive listings to be serious efforts to sell the property.

Creating your listing strategy

Deciding on your listing type depends on your needs. If you need to sell quickly, take an MLS listing — your home will get maximum market exposure. If you want the best possible price for your home, the surest way to get the right bid is to advertise to as many people as possible that your home is for sale. An MLS listing ensures that your home quickly reaches the right network of real estate agents. The Canadian Real Estate Association's MLS Web site allows access to nearly all the MLS listings in Canada, through its links to local real estate boards across the country: www.mls.ca/crea. (See Appendix C for more details on this resource.) In addition to the Internet, MLS listings also appear printed in your local real estate agent's catalogue.

Detailing your listing contract

A *listing contract* is a legal document that must be signed by both you and your agent, usually via standard forms that are supplied by your local real estate board. All the particulars about your home appear on the listing contract; it also states under what conditions you are willing to sell, and you and your agent's obligations. Make sure you obtain a copy of your listing contract and that you put it somewhere safe (not the same safe place you put that spare house key you haven't been able to find in five years).

If it makes you more comfortable, or if you are concerned or confused about something in your contract, you can have your lawyer review it before you sign. Remember that although you are listing with an individual salesperson, the listing contract is with the salesperson's *agency*. (So if Suzanne Smith, your real estate agent, works for Royal LePage, your listing contract is with Royal LePage, not with Suzanne.)

A listing contract deals with three sets of issues:

1. **The exact details of the property for sale.** Your home's lot specification, size, building materials, heating and air conditioning systems, number and descriptions of rooms, and other details are presented in the listing contract. Any extra items (movable things, such as appliances or furniture), or chattels included in the sale are also shown on the listing contract. (The contract also specifies if any items are *excluded* from the sale of the home; for example, the chandelier in the dining room or the hot tub.)

2. **The financial particulars relating to your home.** The listing contract establishes the asking price for your home, and discloses all information concerning your mortgage (such as balance, payment schedule, maturity date), property taxes, and any legal claims on your property.

FYI

If you ever think of selling, would you let us know?

If a neighbour or friend expresses an interest in your home, you can add an exclusion to the listing contract (exclusive and MLS listings only) that states that you don't have to pay your agent a commission if that neighbour or friend (they must be specifically named in the contract) buys your house. After all, it was you who got them thinking about your home in the first place — not your agent!

Prior to signing the listing contract, notify your agent that your neighbour (or your rich cousin Aubrey) may want to buy your property and that you do not wish to pay commission if either follows through. Put the exclusion in writing before you sign the listing. Give the names of the excluded parties to your real estate agent before he comes to list your house. Your agent prepares a letter stating the exclusion, which is signed by his manager. The letter should read something like this:

"This letter is to confirm that XYZ Realty acknowledges that the following parties are excluded from the listing contract dated May 1, 2000, and should either party purchase the property at 123 Main Street, Kamloops, there will be no commission payable to XYZ Realty.

> Mr. and Mrs. Neighbour,
> 125 Main Street, Kamloops

> Aubrey McCousin,
> 18 Showoff Lane, Moneysville

Signed by both the agent and the agent's manager"

Keep in mind that additional clauses such as this may slow down your home's sale. The existence of exclusions may show on your home's listing and can discourage agents and buyers who don't want to deal with any possible complications to the sale.

---

3. **The precise terms of employment for your agent(s).** Your listing contract specifies who's allowed to market your home and in what manner, as well as stating the time period your home can be marketed by the agent, and what you will pay the agent for marketing your home.

Multiple Listing Service (MLS) listings all come with a standard disclosure statement so you can reveal all your deep dark secrets — just kidding! We discuss disclosure statements in detail a little later in this chapter.

Your listing contract does *not* obligate you to accept any offers on your home, even if the buyer fully meets the conditions of sale stipulated in the contract. A listing contract creates an agency relationship between you, the seller, and your selling agent. Throughout the selling process, your real estate agent acts in your best interests to sell the home, without misleading or making any misrepresentations to potential buyers. Refer to Chapter 5 for more information on agency relationships.

Disclosure Statements

When you sign the listing contract, you will likely be required to fill out a *disclosure statement*, also known as a Property Condition Disclosure Statement. The disclosure statement is a legal document in which you describe your property and all other items included in the sale to the best of your knowledge. On making an offer, buyers see your disclosure statement and they must sign it to acknowledge it has been received. For *all* MLS listings in Canada, disclosure is mandatory, or will be soon; for *most* exclusive listings, disclosure is recommended.

Basically, the disclosure statement informs the buyer and your agent about the condition of your home, and protects you and your agent from any litigation in the event that a buyer discovers some dreadful problem with your property that you were not aware of. By providing detailed information on the condition of your home, you ensure that your agent accurately represents your property to potential buyers. You *are* responsible, however, if deliberately concealed information about your property comes to light after you have signed and submitted the disclosure statement.

Who sees my disclosure statement?

Disclosure statements are designed for the benefit of all parties in the transaction. The sellers disclose what they know about the property, and the buyer receives the disclosure statement, often using it as a starting point for a professional home inspection. Both the buyer's and seller's agents refer to the disclosure statement while viewing your home and they may point to any disclosed deficiencies when negotiating the contract.

The disclosure statement puts the onus of accuracy on you, the seller, and any misrepresentation is potentially dangerous. As the seller, you must disclose everything you know about your home, and you're obligated to disclose anything that *you should have been reasonably expected to know*. For example, if there's a minor water leak in your basement that only appears once a year under heavy rains, you should disclose that there's potentially a problem with the drain tile or foundation. The buyers will inevitably find small problems you try to hide.

By signing a legal document that states you have disclosed all knowledge of the condition of your property, should a buyer pursue legal action after becoming aware of some previously undisclosed information, *you* (the seller) are responsible for any concealment — usually *not* your agent. You are only liable, however, if you *intentionally* conceal information. If you don't disclose information because you aren't aware of the issue, it's simply a case of bad luck for your buyer. Your agent would be liable if *she* fraudulently misrepresented any details that are contrary to the information represented by the seller.

Bear in mind that most buyers will do a building inspection, and by doing so, the buyer assumes some responsibility for the condition of the house. The buyers will do their due diligence as they inspect and investigate the house. If the seller has completed a disclosure statement to the best of their ability, and a problem surfaces that the seller was unaware of and the home inspector missed, the buyers' dispute will likely be with the home inspector and not the seller.

What do I need to disclose?

The disclosure statement deals with all aspects of your property. It asks you about both land and structures. A typical disclosure statement deals with three categories:

General information

This section is geared toward the land areas surrounding your property. You include information about the following, if applicable:

- **Public systems.** Is your home connected to public water and sewage systems, and are you aware of problems with either of these systems?
- **Rental units.** Do you have rental units, and are they authorized?
- **Encroachments, easements, and rights-of-way.** Are there any that aren't registered in your title?
- **Ownership issues.** For example, have you received any notices of claims on the property?

Structural information

Here you disclose information specific to your home itself. It may include any or all of the following:

- **Insulation and ventilation.** What kind of insulation and ventilation do you have, and are there any problems with it?
- **Electrical, plumbing, heating/cooling systems.** Again, are there any problems you are aware of?
- **Structural damage.** Is there any flooding, fire, or wind damage to your home?
- **Pests.** Have you had any insect or rodent infestations?
- **Inspections.** Has your home passed a full inspection? Do fireplaces, security systems, and safety devices meet local standards?

Additional information

This section provides blank space for any extra information that is relevant to the condition of your property, or for explanations of any problems or conditions that have previously been mentioned, or repaired in the past.

If you are selling your condominium, you need to include information about current restrictions (regarding pets, children, rentals, or use of the condominium unit) and any future restrictions you are aware of (for example, new bylaws or proposals). You also need to disclose information about anticipated repairs or major construction projects planned for the building.

It won't help you to be dishonest when filling out the disclosure statement. Even though your buyer will be relying on the word of your agent, he or she will also read the sale contract carefully — and you're legally obligated to disclose any known adverse conditions in the disclosure statement that forms part of the sale contract. If you lure an unwitting buyer into making an offer by misrepresenting your property in the disclosure statement, you look foolish when the buyer does his inspection and shows you to be ignorant at best, or a liar at worst. You don't want to lose a ready, willing, and able buyer because you didn't disclose all the necessary facts on the disclosure statement. And you definitely don't want to face a legal battle if your buyer later sues you for not properly disclosing the condition of your home.

Chapter 18

Inspections and Appraisals for Sellers

*W*hen you're purchasing a new home, you need to make sure that you know what you're buying. This is why home inspectors and appraisers are so important to house-hunting — they help you make sure it's a good investment.

And now that you've decided to sell your house, it's just as important to make sure that you know what you're selling. Having an inspection and appraisal done isn't just something buyers do — you should consider it as well. Maybe an inspector will tell you that that leak in the basement is actually just a tiny tear in a water pipe, rather than the massive problem you assumed it was (and were willing to lower the price for). Or, perhaps an appraiser will alert you to a new bylaw that prevents you from making that improvement that was going to raise your asking price. Without the appraiser's advice, you might have had to tear down the illegal renovation.

Inspections for Sellers

We know what you're thinking: "Why would I want to pay hundreds of dollars for an inspection when my buyer will have one done anyway?" You're right, your buyer will, almost certainly, have an inspection performed on your home. Some lenders will only approve a buyer's mortgage subject to the home passing a full inspection, as you, a homeowner, are no doubt aware. Most buyers' offers are also contingent on the seller's home passing a full inspection.

If your house is well maintained, then an inspection is generally not necessary — don't waste your money. However, if there are common problems that affect the real estate in your vicinity — like radon in the Maritimes, contaminated well water in rural areas, or leaky condos in British Columbia — it may be advisable to have an inspection done. A positive inspection report is a great marketing tool to relieve buyers' concerns.

Why you should have your home inspected

If you have your home inspected before you put it on the market, you realize the following benefits:

✔ An inspection alerts you to any defects that require repair. You may want to do the repairs to help raise the value of your home, as well as to avoid haggling with the buyers over the cost of the repairs that in turn affect the asking price for your home. Also, by doing the necessary repairs before you list the home, you cut down on the amount of time your home might spend on the market — an important consideration when trying to interest prospective buyers.

✔ Having a professional home inspection performed before you list may save you from having to redo any cosmetic improvements. For example, if an inspection reveals you have to take out part of the walls of your home office to update the wiring, then you want to find this out *before* you add a fresh coat of paint.

✔ Providing a full inspection report to potential buyers gains their respect and fosters trust in both you and your home.

✔ If you're selling your home privately, a professional home inspection may help you determine the value of your home, and in turn enables you to set the right list price for your property.

Why not to have your home inspected

We have to point out the two main drawbacks to having your home inspected before putting it on the market:

✔ If your inspection reveals any serious problems, you are legally obligated to disclose that information to potential buyers (and to your agent if you are required to sign a disclosure statement — see Chapter 17 for details on disclosures). You may prefer the "ignorance is bliss" approach, but chances are your buyers (and their lawyers) won't share this point of view.

✔ The inspection costs you hundreds of dollars, and any buyers who make you an offer will have their own inspection performed, regardless of whether you have already done so.

If you don't feel you need an inspection report to inspire buyer confidence, and you're certain that your property meets safety standards, don't waste your money on an inspection. If you're afraid that there *are* serious problems and you'd rather take the chance that your buyer's inspector won't notice, it's your decision, but consider yourself warned. Having your home inspected before putting it on the market eliminates one more uncertainty from the selling process, and that means one less thing you have to worry about. The real benefit of a pre-listing inspection is *peace of mind*.

What your inspector looks at

An inspector examines closely all the major functional systems in your home, including:

✔ Structural components: roofing, foundations, floors, walls, columns, and ceilings

✔ Exterior components: exterior wall cladding, doors, windows, eaves, balconies/decks, and vegetation

✔ Interior components: walls, stairways, counters, cabinets

✔ Heating and cooling systems: furnace, air conditioning

✔ Electrical systems: wiring, voltage

✔ Plumbing: condition of pipes and faucets

✔ Insulation and ventilation: insulating materials, ductwork

See Chapter 11 for more information on inspections.

How to prepare for the inspector

Your inspector isn't authorized to turn on any systems that are not already operative in your home. So you need to have all your home's systems turned on and ready for the inspector's visit, including gas, water, electrical, heating, cooling, and plumbing systems. Be on hand to help if the inspector needs to rearrange your personal property in order to gain access to blocked-off areas. There are a few steps you can take to make sure the inspector can do the job easily and thoroughly:

✔ Make sure electrical panel boxes are unblocked.

✔ Remove clutter blocking access to electrical panels, the attic, basement crawl spaces, the foundation, heating and cooling systems, water heaters, and pipes.

✔ Restrain your pets so they don't interfere with the inspection.

✔ Have a copy of each of the following:

- Any service records, warranties, or information on age and performance for appliances that will come with the home

- A written list with the age of all major structural components and systems components, and any service records and warranties

- Your utility bills for integrated systems (e.g., electric, gas)

What common problems to expect

No matter how conscientious a homeowner you are, some things are simply beyond your control. There are some common problems — most are simply the effects of age and improvements in standards for home safety and efficiency — that your inspector is likely to uncover.

Exterior

Here's where you (somewhat sheepishly) admit to ignoring for years that tiny river of a crack beside one of your basement windows. Guess what? It's growing — fast — and might cause serious structural problems down the road. This is one exterior problem your inspector might dig up. Some others include:

✔ Aging roof surface. If the problem is advanced it will be obvious, but in the early stages can be quite subtle, and easily overlooked.

✔ Defective windows.

✔ Wear on siding.

✔ Ground that is not properly sloped away from the home. A proper gradient prevents water drainage into the basement or foundation.

✔ Cracks, bulges, or deformities in the foundation. These abnormalities could indicate a more serious structural problem.

Interior

The insides of peoples' homes can hide a multitude of sins. Here are a few that your inspector could unearth:

- Signs of flooding or leakage into the basement. Waterproofing a home is extremely expensive (as you already know if you looked into it after your basement flooded). If you have installed any waterproofing measures, a sump-pump, or other additions, make sure the inspector takes note.

- Improper insulation or ventilation. If air can get in, water can get in. One of the first things they teach to budding architects is that *water is your worst enemy.* If your home leaks or doesn't allow moisture to evaporate, all of your major structural components are at risk. And to mention the obvious, if your insulation is shoddy, heating and cooling will be inefficient and expensive.

- Interior components that no longer meet safety standards. For example, old paint that contains lead, or missing railings on staircases.

- Outdated electrical, heating, or plumbing systems. If your home is very old, be especially observant of these systems, as they may be both inefficient and unsafe.

A final note: If you're a handyman who's done work over the years on any of the major operating systems in your home, have them looked at thoroughly. Unless you're a professional electrician, plumber, or HVAC installer, you should be aware that just because "it works" doesn't mean you've fixed things properly or safely.

The inspector does not *evaluate* your home — if you want an evaluation, hire an appraiser. An inspector merely *reports.* For example, your house may be of the "they don't make them like they used to" persuasion, but the inspection report only states that your furnace is 48 years old and it is functional and presently operational, not how well it heats. If you want a report that includes how well your systems function, hire the necessary heating or plumbing contractors to evaluate these systems.

Appraisals for Sellers

If you are selling privately — that is, without an agent — an appraisal makes a lot of sense. You obtain a professional, objective assessment of what your house is worth on the current real estate market. Based on your appraisal you can realistically set the price for your home. (See Chapter 14 for the perils of pricing.) And if you're selling your home through an agent, there are some circumstances under which it makes sense to have an appraisal done.

Does a homeseller need an appraisal?

Whether or not you have your home appraised, buyers almost always need to have an appraisal when they apply for a mortgage. If your buyer does not need a new mortgage — for example, if your buyer is assuming your mortgage — then you don't need to worry about appraisals.

However, under some conditions it can be a good idea for you to have your home appraised before you put it on the market. The chief benefit of having a professional appraisal performed before you list your home for sale is that you eliminate uncertainty and get a realistic price range for your home. This is especially important if you require a certain amount out of your house to plan your next move. An appraisal lets you know if your plans are financially viable. Although you may not be required to get an appraisal on your property, the assurance it gives you means one less thing to worry about. In addition, if your home is special or unique in some capacity that makes it difficult for you and your agent to compare and gauge its value, you should probably hire a professional appraiser.

The majority of homesellers do not hire an independent appraiser before listing their homes for sale, unless they're selling privately. Most real estate agents are well versed in the factors that influence the market value of a home, and can provide you with a reasonably accurate estimate of your home's worth. What's more, your agent uses the same process as an appraiser to judge your home's value — a Comparative Market Analysis (CMA) — and they do it free of charge.

Even though a real estate agent and an appraiser use the same process to appraise a home, there are differences. You hire an appraiser for the specific task of supplying you with an expert, unbiased opinion. A real estate agent, however, is a professional *sales* agent, and the opinion of an experienced and reputable agent may take into account intangibles — the "Wow!" factor — because the agent knows a certain type of buyer will pay big bucks for your home. An appraiser may not be aware of the perceived value of your pristine white shag wall-to-wall carpet that really strikes a chord with urbanites in love with 1970s kitsch. Furthermore, most agents will perform a Comparative Market Analysis free of charge, saving you the few hundred dollars you would pay an appraiser.

Hopefully, you've done a little investigation on your own and have some idea of what comparable homes are selling for in your neighbourhood. If your agent's suggested price is wildly out of whack with what you've seen on the market, or you're willing to pay the few hundred dollars for greater peace of mind, you should contact an appraiser.

How is an appraisal performed?

The first thing you'll want to know about an appraisal is how much to budget for it. A standard home appraisal (which could be a bungalow in a neighbourhood with a fair amount of owner turnover) will run you anywhere from $200 to $500, depending on the size and location of the property and the depth of the assessment. Basically, the rate is determined by how much work the appraiser has to do to figure out the value of your property. If there have been a lot of comparable sales in the recent past, it's a fairly easy job. If the last time a house sold in your neighbourhood was in 1957 and it was nothing like yours, an appraisal will be a little more complicated, and thus more expensive.

What will I get for my money?

Appraisers will be very quick to tell you that they are *not* home inspectors. Having said that, they do look at a lot of the same things. Here's a list of some of the things an appraiser notes about your home:

✔ The size of your home.

✔ The age of your home.

✔ Condition — does it need repairs that will impact on the value of the home?

✔ Upgrades, finishing — what work have you put into it recently that will increase the value? Bathrooms and kitchens are usually the focus here.

✔ Infrastructure — heating, plumbing, power: Do they all function properly? Or are there costly repairs needed?

✔ Amenities — especially in condos, but in houses too: sauna, pool, hot tub, deck, garage.

✔ Neighbourhood — schools, shopping, transportation, safety.

✔ Immediate surroundings — what does your yard back onto, a park or a high-rise apartment? Which way does your condo face, south for the best light, or east for the morning sun?

✔ Anything that makes your home special — unique features that can boost the value of your home.

The appraiser is required to do a visual-only inspection of all the items on the above list — but may investigate more closely — by measuring the property and probably taking photos. Any signs of problems or potential problems, like cracks in the walls that could indicate excessive settling, will be documented.

If you live in, say, a Victorian neighbourhood, don't hire an appraiser who specializes in suburban homes built after 1980. Choose an appraiser who's familiar with the special attractions a home like yours offers prospective buyers.

An appraiser may use one of three methods to evaluate the subject property:

- ✔ **A Comparative Market Analysis (CMA).** This evaluation is based on a comparison of your home to the recent sale prices and current asking prices of comparable homes in your neighbourhood, taking the condition, amenities, and other particulars associated with your home into account to adjust that figure up or down. See Chapter 14 for an example of a Comparative Market Analysis.

- ✔ **A replacement cost approach.** This method determines the value of your home based on how much it would cost today to rebuild your exact home. It is used less frequently than the CMA because it provides a less accurate picture of how much buyers are willing to pay for your home.

- ✔ **A rental income approach.** This is used for homes that include rental units, and is essentially a CMA that factors in the income and expenses generated by those units.

Regardless of the method employed by your appraiser, the value he or she determines is a professional *opinion*. The nature of an appraisal is such that two different appraisers, for example yours and your buyer's, may come to different conclusions about the value of your home. If your buyer's appraiser (or the appraiser sent by your buyer's mortgage lender) determines the value of your home to be less than the offered amount, you may lose the offer. The buyer may no longer be willing to pay the offered price, or the buyer's mortgage lender may refuse to finance the offered amount. In this case, the buyer and/or seller may want to get a second appraisal if the first is not satisfactory . . . even appraisers make mistakes sometimes.

How long will an appraisal take?

Believe it or not, an appraisal does not take much time. Depending on how "ordinary" your home is, it could take from 15 minutes to an hour. The more unique features your home has, the longer it takes to note all the items. A standard appraisal should take under an hour.

After the visit to your home, the appraiser researches other sales in your area in the recent past, to compare what other homes similar to yours have sold for. This helps put a market value on your home and will also highlight any unique features of your property. The research process takes a little longer, but again, for a standard home, you can expect the report in two to three days. If your home is in that old money, leave-it-to-the-grandkids neighbourhood where sales are uncommon, the research will be harder and will definitely take longer.

Appraisals for condominiums

The appraisal process is almost identical for condominiums and houses (go back and read the above section if you skipped on to this one). The costs are the same, although a really posh condo may run you a little more. One thing that does make a difference in condos is the maintenance fee. A very high monthly fee that clearly supports extras like a concierge, swimming pool, and meticulously maintained property, will not detract from the value assigned to a condo. However, a high monthly fee on a condo without a lot of frills reduces the price that a buyer is willing to pay.

Be aware that the appraisal may not take into account the status of the condominium corporation — and this is a factor that significantly affects how much a buyer offers for your home. (See Chapter 4 for more information on condominium corporations.) Even though the state of the building management's finances has a bearing on the value of each unit, appraisers do not usually have access to this information. For example, if there's no money in the building's reserve fund, underground parking upkeep or security may be neglected, possibly decreasing the value of the property. If you want a more accurate estimate, you can provide your appraiser with a copy of your condominium's documentation, which will include all the relevant information about maintenance, finances, and legal obligations of the condo corporation. In some provinces this is referred to as the *estoppel certificate*, *condominium certificate*, *status certificate*, or *information certificate*.

Condominiums are often harder to price than houses, so you may find a larger discrepancy between various appraiser's figures or between your condo's appraised value and the price buyers are willing to pay.

Preparing for an appraisal

There are a few steps you can take to make a favourable impression on any appraiser:

✔ **Showcase your home.** Although, technically, cleanliness and tidiness (or lack thereof) should not affect the appraiser's "objective" opinion, appraisers are human, and it never hurts to show off your home for the appraisal. If the appraiser thinks you are a conscientious homeowner, she may give you the benefit of the doubt and place your home at the upper end of a range of values for your home.

✔ **Make sure the appraiser has all the relevant information about your home.** Everything from appliance warranties and inspection reports to receipts for any recent work done on structural, electrical, heating/ cooling, or plumbing systems should be available. Feel free to give the appraiser any information you have on recent asking prices or sale prices in your area, especially any private sales that may not show in sales statistics. While the appraiser will research the most up-to-date information, it never hurts to make sure.

✔ **Follow along as the appraiser tours your home.** Discuss factors that you, or the appraiser, feel influence the value of your home, and make notes. This will help you understand why the appraiser may or may not agree with your own assessment of the value of your home.

✔ **Only use a certified, reputable appraiser.** There are unlicensed appraisers out there. Whatever identification is presented to you should show the appraiser to be AACI (Accredited Appraiser Canadian Institute) or CRA (Canadian Residential Appraiser) designated. If you have any friends who have recently hired an appraiser, ask if they were satisfied that they received a fair appraisal, and if so, ask for the appraiser's phone number. Only work with an appraiser you trust.

Get a written copy of the appraisal if you can. Remember that if you are the seller, you will not have access to the buyer's appraisal. If you disagree with any of the factual information that is reported, you can argue to have the report adjusted. But if you don't have a copy of the appraisal, you won't be aware of any errors. If a certified appraiser refuses to correct factual errors, you can report them to the appropriate authority, the *Appraisal Institute of Canada* (www.aicanada.org). Note that if a bank is doing an appraisal for the buyers, the buyer may not get a copy of it, especially if the bank is paying for the appraisal. If, as the buyer, you are paying for the appraisal (and you couldn't negotiate for the bank to pick up the cost) you may be in a stronger position to get a copy of the appraisal from the bank.

Be sure the appraiser knows why you need his services. The purpose of the appraisal has an effect on the final cost and on the amount of time it will take. Homeowners also get appraisals done when they're considering refinancing or renegotiating their mortgages, dividing property after a divorce, or in connection with other legal concerns. The fees for a home appraisal for litigation purposes are far higher; they can go well into the thousands of dollars because the report is more comprehensive and includes more detailed and slightly different material, and the research just takes longer.

Part VI
Sealing the Deal

The 5th Wave

By Rich Tennant

"WELL, IT ALWAYS HELPS TO PUT FRESH FLOWERS AROUND, AND SIMMER SOME POTPOURRI ON THE STOVE. OH, AND LET'S GET RID OF THOSE ALLIGATOR MOTELS."

In this part . . .

*W*hen the curtain rises on your market-ready home, we want you to be prepared. So we're going to be your coaching and cheerleading team to help you transform your home into an open house. We'll also give you pointers on how to handle buyers once you've wowed them into making offers. And finally, we'll walk you through sale contracts and negotiations, right up to when you pass the keys on to the new owners.

Chapter 19

Making Your House Shine

*N*ow that you're sure about selling your old place and finding a new place to call home, you'll start to notice a big change in your attitude. Your *home* — the place where you relaxed, slept, worked, ate, raised kids, and cuddled pets — will slowly become a commodity, a *house*. And if you get top dollar for this house, the better position you'll be in to buy a great new home.

Here's where some old-fashioned elbow grease gets acquainted with a positive, objective viewpoint. In this chapter, we'll walk you through a good, hard look at your house, to help you determine what needs to be done to improve it, and what improvements are unnecessary. Once you've decided what needs to be done, we'll give you tips on how to roll up your sleeves and make your house the shiniest on the block.

Undertaking Home Improvements

One of the most common selling mistakes is to make major renovations before a sale. Pouring thousands of dollars into renovations does not result in an equivalent increase in the market value of your home. Some renovations are "good" and others are "bad" in terms of a return on your investment, and you need to know which is which before jumping in with both feet. Renovations that would have fallen into the good category or the bad category will, if poorly executed, fall into the "ugly" category and knock money off your sale price.

Improvements that save your buyer money as the new owner of your home do increase the value of your home to some degree. For example, making your home more energy efficient means your buyer saves on heating and cooling costs. However, this renovation will probably not return more than 30 to 50 percent on your investment. In fact, there are few, if any, renovations for which you will get back all of what you put in. Here are some guidelines as you spruce up your home to sell it.

- **Inexpensive cosmetic improvements, such as repainting, are always your best bet.** Select colours from a neutral, conservative palette to repaint your house inside and out. This will make your house look brighter, larger, and well maintained. Statistics show that when you sell your house, you will recuperate 60 to 65 percent of the money you spent on painting.

- **If interior or exterior structures of your home need improvement to make it saleable, then larger renovations may be worth the time, money, and hassle.** For example, if you neglected to add an extra bathroom to go with those two extra bedrooms you built back in 1995, and your daughters have grown up having to run across the house when nature calls, then it makes sense to add one now. As a general rule, kitchens and bathrooms are good places for renovations. Upgraded features of kitchens and bathrooms make good selling points and on average, home sellers get about 65 to 75 percent back on the money they put into modernizing.

But if you'll never make back the money you spend, why would you even consider renovations? The fact is, if buyers recognize your home needs work, they'll factor into their offering price a large margin of error for the cost of renovations. You can either sell your home "as is," which means the buyers will pay a lower price and undertake renovations and improvements themselves, or you can finance some good renovations yourself before you sell. Although you may never get a 100 percent return on the money you spend renovating, you may *lose less* than if you were forced to drop the sale price into the "as is" category.

If your timeline for selling your home is a few years down the road, you might want to make a major addition to your home. That way, you get to enjoy the new features, plus they'll add value to your home when you eventually sell. But if you're looking to sell *immediately*, leave well enough alone — it's just a bad idea.

Sometimes renovations are simply not warranted. Even though your 30-year-old bungalow could badly do with fixing up, it might not be worthwhile if you notice that all the houses that have sold on your street have been torn down to build spanking brand new monster homes. If people are buying into the neighbourhood for the land, rather than the house that sits on the land, don't waste effort and money on what will become demolition debris.

Lose a little or lose a lot…

When Ken and Barbi decided to sell their dream home after 20 years, they listed it at $250,000. Along came Shelley, who loved the house but could see that the bathrooms — which had never been upgraded — were due for some major renovations. This was a common complaint from everyone who viewed the house. The contractor she called said it would cost $7,000 for all the renovations, but just to be on the safe side, she budgeted $10,000 — so she made an offer of $240,000. Ken and Barbi weren't thrilled at the idea of knocking $10,000 off the price of their biggest asset. So Ken phoned a contractor friend who said he could do it for $6,500. They went ahead with the renovations and re-priced their house at $255,000 (original price $250,000, plus $5,000, approximately 70 percent of the renovation cost). In a perfect world, a new buyer would have come along, seen the beautiful new bathrooms, and have been willing to pay the full asking price. No such buyer appeared, however, but the house did eventually sell for $246,000. By renovating

the bathrooms, Ken and Barbi overcame buyers' objections to the bathrooms, and ended up recovering all but $500 of the renovation cost.

A few streets over, Flo and Harry couldn't resist adding the purple porcelain bathtub and the fuschia tiles imported from Italy — to the tune of $12,000. Like Ken and Barbi, they'd been in their house for 20 years and had also priced it at $250,000, the standard market value for the neighbourhood. Predictably enough, few buyers shared Harry and Flo's taste for pink and purple porcelain, so the highest offer they received was $240,000. Everyone was factoring in the cost of ripping out that crazy purple bathtub. So Flo and Harry were out the $12,000 they initially spent installing those vibrant-coloured fixtures *plus* the $10,000 that got knocked off their asking price by the potential buyers. Try to make sure your home improvements appeal to mainstream tastes, and you'll have better luck with your investments.

 If you're thinking about renovating, you should talk to your real estate agent. If you aren't using an agent, a good place to go for information is the Canada Mortgage and Housing Corporation (CMHC) or the Canadian Home Builder's Association. Both organizations offer many products dealing with home renovations, and have plenty of free information available on their Web sites (www.cmhc-schl.gc.ca and www.chba.ca). If you need more specific information, talk to a real estate appraiser.

Creating curb appeal

Making a good first impression is crucial to selling your home. Potential buyers don't walk up your driveway blindfolded; their first view of your property is from the street. Your home has to look good outside as well — this is often called *curb appeal.* You never know who's going to drive by your front yard, so consider it part of the marketing strategy.

Pretty on the outside

In case you're wondering where to begin, here's a checklist of tasks to help enhance the exterior of your home and yard:

- ✔ Clean out the garage, and move any large, infrequently used items into storage elsewhere.

- ✔ Clean windows, shutters, eaves, doors, and mailboxes.

- ✔ Replace damaged window or door screens.

- ✔ Do any necessary repairs and touch up paint.

- ✔ Get out the gardening gloves: trim hedges, trees and shrubs; rake leaves; mow the lawn; weed gardens; tend to flowers.

- ✔ Clean oil marks and stains off the driveway.

- ✔ Ensure the garage door opener is working properly.

- ✔ Clear and clean paths, patios, and patio furniture.

- ✔ Make sure your house number is visible from the street.

- ✔ Do last minute dusting and tidying to get rid of any clutter that's accumulated over the past week.

A big "For Sale" sign in front can go a long way to getting your home noticed, but you want to make sure the next reaction will be, "And it looks great!" You have to draw buyers in before you can dazzle them with the built-in cabinetry and the lakeside glass walls that offer the stunning panoramic view of your private shoreline. Getting the right kind of attention requires a plan of attack.

Pay attention to other special areas that might need improvement, such as dirty backyard pools and rusting swing-sets. Take the time to look around and tidy carefully, and don't just shove all the clutter into the garage and close the door. If a buyer decides he wants to take a peek to make sure both his mini-van *and* SUV will fit inside, it doesn't look good — and that could cost you a sale.

If you are planning to have an inspection or appraisal performed, now is the time to do it (see Chapter 18 for more on both inspections and appraisals for sellers). As part of the spiffing-up process, you'll want to make any repairs suggested by your inspector or appraiser.

An inviting inside

Hardly know where to begin? Take a look at this list and plan to perfect your home's interior appeal:

- Hold a garage sale.

- Make renovations that you were planning on (see the beginning of this chapter for information on "good" and "bad" renovations).

- Repaint or touch-up paint, and repair cracking plaster.

- Fix leaky faucets, wobbly doorknobs, loose cupboard handles, and squeaky hinges or floorboards.

- Clean draperies and upholstery; shampoo carpeting.

- Move excess furniture and belongings (especially toys) into storage — visitors will have an easier time walking around and the rooms will appear larger.

- Get rid of any unwelcome visitors (like those cute little squirrels that live in your chimney, and the family of mice in the crawl space) — call an exterminator if you must.

- Wash inside windows, walls, panelling, and any other surface that might have smudges or fingerprints.

- Put away all small appliances and clean any large appliances that are included in the sale.

- Lock away jewellery and valuables.

- Add comforting touches like candles or flowers; light the fireplace (if you have one and it isn't August).

- Have fresh towels in bathrooms.

- Be aware of odours (especially those you may have become accustomed to, such as cigarette smoke or pets) and take countermeasures (try baking bread or putting a few drops of vanilla in a warm oven just before a showing).

- Weather permitting, open windows to let in as much fresh air as possible.

- Place any inspection reports, records, or information sheets outlining the features of your home in plain view, with enough copies that buyers can take one with them.

Alluring interiors

So, your home positively sparkles outside in the sunshine — great. But once a buyer moves beyond the exterior, you need to back up that great first impression with something even better inside. Just clean and tidy is fine for the outside, but inside your home there are two extra qualities you must be concerned about: neutrality and ambience.

A garage sale is a great way to get rid of closet clutter. It not only improves the look of your house for showings, but it will make moving that much easier. Now you finally have an excuse to get rid of those extra 12 toasters you got as wedding gifts.

It's not enough to be organized and spotless. Buyers who are touring your home need to be able to see themselves living in it, and that means you have to erase, as much as possible, your personality from the interior. A neutral setting lets buyers start to think seriously about your house as "my new home," and this is the first step toward an offer. Once you've visibly neutralized your house, you need to take care of all the other senses that create ambience — the smells, sounds, and feels that will make your home comfortable and inviting. Use the list below to make sure you've covered all your bases.

If you plan to repaint, or if you are replacing countertops or fixtures, choose light, neutral colours. Painting is better than wallpaper — it is much easier for a buyer who does not share your design sense to repaint than to strip wallpaper. Light, neutral paint will make rooms brighter and feel larger, and will remove some of your personality from the decor. Simple cosmetic improvements are relatively inexpensive and make a big difference to the appearance of your home.

Be prepared to show at any time of day or night, and on short notice. Keep things clean, and have a contingency plan for your family and pets in case you get an unexpected call from your agent.

Going to Market

So your home sparkles inside and out and you're ready to get the word out that you want to sell. From the sign on your front lawn to your open house, your marketing techniques are a key part of the home-selling process. Although you may be able to advertise a garage sale with a flyer posted at the end of your street, we suspect selling your home will take a bit more effort. To sell your home with the least amount of hassle — and for the highest price — you need to have a marketing plan.

The more professional you are about your advertising, the more trusting your buyer is likely to be. If you're selling with the help of a real estate agent, you'll automatically benefit from the credibility of the company image your agent works for, and their marketing expertise.

If you're selling your house on your own, take a page from the real estate agent's book: a co-ordinated effort is better than a haphazard one. An agent will explore all avenues for sale and *act* like a salesperson. You should, too. Make the most of the resources available to you, type any information sheets instead of handwriting them, use professional signage, and be polite when the buyers come calling.

Your basic "For Sale" sign

If you have a yard, posting a "For Sale" sign in it is one of the best ways to attract buyers. If they're interested in your neighbourhood, buyers will tour the area looking for potential homes. Don't let them miss yours. Your sign should be prominently displayed (perpendicular to the road) and list a number where your real estate agent or you, the homeowner, can be reached. If it's a corner lot, maximize your exposure by putting a sign facing each road, providing local bylaws allow more than one sign.

Consider yourself warned: Unless you put the words "shown by appointment only," your buyers may come knocking at any time of the day or night. In fact, they may come knocking at any time, regardless.

If you're selling on your own, give yourself an edge by investing in a quality "For Sale" sign. On the Internet, check out www.privatelist.com — a Web site for private homesellers — for information about spiffy signs and other issues related to selling privately. You can also look up signs in your Yellow Pages and call local shops for quotes. The sign should say "Private Sale" or "For Sale by Owner" and include a phone number or pager number where you can be reached easily.

Advertise, advertise, advertise

The purpose of placing an advertisement is to get people to phone and book an appointment. You want to give the basic information — like number of bedrooms, general location, kind of house (bungalow, split-level), and key selling features. Make sure you include the price, which will encourage only serious buyers to call. A good ad will tempt, but not give it all away: After all, you want to entice buyers to actually come by and see your home.

Listing in the newspaper

If you're selling with the help of an agent, you won't have to take care of writing and placing ads in local newspapers and real estate weeklies. However, you can help out your agent by identifying the key selling features of your home. Make a list of the top five or ten reasons you bought the place, and incorporate these factors in the ads if they help increase your home's appeal.

Remember that weekend ads generally have a greater readership, but the best coverage is achieved by taking out both a weekend and a daily ad.

Check out the competition. How can you make your house stand out in comparison? Buyers read through real estate advertisements with their own criteria in mind, so put front and centre the amenities that will capture the attention of your target market. Your home's proximity to great schools, its waterfront location, the award-winning design, or an unbeatable view deserves mention in your print advertisements.

If you're selling privately, use the words "Private Sale" or "For Sale by Owner" in your ad. The potential to get a good deal through shared savings on the commission is an excellent selling feature. If you are willing to co-operate with buyers' real estate agents, put "courtesy to agents" or "will co-operate with agents" in your ad. Some buyers will not deal directly with a seller and would prefer to have their agent contact you to co-ordinate a showing. Some agents will call with prospective buyers for your house, others will be interested in listing your house. Whether or not you decide to use an agent's assistance in selling your home, take the time to talk with them. An agent can offer you great advice on competitively pricing your home.

Many real estate agents will be pleased to work with you. If an agent brings you a buyer and you can negotiate a reduced commission, you may just have a deal. And since the point here is getting your house sold, it's definitely worth considering.

Real estate agents are a homeseller's number one marketing tool since they're constantly in touch with potential buyers and other agents. A majority of home sales are completed through agent-to-agent contact, not by advertisements or "For Sale" signs.

Reaching beyond your local newspaper

Where else should you advertise? Specialty real estate publications are the most targeted, but you should also advertise regularly in the newspapers, particularly the issues that run the most house listings. You may also want to advertise in national or city-specific papers, as some buyers may be relocating.

Buying a home is a serious business, so you will be wise to treat it as such. Buyers will be wary of giveaways, gimmicks, or anything else that smells of double-dealing. In any advertising, be flattering, but sincere, when you describe your home. In the end, your home will speak for itself.

In this Web-savvy time, realize that many homebuyers let their fingers do the surfing when they're looking into new homes. Advertising your house on the Internet is a great way to maximize your house's exposure. If you're dealing with a selling agent, ask her whether she'll be listing your home on the company Web site, or even better, the MLS site. In Chapter 7, we've listed this site, as well as a whole bunch of other excellent home Web sites to visit.

When people phone you, ask them how they heard about your house, and when it comes time to review your progress, you can stop advertising that isn't producing any results. Advertising will cost money, but missed buyers will cost you more.

Sexy feature sheets

A *feature sheet* is the classy, showy, older sister to the newspaper ad. It includes the same basic information — kind of house, number of bedrooms and bathrooms, approximate square footage, neighbourhood, price, and contact telephone number — but it also uses colour and strong design elements to make an impressive pitch for your house.

Selling with the help of an agent? If so, chances are your agent will prepare the feature sheet for you. If you're selling privately, here are some suggestions for making up your own feature sheet:

- Attend some open houses and ask for their feature sheets. If you see a well-designed form, model your own in the same manner. Of course, you can't use any copyrighted text or illustrations, so don't plagiarize, but do take note of what information is specifically outlined and how it's presented most effectively.

- Put a great photograph of your house looking its very best on your feature sheet. If you don't already have the right shot, hire a photographer or get a talented friend to take photos using a wide-angle lens and a film type that allows for multiple prints. You may even want to use pictures of your house at different times of year, so prospective buyers can see how cozy your home looks with a dusting of snow and how magnificent the gardens are in the summertime.

- Ensure the pages of the feature sheet are detailed, but also readable. Don't feel you have to fill the page completely — white space allows people to focus on the important elements of your feature sheet without feeling overwhelmed. Stick to a standard, easy-to-read font for the text and a simple, bold headline. If the elements of good typography are beyond you, ask a design-savvy friend to help you, or look for a professional you can pay to create the feature sheet for you.

If you have a scanner and a colour printer, you can create your own brochure. If you don't, waltz down to the nearest photocopy place; many copy shops now have computer, scanner, and quality colour photocopying facilities. Sometimes this creates a more professional-looking product.

Keep a stack of feature sheets handy to give to prospective buyers who visit. It provides a good reference when they are comparing homes and gives them a reminder of all the features your house offers. The feature sheet is a marketing tool that will keep selling your house even while you're on the golf greens or taking a nap.

Showing (Off) Your Home

Remember that a house showing can be a painful experience for any home-seller. If the reality of moving out of the beloved family home hasn't hit yet, it certainly will now. Try to focus on the excitement of finding a new place to live. If you're selling on your own, find a balance between showing all the features of your house and letting people move through it at their leisure. Nothing annoys a buyer more than a seller hovering nervously over her shoulder.

If you're working with a real estate agent, he'll show your home to potential buyers for you. If you're selling privately, you may still allow other agents to show your home. Some agents will use a *lock box system* to facilitate showings when you can't be around. A lock box contains your key and is secured with a coded lock. If a buyer's agent wants to bring prospective buyers into your home, she can call your agent for the code to the lock box, and then return the key to the lock box when they leave. All entries are recorded so you know who has gained access to your home and when.

Lock boxing — no, it's not like tae bo

The lock box system makes life infinitely easier for you. You don't have to automatically drop what you're doing as soon as you get wind of someone else who wants to see your house. Let your agent take care of the showing — that's one of the reasons you hired her. Your agent will leave a key to your house in an outdoor lock box. This allows other agents to show your house when your own agent can't be there. Now, there are pluses and minuses to this setup. On the one hand, your house may get shown to more buyers because the lock box is really convenient. However, it also means that your agent won't be there to point out the fantastic features your house has to offer, draw buyers' attention to the built-in bookcases in the study, the breakfast nook that gets the morning sun, and the short walk to the local school and shopping centre.

Nevertheless, buyers often want to look at homes with their own agent, not the seller's. A good agent chooses the right buyers to show the home to and doesn't need to go over each feature point by point with an overeager sales pitch. Agents try to identify a good fit based on the needs of buyers and sellers, so your home sells itself.

If your agent recommends a lock box, find out what security precautions are taken. Most companies verify the identity of the agents who want to show your house before giving them an access code to the lock box. The access code should change regularly.

Nevertheless, you are not obliged to use a lock box if you would prefer to have your agent present at every showing. In fact, you can make it a condition of the listing that your agent is present at every showing of your house. Remember, you pay the commission and you call the shots.

If you are selling privately, make it easy for buyers to get in touch with you. You might want to get a cell phone or a pager so you can receive and return calls promptly. If your answering machine greets callers with the singing efforts of your three-year-old, it's time for a change! Your outgoing message should state that the house is for sale and that you'll return calls as soon as possible.

Handle phone calls as professionally as you can. Explain to your kids that if prospective buyers call when you're not available, they should simply take down a name and phone number, and tell the person that you'll return the call as soon as possible. Get back to buyers as quickly as you can, and have all the information they may request on hand so you can let them know that you're serious about selling your home.

Fielding the calls

If you're selling privately, you take all the calls from people interested in your home. Many people, both buyers and sellers, find the initial phone call a bit awkward. You'll quickly find ways of putting yourself and your callers at ease, so don't be annoyed or defensive if the caller sounds wary at first.

Always, always have a pen and paper by the phone. Try to engage callers in a regular conversation so they don't feel as if they're being grilled. Respond to their questions frankly, and ask them questions as well. Find out as much as you can about your callers. Open-ended questions work best. What are they looking for in a house and neighbourhood? How familiar are they with the neighbourhood? Do they have school-aged children? Will they have to sell their own house before they buy?

As you learn more about the callers, you will be able to demonstrate some of the ways your house might fit their needs as you answer their questions. For example, if they have children, you would want to emphasize the excellent reputation of the local schools, the recreational facilities across the park, and the polite, well-adjusted teenagers down the road.

You want to find out where they work and if there is a number you can reach them at there. This is useful for checking the identity of callers, and if you need to reschedule at the last minute you know where to find them. Also, ask how they heard about your house and make notes for when you review your marketing plan.

You don't want to negotiate with buyers over the phone. If they say the price is too high, urge them to come and look at the house. If you think they are serious buyers, ask them *when* they would like to come and see your house. Make it specific. Would Thursday evening or Saturday morning be better for you? Try to line up successive appointments, maybe 45 minutes apart, so that as one set of prospective buyers is arriving, the earlier one is leaving. This way they will get a sense that there is a fair bit of interest in your property . . . and you only have to get your house ready once.

Call to confirm all appointments. People are less likely to stand you up if you have called to confirm.

Be prepared for a potential buyer to walk through the door on short notice. One of the joys of cell phones is that someone may be standing on your front lawn asking when they can see your house. If you are working with an agent, he will schedule the appointment at a convenient time. If you are selling on your own, you'll have to get the buyer to come back when it is convenient for you, or let them in on short notice. You'll also have to keep your home in tip-top shape on a full-time basis. While all this may seem inconvenient (it is!) it'll all be worth it when you close that sale.

Staying secure

Real estate agents work with buyers all the time, and become very good at screening people who are either not serious about buying, or genuinely creepy. Likewise, if your home's showing is with another agent, that buyers' agent will have pre-qualified the buyer to make sure they can afford the house and ensure that they are ready to buy the right house should it come along at the right time.

When you're selling privately, you do have to talk to strangers, but you do not have to let them into your home. Trust your instincts. For your own safety, don't allow anyone who just knocks on your door to tour your home right away. If someone shows up without an appointment, speak to them at the door, and cover the same topics you would discuss if they called to arrange to see your home. Take their names, phone numbers, and any other details. Explain that you can't show your home immediately, but can make an appointment with them later. You may want to leave a list with a friend or neighbour of the names and phone numbers of everyone who schedules appointments.

Another tip for selling your home privately: It's a good idea to have a partner or a friend with you in the house when you're showing it. Take precautions against being robbed or attacked. Ask people to sign a visitor information sheet so you know exactly who has been in your home, when they came in and how long they stayed. This list will be useful for assessing the amount of interest in your house and keeping track of prospective buyers with whom you will want to follow up. However, in the event of theft or damage, you will have some information about everyone who has been through your home.

The open house

The open house is your home's big day. The basic idea is that your home is open for showing on certain designated days (usually during the weekend). An open house may cut down on the number of private showings you have to give, thereby reducing the disruption to your daily life. Also, many buyers feel more comfortable and leisurely being "one of the crowd," rather than touring on their own.

Some people feel the open house serves to introduce the agent to the buying public in general, as opposed to specific buyers for your house. This may be partly true, but in the end, the more people who see your home, the more chance there is that someone will fall in love with it. Your home should be at its best on the day of the open house, so follow our preparation tips in this chapter. If you haven't already overhauled your home, now's the time to do it.

If you're selling privately, announce the times and dates of your open houses in the classifieds, and post an open house sticker on your "For Sale" sign with the appropriate hours showing. Buyers who happen to drive by and see the notice will think it's their lucky day. Make sure everyone who comes to the open house gets a copy of your feature sheet. Plan ahead so you don't book an open house on a long weekend — it will probably be a waste of time. If you're not selling privately, you can rely on your agent to take care of all the organizational details of your open house.

All of your neighbours — and your neighbours' friends — may troop through your house. Maybe they _are_ just being nosy, but remember that word of mouth can be a great marketing tool, too. So let them talk. Give them a reason to talk! The more people who know about your fabulous home, the more potential buyers you may attract.

Whatever you do at the open house, here are three basic rules to observe:

- **Don't negotiate the price.** Be firm that you will seriously consider all _written_ offers.

- **Don't give a particular reason why you are selling your home.** A good standard response is: "We've enjoyed this house, but it's time to move on."

- **Don't indicate you are under time pressure to leave.** This gives potential buyers an edge when negotiating.

But nothing seems to be working!

If you've taken all of your real estate agent's expert advice, had plenty of open houses, and still haven't received any offers, you must be wondering, what's gone wrong? It could be one of many things, but the following are the most common problems:

- The asking price for your home is too high

- Your home's in poor condition

- Your home's located in a less desirable neighbourhood

- Buyers don't know about your home

Don't give up. It's important to get feedback from potential buyers, either directly or through your agent. If you've heard from several buyers that they love your home and it's in great shape but it's just a bit beyond their budget, you might consider lowering the price. If the general feeling among buyers is that the price and location are great, but they're wary of the amount of work they will need to put in to spruce the place up, you may want to get cracking on some of those improvements yourself.

Make sure you talk to your agent about how many buyers have come through your home and what they are saying. You can drop your asking price, refresh your advertisements, or do some home improvements, but whatever the problem is, you can only fix it if you take the time to figure out what's stopping your home from selling.

Chapter 20

The Legal Stuff

In This Chapter

▶ Understanding the basics of sale contracts

▶ Knowing which parts of the sale contract concern you (the home seller) the most

▶ Taking into account important differences in condominium sale contracts

▶ Learning about legal terms and documents involved in transfer of ownership

*O*nce you've found a buyer, you need to take care of all the legal stuff. Think of this chapter as being sponsored by the most sober and respectable advisor you can imagine . . . picture us in conservative clothing with horn-rimmed glasses if it helps. Take this seriously! Selling a house is a wonderful accomplishment. We do not want you to trip up on the legalities.

Recipe for a Successful Contract

Unless your current house was picked up off an abandoned lot by a tornado, carried hundreds of kilometres, and plopped onto your land, you already know about sale contracts. (Take a look at Chapter 9 to see the Contract of Purchase and Sale from a buyer's perspective.) Here we review the contract from a seller's point of view.

If you've made any radical changes to your home since you bought it, or if there have been new developments in the community that may complicate the sale of your home, certain aspects of the Contract of Purchase and Sale may take priority where they did not in the past. (In some provinces, you use an Agreement of Purchase and Sale, and in others you use a Contract of Purchase and Sale; the term may be different from place to place, but the results are the same.) If you didn't buy your current home, or if it's been so long since you bought your home that you can't remember a single thing about signing the contract, pay very close attention because the paperwork has changed, agency relationships have changed, and disclosure requirements have changed as well.

When excited and happy buyers decide that they'd like to buy your house, they fill out the Contract of Purchase and Sale on their end, writing out their bid, terms, and conditions (for example, seller must fix roof and leave garden gnomes as they are), and all other applicable sections of the contract. Then, the buyers (or their real estate agent) give the written offer to you (or to your agent if you have one). At this stage, the contract is called an "offer" until you and the buyers have agreed to all the terms of the contract (like the price and the deposit) and all of the conditions in the contract are met. Say the buyers' offer to purchase your home is conditional upon you fixing the roof, then you have to patch up that leak in order to meet the buyers' "condition." Get together with your agent (or your lawyer if you're not using an agent) to review all offers. If the offer is coming through another agent, the agent will usually present it to you in person to give you some background on the buyers and how they arrived at the starting point for the initial offer.

The offer can be presented anywhere, but it's customary to do it at the seller's house. If there are too many distractions at your house (kids, pets, in-laws) you may want to meet at your agent's office, or the buyer's agent's office if it is closer. Wherever you meet, you should feel comfortable and relaxed as you review the offer.

Your agent will take you through the offer step by step and point out the key features, while the buyers' agent explains how or why the buyers made their offer subject to various terms and conditions.

Reading the Recipe: Basic Contract Know-How

Many real estate agents use computer software packages that contain standard forms for Contracts of Purchase and Sale, as well as certain phrases that can be inserted into the contract. So you may receive a completely computer-generated document, though it's also common to receive a handwritten contract.

Real estate laws differ from province to province. Consequently, there's no single standard contract for all of Canada. Provincial real estate boards or associations each have their own standard contracts that they make available to agents. However, most *local* real estate boards or associations have their own contracts, too — which are generally variations on the provincial forms. Most home sales use a contract supplied by the local real estate board. Be prepared to receive a lengthy document: the offer — the partially completed contract you receive from the buyers — may be six or seven pages (or longer).

Don't worry if your sale is particularly complex or unique. The standard forms are only a guide — they can be modified to suit the particulars of your sale, and you can add as many *schedules*, less commonly known as *addendums*, as you need. These add-on forms specify all the clauses and conditions of sale that simply wouldn't fit in the space allotted on the standard agreement. Some schedules come with pre-printed clauses; others require you and your agent to fill in the particulars.

A Contract of Purchase and Sale has a typical structure with three main sections: First it lays out the terms of the offer, then the conditions of sale and any restrictions or obligations involved in ownership of the property (known as *covenants*), and finally the signatures for acceptance. In the next section we explain all these contract components in detail.

The Ingredients

Sale contracts are a bit like pancakes. Basic pancakes need flour, eggs, and milk, but beyond that you can add blueberries, bananas, cinnamon, maple syrup, and anything else you like whether it's in the batter itself or on top. There's no set recipe for great pancakes, but there are some common ingredients. The same goes for real estate sale contracts. The bulk of the recipe will depend on the particulars of your situation. Since we can't tell you exactly what your recipe should be, we will instead tell you what sorts of things will be of particular concern to you, the seller, in some key areas. After all, when you cook with quality ingredients, you're much more likely to end up satisfied.

A dash of offer

The first part of a Contract of Purchase and Sale is the *Offer to Purchase*. (For an example, check out our copy of the Ontario Real Estate Association's Contract of Purchase and Sale appearing in Chapter 9.) The "Offer to Purchase" section has a threefold function. First, it identifies the parties involved in the transaction: you (the *vendor*), your buyer (the *purchaser*), and your real estate agent (usually referred to as the *agent*). If your home is owned jointly by both you and another party (perhaps your spouse or partner), both owners will be identified in the vendor section. Second, the offer will identify the home as it is registered with the local land registry office, the lot and plan numbers, and sometimes the approximate dimensions of the lot. All this information is taken from the listing contract or from the title search that either the buyer or seller (or their agents) has obtained. (Lastly, the offer will set out the major financial details — usually consisting of the offered price and amount of deposit.

Every offer has some common elements. Make sure all of this information is supplied in the buyers' written offer:

- ✔ The name and address of the buyers
- ✔ The amount of the initial deposit accompanying the offer, or payable on acceptance of the offer
- ✔ The civic and legal address of the property being sold
- ✔ The amount of the buyers' initial offer
- ✔ Subjects and terms and conditions of the offer
- ✔ Items included and excluded from the sale
- ✔ Completion, possession, and adjustment dates
- ✔ Time that the offer is open for acceptance
- ✔ The buyers' signatures (witnessed where necessary)

Now, we'll go into these points in more detail.

Name and address of buyers

The buyers supply their names and addresses, so you know whom you are dealing with. If the offer is made in a company name, you will need to know the position the buyer holds in the company, and whether or not the buyer has signing authority on behalf of the company. You should also be very careful if the buyer's name is followed by *"and/or nominee."* The buyer may intend to assign the contract to a third party (maybe the daughter who's graduating medical school in the spring, maybe the money-laundering subsidiary of Crooked Mile Inc.), and ideally the buyer should specify who that third party (or nominee) is on the contract. If the name of the third party is not specified in writing, it *may* create ambiguity in the contract and possibly make the contract unenforceable. Your agent or lawyer can explain the proper way to assign the contract and deal with any potential problems.

Initial deposit and deposits in general

A deposit is an initial amount of money to confirm that the buyers are serious about their offer to purchase your home. A deposit that accompanies your buyers' offer forms part of the down payment when the sale is completed. We recommend that the deposit be made by certified cheque or bank draft. Indeed, in some parts of Canada, the deposit *must* be presented in this fashion.

There's no standard figure for the deposit, but from the seller's perspective, the bigger the better. If the deposit is substantial (a reasonable and substantial deposit is about 5 to 6 percent of the purchase price, depending on price range), it's less likely your buyer will consider walking away before the sale is completed. If you're buying another house based on the sale of your current home, the deposit gives you assurance that your buyer is committed to the purchase of your current home. You do not want to commit to buying a new house unless you feel secure that your buyer's offer is sincere.

Initially, the offer may be presented with a small deposit ($500 or $1,000) that the buyers will increase when all their conditions are removed from the contract. If the buyers collapse their offer, they risk forfeiting their deposit. So, by making a small deposit the buyers risk losing less money if they change their minds about buying your home.

The buyers' deposit can be placed in an interest-bearing trust account, so at least the buyer will earn interest on their money until the completion of the sale.

Civic and legal address of the subject property

Your home's address is included to make sure you are selling the right property. While it's not that much of an issue in towns and cities, if you are selling vacant land you should always check legal descriptions at the land registry office, especially where there may not be a street number and address. If you're unsure about your home's legal description, check your property tax notices or contact the land registry office in your area. You can find a listing in the Blue Pages of your telephone book.

Price of the initial offer

The price is your starting point for negotiations, and probably the first thing you'll want to look at when the offer comes in. If the initial price the buyers offer is at least reasonable, you can probably negotiate an acceptable price for you and the buyer. In an ideal world, the initial offer will be at exactly the price you asked for or better, and you can skip to the part where you negotiate the other terms of your sale contract. If the offer isn't everything you hoped for, see our negotiating tips in Chapter 21.

A handful of covenants, a sprinkle of conditions

The most important part of the agreement is the conditions of the sale. We know what you're thinking: "Of greater concern than the price?" Yes. The financial details contained in the "Offer to Purchase" portion of the sale contract are easily and quickly verified. The conditions of sale may be much more complex and can be treacherous if you don't review them carefully.

In Chapter 9 of this book we discuss various *"subject to"* clauses that are common in Contracts of Purchase and Sale. Most buyers will ask the seller to meet certain conditions, like repairing the handrail on the staircase or fixing the kitchen faucet in order to make the house acceptable for their purchase. These conditions are noted in the contract as *subject to* clauses. (In effect, the buyers are saying, "We will buy your home *subject to* the repair of the second floor staircase," or some other specified condition.)

Remember that all terms and conditions included in an Offer to Purchase for your home are negotiable; both parties (you and your buyer) must agree to them. You'll almost never see an offer that doesn't contain any subject to clauses. Sometimes, in a very active market where there are competing offers, the buyer will keep the subject to clauses to a minimum to make the offer as attractive as possible to the seller. Even with a plethora of competing offers, you'll usually find a quick "subject to inspection" clause inserted in the offer. You can choose to reject one or all the subject to clauses the buyer has attached to the offer, but if you do, you risk losing the offer altogether. Use good judgment; if you think the buyer's requests are reasonable, then accept them and go about fulfilling the conditions. If one or two of them seem completely ridiculous, talk to your agent about making a *counteroffer* that excludes the conditions that you find unacceptable. Of course, if you're selling privately, you have to take care of this yourself, but do consult your lawyer for help so you can state your terms clearly in a counteroffer.

Assuming that you do accept a few of the buyer's conditions specified in the subject to clauses of their offer, you must confirm that the items have been addressed. In effect, you're saying that yes, you have reshingled the roof, or yes, you have removed the cedar hedge that obscured the driveway, in accordance with subject to clause A, B, or C. Your buyer must acknowledge you've met these conditions so they can be removed from the offer.

Procedures vary from province to province for removing subject to clauses from an offer. In Nova Scotia, for example, clauses are typically worded so that if no written notice from the buyer to the contrary is received by the seller, the seller can assume the buyer is satisfied. In most provinces, a standard form is attached to the offer stating that X, Y, or Z condition has been satisfied; in Ontario you attach a *waiver*; in Saskatchewan you attach a *condition removal form*. In British Columbia, subjects are removed using a separate *amendment*. Subject removal documents are usually prepared by the agents on the applicable standard forms. Standard contracts and add-on forms are suitable for about 99.9 percent of home sales and are mandatory in some provinces. These standard forms are supplied by the real estate agent. If you are not using an agent, your lawyer will have these forms available.

We'll go over some of the most common subject to clauses so you have an idea of what your buyers may include in their offer.

Subject to financing

This is the condition that the buyers include in the offer basically as a safeguard until they obtain proper mortgage financing. In some cases the buyer's financing can require that the home be appraised at an equivalent or greater value than the purchase price. With mortgage pre-approval offered by most lenders, many of today's buyers come to the negotiating table with the security of financial backing. Even if they have a pre-approved mortgage, most buyers should make their offer subject to financing for a short period (a couple of days) to allow the lender to do an appraisal and confirm that the accepted offer is fair market value. If the buyer does not have a pre-approved mortgage, five to seven business days should be adequate for a bank to arrange a new first mortgage. Like all subject to clauses, the subject to financing clause must include a date by which it must be removed. A commonly worded subject to financing clause reads like this:

> "Subject to new first mortgage being made available to the buyer by _____, in the amount of $_____ at an interest rate not to exceed ____% per annum calculated semi-annually, not in advance, with a ____ year amortization period, ____ year term and repayable in blended payments of approximately $_____ per month including principal and interest (plus 1/12 of the annual taxes, if required by the mortgagee). This condition is for the sole benefit of the buyer."

 Subject to financing clauses require the buyers to make a true effort to arrange the required financing. They're not permitted to just sit at home and say, "We couldn't get it." If you think that a buyer did not make a good-faith effort to get financing, and can prove it, you may be in a position to refuse to return the initial deposit if the offer falls apart because this condition has not been met. This is where lawyers get involved, but keep in mind that a clearly worded subject to financing clause and a true concerted effort by the buyer will eliminate the need for lawyers and disputes related to financing subjects.

Subject to inspection

Most offers these days have a subject to inspection clause, the condition that the home passes a full inspection. No matter how well you have maintained your home, be prepared to have an inspection conducted by the buyer. If you had your home inspected prior to listing, you shouldn't have any surprises with your buyer's inspection. If your home is relatively new and it passed an inspection before you purchased it, and you have not seen any evidence of problems, you probably don't need to worry about an inspection turning up anything significant. If you own an older home in which the major operating systems and structural components have not been updated or replaced in decades, this condition may become an issue. Even if your home seems to be running smoothly, you may be in for some unpleasant surprises come inspection time. Typically, the clause will read something like this:

"Subject to the buyer, at their own expense, receiving and being satisfied with an inspection report from a certified building inspector of their choice on or before _____. This condition is for the sole benefit of the buyer."

Chapter 17 discusses the main reason against having a pre-listing inspection: should it reveal any problems, you are legally obligated to disclose that information. This does not apply only to the disclosure statement. It is possible that the sale will be null and void if there are any conditions or encumbrances known to the seller that are not listed in the contract. Disclose everything in writing to avoid future problems.

Subject to sale

Buyers often make an offer conditional on the sale of their previous home prior to an agreed-on date. Perhaps your buyer doesn't expect to have any problems selling his home, but is simply playing it safe. But perhaps he's only in a position to make a conditional offer because he thinks he'll encounter difficulties in unloading his own property, and he has to sell his home to be able to buy your house. We discuss in Chapter 15 why buying before you sell is dangerous. It's your call whether you should accept an offer with this sort of condition. If you are confident in your buyer's ability to sell their previous home, or if you feel you are not in a position to be rejecting reasonably priced offers (conditional or otherwise), then accepting may be the best course. But if you are in a seller's dream market (e.g., downtown Toronto) and you have no doubt that another, unconditional offer will be forthcoming, you may wish to hold out for the better offer. Talk to your agent about market conditions in your area and how they should influence your perception of a "good" offer. The sale clause could be written as follows:

"Subject to the buyer entering into an unconditional agreement to sell the buyer's property at 123 Main Street, Anywhere, Saskatchewan, by _____. This condition is for the sole benefit of the buyer. However, the seller may, upon receipt of another acceptable offer, deliver a written notice to the buyer or the buyer's agent (enter name of the buyer's agent and company name) requiring the buyer to remove all conditions from the contract within 12/24/48/72 hours (choose one) of the delivery of the notice. Should the buyer fail to remove all conditions before the expiry of the notice period, the contract will terminate, and all deposit monies will be returned in accordance with the Real Estate Act."

The portion of this clause from "However" on is known as the *time clause*. This clause is extremely important if you think that you may receive other offers while this buyer is trying to sell his home. The length of the notice period is negotiable and can be as short as 12 hours, but this puts a lot of pressure on the buyer and you will find that many buyers won't agree to this. If you are in a seller's market, you'll want to keep the notice period as short as possible, since this will allow you to deal with a back-up offer relatively quickly, if one comes in. From the buyers' point of view, the longer the notice period, the longer the buyers will have to arrange interim or bridge financing. And the longer they'll have to consider all their options, and the longer they'll have to sell their house.

If you need to invoke the time clause, you may want to get confirmation that the notice was actually delivered at a certain time. Although technically this is not necessary to make the notice valid and enforceable, it helps keep everyone clear on the process. The delivery can be witnessed by someone, or the buyer or the buyer's agent can sign a copy of the notice to acknowledge they have received it. At this point, there is no negotiating and you are just waiting to see who will buy your home. The notice to invoke the time clause will look like this:

> "This notice constitutes written notice from the seller to the buyer requiring the removal of all conditions (or condition) from this contract within (24/48/72) hours or this contract will terminate at the end of the (24/48/72) hour period and the deposit will be returned to the buyer. This time clause will start running on delivery of this notice to the buyer or (the buyer's real estate agency) which will be at _____ o'clock am/pm on (date), 2000. Therefore, the (24/48/72) hours will terminate at _____ o'clock a.m./p.m. on (date), 2000."

In some provinces, you may have to exclude Sundays and statutory holidays from the time clause. In this case, the clause will read "24/48/72 hours excluding Sundays and statutory holidays." Your agent or lawyer will know local provincial regulations.

Escape clauses

Another category of subject to clauses depends on a third party or requires the approval of one party to the contract. These *third party subject clauses* are often called *escape clauses* or *whim and fancy clauses,* because either party can simply withhold approval and walk away from the contract.

One of the most obvious escape clauses is *subject to a relative or friend reviewing the contract*. This is very ambiguous and hard to enforce, and you should do everything you can to avoid such a condition. Another escape clause would be *subject to the buyer obtaining financial advice*. The buyer should have received financial advice before writing the contract—this is an extremely obvious escape hatch.

You or your agent should recognize escape clauses and try to keep them to a minimum, and where they are necessary keep the time frame as short as possible. Generally, a contract with an escape clause is unenforceable until the subject is removed.

Clauses introduced by the seller

Few vendors are concerned with what happens to the property once it has been sold. However, there may be some cases where the vendor would like to place restrictions or obligations on the new owners of the property. For example, when history buffs and activists Pierre and Marie decided to sell their Vieux Quebec home, which had narrowly missed being designated a Canadian heritage site, they wanted to stipulate in the Contract of Purchase and Sale that the new owners respect the home's historical significance. So they introduced a clause stating that the new owners were forbidden to undertake any major additions or renovations to the original structure other than restorative projects to preserve the character and historical importance of the building. However, most covenants of this sort come with the land and are not the prerogative of the seller to introduce.

If your property has municipal or provincial conditions restricting the use of the property, they should be clearly outlined in the contract to protect you from any future actions by the buyer. If you are not in an unusual position like the one mentioned above, and there were no restrictions or obligations placed on you when you bought the property, you should not attempt to introduce these sorts of clauses.

Subject to seller's purchase

Another clause that you as a seller may need to include is a *subject to purchase* clause. This condition stipulates that the buyer's Offer to Purchase will only be accepted if the seller's Offer to Purchase another home is in turn accepted.

For example, Lars and Jorge wanted to sell their house, but only if they could get the house of their dreams. They did find one house that fit the bill, but their offer, subject to the sale of their own house, was rejected. The couple decided that in such a busy market, they had better list their house and keep an eye on their dream home. After a couple of weeks, Lars and Jorge got an offer on their house, and notified the prospective buyers that they would only sell if they could come to an agreement on their dream house. The buyers were in no rush so they accepted a *subject to purchase clause*. It was written into the Contract of Purchase and Sale as follows:

> "Subject to the seller entering into an unconditional agreement to purchase the property at _____ by _____.
> This condition is for the sole benefit of the seller."

Subject to purchase clauses are not very common, and in a situation like Lars and Jorge's, it is always a good idea to let the buyers know the seller's plans in advance so that the buyers won't be surprised to see a seller's condition added to the contract.

What's included — fixtures and chattels

Anything that is fixed to the structure of your home (known as a *fixture*) is assumed to be included in the purchase price unless otherwise stated. Anything movable — appliances, furniture, and the like, known as *chattels* — is assumed to be excluded from the sale. Nonetheless, in some provinces, appliances are typically included in the sale price. Find out early in the process what the conventions are for your area. Now is the time to exclude from the sale anything the buyers might think they will be getting, whether it's your fabulous new and astonishingly silent dishwasher, or the antique chandelier from your great-grandmother.

The Contract of Purchase and Sale will list exactly what is, and what is not, included in the sale. How would you like to buy a home in Moose Jaw, and take possession in February only to discover the furnace had been ripped out of the basement? These kinds of events are not common, but they have been known to happen. Clearly this section of the contract is of greater importance to the purchaser — the one likely to get the short end of the stick. But you need to do a quick review of this section as well, just to ensure that everything you want to take with you will be yours come moving day.

Time frame of the offer

The time frame of the offer is one of the most important elements of your Contract of Purchase and Sale. This element states that the offer is only valid for a certain length of time. If this length of time expires before the offer is accepted, the offer is null and void and the deposit is returned to the purchaser unless both parties agree to extend the time for acceptance.

The *completion date* is the date on which the buyers pay their money and have the house registered in their name. The *possession date* is the date the buyers assume possession of the property. If all conditions have not been met by the *subject removal date*, the offer can be withdrawn and the transaction terminated.

Pay extremely close attention to these dates. Most contracts hold the vendor responsible for the property until the completion date. If a fire ravages your home the day before the completion date, it's *your* problem. From 12:01 a.m. on the completion date, the property and all included items will be at the risk of the buyer. The buyer will actually have insurance on the house hours before the house is registered in his name.

Arrange to have your insurance policies terminated on the closing date and not before. If possible, avoid the last day of a month or year as a closing date. These are busy days for banks, creditors, insurance providers, and most administrative staff that will be involved in processing the new information generated by the sale. This means you are at an increased risk of otherwise avoidable delays in registering the sale of your home.

If you have rental units

The Contract of Purchase and Sale becomes considerably more complex if your home has rental units and your buyer intends to continue renting out these parts of your property. This aspect is typically a larger headache for the buyer than for the seller. However, if you have tenants at the time of sale, be prepared for some extra hassle. For example, if you live in Ontario, you will have to sign a statement to the effect that you are charging a legal rent. If it turns out you are not charging a legal rent, you're not only in trouble with your tenants, but also with your buyer. The possible obstacles are far too case-specific for us to deal with here — so all we can do is give you some general advice:

If you have a rental unit and are selling to a buyer who intends to continue the tradition, speak to your lawyer about the legal and contractual consequences *before* signing the Contract of Purchase and Sale. If you are getting close to an agreement on price and you want to keep negotiating, you can go ahead and accept the offer, but make it subject to you consulting with your lawyer. In many parts of the country, a copy of the rental agreement may become an addendum or schedule to the contract. If the buyer wants to terminate the tenancy, the buyer will request in the contract that the seller give legal and binding termination notice to the tenants in accordance with the provincial tenancy legislation.

A pinch of acceptance

This final section of the contract is quite simple. Once the contract has been negotiated to your and the buyer's satisfaction, all that remains is to sign on the dotted line (as well as filling in the appropriate dates and seals), and accept the offer subject to the terms and conditions outlined. You must make sure that both parties have initialled any changes made to the contract, and all signatures have been witnessed where necessary.

Especially for Condo Owners

The legal workings of selling a condominium are slightly different than those for selling a house. First of all, condos may have separate standard legal forms. In essence, these forms are similar to the standard Contract of Purchase and Sale for a house — both kinds of forms cover the details of the offer, the conditions of sale, and the acceptance. But there are two very important elements specific to condominium sale contracts: the financial status of the condominium corporation and its bylaws. In many areas you will be using the standard forms, and adding the condo clauses just as you would add financing clauses to the contract.

In most provinces, these details are included in a document known as the *condominium certificate*, *estoppel certificate, information certificate,* or *status certificate*. It lists the expenses for a specified unit, discusses the status of the complex in its entirety, explains the regulations and procedures for the administration of the complex, outlines the rules governing behaviour of residents and the corporation, and stipulates all financial obligations. See Chapter 4 for more on this important document.

In B.C., new legislation known as the *Strata Property Act* (also called the *Condominium Act* in some provinces) came into effect on July 1, 2000. Under the new legislation, the *strata corporation* (the condominium corporation) prepares a package for the seller or the seller's agent to give to potential buyers. This package, usually put together by the property manager of the condominium, includes current financial statements and bylaws for the building, minutes from the buildings meetings for the last year or two, plus any rules or regulations regarding the use of the suite. All of these items are specified in the contract, and the offer is subject to the buyer receiving and approving all of these documents.

It is extremely important for buyers to have a lawyer review the condominium certificate or equivalent documentation before removing the subjects from your offer. In B.C., the buyer's lawyer can review any aspect of the information package that concerns the buyer. The lawyer may also want a copy of the building's insurance policy to make sure the building has adequate coverage.

As a vendor, you can anticipate your buyer's request by ensuring your agent has a copy of all relevant papers, and by providing copies to potential buyers at showings. You must make all these documents available to the buyer, and if you can provide everything promptly, it may help to solidify a trusting relationship with potential buyers and speed up the process. The condominium corporation must provide you with a copy, but they often take quite a while to process requests. The moral of the story is, send in your written request for all the required documents at least a month in advance.

Your buyer will also be interested in the state of the condominium corporation's *reserve fund*. This is the fund that supplies money for structural repairs, and any renovations or work needed on the complex. This information is generally contained in the condominium certificate, or the financial statements for the building. Your agent will need this information as he presents your suite to potential buyers. You can win points with potential buyers by being knowledgeable about the status of the corporation and the procedure if repairs are needed on the building.

Deeds and Titles

You've got some great buyers lined up who plan to keep up your much-loved backyard "Wizard of Oz" topiary. Oh, and they've also offered you a great price for your home. Time to call the moving truck, right? Well, before you sign the contract and hand them the keys (and the topiary clippers), you have to prove to them what it is you really own — and then legally transfer this ownership to them. You may think of that gurgling stream out back as yours, but is it your property? Do you owe anything to anyone in relation to your house? You're not off on the Yellow Brick Road yet — but read this section and you soon will be.

Conveyance

The process of transferring ownership is known as *conveyance*. When you sell your home, whether it's a house or a condo, your lawyer will prepare a legal document called a *deed*. The deed certifies that all the conditions of sale have been met, and transfers ownership of the property to your buyer. A deed may not always transfer full ownership, it may transfer partial ownership, or any other specified interest in the land.

We found the reader-friendly definitions in *Duhaime's Law Dictionary* to be an accessible and indispensable online source of legal terminology — and it's free! Visit the Web site (www.duhaime.org) to look up any legal terms you find baffling.

Any claims or encumbrances against the property such as Crown grants or rights of way can also be transferred along with ownership. The term *conveyance* also applies to the transfer of these encumbrances. Once your lawyer has dealt with all aspects of conveyance, the information becomes collectively known as the *title* to the property. The title identifies the property and the owner of the property, and lists any debts or claims against the property.

All the transfer of title information has to be registered with your province (generally at a provincial land titles office) in order to guarantee that you will no longer be held responsible for that property. The drafting of the conveyance documents is the responsibility of the buyer. When the documents are submitted for registration, they will be issued a *Certificate of Title*, and you will no longer have any claim to the property.

It is usually the buyers' responsibility (or more precisely, their lawyer's) to do the title search. The title search ensures that you do, legally, own the property and that there are no debts or claims against it that you have not disclosed. Many provincial registry offices are now automated and keep original documents only on microfilm. Those that still keep paper documentation do not allow original documents to be removed from the registry office. If your property is over a hundred years old, it is possible that the original documents have been archived. Restricted access to documents means that your lawyer and your buyers' lawyer may have to meet in the local registry office to perform some of the necessary tasks.

Land registries

Just as the various provinces and territories support distinct real estate laws, they also support many different systems of land registration across the country. It is not always the same department or division of government that is responsible for registering land titles. For example, in Alberta, "Land Registries" is a division of Alberta Municipal Affairs, and in Saskatchewan it is the newly formed "Saskatchewan Land Information Services Corporation" that is the registration agency. In the Northwest Territories it's the "Legal Registries" division of the Department of Justice, and in Newfoundland it is the "Commercial Registrations" division of Government Services and Lands.

Different provinces and territories have divided the land differently. B.C. is divided into seven regions for the purpose of registration, whereas Alberta is divided into only two. This means that the identification information for your property will take a form dictated by your provincial government. If you desperately want to know exactly how it works in your area, you can contact your provincial or territorial government, or the land surveyors' association, but there's no pressing need to be an expert on systems of land registration.

You do, however, need to know about the documents that are typically required for registration. In all cases, these include the *transfer deed* (prepared to change the registered ownership of the home) and your *mortgage discharge statement* (instructing your lawyer regarding the paying of applicable funds back to the bank). If your buyer is assuming your mortgage, you must register the conveyance and your buyer must register the new mortgage on the property, as well as any new rights-of-way or minor easements for utilities. In those cases involving properties with outstanding debts or claims, these must be registered or *discharged* as well (if they have not been already). And should an up-to-date survey be required, register that too.

There is a separate charge for almost every registration or service provided by your local registry office. Registering the transfer of land usually entails a base fee plus one or two dollars per thousand dollars of the value of your home. For example, if your home sold for $250,000, you may have to pay a $35 base charge plus $250 to register the transfer deed. Registration of a mortgage discharge will carry a separate fee, as will the survey plan, and any other documents. If you need to obtain copies of official documents, you will have to purchase them, usually for around $10 a copy. The cost of any registrations that your lawyer makes on your behalf will filter down to you as disbursements — in other words, you will pay for them as part of your legal bill. When you get a quote from a lawyer for your conveyance, make sure the price includes all fees and disbursements.

Clearly, the registration of some of these documents falls to your buyer. However, they may become of interest to you if the documentation for *your* title to the land was not registered properly.

Western Canada primarily uses the *"Torrens System"* of land registration. This system holds that regardless of the existence or status of any previous titles, the certificate of title that you possess is "indefeasible." This means that so long as you have a certificate of title, ownership of your land cannot be taken away from you under any circumstances. Claims, debts, or other ownership issues not spelled out in your certificate are irrelevant to your title.

In other parts of the country, your title must be validated before you can transfer it to another party. If there happen to be any previous titles with unresolved ownership issues, these can affect *your* right to ownership. The Torrens System was adopted to make the validation of titles unnecessary, and therefore to make transfers of titles simpler and easier to record. But even under the Torrens System, there can be hindrances to a smooth title transfer.

Chapter 21

Negotiating Tricks and Bargaining Chips

· ·

· ·

*H*ammering out a final deal with the buyers of your home involves several elements. Yes, price will be the first thing on your mind, but pay attention to other key details, such as possession date, conditional clauses and their expiry dates, the extras you'll include in the sale (chattels like your washer and dryer), and the amount of the buyer's cash deposit (we discuss all of these items in Chapter 20). Everything is negotiable, so have a clear idea of what is most important to you and be flexible in everything else.

Set the Stage to Negotiate the Offer

All property owners should be present when you're negotiating an Offer to Purchase since all signatures will be required to seal the deal. If you and your spouse (or your sister, or parent, or other partner) jointly hold the title to your home, then both of you should be at the negotiations. Turn the ringers off the phones and keep children and pets out of the way.

Make yourselves comfortable; it may take a while. Have refreshments like juices and tea or coffee ready, but don't offer any alcohol until after the deal has been signed (if at all). Believe it or not, the Contract of Purchase and Sale may be deemed null and void if the buyers are under the influence of drugs or alcohol when they sign (likewise, if your buyer's proven to be insane, coerced with force, or under-age!).

Keep Your Eye on the Prize: What's Really Important

You love your home. You may have raised your kids there and decorated it to your taste and style, making it a reflection of you. And we know you're a wonderful person, so who wouldn't love your humble abode? Imagine your horror when the people making an offer on your home want to rip out everything — the red velvet wallpaper and even the orange shag carpet! You may feel so offended that you want to throw their offer in the garbage, but If the dates are perfect and the offer is only subject to inspection, and their initial deposit is a fair starting point, you'd better give the negotiations a try.

Remember that the point here is to sell your home — for a fair value as quickly and simply as possible. There's no one-size-fits-all negotiating strategy, but you should have an unemotional, business-like game plan that allows you to make rational decisions as you go through the buying and selling process. Unfortunately, your buyers may not share your negotiating style and approach. *Try not to take the proceedings personally.* You're working on a business deal, and you share a common goal — the buyers want to have your home and you want them to buy it, at least if the price is right. If you've received a fair offer from the buyers, put personalities aside, and deal with the terms of the offer!

Work out your strategy in advance, taking into account whether you're in a buyer's or a seller's market, and therefore whether you're negotiating from a position of relative weakness or strength. (See Chapter 13 for market definitions.) If you're negotiating in a buyer's market, purchase offers can be scarce and you may have to take a lower price for your home than you had hoped for. In a seller's market, you may be able to capitalize on the competitive conditions and hold out for a bigger and better offer if your negotiations go poorly.

Even the most stoic of sellers may find themselves getting worked up at the negotiating table. Stay cool, act calm. You're making big decisions here and you don't want to do anything rash. This is particularly important if you're selling privately because you won't have an agent at your side to help you stay calm and objective.

The Negotiating Process

In reality, the first step you'll take as a seller in the negotiating process is setting the asking price for your home. (See Chapter 14 for more on setting the price.) Whether or not you're using a real estate agent, your asking price lays the groundwork for the selling process. It can affect how many offers you receive, and is the springboard from which you'll dive into the deep and murky waters of conditions, terms, and clauses.

Only consider written offers

Don't negotiate until you get a written offer. And don't sign *anything* until you've consulted with your real estate agent or your real estate lawyer (or notary public, if you live in Quebec). You need a professional to make sure the contract is legally binding and the terms and conditions represent you properly. This is tricky stuff. If you even have a signature in the wrong spot, the contract may be null and void.

Don't dismiss early offers. Houses often generate the best offers earliest in the process when they're fresh on the market . . . and you never know when, or if, the next serious offer will come. Remember that an offer represents an opening bid to start negotiations. Both the buyer and the seller want the same thing: the best possible price and terms of sale. Each party can make certain concessions and certain gains.

The offer may seem to be overly detailed and specific, but to ensure you have a binding contract with no misunderstandings, every detail should be written into your purchase agreement. It may seem silly to include little things like remote garage door openers in the contract, but it's those little things that can drive you crazy if they're not clearly specified in writing.

When you get an offer, your options are to accept it, reject it, or "sign it back," that is, return it to the buyer with a counteroffer proposing a different price or different terms. Review the offer with respect to each of the following considerations.

How low will you go?

First and foremost, we're all interested in the prices we pay for our purchases. Your home is not just a purchase, though, it's an investment and if you've cared well for your home, you should be able to make a profit when it comes time to sell the place. Determining what your home is worth in the current housing market takes a bit of analysis. In Chapter 14 we provide you with detailed information on estimating a realistic sale price for your home. Once you've figured out your listing price, though, you also need to decide what is the lowest offer you'll accept.

Remember that the initial offer is the buyer's starting point, just as the list price is your initial bargaining position.

Entertain any and every offer you receive. Don't reject anything out of hand, unless your lawyer or real estate agent strongly advises you to do so; make a few changes to the agreement and counter your buyer's offered price. If a buyer is interested enough to write up the paperwork, you have a better-than-decent chance of negotiating a price you're willing to accept.

Remember that negotiating requires give and take. If you don't give buyers an idea of your flexibility, they won't take the time or effort to pursue an agreement. A buyer may be truly interested in getting your house, but puts in an offer that cuts $25,000 off the asking price. Don't tear it up; he may be following the "you can't blame a guy for trying" philosophy. The response to your counteroffer may surprise you by being, "Yeah, okay."

"Only if you promise to . . .": Negotiating the subject to clauses

Subject to clauses are a buyer's safety-hatch — a way to escape the Contract of Purchase and Sale if something goes wrong. If a buyer needs to sell his home before he can afford to buy yours, he may make his offer "subject to sale" (meaning that his offer to buy your home will only be confirmed once he's been able to secure the sale of his own current residence). See Chapter 20 for details. Three of the most common clauses on an offer to purchase are *subject to financing*, *subject to inspection*, and *subject to sale*.

- ✔ **Subject to financing clauses** don't offer much room for negotiation. Buyers can't remove this subject clause during the offer/counteroffer process, unless perhaps they have a lot of equity and don't really need a mortgage, or require a small and easy-to-get fast mortgage. Remember, if the buyer didn't need a mortgage, she likely wouldn't have made the offer subject to financing in the first place. You can try to negotiate a shorter time limit for the buyer to arrange her mortgage, however. Often too, a buyer will have a pre-approved mortgage — it's usually only a matter of an appraisal to have the mortgage finalized. If this is the case, then allowing the buyer this clause may put you in a better position to negotiate other things.

- ✔ **Subject to inspection clauses** are commonly included in a buyer's offer to purchase a home. Since it should take no more than two or three days to arrange an inspection, this is an easy clause to negotiate. As with the subject to financing clause, though, you can try to negotiate a shorter time period for the inspection's completion to speed things up. Most inspectors can deliver a copy of the inspection report at the end of the inspection.

- ✔ **Subject to sale clauses** can be negotiated with regard to the length of time you give your buyers to sell their current home. Any buyer who already owns a home probably can't afford to carry the expense of two homes at once. You have to be reasonable here. No matter how anxious you are to move, allow the buyer a decent amount of time to list and sell his home. Usually four to six weeks is considered fair, and (depending on how badly you want to sell to this particular buyer) you can agree to extend the time period if the buyer can't meet the original deadline.

In conjunction with the subject to sale clause, also include a time clause to keep your options open. If you're waiting for your buyer to secure financing or sell her residence, your time clause can release you to pursue another offer that arrives in the meantime.

The time clause gives the first buyer a specified time period to remove all the subject to conditions from the contract and close the sale. If the first buyer can't remove all the subjects in time, your time clause releases you from the contract and allows you to pursue other offers. See Chapter 20 for more about the time clause.

If you extend the subject to sale clause, you'll probably have to extend the completion and possession dates stated on the Contract of Purchase and Sale. Whatever dates you choose, they'll probably change once your buyer has a buyer for his own house. Your closing date for the sale may depend on your buyer's yet-to-be-negotiated closing dates.

If you've found a house you really want to purchase after selling your own, you can try to add a *subject to purchase* clause that makes your home's sale conditional on whether you can still get the house you wanted. Be prepared that your buyer may not be happy with this condition and may not accept its inclusion in the contract. These clauses are not at all common, but in some situations it can give you peace of mind that you won't be homeless if your dream house was snatched up before you had a chance to sell.

If you're selling a condominium, you may encounter a *subject to viewing condominium bylaws and financial statements* clause. In many provinces, the law requires that a condominium corporation provide the buyer with full information on the condo complex and its regulations. Your buyer must acknowledge in writing that the information's been received and approved. There aren't too many negotiating points here, except for the time frame and how far back into the building's history the buyer would like to go.

Expect some regional differences and extra information to be required in different parts of the country. For example, around Vancouver (where there are a number of leaky condominiums), the buyer may ask for any engineering reports or building envelope studies that are available, and the seller must provide the information to the buyer.

In most provinces, once a subject to condition in the Contract of Purchase and Sale has been met, it's formally removed from the contract with a written *waiver, amendment,* or *condition removal form.* These legal documents are usually signed by both parties (the buyer and the seller) to confirm that a condition has been fulfilled and is no longer part of the offer.

"I never liked those drapes anyway": Including appliances and household decor

Anything permanently attached to the property is considered to be part of the package. So any built-in cabinets, built-in appliances, or wall decorations — legally considered *fixtures* — are things you'll be leaving behind for the next owners. Anything portable (*chattels*), on the other hand, is yours to keep, if you want it. Under this logic, the drapes are still yours, but the tracks they hang from aren't; Grandma Bertha's bedside lamp comes with you to your new home, but the beautiful chandelier in the entrance hall belongs to the new owners.

Anything portable that you *do* want to leave behind (the drapes, the refrigerator, the pool-cleaning accessories you won't need in your new condo) must be written into the contract specifically and listed item by item. Something else to keep in mind, though: Anything you *don't* want to leave behind is best removed before showing the house at all. If you can't do that, be sure to make it clear to everyone who walks through the door that those items are not part of the deal. You don't want prospective buyers to fall in love with a piece of art or furniture that you would never consider parting with, and make an offer that turns on whether or not it's included in the sale. And build *everything* (exceptions and inclusions) into the property section of the contract. If you include a built-in vacuum system, make sure you also include the attachments and powerhead for the system.

Even if you plan to include portable items in the sale of your home, do it at the last minute. If the portable items are listed in the contract right from the start, they don't seem like bonuses when you're negotiating, since potential buyers will try to talk down your price anyway. If you wait until *after* the buyers try to talk you down, "throwing the drapes in" or including the washer and dryer may appease them as much as lowering the price.

Don't include any leased items as part of the sale. Many companies lease security systems and water filtration systems, and if they're left with the house, the buyer will be charged. The last thing the buyer wants is to get a bill for a security system she thought she'd bought outright with the house.

Buyers might also specify that certain items be *removed* as a condition of the offer. Some people just don't want the brown and gold linoleum and faux-wood panelling greeting them on moving day. Some buyers make big requests. For example, you might receive an offer $5,000 below your asking price and with the condition that you remove the shag carpeting. Part of your negotiations will include figuring out the buyer's priorities. Are they just looking for any excuse to cut the price? Are they willing to budge on the rug? As a concession,

Of course, sometimes people surprise you

Jed and Daisy were being relocated to the southern U.S. and needed to list and sell their home fast. They didn't have a chance to clean up the really big problems around their house, like the car-on-cinder-block flower planters in the front yard. So they trimmed, weeded, watered, and crossed their fingers. Most of the prospective buyers turned around without even getting out of their cars and Jed and Daisy were just about ready to give up. But — surprise! — the next couple to view the house not only weren't put off by the dead car museum out front, they asked that it be included in the sale contract! You just never know when someone like Spyder and the missus will want to keep what you can't bear to take with you.

you might agree to remove the rug but cut less off the price. Or you could try dropping your price and leaving the rug with the property. Your agent or lawyer won't recommend any substantial changes to your home before closing — just in case your home doesn't close for some reason — but, hey, if your buyers insist that if you remove all the tacky light fixtures, they will agree with the price of your counteroffer, you can probably agree to remove those lights.

The closing date

After having spent a couple of hours reviewing the price, the subjects, and all the inclusions and exclusions, the dates may seem relatively minor. Give yourself a breather from the contract and then refocus. The dates will be the most important factor when moving time comes around. If you can negotiate a sensible and relaxed set of dates now, your move will be much easier at a time when stress will be at an all-time high. Again, if you can get ideal dates scheduled, you may drop a little bit off the price in return for the buyer's flexibility.

The *closing date* (or *completion date*) is the day when the money changes hands and the title is conveyed to the buyer. The *possession date* is the day you receive (or give) the keys to the other party. The *adjustment date* is the date that property taxes, condominium fees, and any other annual municipal fees and utility bills are adjusted to. These last two dates should be one and the same: you get the keys, you start paying the bills.

Ideally, give yourself a one- or two-day overlap where you have the keys for your new house as well as the keys for the house you've sold. The following would be a perfect scenario, starting on a hypothetical Monday:

✔ *Monday* — Completion date on your present house

✔ *Tuesday* — Completion date on the house you're buying

✔ *Wednesday* — You get the keys for the house you're buying at 12 noon (usual time of key transfer) unless you negotiated an earlier time to get the keys

- Adjustment date for the house you're buying

✔ *Thursday* — You give the keys to the buyers of your old house at 12 noon

- Adjustment date for the buyers of your house

This scenario gives you a chance to have a relaxing move, and still go back to clean up your old house Thursday morning before you give the keys to the buyers of your old home. The downside is that the buyers pay their money on Monday but don't get their keys until Thursday noon. This is fairly common in some provinces, and for the right price, the buyers will accept the dates once they have negotiated with you on all the terms of the agreement. In other provinces such as Ontario, it's common to have the closing date and the possession date as the same day. If this is the case, it may be worth arranging interim/bridge financing to close the house you are buying a couple of days before your present home's closing date so that you don't have to store all your possessions, especially if something is delayed.

Discuss with your real estate agent or your lawyer how many days you'll need for the closing. If you're working with a real estate agent, you may still want one or two days to run the contract by a lawyer. In some provinces, legal documents can't be signed on Sundays or statutory holidays.

The *Transfer of Title* officially closes the contract when you file the paperwork at the land registry office. These offices are typically open from 9:00 a.m. to 3:00 p.m. weekdays. No matter how pressed for time you are, don't even try to officially close two contracts on the same day. Leave at least one day to close the sale of your current house and transfer money before you go back down to the land registry office and close the purchase of your next house. (See Chapter 9 and Chapter 15.)

Open for acceptance until . . .

When you realize how many changes can be made to the contract, you may realize you'll need more time to reach an agreement. If both you and the buyer agree, the offer can be extended until an agreement is reached on all the terms. If the offer expires before you reach full agreement with the buyer, it should be rewritten with a new time frame for acceptance.

Signatures

Both the buyer and the seller have to sign the contract, and, usually, have their signatures witnessed on each page. In some jurisdictions, it's sufficient to have the first page of the contract signed and witnessed, and then have both parties initial the bottom of every page. Your agent or lawyer can advise you on the proper way to sign or initial the contract.

Multiple Offers

If you're lucky enough to be selling your home in a red-hot seller's market, you may get competing offers on your home. This embarrassment of riches has to be treated carefully to ensure you get the offer you want in place without having to go through the whole process twice.

Keep these guidelines and practices in mind to ensure everything goes smoothly.

- **Keep everyone informed.** If more than one group is interested in your home, it's in your best interest to make sure everyone is kept up-to-date once offers are starting to be written. In the ideal scenario for the seller, the buyers enter into a bidding contest and pay up to, or over, the asking price.

- **Act in good faith.** Many buyers will not compete with another group when making an offer. Remember that what's good for the seller is not always good for the buyer. If a seller tries to get cute and delay one offer hoping to get a second competitive offer, both potential buyers may cancel their offers.

Let's imagine Ken and Sue have listed their fabulous heritage house for sale. It's a hot seller's market, meaning buyers outnumber sellers, and the low inventory of homes means Ken and Sue should get close to their $499,000 asking price.

Buyers A, B, and C all see the house the first day it's listed for sale, and all come to the same conclusion: The house is gorgeous, the house is well priced, and they want it.

Ken, Sue, and their agent get together to review the offers. Buyers A were the first to notify the listing agent that they had an offer, so their offer is presented first, followed by the offers from B and C. Before making changes to any offer, Ken and Sue discuss all three offers with their agent and decide which offer has the most potential. Buyer C offered $475,000, which was all he could afford. Both A and B offered the full price of $499,000 with similar terms and conditions.

Ken and Sue decide to deal with offers A and B. A's offer is $499,000 and only subject to inspection. The dates are perfect and the $50,000 deposit is attractive. B's offer is $499,000, but it's subject to financing (with B stretching to afford the price) and inspection, with a $25,000 deposit.

Ken and Sue have a couple of options: They can choose to accept one offer as is, or with minor changes that both parties agree to, and hope that the conditions go through and the contract is fulfilled. Or, they can reject both offers as presented and ask A and B to present better offers and hope for an even more advantageous offer. In the end, Ken and Sue decide to accept A's offer. But they actually have a third option: accept B's offer as a *back-up offer*.

Back-up offers

In some provinces, a second offer can be accepted as a back-up offer, subject to the collapse of the first offer. Your agent or lawyer will advise you what is acceptable in your province. The offer would be worded something like:

> "This is a back-up offer only and is subject to the seller being released by the buyer from all obligations under the previously accepted Contract of Purchase and Sale by _____ , 2000. This condition is for the benefit of the seller."

Looking at Ken and Sue's situation again, they could accept B's offer as a back-up offer subject to A's offer collapsing. B has nothing to lose by being a back-up offer for a couple of days while A has an inspection done. Should A not be thrilled by the inspection, then B would have their chance to purchase the house, subject to their own inspection and financing. If A buys the house, then B's offer would not proceed and B would get the deposit money returned to them.

The other common situation for a back-up offer is when the buyer has added a subject to sale clause to the offer and a second offer comes in, subject to the collapse of the first offer. In this scenario, the first offer should have a time clause in it, giving the buyer 24, 48, or 72 hours (or whatever was negotiated) to remove all subjects from the contract. Once the sellers have a second acceptable offer, the sellers give written notice to the first offer to remove all subjects within the prescribed time frame, or step aside so that the back-up offer will be the offer in effect. An example invoking the time clause can be found in Chapter 20.

In the best of both worlds, the seller wants to sell at their listing price and the buyer wants to buy at their originally offered price. Negotiating is what falls in between.

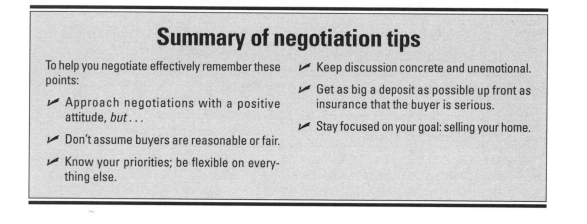

Summary of negotiation tips

To help you negotiate effectively remember these points:

✔ Approach negotiations with a positive attitude, *but* . . .

✔ Don't assume buyers are reasonable or fair.

✔ Know your priorities; be flexible on everything else.

✔ Keep discussion concrete and unemotional.

✔ Get as big a deposit as possible up front as insurance that the buyer is serious.

✔ Stay focused on your goal: selling your home.

Part VII
Part of Tens

The 5th Wave   By Rich Tennant

"Most of the gingerbread is still in good shape, and I had the roof re-frosted just last year."

In this part . . .

There are all sorts of folk traditions around setting up house. You'll find some entertaining lists here, as well as practical advice on making your new house a safe and well-maintained home. We've also compiled information on a host of regional issues which may affect you depending on where you live.

Chapter 22

Ten Regional Concerns When Buying a Home

In This Chapter

▶ Special considerations for urban and rural homeowners

▶ Points to remember if you're buying on lease land

*T*he Canadian poet and critic George Bowering once wrote, "The best thing about Canada is that it is not this. It is this and that." And was he ever right — just think about all our different provinces, with their different weather patterns, geography, and demographics. The incredible variety of this huge country of ours can make homeownership very different from region to region. Moving to a new part of Canada can be the best thing you'll ever do. But before you peel off your "I Love Toronto" bumper sticker and head for Trout Creek, or ditch your one-horse town for the bright lights of Halifax, keep these tips in mind.

Check Transportation Routes in Cities

The fact that a city has a public transportation system doesn't necessarily mean that everyone in the city can get from point A to point B with ease. When researching an urban property, call the city's transit commission to get information on nearby routes. If the townhouse you've got your eye on has streetcar access only, realize that it may take you longer to get anywhere than it would from a property with bus or subway access. If you move to a subdivision in the northern periphery of the city, find out how often the commuter train runs. It could well leave you stranded downtown if you miss that packed six-o'clock train.

Be Cautious about Industrial Sites

There are plenty of horror stories about people developing all kinds of illnesses that turn out to be directly related to emissions from the factory half a kilometre away or the pollutants contained in that dumping ground over the hill. If your new home is anywhere near large power generators, factories, dump sites, or on reclaimed industrial land, start by doing some research in the back issues of the local paper. Have there been any articles, disputes, or series of letters to the editor about said industrial site? Next, seriously consider getting the soil and water of your new home tested. That's where pollutants leaching into your property will likely turn up.

Stay Away from Major Roads If You're Noise-Sensitive (or Nose-Sensitive)

If you commute, it can be extremely tempting to buy into that new subdivision along the highway. But before you do, get the whole family to do a sound check. Stand in the yard, close your eyes, and listen. Can you handle the level of noise you hear on a daily basis? Repeat the check in all rooms of the house, with the windows open and closed. The same rule applies for a property on any major road in a town or city. Constant traffic can become extremely disruptive to your sleep and relaxation. Also try to check noise at different times of the day, and if possible see how loud the noise is in the evening when you might be trying to go to sleep. Next, do a smell check in your new neighbourhood. Vehicles on highways and busy roads can emit a lot of stinky exhaust that can affect the air quality of your region.

Steer Clear of Emergency Routes

If you're moving into a town or city, it could at first seem like a plus to be near a hospital. After the first week, however, you may have heard more than your fill of ambulance sirens. The same goes for fire routes. It doesn't hurt to make some phone calls to see if that semi-detached is on a fire truck or ambulance route.

Very noisy routes aren't always necessarily around the corner from the fire station or hospital. If you're on the only road that leads to the bridge dividing the town, you may be in line for some serious siren-wailing.

Be Certain Your Street's on the Level

Melody found a beautiful house in a good area of a major city. However, she noticed something very odd — all the houses across the street looked significantly shorter than those on the side where she wanted to buy. In fact, it looked as though they had sunk partially into the ground!

Melody called her municipal Building Department, and they confirmed her observation. Turned out that the houses on one side of the street had been built over an improperly filled gravel pit, and they had begun to sink some 30 years ago. The Building Department had on file the exact perimeter of the gravel pit, and it turned out that Melody's new house was on solid ground.

Even if your street looks picture perfect, calling the Building Department is a good idea. It can tell you what was on your property before your house, when your house was built, and by whom. Even if your house is on the level, it's always good to have that information on file.

Make Sure You're in the Good-School Region

If you have children or are planning to have them in the next little while, do some research into the school *catchment area* for your new home. The catchment area is the geographical boundary that determines which children go to what school. Catchment maps are available from the local school board or district. If you're outside the catchment area of the school you'd like your children to attend, contact the school. Sometimes, children will be permitted to enroll in a school outside their catchment area — but they may be outside the bus route, making you responsible to get them there every day.

Avoid Rainy-Day Regions If You're a Sun Worshipper

Anyone who has lived in Vancouver can tell you stories about the interminable stretches of rain. On the upside, living in a coastal area can be mild; when that sun *does* come out, you can play golf in December. Just realize that there's a downside: though it's wonderfully snow-free, there's a good chance that the Christmas-day golf tournament you planned could be rained out. It doesn't hurt to do some research into weather patterns before you move; you can do this easily at www.relocatecanada.com. You may be surprised at how much a rainy-day region can affect you.

Watch Out for Waterways

There's no doubt about it: Homes by the river, lake, or stream can be real showstoppers. But the waterway can spread with a serious spring thaw, and your rosebushes may quickly become underwater plants. In the case of extreme rainfall or storms, you, your partner, and Spike the hamster may have to vacate. Also, water safety will be an extremely vital lesson to teach your children; after all, a potentially dangerous element will be a part of their backyard.

Research Services in Rural Areas

That charming lakefront cottage out on Rural Route 12 may seem to you like a promise of pastoral bliss, but there's a chance it could leave you in no man's land. Call the town hall or your region's public works office to find out exactly what municipal services are available to the property. How often is garbage pick-up? Is there any recycling pick-up? Do you have an emergency 911 locator on the property? Is there snow removal on your road in the winter? Will you have to get propane delivery or pay through the nose for electricity to heat your house?

Think Twice about Lease Land

Many recreational areas across Canada are built on lease land held by the provincial government or First Nations peoples. Typically, there are cottages or summer homes built on this land. It is possible that your lease may not be extended, and there may not be any compensation if you build your cottage or summer home on lease land. Although compensation may have been stipulated in the lease, you may walk away with no compensation after a court dispute.

If you want to buy a property on lease land, do your research well. Have a lawyer carefully review all aspects of the lease, with special attention paid to any escalation in lease payments, what may happen to the land, and any improvements at the end of the lease. Because of the uncertainty related to lease land, the price will generally be lower than freehold property, and lease land will always be harder to sell and finance than freehold land.

The Musqueam situation in Vancouver illustrates what can go wrong. In the Musqueam Park subdivision there are two parcels of land — one with a prepaid lease and the other not prepaid. In the prepaid area, there are no monthly lease payments, but the Musqueam band can set the property tax rates, which has led to property taxes being higher than property taxes on adjacent non–lease land in Vancouver. At present, the homes in the prepaid section appear to be holding their value, although they have been tarnished by the dispute in the adjacent "not prepaid" area.

So, while that lakefront property may be stunning, lease land requires careful investigation before buying. Make sure that your lawyer studies the many variables that could apply to your newfound dream cottage on leased provincial land or First Nations land.

Chapter 23

Ten Tips for Condo Buyers

• •

In This Chapter

▶ Getting to know your board of directors

▶ Reading a strata plan

▶ Avoiding getting scalped by commercial properties

• •

*C*ondominium comes from two Latin words: *con*, which means "with," and *dominium*, which means "ownership." And when you think about it, the name really fits what you're about to invest in. A condominium lets you take advantage of owning your own home, but it also lets you share this ownership with others.

But before you sign that offer and run off to a cocktail party to flaunt your new Latin skills, think of this: If you make an ill-informed decision, a condominium could make you suffer the very *worst* of both worlds. You could get locked into owning a cramped, restrictive unit, and you could be stuck in a bad building with irresponsible owners you can't stand.

The whole reason you want a condo is to get the *best* of both worlds, and we don't want you to end up with a lemon. So read these tips, and do some research into your prospective new home in the sky.

Insist on Documentation and Read It As If Your New Life Depends on It

When you leave the condominium sales office, you should have in your possession a condominium certificate, which will contain different documents given different names from province to province. However, whatever package you get should include variations of a sample deed, a *strata plan* (the equivalent to a land survey), homeowners' bylaws, and a budget. Make and keep a copy, and get the originals to your lawyer ASAP. Then, dive into everything yourself. This stuff will look terribly boring, but you must read it! You may find out that your silverpoint Persian cats, Mutt and Jeff, will be uninvited, or your tribal drumming circle will only be allowed to meet on Tuesday mornings from 10:30 to 11:15.

Put It Under a Microscope: Condos Need Inspections, Too

Buying a condo can be as big a financial commitment as buying a house. For this reason, get an inspector on your team before you remove the subjects from your offer to buy. The inspection should cover most of the same things that a standard home inspection would cover (as detailed in Chapter 11): the exterior upkeep of the building, the basement, the heating, water, and ventilation systems, and interior problems such as possible leakage in your unit.

Use Your Measuring Tape If You Buy New

That condo development so wonderfully close to your workplace is already zooming into full occupancy. The catch? It's not built yet. To get the condo of your dreams, you may have to invest in an unfinished project. But if you do, make sure you figure out the differences between the spacious, pristine model unit and *your* unit — the one that will be built from the floor plan that the condo developers have shoved into your hands.

This plan is also called a *strata plan* — the condo owner's equivalent to a land survey. The strata plan will give you the exact dimensions of your condo, as well as its situation in the building, the number of condos on your floor, and whether that beautiful bay window you'll have in your living room has north or south exposure. You should also get the strata plans for the parking areas, basement, laundry, gym, and any other parts of the building that you will partly own.

Take a thorough look at your plan before you buy. It's not uncommon to hear people raving about how well laid out the floor plan of their new condo is — until they realize that they've bought a 900-square-foot two-bedroom that may be smaller than they expected. Figure out if the rooms in the unit will really be big enough for you. How does your prospective new condo's "spacious" master bedroom compare with your current, humble boudoir? You may be surprised to find that it could be significantly smaller.

Get to Know the Board of Directors

Taking the time to get in touch with your homeowners association's board of directors will give you an idea of the kinds of people with whom you'll be sharing your new home. If the treasurer ran off to Maui last year with the funds for that upcoming renovation, you'd want to know, right?

Stay Away from High-Rent Developments

If you buy a house, you want to make sure your new neighbourhood is made up of people like you, who really make a commitment to the upkeep of their homes and the safety of their street. That's why it's not the best idea to move onto a street where most of the homes are rented. The same goes for condos. When you're thinking of buying into a condo development, ask the condo corporation what percentage of units in the development are rented. The higher the percentage, the more concerned you should be. The more renters there are in the building, the fewer people you'll see raising their hands to pitch in for long-term improvements, like extensive roof repair, landscaping, or plumbing.

Watch Out for Maintenance Fees That Are Too Good to Be True

If you're looking into a new building, don't jump to buy if you see low monthly maintenance fees. It's possible that your condo developers are keeping these costs artificially low to lure new buyers. Once the developers are done and the homeowners' association takes over, the grim truth is uncovered as actual monthly costs are determined.

To prevent getting duped, compare the developer's stated maintenance fees with the actual maintenance fees of an established building of a similar size.

Ask About the Building's Commercial Property

Alyssa was overjoyed when the salesman in the condo showroom told her that there would be a convenience store, dry cleaner, and dental clinic on the first floor of the building. However, her joy turned to anger at a homeowner's meeting six months later, when she discovered that these properties paid ludicrously low maintenance fees, and were given extra parking places for free. If you're thinking of buying into a new building, ask how many commercial properties there will be, if any. Then, ask to see documentation of how much in maintenance fees these businesses pay, as well as any other perks they may be getting, such as extra parking. If you look into this carefully, you won't end up paying for that video kiosk in the Speedy Mart.

Share As Few Walls As Possible, Especially If You Crave Quiet

A good rule when looking at condos is that the more walls you share with other condos, the greater your chance is of hearing the odd voice or thump. The same goes for the floor and ceiling: it will be quieter to just have someone below you than to have people above and below you. (Anyone who's lived underneath a tae bo video addict can attest to this.) This is one reason why corner suites are usually more expensive, and why top-floor corner suites are the crème de la crème.

Own Your Locker

When you're told that you'll have a big storage locker and a parking place, make sure you determine whether you own them, or are given *exclusive use* of them. If they are for exclusive use, you don't own them, you can't sell them, and you may not be able to transfer use of them to someone else. If you own them, you can make a little side money by renting them out or selling them if you decide to give up your car or have a big garage sale.

Check For Signs of Aging

Condominiums built in old apartment buildings can be really charming, especially if the modern, cement-block ones look like big warts on the skyline to you. But it's important to make sure that the old-fashioned vibe you get from the building won't put you in the Middle Ages once you move in. If you're looking at a condo in an old apartment building, check for signs of dilapidation, such as crumbling walls or roof. Also, check to see whether the heating, cooling, ventilation, and security systems are up-to-date. If they're not, you may soon be paying extra maintenance fees to fix a big breakdown.

Chapter 24

Ten Ways to Protect and Maintain Your Investment

In This Chapter...

▶ Keeping an eye on your surrounding property

▶ Servicing your heating and cooling systems

▶ Safeguarding your home

Many people subscribe to the "if it ain't broke, don't fix it" view of home maintenance. But it will cost you so much more to repair water damage than it will to check the roof for loose or damaged shingles every six months. Just as you should change your car's oil every 10,000 kilometres, so should you change your furnace's air filter at least once a year — you may dote on your car, but ultimately, your home is a much larger investment, so take care of it! Imagine selling your home for $50,000 less than you want because of water damage in the basement. And if you checked your home's foundation regularly, you may have been able to prevent the damage altogether. Whether it needs to be done monthly or yearly, take the time to inspect as well as repair your home's interior and exterior. We guarantee you'll enjoy living in your home much more, and you're likely to be very happy with its resale value.

Inspect the Exterior

Do an exterior inspection twice a year. Check your home's foundations for signs of cracking, bulges, or deterioration. If you have a brick home, you should watch for deteriorating bricks or masonry; aluminum siding should be checked for rot, dents, cracks, or warping.

Clean and check your eavestroughs at least once a year in the fall. Trim vegetation away from gutters and downspouts to avoid blockage. One of the best ways to examine your eavestroughs is to watch them when it rains. Do they drain properly, or do they overflow, or are there holes? Where does the water drain? Downspouts should direct water away from your home, not toward the basement.

Don't force yourself to climb on your home's roof — you can just use a pair of binoculars to take a quick survey. Look for damaged or missing shingles, especially if water is leaking into the interior of the house. Check the flashings (the metal or plastic reinforcing the angles and edges on a roof) too for deterioration. Call a roofing specialist in to do a full inspection if you notice anything. Watch chimneys for loose or deteriorated mortar, and watch the flashing around the chimney. Look for birds' nests in them, too.

Look at What Surrounds Your House: Landscaping, Yard, and Deck

Inspect the property around your house before and after winter. Have a look at the trees — are they healthy? If a branch has no leaves while others are in full bloom, that branch is probably dead and needs to be removed before it falls onto the new addition or onto an innocent passer-by. Have a look at any exposed tree roots near the house; they can sometimes grow into your sewer system. Trim any shrubs around your doorways and windows so that prowlers can't hide behind them.

If you have a lawn sprinkler system, check it once a year in the spring for leaky valves or exposed lines. Get rid of any garden debris that could attract wood-eating insects — you don't want your home to be a termite hotel! Check out your pool and hot tub: Look for leaks or damage. Look at your walkway for unevenness.

Finally, don't forget to inspect the garage: its foundation, roof, and walls. In the summer, if you have an asphalt driveway you should check it and patch up any cracks.

Maintain Heating and Cooling Systems

Service, service, service. That's all we have to say about your heating system. It's cleaner and also easier on your wallet if the system is working at its highest efficiency. Have your system inspected and serviced once a year — a good time to do it is just before you start using it for the winter. If you have a forced-air system, clean or change your furnace filters at least once a year. Have the ducts cleaned out too so that the air can travel freely around the home without moving lots of dust around. Include the chimney on your "to clean" list: a blocked chimney is a big fire hazard.

A central air conditioning unit should also be serviced once a year. Remember to cover it before the winter when not in use. If you rely on window air conditioning units to keep you cool in the summer, make sure to store them in a safe place for the winter (not on your garage floor where de-icing salt can leak onto them) or protect them from snow with plastic sealed with duct tape. When window units are in place, make sure to fill any gaps between the window and the unit — gaps reduce the unit's efficiency and stability.

Stay Warm: Insulation

If you've ever had frozen pipes in the winter, you know the importance of having good insulation. Even if you're not worried about frozen pipes (you live in B.C., don't you . . .), insulate your hot water pipes to keep them from losing heat when in use. If you notice small drafts around your home, you may be able to block them with the addition of spray foam insulation. Ask at your local hardware store for tips on convenient mini-insulation materials. Watch for drafts especially near electrical outlets and light switches on exterior walls, under baseboards, around window and exterior door casings, and around entrances to un-insulated areas in your home, like the cold storage room.

Speaking of un-insulated areas, you should think about insulating some of them: Your attic and your basement are two good places to start. Good insulation will make your home more efficient, keeping your heating and cooling costs low.

Breathe Easy: Ventilation

Clean air is particularly important to create a healthy living space, especially if you or someone in your family suffers from allergies or asthma. Make sure your home "breathes" so there's an adequate exchange of air inside your home. Don't seal all your doors and windows so that they're absolutely airtight or you may have trouble with a buildup of moisture or harmful gases inside your home. Because modern homes are so airtight, some have built-in air exchange systems to keep clean air flowing through them. Ventilation options include attic fans, heat recovery ventilators, and balanced mechanical ventilation systems — or keeping windows open.

Again, like the heating/cooling systems in your home, have your ventilation system serviced yearly. Your home's ventilation includes kitchen exhaust hoods, bathroom fans, and dryer exhausts, so don't neglect these either. On the outside of your home, check around the ventilation openings for any cracks, leaks, or damage. On the inside, clean or replace ventilation screens or filters, and turn on your fans and fume hoods at all settings to make sure they work properly.

Sleep Soundly: Home Safety

Here's ten things to do regularly to safeguard your home:

1. Replace batteries in smoke detectors at least once a year.

2. Test all your smoke detectors, fire alarms, and carbon monoxide detectors once a month.

3. Don't leave any inflammables near the furnace, water heater, or space heaters.

4. Pay attention to the condition of stairways and their railings; make repairs if they are unstable.

5. Plan out fire escape routes for your home and make sure your children know how to get out if they can't use regular doorways.

6. Test locks on all the doors and windows, and change them if you've had a break-in or lost a key.

7. Ensure extension cords are tucked away from people's feet and pets' teeth.

8. Check any exposed wiring — including those extension cords, phone cords, cable lines, and appliance cords — for broken or frayed wires; replace them if you find anything.

9. Test your circuit breakers every six months.

10. Update that list of emergency numbers and information on your fridge, especially if you have a caregiver.

Keep an Eye on Your Doors and Windows

Inspect all window and door screens for rust, holes, and tears, and mend or replace them. Give the screens and windows a good wash. Replace any broken or cracked panes of glass. Open and close all doors and windows: do they stick? Oil door hinges or apply car wax to where they bind. Test window locks. Look at your windowsills for signs of water damage. If the wood framing feels damp or looks warped, rainwater may be getting through. Look for deterioration of window trim, seals, putty, caulking, and weather-stripping on both the exterior and interior. If you notice problems, fix them immediately. The longer you allow water damage to occur, the more expensive it becomes to repair. Test outdoor lighting to make sure your entrances are lit adequately at night.

Cook Up a Storm in a Safe, Sumptuous Kitchen

The kitchen is a fine place for water problems, so inspect it thoroughly. Check for leaks under the sink and around the dishwasher (if you're lucky enough to have one of the mechanical ones, that is). Watch around the sink and faucet for places that need resealing.

Every outlet near the sink should be a GFCI receptacle (ground fault circuit interrupter) that will protect you from being electrocuted if it comes in contact with water. You should test it every six months (press the little test button; it's that easy!).

Clean out that fridge and defrost that freezer. Get rid of the dust that builds up on the refrigerator coils — you know what dust we mean! Make sure the seal on the fridge door is tight. Give your stove and oven a thorough cleaning, especially if you use them often. You'll find the cooking elements produce less smoke and odours and have less chance of causing a grease fire if you keep them clean.

Check the burner operation on your stove to avoid fire hazards. Make sure your fire extinguisher still works and that it's within easy reach in case of an emergency. You should also have a kitchen exhaust hood above your stove to remove the smoke and odours while you cook. Change or clean the filter every month or two, and maybe more if the fume hood doesn't connect to the exterior.

Get Away From It All in a Leak-free Bathroom

Every six months you should inspect your bathrooms. As in the kitchen, test the GFCI receptacles in your bathroom (see the kitchen section). Check for water leaks around the faucets, toilets, and pipes. Watch for water damage (typical signs include brown patches, warped wood, and mould) in the flooring, walls, and ceiling. Re-grout what you need to, especially in the corners of your shower and where the tub meets the wall. Make sure the toilet flushes properly, the handle doesn't stick, and that it seals properly after a flush. For plumbing repairs, consult a professional; if you're a novice, you may make a minor problem into a major one.

Confront Your Childhood Fears: Visit Your Basement/Attic

You may not spend much time in either your basement or your attic, but don't ignore them altogether. Although you may use both areas for storage, go through them once a year and get rid of unnecessary clutter; if you've left paint, varnish, or oily rags about, make sure you properly dispose of them — they're a major fire hazard.

Basement and attic leaks are the major cause of water damage, so inspect them carefully. Watch for water leakage in crawl spaces, on ceilings, on walls and around windows. A brown patch on a white wall is a bad sign. Use your nose: A damp musty smell is a good indication of water leakage, even if you don't see anything.

Look for signs of termites or other pest infestations: hollow-sounding beams, holes in wood, droppings, and bite marks are a good indication that you're not living alone. In the summer, look in the attic for bigger freeloading visitors. You may be able to set a few mousetraps yourself, but if you discover a raccoon or some other large varmint, you're better off to call a professional pest remover.

Part VIII

Appendixes

In this part . . .

Don't skip this section! This part contains samples of key documents and a glossary of terms that will help you navigate the wilds of real estate as though you've been doing it forever.

Appendix A

Glossary

• •

*T*he terms that appear in *italic type* throughout the book are defined in this glossary.

addendum: See *schedule*.

adjustment: The amount of money owed by the buyer, usually to the seller, to compensate for any prepaid utilities, property taxes, etc., that extend past the *closing date*. Adjustments should be calculated by a lawyer and presented in a written statement.

adjustment date: The date on which the buyer takes responsibility for all tax rates, local improvement assessments, and utility charges related to the property. This is the date used to calculate the amount of any *adjustments* owing.

affidavit: A sworn, written statement made before a notary public or some other person authorized to administer an oath.

agency: A legal relationship between a seller or buyer and the person(s) they have authorized to act on their behalf in selling a home (seller's agent), or in purchasing a home (buyer's agent).

agent: Also known as a salesperson or registrant. A term used to describe a real estate salesperson. In some provinces, a salesperson can have an "agent or broker" licence that would allow her to be an office manager and administer office trust accounts. See *broker*.

Agreement of Purchase and Sale: See *Contract of Purchase and Sale.*

amendment: A legal document that is added on to the *Contract of Purchase and Sale* to indicate that a particular condition of sale has been satisfied by a specified date and that condition may now be removed from the contract (also known as a *condition removal form* and a *waiver*). Amendments may also be used to extend a *subject removal date* or to change the *closing date* and/or *possession date* once all conditions have been removed from the contract. Standard forms are used for most amendments.

amortization period: The length of time upon which the calculation of the size of the periodic *mortgage* payments is based.

appraisal: An assessment of the *fair market value (FMV)* of a property. Appraisals are often required by lending institutions to approve financial backing for the purchase of a home. Appraisals are performed by specialists certified for this purpose. However, buyers and sellers often rely on the informal evaluation of an experienced real estate agent to help estimate the amount of a reasonable offer or asking price.

appraisal, rental income approach: When appraising a property that has income-generating suites, the appraiser will consider the income (and expenses) to determine the value of the subject property.

appraisal, replacement cost approach: An approach used by appraisers to determine the value of a property based on how much it would cost today to rebuild the exact home.

back-up offer: If the sellers of a property have accepted a *conditional offer* that they are uncertain about, the sellers can accept a back-up offer subject to the first offer not proceeding. Should the conditions not be removed from the first offer, at that time the back-up offer will be the offer in effect.

blended payment: A mortgage payment that goes towards paying down both the *interest* and *principal*. Over time, as the amount owing becomes less, the portion of the payment going towards the interest decreases and the portion going towards the principal increases. The amount of each payment remains constant.

bridge financing: Money loaned to a buyer to help finance the purchase of a new home, while their current home has not yet been sold. The financing usually involves a personal fixed rate loan, often a lump sum, which can be repaid in one lump sum at maturity or prepaid at any time without penalty. There are no standard maximum or minimum amounts for bridge financing.

broker: The real estate broker (in some provinces referred to as the nominee) is often the office manager who supervises the salespeople in the real estate office. The broker can also sell real estate if he or she so chooses. The broker has an upgraded licence that qualifies the broker to administer trust accounts and assist any salespeople having problems with real estate transactions.

buyer's market: Housing market conditions in which there are more homes listed for sale than buyers looking for homes (also known as a slow market). These are generally favourable conditions for buying, since more sellers are competing for fewer buyers.

Canada Mortgage and Housing Corporation (CMHC): The CMHC is the federal government's national housing organization. It is responsible for administering the National Housing Act, provides information to the public, and offers *mortgage insurance.*

Canadian Association of Home Inspectors (CAHI): An association of building inspectors that maintains education requirements and a code of conduct for property inspectors across Canada.

Canadian Home Builders Association (CHBA): Representing over 6,000 firms, the CHBA represents every aspect of the construction industry and works to ensure a stable construction environment, and offers opportunities for its members to keep up with the latest trends, techniques, and education matters in the construction industry.

Canadian Home Income Plan (CHIP): A plan that finances *reverse mortgages* to qualified applicants, who generally own their home clear title. The Canadian Home Income Plan is one of the few plans offering reverse mortgages in Canada. See *mortgage, reverse.*

capital gain: Income from the sale of investments or property — for example, the profit from the sale of a home. Capital gains from the sale of property are usually taxable, although tax exemptions are available for the sale of a *principal residence* and qualifying farmland.

carriage house: One of two houses that share a garage — usually separated into two garages that share a common wall that provides a joint access route to the two backyards. Often these houses share a basement wall as well, although they appear detached to passers-by.

catchment area: The geographical area that outlines the boundaries of the neighbourhood that qualify for admission to a certain school. Maps of school catchment areas are available from local school boards.

Certificate of Completion: A legal document (also known as Certificate of Completion and Possession) signed by a new homeowner of a newly built home and the builder. It states that the homeowner has inspected the completed building and that all contracted tasks were finished properly. This certificate is necessary to initiate home warranty coverage under provincial *New Home Warranty Programs.*

Certificate of Title: A legal document that is issued to a buyer. It states that ownership of a property has been transferred to the buyer from the seller, and lays out any debts or claims against the property. The certificate is issued by the appropriate land registry office upon submission and approval of all the necessary documents. These documents typically include a *deed*, a recent *survey*, a *mortgage discharge statement* from the seller and mortgage papers for the buyer, and statements of any debts or claims against the property that are not already listed in the deed.

chattel: Movable personal possessions that would not normally be included in the sale of a home. They must be named to be included in the sale. Different regions have different customs regarding which objects are commonly included in the sale.

clause: This is a legal statement included in the *Contract of Purchase and Sale* that stipulates a term and condition of the contract. A clause may stipulate a condition that must be met, usually within a specified time period, for the sale to be completed. Common clauses are time clauses, which specify a time frame for a particular condition to be met. Another type of clause is the subject to clause, which stipulates a specific event that must occur before the sale is completed (e.g., the home passing a full *inspection*, or the sale of the buyer's previous home). A holdover clause (sometimes called a holdover period) may also be present in a listing contract, which may require the seller to pay commission to the listing agent if a party introduced to the property during the listing period proceeds to buy the property directly from the seller once the listing has expired. A third-party subject clause (or escape clause or whim and fancy clause) may allow a buyer an easy escape from a contract, and if such a clause is in a contract the time frame to satisfy the condition is usually as short as possible.

closing: The final stage of transferring ownership and possession of the property to the buyer.

closing date: The day on which the sale becomes final (also known as the completion or settlement date). In some provinces, it is also the day on which the buyer takes possession of the property.

collapsing an offer: If the *clauses* are not removed from a sale contract and the sale of the property does not proceed, the offer is said to have "collapsed" and any deposit monies will be returned to the buyer in accordance with the applicable provincial Real Estate Act.

commission: A fee, usually calculated as a percentage of the sale price, paid by the seller to their *agent*, or split between the seller's and buyer's agents, upon *closing* of a sale. The amount or percentage of the commission is agreed upon and stated in the *listing contract*. A typical commission might be 4 percent to 6 percent of the sale price.

commitment letter: See *mortgage note*.

Comparative Market Analysis (CMA): The process most widely used to evaluate the market value of a property (also known as Competitive, or Current Market Analysis). It involves comparing a property to similar homes in the same neighbourhood. The current asking prices and recent sale prices of these homes are then taken as benchmarks for the market value of the property in question. A CMA is often the best method for determining what buyers will actually pay for a home.

completion date: See *closing date*.

condition removal form: See *amendment*.

condominium: A type of ownership in which buyers gain sole ownership of their unit and share ownership of common areas with other unit owners. Condominium dwellers share in the running of the *condominium corporation*.

Condominium Act: See *Strata Property Act*.

condominium certificate: Also known as estoppel, information, or status certificate. Each unit in a condominium complex has a corresponding condominium certificate. This document describes the monthly fees for a particular unit, then lays out exactly which expenses are the responsibility of the *condominium corporation*, which fall to individual owners, which will be shared by all unit owners, and how those shared costs will be proportioned. It will also lay out the bylaws that govern conduct of unit owners and how the condominium corporation is run. Condominium certificates also include information on the financial status of the condominium corporation.

condominium corporation: All the owners in a condominium building form a condominium corporation (or strata corporation), with each unit having one equal vote in the running of the condominium corporation.

condominium unit: An individual unit in an apartment or condominium building (also known as a strata unit).

Contract of Purchase and Sale: The sale contract, also known as an Agreement of Purchase and Sale or an Interim Agreement. This document is usually a standard form provided, often through your agent or lawyer, by a local or provincial real estate board.

conveyance: A legal term for the process of transferring full or partial ownership of a property, including all debts and claims associated with it. The legal document associated with conveyance is called a *deed*.

co-operative corporation: The governing body that oversees the *co-operative housing* complex.

co-operative housing: A type of housing complex in which owners do not own their specific unit. Instead, they jointly own, with the other co-op owners, the *co-operative corporation*. A share in the co-operative corporation gives an owner the exclusive right to occupy a specified unit. With co-operative housing comes the expectation that owners will participate in the maintenance of the entire property and in the running of the corporation.

counteroffer: An offer sent back to the buyer by the seller, or vice versa, with changes or conditions suggested that would make the offer acceptable to the other party. A counteroffer (or counteroffers) is a typical part of negotiation for purchase of a property.

covenant: Restrictions or obligations that are entailed by ownership of a property. These are explicitly stated in the *Contract of Purchase and Sale*.

deductible: The amount that the insurance policyholder pays the insurance provider toward the cost of replacing damaged or stolen items covered under the *insurance policy*.

deed: The legal document that transfers ownership from the seller to the buyer. It states any debts or claims against the property and what obligations come with ownership of that property, if any.

deed of trust: See *mortgage*.

deficiency inspection: Prior to the change of ownership of a newly built home, the buyer and a representative of the builder will walk through the property and note any deficiencies in the construction and the finishings. Any noted deficiencies will be repaired by the builder at the builder's expense prior to the change of ownership.

deposit: Money paid by the buyer when the *Offer to Purchase* is made. It is held in trust by a real estate agent or lawyer until *closing*, at which time it is paid to the seller. A deposit signifies that the buyers are sincere in their desire to purchase the property.

disbursement(s): A fee paid to a lawyer in compensation for any fees that they have paid on your behalf while working for you (e.g., courier costs, travel expenses).

discharge fee: See *prepayment charge*.

disclosure statement: More formally known as a Property Condition Disclosure Statement or a Vendor Property Information Statement. A legal document in which the seller describes the property and all other items included in the sale to the best of their knowledge. It is usually filled out and signed on entering into a *listing contract*. It requires the seller to list any defects of the property, and any known debts or claims against the property. The purpose of a disclosure statement is both to inform the buyer and the seller's agent about the condition of the home, and to put the onus on the seller to honestly represent his home, aware that he may be subject to future litigation in the event that a buyer discovers some undisclosed problem with the property.

down payment: A lump-sum payment made to the seller on purchase. It is the difference between the amount of the *mortgage* and the full *purchase price*.

dual agency: A situation in which the buyer and seller have the same *agent*, or have different agents that work for the same brokerage company. Both buyer and seller have a legal right to be told when they are in a dual agency situation, and in most cases, buyer and seller will both be asked to sign a written statement that they understand and approve of the situation.

duplex: A type of housing involving a single structure divided into two dwelling units — often top-to-bottom so they share a common floor/ceiling, although sometimes side-to-side so that they share a common wall. The owner typically rents out one of the units. It is possible to purchase a half-duplex, where the property is divided into two units, with both suites being sold and owner-occupied.

easement: A privilege acquired by a landowner for the benefit of his land over land owned by someone other than the benefiting owner. Easements do not entitle their holder to possession of the property, but they do allow their holder to use that part of the property for a specific purpose. (In rare cases, easements prevent the owner of the property from using a part of it in a specified manner.) Typical easements might be held by electrical power suppliers or telephone companies to allow them to put in-ground or overhead wiring across residential properties.

encroachment: A section of a structure or property sitting on one lot that intrudes illegally onto land belonging to someone else.

encumbrance: Any financial charge owing against a property (a *mortgage* is an example of an encumbrance).

endorsement: A statement added to your *insurance policy* that extends your coverage.

equity: The difference between the value of your property and the outstanding debts against it. Equity can be used as collateral for securing loans or lines of credit.

estoppel certificate: See *condominium certificate*.

exclusion: A term used in *insurance policies* to denote a specific event causing loss or damage that is not covered by the policy. See *property coverage, all-risks* and *property coverage, standard*. Also used to exclude a specified item (i.e., a chandelier) from the sale of a house.

fair market value (FMV): The value of a property as determined by an *appraisal*. In other words, the price for which a property should actually sell given its condition, location, and the current market conditions.

farm area: An agent who specializes in one specific area (either a geographical area or specific market segment) will "farm" that area by keeping residents up-to-date with area listings and sales, either by newsletters or frequent advertising.

feature sheet: A list of the attributes of a property. A feature sheet is usually compiled by the seller or their *agent*, and given out to prospective buyers when they tour the home. It may include details such as lot size, number of bedrooms and bathrooms, type of house, facts about the neighbourhood, amenities and perks, as well as pictures of the property and contact information for the seller or their agent.

finder's fee: A fee paid by the buyer to the buyer's *agent* for finding a suitable home.

fixture: A built-in, or non-movable, part of a property that is typically included in a sale. Fixtures are assumed to be included in the sale unless it is explicitly stated otherwise. Different regions across the country have different customary practices regarding fixtures that are commonly included in a sale.

flue: The vent from the chimney that must be unobstructed to operate properly. A building inspection will make sure the flue is functional.

foreclosure: The repossession of a property by the lending institution on default of mortgage payments by the owner.

gradient: The grade or slope of the property. Ideally the gradient of the land and any surrounding patios or sidewalks should be away from the house to minimize the chance of water getting into the basement of the property.

gross debt service (GDS): The amount of all housing-related costs. This includes mortgage payments, property taxes, and hydro, water, and heating costs. The GDS can be calculated monthly or annually.

gross debt service ratio (GDSR): The percentage of gross annual or gross monthly income needed to cover all housing-related costs (including principal and interest on the mortgage, property taxes, and hydro, water, and heating). The GDSR is used to help determine how large a mortgage a borrower can afford.

Ground Fault Circuit Interrupter outlets (GFCI outlets): Found where water is present (kitchens and bathrooms), these outlets ensure that if an appliance is dropped into the water the electrical current will be interrupted to prevent electrocution.

half-duplex: See *duplex*.

home equity loan: See *mortgage, second*.

information certificate: See *condominium certificate*.

inspection: A report on the presence and apparent condition of the structural and operational systems of a home. Inspections are visual and physical investigations — they are not evaluations of the value of a property.

insurance policy: A policy covering loss or damage to your property (*property coverage*) and the loss or damage of someone else's property that was caused by you (*liability coverage*).

interest: A fee paid to a lender in return for financing a *mortgage*. Interest is usually calculated as a percentage of the amount borrowed.

interest rate: The annual fee for borrowing money as a percentage of the amount borrowed. Interest rates on mortgages may be *fixed*, *variable*, or *capped*.

interest rate, fixed: The percentage of the *mortgage principal* that the borrower pays, for a *mortgage term*, that remains unchanged for the duration of the term. The borrower knows in advance the exact amount of her payments for the term.

interest rate, variable: The percentage of the *mortgage principal* that the borrower pays, for a *mortgage term*, that fluctuates in accordance with changes in the lending rates during the term. The advantage of a variable rate mortgage is that, should interest rates go down during the term, the borrower will have saved money over a fixed rate mortgage for the same term. Conversely, if mortgage rates rise, a variable rate exposes the borrower to the risk of higher payments. For this reason, variable rates can often be converted to fixed rates for a specific term if the borrower believes interest rates will continue to rise.

interest rate buy down: An incentive to make a property more affordable to the buyer. The seller (or sometimes the builder) will "buy down" the interest rate a percentage point or two to help the buyer qualify for a mortgage at a lower rate. The seller will usually add the amount of the interest rate buy down to the *purchase price*.

interest rate differential: If a homeowner wants to discharge his mortgage before the term is up, and if interest rates have fallen since the mortgage was taken out, the penalty to the homeowner will usually be the difference between the current lower rates and the rate of the original mortgage, calculated for the balance of the term of the original mortgage, or a three month interest penalty…whichever is the higher amount.

Interim Agreement: See *Contract of Purchase and Sale*.

irrevocability/time for acceptance: The amount of time a seller has to respond to a buyer's offer to purchase their home. This time period is written into the Contract of Purchase and Sale.

key box: See *lock box*.

Land Titles Office: The office where the *title* of the property is formally transferred from one party to another.

Land Transfer Tax: In many provinces, tax is payable to the provincial government upon the transfer and registration of any real estate. The amount of tax and any exemptions will vary across Canada. Consult with your agent, lawyer, or bank to determine which taxes are applicable in your province.

lawyer's disbursements: See *disbursement(s)*.

leased items: Items that are leased or rented in a home and should be dealt with separately in a Contract of Purchase and Sale or excluded from the sale. Items such as water purifiers, security systems, and service/warranty contracts would be considered leased or rental items.

liability coverage: A home insurance policy that covers you personally in the event that you cause loss or damage to someone else's property for which they request compensation.

lien: A claim against a property for money owing. Usually, liens are held by builders or suppliers who were not paid for labour or materials that were provided for work done on the home. A lien holder may take legal action forcing the homeowner to settle the debt, but liens are usually settled by lawyers when the property is transferred from the builder to the buyer.

link house: See *carriage house*.

listing contract: A legally binding agreement between a seller and one or more *agents* authorizing those agents to market a home. The contract states what services will be provided by the agent(s), describes the property being marketed, and specifies the *commission* to be paid upon *closing* of a sale. Listing contracts can be *exclusive*, multiple, or open.

listing contract, exclusive: A *listing contract* that authorizes a single *agent* to market a home. With an exclusive listing, the agent (the seller's agent) does not have to co-operate with other agents who want to show the home to potential buyers. Exclusive listings may be at a lower than average *commission*.

listing contract, multiple: A *listing contract* that authorizes the seller's *agent* to work with other agents in marketing the home. A multiple listing gives a home the greatest possible exposure to the market. If an agent other than the seller's agent finds a buyer, the commission may be split between the two agents.

listing contract, open: A *listing contract* that authorizes one or more agent(s) to sell your home while protecting your right to sell it yourself. You do not have to personally deal with any of the agents who are working on your behalf, and if you are the one to find a buyer, you are not obligated to pay any commission fees.

lock box: Sometimes referred to as a key box, a lock box is a secure box attached to the property that contains the keys to the property for sale. Agents can show the property to prospective buyers without the owners being present.

median home selling price: The statistical halfway point between the highest and lowest prices in a specific sales search, as opposed to the average of all selling prices. Also referred to as median sale price.

mortgage: A contract between a lender and a borrower (also known as a deed of trust) that allows the borrower to purchase a property, with the repayment terms outlined in the mortgage itself.

mortgage, assumable: An option in a mortgage that allows the buyer to take over responsibility for the outstanding portion of the seller's mortgage on their home. In the past, sellers have remained liable should the buyer default on mortgage payments; however, it is now standard practice in all provinces for the seller to be fully discharged from any responsibility when a buyer assumes the mortgage.

mortgage, conventional: A mortgage that is less than or equal to 75 percent of either the *purchase price* of a home or the lowest appraised value of a home. Conventional mortgages do not require mortgage loan insurance.

mortgage, high-ratio: A mortgage that is greater than 75 percent of the total purchase price, or appraised value (whichever is lower), of a home. High-ratio mortgages must be insured, either by the CMHC or GE Capital Mortgage Insurance Canada.

mortgage, portable: An option in a mortgage agreement that allows the mortgage to be transferred from one property to another.

mortgage, reverse: An agreement with a lender allowing a homeowner to borrow against the equity built up in her home. Reverse mortgages can involve a single lump-sum payment, regularly scheduled payments, a line of credit, or some combination of these options. The maximum amount that can be borrowed is determined by the lender and usually cannot exceed about 45 percent of the value of the home. Reverse mortgages are only available to homeowners over the age of 62. The *Canadian Home Income Plan* is one of the few providers of reverse mortgages in Canada.

mortgage, second: A mortgage taken out on a property that already has a mortgage against it. People sometimes take out a second mortgage to finance substantial renovations or ventures. Second mortgages generally involve a higher interest rate than the current lending rate. Also known as a home equity loan.

mortgage, vendor take back (VTB): A mortgage in which the lender is the seller of the property (as opposed to a financial institution). It is common for sellers in this situation to hire a *mortgage broker* to deal with buyers on their behalf.

mortgage broker: A person or company that arranges mortgages for buyers. Buyers deal directly with their mortgage broker and the broker usually gets paid a fee from the lender, not the buyer. If the buyer has bad credit or requires special assistance to qualify for a mortgage, the broker can charge the buyer a fee.

mortgage discharge statement: A legal document that will be given to the borrower by the lender when the mortgage has been paid in full. This document releases the borrower from all obligations to the lender.

mortgage life insurance: Insurance purchased by a borrower in case the borrower dies before repaying their mortgage in full. The insurance will cover whatever amount remains owing on the mortgage. Mortgage life insurance is usually available from the lending institution or from an insurance broker.

mortgage loan insurance: Insurance bought by the borrower in case she for some reason is unable to repay the mortgage in full. Mortgage loan insurance can cover up to the entire amount that remains owing on the mortgage. All *high-ratio mortgages* must be insured. This kind of insurance can be purchased through the *Canada Mortgage and Housing Corporation (CMHC)* or through GE Capital Mortgage Insurance Canada.

mortgage note: Also known as a commitment letter, a mortgage note is the signed document confirming that a lender accepts the terms of the mortgage, including when and how the mortgage must be paid, and any penalties that may apply.

mortgage pre-approval: An agreement between a lender and a prospective homebuyer reached before the buyer makes any specific *Offers to Purchase* stating that the lender will provide the buyer with a mortgage up to a specified amount.

mortgage principal: The actual amount of money borrowed under a *mortgage*. Repayment of the mortgage includes both the principal (amount borrowed) and interest (fee for borrowing).

mortgage refinancing: If a homeowner has considerable equity in her home, and wants to borrow more money to do substantial renovations, she can increase her present mortgage by refinancing the home at current interest rates.

mortgage term: The length of a *mortgage*; not to be confused with the *amortization period*. The term of a mortgage is usually a shorter period (anywhere from six months to ten years) during which time the method of calculation of the *interest rate* is specified for the entire term. The full amount of the mortgage becomes due at the end of a term; however, most homeowners require more than one term to repay their mortgage.

If a mortgage has not been paid in full by the end of a term, it may be renewed for a further term under a new contract that may involve new conditions. Mortgage terms may be *closed*, *convertible*, *open* or *partially open*.

mortgage term, closed: During a closed-term mortgage a borrower is not allowed to pay off the mortgage in full without incurring penalties. The borrower may make some prepayments on the anniversary date of the mortgage, but any prepayment options will be clearly outlined to the borrower before they agree to commit to the mortgage. See *penalty fee*.

mortgage term, convertible: A short-term (6–12 months) closed mortgage that lets the borrower convert the mortgage into a longer term without penalty. This type of mortgage also allows the borrower to prepay a specified amount at previously determined intervals without penalty.

mortgage term, open: A *mortgage term* during which the borrower can prepay as much of the mortgage as he chooses, even all of it, at any time, without incurring a *penalty fee*.

Multiple Listing Service (MLS): A database of information on homes for sale. It is available only to real estate agents that are members of the Canadian Real Estate Association, and is a trademark of the Canadian Real Estate Association. Agents have access to their local MLS systems, but generally do not have access to MLS systems across the country.

named peril: An event causing loss or damage to a property that is specifically named in the terms of a home *insurance policy*. If a policy works on this basis, it covers only those named perils identified in it. See *property coverage, standard*.

New Home Warranty: An insurance policy that protects builders of new homes during construction. Once the *Certificate of Completion* has been transferred over to the buyer, it becomes a kind of consumer warranty. Although the builder buys the warranty, the buyer usually ends up paying for it, as the cost is tacked on to the *purchase price* of the home.

New Home Warranty Program(s) (NHWP(s)): Provincial organizations created to protect the interest of new home-owners by offering *new home warranties* and promoting high standards of quality and service among home builders. Only builders who meet stringent criteria can become members of an NHWP.

nominee: See *broker.*

Offer to Purchase: The legal document (also known simply as an offer) in which a buyer agrees to pay a specified price for a particular property. An offer can be *conditional* or *unconditional.*

Offer to Purchase, conditional: An offer to purchase a property stipulating specific conditions that must be satisfied before the sale can be finalized.

Offer to Purchase, unconditional: An offer to purchase a property (also known as a firm offer) that has either had all the specific conditions satisfied or had no conditions to start with.

open house: A *showing* of a home, advertised for a specific date and time, during which anyone who is interested may come and tour the home, without needing an appointment.

penalty fee: A fee (also known as a discharge fee or prepayment charge) owed to a lender when the borrower repays more than the amount of the scheduled mortgage payments for a term. A typical penalty fee might be equal to three months' interest, or an *interest rate differential.* Many lenders offer mortgages with "prepayment options" that allow borrowers to prepay a specified portion of the total mortgage or principal at regular intervals.

personal liability insurance: See *insurance, personal liability.*

possession date: The date on which the buyer may move into a new home. In some provinces, the possession date is the same as the *closing date.*

premium: A fee paid for money loaned (mortgage premium) or insurance provided (insurance premium). Mortgage premiums are usually calculated and stated as a percentage. Insurance premiums may be a flat rate and are typically stated as the amount due at each scheduled payment.

prepayment: Most mortgages offer the homeowner a number of options to reduce the outstanding principal of the mortgage without incurring any penalties. The home-owner may be able to pay off 10 or 20 percent of the principal once a year on the anniversary date of the mortgage, or increase the mortgage payments by 10 or 20 percent once per year, effectively allowing the homeowner to prepay their mortgage.

prepayment charge: See *penalty fee.*

principal, as applied to relationship between seller and agent: In an agency relationship between the agent and the client (either buyer or seller), the client is referred to as the *principal* in the relationship, and the agent is authorized to act on their behalf.

principal residence: A dwelling, within Canada, that is owned and inhabited for the majority of a year. A person may designate only one property as their principal residence for any given year.

Principal Residence Exemption: A tax exemption available on the proceeds of sale of a home that was designated as the owner's principal residence for the entire length of time that the property was owned. Under these circumstances, all profits from the sale are tax exempt.

property coverage: A home insurance policy that covers the structure and contents of your home, each to some specified degree, in the event of loss or damage.

property coverage, all-risks: A type of property coverage that covers all risks to your dwelling, with the exception of specific events named in the policy contract. See *exclusions*.

property coverage, standard: A type of property coverage that covers only those damage-causing events that are specifically named in the policy. This coverage works on a *named perils* basis. See *exclusions*, *named perils*.

Property Condition Disclosure Statement: See *disclosure statement*.

Property Transfer Tax: See *land transfer tax*.

purchase price: The agreed selling price of a property.

real property: Consists of land and whatever is erected or growing on or affixed to the land, and the right to use that land (also known as realty).

Realtor: A trademarked term held by the Canadian Real Estate Association designating real estate agents that are members of the Canadian Real Estate Association.

rescind a condition: To remove a condition (or *clause*) from a sale contract in order to proceed with the sale of the property. It is usually the buyer who rescinds conditions.

reserve fund: A fund kept by a *condominium corporation* to cover the cost of any repairs, upgrades, or emergencies that arise.

rider: An *insurance policy* that is added on to an existing policy to extend coverage.

rowhouse: See *townhouse*.

schedule: A legal form (also known as an addendum) that can be added on to the *Contract of Purchase and Sale* to specify conditions of the sale. It is used when there is not enough room on the standard sale contract to fill in all the conditions of sale.

seller's market: Housing market conditions in which there are more buyers looking to buy than homes available for sale (also known as a hot market). These are generally favourable conditions for selling, since there are more buyers competing for fewer homes.

semi-detached house: A house joined with another house by a shared wall. Ownership includes half of the structure and land, and owners are responsible for all the costs and work associated with their half.

showing: A tour a prospective buyer takes of a home that is for sale. Showings are usually arranged by appointment and guided by the seller's agent.

single-family detached house: A house that stands alone on a lot and shares no common structures with adjacent houses. Ownership includes the structure and lot in their entirety. All responsibility for repairs and maintenance, property taxes, and associated costs rests solely with the owner(s).

status certificate: See *condominium certificate.*

strata corporation: See *condominium corporation.*

strata plan: A registered survey for a condominium building that outlines the exact size of all the condominium units in the building and outlines which areas are common property and which areas are for the exclusive use of individual units (e.g., balconies).

Strata Property Act: Known in some provinces as the Condominium Act, this Act identifies the regulations that govern condominiums and outline the responsibilities of the individual owners, the condominium corporation, property managers, and developers.

strata unit: See *condominium unit.*

subject removal date: The date by which a specific subject *clause* (or condition) must be removed from the sale contract. The date can be extended if both parties agree that more time is needed to satisfy the clause or condition.

sump pump: An electric pump located in the basement of a building (or nearby on the outside) that will activate and pump water out if the water in the drainage system hits a predetermined level. A sump pump will keep a basement (or underground parking in a condominium building) from flooding during heavy rains.

survey: A document (or the process by which it is generated) showing property boundaries, the location of all structures situated on the lot, and any *easements* or *encroachments* associated with the property. If the seller does not have an up-to-date survey for a property, a lender may require the buyer to provide one before approving a mortgage, and in some provinces, one must be provided when a buyer registers the *Transfer of Title* in order to be approved for a *Certificate of Title*.

tenancy, joint: Ownership of a property in which two or more people equally own the property in question. When one owner dies, their share of ownership is transferred to the surviving owner(s).

tenancy in common: Ownership of a property is divided equally among two or more people. But, when one owner dies, her share of the property is transferred to her estate, as opposed to being transferred to the surviving owner(s).

time allowed for acceptance: See *irrevocability.*

title: Full, exclusive, and legal ownership of a property. Title is secured when a buyer receives a *Certificate of Title* from the appropriate land registry office.

title search: A search of the land registry office records to ensure that there are no past debts or claims against a property that may challenge the *title* of a buyer.

Torrens System: A system of land registration used in the Western provinces. It operates on "indefeasible" ownership — meaning that the ownership of a title-holder cannot be challenged under any circumstances. The Torrens System was developed to avoid lengthy *title searches* and legal disputes arising from past claims or debts that were not cleared by previous owners and yet not disclosed upon sale of the property.

total debt service: The total amount of gross income required to cover all debts, including housing-related debts. This includes any credit card debt, car payments, line of credit payments, and other regularly incurred debt payments. Total debt service can be calculated monthly or annually.

total debt service ratio (TDSR): The percentage of gross income, annually or monthly, required to cover all debts, including housing-related costs. The TDSR can help determine how large a *mortgage* a borrower can afford.

townhouse: A house (also known as a rowhouse) that shares a common wall with the two houses on either side or is part of a single structure that contains such houses. Townhouses can be owned independently or as a unit in a condominium complex.

Transfer of Title: The process of transferring ownership of a property from one party to another. See *conveyance*.

Vendor Property Information Statement: See *disclosure statement*.

viewed date: The date as specified on the sale contract when the buyers last viewed the property in question before making their *Offer to Purchase*. The contract will specify that the property and all included items will be in the same condition on *possession date* as when viewed by the buyers on the viewed date.

waiver: See *amendment*.

Appendix B

Sample Inspection Report

· ·

BAKER STREET HOME INSPECTION SERVICES INC.

3335 Yonge Street, Suite 402
Toronto, Ontario M4N 2M1
Telephone: 483-3535
Fax: 483-9756

BUILDING INSPECTION REPORT

Property Inspected _123 EASY STREET   UTOPIA_

Inspection Date _JANUARY 1, 2000_   Inspector _JEFF CLARKE_

SUMMARY (GENERAL COMMENTS)

In comparison to other homes of similar vintage in the vicinity that we have inspected, the functional condition of this building/dwelling is . . . . ☐ Below average ☒ Average ☐ Above average

Recommended improvements or repairs to the building/dwelling have been addressed in the report.
It is suggested that the highlighted concerns be attended to within the next year.

	MINOR REPAIRS	MAJOR REPAIRS		MINOR REPAIRS	MAJOR REPAIRS
Roofing	☐	☒	Structure	☒	☐
Exteriors	☒	☐	Electrical	☐	☒
Interiors	☒	☐	Heat/Cool	☒	☐
Maintenance	☒	☐	Plumbing	☒	☐
	☐	☐			

Comments: _See "PRIORITY INDEX" for timeframes and budget costs._

1. The report, issued by the inspector, is prepared with reasonable skill and care within the limitations of a visual inspection on the inspection date.
2. The required repairs to the building include, but are not limited to, what is reported herein due to the limitations and restrictive nature of a visual inspection. The client is hereby warned that not all deficiencies will be revealed.
3. The inspector's role is principally educational; to provide you with a better understanding of the building.
4. The inspection is partially designed to reduce your risk of buying an older home, however we cannot eliminate this risk. The inspector/inspection firm will not absorb any of your risk in buying an older property.
5. The client is hereby advised to budget at least 1% of the building's value annually for maintenance and unforeseen repairs.
6. Cost estimates provided in this report are minimums and are intended to be a rough guideline only. Estimates are based on the most cost effective solution to address the problem and will not include betterment.
7. The inspection does not cover code compliance issues set by governments or other regulatory authorities.
8. The inspection does not take into account eligibility for mortgage insurance, building or home owners insurance.

I have read this report from Baker Street Home Inspection Services Inc. and am aware of the limitations of the inspection process. I accept this 14 page report and supplements according to the conditions as stated herein. I am aware that this inspection is not a guarantee of present and/or future conditions.

Name of Client _MR. & MRS. SMITH_   (Bus.) _____ (Res.) _855-6793_

Current Address _46 MAPLE ST.   OAKVILLE, ONTARIO   L5J-1T4_

Signature of Client _E Smith_   Signature of Client Representative _____

Total payment of _$ 321.―_   Received in full _Clarke_   TERMS: Payment due upon receipt of this report.

_21.―_ G.S.T. Included #R100381029   Cheque ☒   Cash ☐

© Copyright (1999) The Canadian Building Consulting Group Inc.

YOUR BUILDING INSPECTION

The primary purpose of the inspection and this report is to educate the prospective purchaser/owner about the general condition of the building. In addition, maintenance, repair and cost effective improvement advice is provided to increase this understanding. **No claim is expressed or given that all problems with the building will be discovered by the inspection we have just performed.** Every effort has been made to provide this report with the most accurate and practical information for the purpose intended.

Definition of terms used in the report:

Functional .... (1) system was performing its' intended purpose at the time of the inspection.
Monitor .... (1) item is marginal, will require future repair, owner is advised to monitor.
(2) preventative maintenance repairs are required beyond the first year of ownership.
Minor Repair .... (1) minor repair is recommended; costs should not exceed $1500.⁰⁰ and/or the repair is not urgent.
MAJOR REPAIR .... (1) major repair is recommended; costs will exceed $1500.⁰⁰
Good Condition .... (1) no defects were discovered that should require repair within the first year.
Fair Condition .... (1) no repair is deemed necessary within the first year; however the system or component is marginal.
(2) system or component is performing its intended purpose but due to its age can fail at any time
N/A................................ (1) not applicable, not accessible, not inspected, or
(2) not installed or does not pertain to the subject property.

The inspector's objective during the summary portion of the inspection is to discuss the significant aspects of their findings. There is no time limit on these discussions. We encourage you to ask as many questions as you like to ensure we have addressed your concerns. The inspection process is a two-part system: the verbal survey and the report. As such, **this report is not transferable** to third parties as it will not clearly convey the information herein.

Enclosures: ☒ LEAK PREVENTION ☒ KNOB & TUBE WIRING ☒ CRAWL SPACE INFO ☐ _____
☐ _____ ☐ _____ ☐ _____ ☐ _____

GENERAL CONDITIONS, SPECIAL SITUATIONS & LIMITATIONS

WEATHER CONDITIONS
☐ Snow/rain/_____ limited the extent of the exterior inspection.
☒ Roof/grade/walkways/decks were snow covered at the time of inspection.   **Recent weather conditions:**
☐ Absence of recent heavy rainfall limited scope of basement foundation inspection.   ☐ Rainy ☒ Snow ☐ Clear
☒ The outdoor temperature was too low to safely test the central air conditioning system.   ☒ Average temperature __-10°c__
☐ The outdoor temperature was too high to sufficiently test the central heating system. _____
☒ Weather conditions during inspection: ☐ Rainy ☐ Snow ☒ Clear ☐ Cloudy ☐ Windy   Temperature __- 5°c__
INACCESSIBILITY
☐ Basement/Garage storage limited access/visibility.   ☐ Excessive storage limited access to: _____
☐ Areas/systems not fully visually inspected: _____
☐ Other specific limitations:_____
☐ Work in progress (not fully inspected) _____
☐ Plumbing system winterized (not fully inspected)   ☐ Inspection of plumbing limited due to recent non-usage.
☒ Further inquiries to vendor is recommended regarding: __WATER STAINING ON WEST BASEMENT WALL__ .
RENOVATIONS/REMODELLING
Some recommendations contained in this report are based on the intent of the purchaser/_____ that significant upgrades will be done to the following: ☐ _____ ☐ Exterior ☐ Bathroom(s) ☐ Basement
☒ Addition at: __REAR__   ☐ Heat/Cool ☐ Interior Layout ☐ Kitchen ☐ Electrical ☐ Plumbing
☐ Purchaser to undertake most recommended work: ☐ Personally _____   ☐ By others: _____
GENERAL/ORIENTATION
☒ Orientation: For reference purposes the front of the building is facing: ☒ north ☐ south ☐ east ☐ west
☐ Vendor has warranted the following: _____
☒ Building substantially furnished   ☒ Building occupied   ☐ Building vacant/partially   ☐ Building unoccupied
TYPE OF INSPECTION/SALE
☒ Pre-purchase inspection   ☐ Pre-sale inspection   ☐ Newly built house inspection   ☐ Post-purchase inspection
☐ Home owners inspection   ☐ Estate sale   ☐ Power of sale   ☐ Private sale   ☐ Pre-lease/rental   ☐ _____
ATTENDANCE
☐ Purchaser/client not present at inspection ☐ Client partially attended inspection ☒ Client fully attended inspection
Also in attendance: ☐ Vendor   ☐ Vendor's agent   ☒ Purchaser's agent   ☐ _____
EXCLUSIONS
☐ The testing of swimming pools & related equipment is beyond the scope of our visual inspection.
☐ Exterior/common elements are the responsibility of the condominium corporation.
☒ **Note:** Appliances, central vacuum systems, trees, heat exchangers, flue interiors, outbuildings, security systems, intercom, spas, wood destroying insects, vermin, underground storage tanks, sub-grade plumbing drains, environmental testing, UFFI, window air conditioners, asbestos containing material, septic tanks, wells, marine structures and other items not specifically mentioned in the report are not included within the scope of this inspection. We do not disassemble equipment, bore holes into walls, floors and ceilings, move furniture and boxes, lift up carpets and rugs, etc.

Clients Initials _____   © Copyright (1999) CBCG (Inc.) (rev 08/99)

ROOF STRUCTURES, COVERINGS & RELATED SYSTEMS

1-Yr. Priority Key

Functional	Monitor	N.A.	Minor Repair	MAJOR REPAIR

METHOD OF ROOF INSPECTION
☒ Fully accessed ☐ At eaves ☐ At ground level with binoculars (too steep/inaccessible)

LIMITATIONS
☐ Majority of the above elements were snow covered. ☐ _____
☐ Flat roof is covered with gravel ☐ Flat roof is covered by decking
☐ Due to the unpredictable and latent nature of roof leaks, no assurances or warranty can be provided
  that your roof will not develop leaks within the approximated expected lifespan stated in this report.

ROOF COVERINGS TYPE
☒ Asphalt shingles are the principal roof covering of the building.
☐ Asphalt shingles cover all sloping roof surfaces of the building .
☐ _____ covers the principal flat roof surfaces of the building.
☐ _____ is the principal roof covering of the building.
☐ _____ covers the flat roof surface at the _____
☐ _____ covers the roof surface at the _____
☒ There is more than 1 layer of shingles presently installed to roof surface.

ROOF COVERINGS CONDITION
Estimated remaining lifespan of roof shingles/coverings:
_____SHINGLES_____ = __0-1__ years ☐ ?   ☐ **NOTE:** Estimated lifespan based on
_____ = _____ years ☐ ?   visible portion of roof only.

General condition of flat roof coverings: ☐ Good ☐ Fair ☐ Poor ☐ ? _____
☐ _____

(Priority: MAJOR REPAIR ☒)
☐ Current repair is required at: _____
☐ Roof covering replacement is required at: _____
☒ High probability of replacement of _____ALL_____ roof coverings within __1__ years.
☐ Repairs/roofing tune-up is required soon/before next application of roof coverings.
☒ Trim tree branches/vines away from roof edge. ☐ _____
☐ _____
☒ BUDGET $ 4,000.- to remove all existing shingles and install NEW.

(Priority: Minor Repair ☒)
ROOF/WALL FLASHINGS & JOINTS
☐ All flashings are in: ☐ Good condition ☐ Fair condition ☐ _____
☐ Repair/replace flashings at: _____
☒ ~~Repair~~/replace all flashings with next roof covering replacement.
☐ Repairs/maintenance required before next application of roof coverings. (ie) caulking or tarring
☐ Caulking recommended at: _____
☐ _____

(Priority: Minor Repair ☒)
ROOF DRAINAGE
Type: ☒ Aluminum ☐ Galvanized steel ☐ Plastic ☐ Copper ☐ Hoppers/Scuppers
☒ Roof drainage is in: ☒ Good condition ☐ Fair condition ☒ Seasonal cleaning required
☐ Gutters ☐ Downpipes require repair/extending/painting at: _____
☒ Extend downpipe(s) at _- ALL -_ corner/side 4'-6' away from building ☒ Add drainage pads
☐ Replacement ☐ Installation of gutters/downpipes recommended at: _____
☐ Gutters & downpipes are approaching end of functional life. ☐ _____

(Priority: Minor Repair ☒)
SOFFIT AND FASCIA
Type: ☒ Aluminum ☐ Plywood ☐ Wood ☐ Vinyl ☐ _____
☒ Soffit & fascia are in: ☒ Good condition ☐ Fair condition ☐ _____
☒ Repairs/~~paint~~ are required/recommended at: _loose piece at N.W. corner_
☐ Replacement/new aluminum cladding of soffit/fascia is recommended in future.

(Priority: Minor Repair ☒)
SKYLIGHTS, ROOF WINDOWS & SOLARIUMS
Type: ☐ Factory built ☐ Home-made (usually of sub-standard quality)
☐ Units are in: ☐ Good condition ☐ Fair condition ☐ Evidence of leakage at: _____
☐ Annual maintenance/caulking recommended. ☐ _____
☒ ~~Repair~~/replace: _New skylight required as part of "New" roofing system._
☐ _____

ADDITIONAL OPINIONS: _____
-tree branches too close to roof edge encourages squirrel and
raccoon activity which is damaging roof surface

Clients
Initials _____

☐ **SEE ADDITIONAL COMMENTS PAGE / INFORMATION SHEET** ☐ _____

EXTERIOR (GENERAL)

1-Yr. Priority Key
Functional · Monitor · N.A. · Minor Repair · MAJOR REPAIR

Approximate age of building is ___65___ years.
Building has been substantially renovated/upgraded ___—___ years ago. ☐ N/A

TYPE OF STRUCTURE/OCCUPANCY

☒ Detached ☐ Wood frame ☒ Single family dwelling
☐ Semi-detached ☐ Brick veneer ☐ Multi-purpose occupancy
☐ Row house ☒ Solid masonry ☐ Duplex ☐ Triplex
☐ Condominium/townhouse ☐ Wood frame-upper level ☐ Basement apt. added
☐ _____ ☐ Brick front only ☐ _____

[☒ Minor Repair] EXTERIOR WALLS/WALL COVERINGS
Brick/Masonry
☒ Masonry units & mortar are in: ☒ Good condition ☐ Fair general condition.
☒ Mortar repair; tuck pointing recommended at: _localized areas at S.E. corner_
☐ Brick repair required at: _____
☐ Non-structural cracks noted which could/should be repaired. ☐ Repair sills at: _____

[☒ N.A.] Wood/Other sidings:
☐ Aluminum ☐ Vinyl ☐ Wood ☐ Insulbrick ☐_____ shingles ☐_____
☐ Good condition ☐ Fair condition ☐ _____
☐ New wall coverings/re-cladding recommended at: _____
☐ Repair work required/recommended at: _____
☐ Application of protective coatings (paint, stain) recommended to most/all wood surfaces.

[☒ Functional] Foundation Wall (above grade):
☒ Foundation wall is in: ☒ Good condition ☐ Fair condition ☐ Non-structural cracks noted
☐ Requires tuck pointing at: _____
☐ Requires parging/repair at: _____

[☒ Minor Repair] CHIMNEYS
☒ Masonry ☐ Good condition ☒ Flue cap recommended
☐ Metal ☐ Fair condition ☒ Requires new chimney cap/drip edge
☐ None required ☒ Requires tuck pointing ☐ Requires removal/rebuilding
(i.e. electric heating) ☐ Requires repair ☐ _____

[☒ Minor Repair] EXTERIOR DOORS
☒ Exterior doors at: ☒ Front ☐ Side ☐ Rear **are in:** ☒ Good condition ☐ Fair condition
☒ Repair/replace: _REAR DOOR; broken frame_ ☐ Install at: _____
☐ Install storm/screen door at: _____
☐ Repair/replace hardware at: _____ ☒ Upgrade locks at: _ALL DOORS._
☐ Upgrade caulking/painting ☐ Upgrade weather stripping ☐ _____

[☒ Minor Repair] WINDOWS (GENERAL)
☐ Aluminum ☒ Wood ☐ Vinyl trim ☐ _____ ☒ wood/aluminum storms
Predominant types:
☒ Single/Double-hung ☐ Casement ☐ Sashless ☐ Horizontal sliding ☐_____
☒ Windows are in: ☐ Good condition ☒ Fair general condition ☐ _____
☐ Storm/screen systems are recommended to be upgraded at: _____
☐ Repair/replace window frame/sills at: _____
☒ Window refurbishing/replacement recommended: _dining room window_
☒ Upgrade caulking/painting ☐ _____

[☒ Minor Repair] GRADING / SITE DRAINAGE / RETAINING WALLS
☐ Good condition ☐ Fair grading conditions exist alongside the foundation(s) of the building.
☒ Grading conditions require improvement at: ☐ Front ☒ Rear ☒ Side _____
☒ Patio/walkways slope towards foundation wall. Correction recommended at: _east side._
☐ Retaining walls are in: ☐ Good condition ☐ Fair condition ☐_____
☐ Retaining walls require repair/replacement at: _____
☐ Window wells are in: ☐ Good condition ☐ Fair condition ☐_____
☒ Window well installation recommended at: _2 rear basement windows_

ADDITIONAL OPINIONS: _____

Clients
Initials _____

☐ **SEE ADDITIONAL COMMENTS PAGE / INFORMATION SHEET** ☐ _____

1-Yr. Priority Key				
Functional	Monitor	N.A.	Minor Repair	MAJOR REPAIR

EXTERIOR (CONT.)

GARAGE/OUTBUILDING/CARPORT
☐ **Attached Garage**   ☐ Good condition   ☐ Fair condition   ☐ Poor condition
☐ Gas proofing measures of common walls with house required; provide gas seal.
☐ Entry door into dwelling requires self-closing device.   ☐ Weather stripping required to door.
☐ _____

☐ ☐ ☐ ☒ ☐
☒ **Detached Garage**   ☐ Good condition   ☐ Fair condition   ☐ Poor condition
☒ Wood Frame   ☐ Solid Masonry   ☐ Brick Veneer   ☒ Eavestroughs recommended
Roof Coverings: ☐ Good condition   ☐ Fair condition   ☒ Replace roof coverings soon
☒ Caution: Unprotected underground/overhead electrical wires are supplying power to the garage.
☒ *Repairs to garage wall sidings recommended.*

☐ ☐ ☐ ☒ ☐
Overhead Door Operation   **Automatic Door Operation** ☐ N/A
☐ Good condition   ☐ Fair condition   ☐ Good condition   ☐ Fair condition
☒ Requires repair/replacement   ☐ Repair/replace operator   ☐ Adjust/no auto-reverse
☐ _____

☐ ☐ ☐ ☒ ☐
WALKWAYS/DRIVEWAYS
☐ Good condition   ☒ Fair overall condition   ☐ _____
☒ Repair work required/recommended at: *front entrance walkway (ie) uneven*
☐ _____

☒ ☐ ☐ ☐ ☐
PORCHES, DECKS, BALCONIES (egress to exterior)
Location: *front*   **Type:** ☐ wood ☒ masonry ☐ steel
Structural supports: ☒ Good ☐ Fair   condition _____
Decking: ☒ Good ☐ Fair   condition _____
Steps/stairs: ☒ Good ☐ Fair   condition _____
Guards/handrails: ☒ Good ☐ Fair   condition _____

☐ ☐ ☐ ☒ ☐
Location: *rear*   **Type:** ☒ wood ☐ masonry ☐ steel
Structural supports: ☒ Good ☐ Fair   condition _____
Decking: ☐ Good ☐ Fair   condition *- replace 3 deck boards.*
Steps/stairs: ☒ Good ☐ Fair   condition _____
Guards/handrails: ☒ Good ☐ Fair   condition _____

☐ ☐ ☐ ☒ ☐
Handrail recommended alongside steps at: *rear steps.*
Other conditions: _____
☐ _____

☒ ☐ ☐ ☐ ☐
EXTERIOR PLUMBING CONDITIONS
Garden hose connection location: ☒ Front ☒ Rear ☐ Side ☐ Garage ☐ None
☒ Good condition   ☐ Fair condition   ☐ Repair/replace at: _____
Main vent stack(s):
☒ Good condition.   ☐ Requires repair/extending from roof   ☐ _____
☒ Good clearance from windows/doors. ☐ No evidence of vent stack for plumbing system visible.

☐ ☐ ☒ ☐ ☐
EXTERIOR ELECTRICAL CONDITIONS
Exterior plug receptacle location: ☐ Front ☐ Rear ☐ Side ☐ Garage   ☒ None
☐ Good condition   ☐ Fair condition   ☐ Requires weatherproof cover   ☐ GFCI recommended
☐ Requires repair/replacement _____   ☐ Receptacle not grounded
☐ _____

☐ ☐ ☐ ☒ ☐
Lighting location: ☒ Main entrance   ☐ Side entrance   ☐ Rear entrance   ☐ Garage
☐ Fixture(s) are in: ☐ Good condition   ☐ Fair condition   ☐ _____
☐ Replace fixture at: _____   ☒ Installation recommended at: *REAR ENTRANCE*

☒ ☐ ☐ ☐ ☐
Service entrance: (electrical cables feeding house from street transformer)
☒ Overhead entrance   ☐ Underground/lateral entrance   ☐ _____
☒ Mast head, conduits/meter base properly affixed to building. _____
☐ Repairs are required at: _____

ADDITIONAL OPINIONS: _____
~FENCING REPAIRS AT REAR RECOMMENDED.
_____
_____

☐ **SEE ADDITIONAL COMMENTS PAGE / INFORMATION SHEET** ☐ _____

Clients
Initials _____

1-Yr. Priority Key

Functional / Monitor / N.A. / Minor Repair / MAJOR REPAIR

FOUNDATIONS, BASEMENTS & STRUCTURES

☐ **LIMITATIONS:** Substantially / partially finished basement restricted observations.
☐ Due to the unpredictable and latent nature of basement leaks, no assurances or warranty can be provided that your basement will not leak in the future. We caution you that it is common for basement leaks to develop at any time in the future where no such leaks existed in the past.

FOUNDATION CONSTRUCTION TYPE
☒ Continuous masonry foundation
☐ Masonry/wood piers
☐ Slab on grade
☐ Wood beam on grade

ACCESS/BASEMENT TYPE
☒ Full basement
☐ Crawlspace
☐ Basement & crawlspace combination
☐ No access of:_____

☐ ☒ ☐ ☐ ☐   **FOUNDATION MATERIAL TYPE**
☐ Brick
☐ Stone
☒ Concrete block
☐ Poured concrete
☐ Foundation wall interiors not accessible for inspection.
☐ Repairs are required at: _____
_____
_____
☒ Non-structural cracks were observed which could be a source of future water penetration.

☐ ☐ ☒ ☐ ☐   ☒ **EXTENSION/ADDITION** at the _____ Rear.
is supported with a different foundation type than the main building.
☒ Continuous masonry   ☐ Crawlspace   ☒ Repairs/improvements are required at:
☐ Masonry/wood piers   ☐ Full basement
☐ Slab on grade   ☒ No visible   - SEE CRAWLSPACE INFO. SHEET.
☐ Wood beam on grade   accessibility   _____

☒ ☐ ☐ ☐ ☐   **INTERIOR COLUMNS & BEAMS/INTERIOR LOAD SUPPORTS (BASEMENT LEVEL)**
Columns & Walls: ☐ Wood   **Beams:** ☒ Wood
                   ☐ Steel   ☐ Steel
                   ☒ Masonry
☒ Support system members are in: ☒ Good condition ☐ Fair condition
☐ Repairs to support load are required at: _____

☒ ☐ ☐ ☐ ☐   **FLOOR (BASEMENT)**
☒ Concrete
☐ Unfinished/exposed soil
☐ Raised wood (limited observations)
☒ Good condition ☐ Fair condition
☐ Repair at:_____
☐ _____

☒ ☐ ☐ ☐ ☐   **FLOOR JOISTS/FLOOR SYSTEM**
Type (floor & ceiling joists where visible)
☒ Wood joists ☐ Wood trusses ☐ Steel joists/concrete deck ☐ _____
☒ Floor joists appear to be in: ☒ Good condition   ☐ Fair condition where visible.
☐ Repair/replace floor joists at: _____

☐ ☐ ☐ ☒ ☐   **BASEMENT WINDOWS, VENTILATION & INSULATION**
☐ Good ventilation ☐ Fair natural ventilation supplied to basement/crawlspace.   ☐ None
☒ Replacement/upgrade of most/some basement windows are recommended.
☐ Supply ventilation to: _____ ☐ Weather strip cold storage room door.
☐ Insulation recommended at: _____

☐ ☐ ☐ ☒ ☐   **WATER SEEPAGE / PENETRATION**
☐ No visual evidence of active water penetration through foundation walls. (limitations in effect)
☐ Dampness/efflorescence noted on foundation walls. ☐ _____
☐ Dampness observed at cold storage room. ☐ _____
☒ Active leaking/seeping observed through foundation walls at: _side wall - west._
☐ Previous leaking/seeping observed through foundation walls at: _____
☐ All areas of all foundation walls not thoroughly inspected due to finished wall coverings and storage of materials/etc. ☒ _SEE LEAK PREVENTION REPORT SHEET._
ADDITIONAL OPINIONS: _____
_____
_____

Clients
Initials _____

☐ **SEE ADDITIONAL COMMENTS PAGE / INFORMATION SHEET** ☐ _____

1-Yr. Priority Key				
Functional	Monitor	N.A.	Minor Repair	MAJOR REPAIR

ELECTRICAL SYSTEM

MAIN ELECTRICAL STATION

Main disconnect rating: **Main power disconnect type:**   **Main service rating:**

☒ 60 A ☐ 100 A   ☐ Circuit breaker   ☒ 60 A ☐ 100 A
☐ 200 A ☐ _____ A   ☒ Knife switch/cartridge fuse   ☐ 200 A ☐ _____ A

Supply voltage: ☐ 120 V ☒ 120/240 V ☐ 347/600 V   **Service entrance conductors:** ☐ Cu ☐ Al
Grounding conductor: ☒ Good condition ☐ Not determined ☐ Requires repair/replacement

[Priority: Functional ☒]

Location of main and distribution panels: ☒ Basement ☐ Garage ☐ _____
Location of auxiliary distribution panels: ☒ Basement ☐ Garage ☐ _____
Condition of main/auxiliary panels: ☐ Good condition ☒ Fair condition
☐ Panel cover missing at: _____ ☐ Repair/replace panels at: _____
☐ Cover holes in panel at: _____ ☐ Access to panel is restricted
☐ _____

[Priority: Minor Repair ☒]

☐ Adequate ☒ inadequate   sized main distribution panel is installed. ☐ _____
☐ Adequate ☒ inadequate   number of circuits are available to properly distribute intended load.
☐ Additional ☒ replacement distribution panels(s) are recommended (for future use).
☐ Labelling of branch circuits at main distribution & auxiliary panels is recommended.
☐ Spare circuits available at distribution panel: ☐ Yes _____ ☐ No _____
☐ _____

[Priority: MAJOR REPAIR ☒]

DISTRIBUTION

Predominant visible branch wiring type: **Branch circuits overcurrent protection:**

    At main distribution panel(s):
☒ Knob & tube (old copper)
☒ Romex (conventional copper)   ☒ Glass fuses ☒ Cartridge fuses ☐ Breakers
☐ BX (metallic sheathed)   At auxiliary panel(s):
☐ Aluminum   ☐ Glass fuses ☐ Cartridge fuses ☐ Breakers
☐ **Note:** Aluminum wiring is the original/principal branch wire type of this dwelling.
☐ Arcing/other unsafe conditions were identified with outlets tested. ☐ _____
☐ No unsafe conditions identified with outlets that were tested. ☐ _____
☒ A SIGNIFICANT AMOUNT OF KNOB & TUBE WIRING IS PRESENT.
☐   - see info. sheet on old wiring

Fuses/breakers
☐ Properly sized fuses/breakers are presently used to protect branch circuits.
☐ Improperly sized fuses/breakers are presently used at: ☐ Main panels ☐ Auxiliary panels
☐ 15 Amp fuses are required for all 110 volt receptacles and lighting circuits.
☐ _____ amp fuses are required for circuit # _____

[Priority: Minor Repair ☒]

GENERAL

☒ Good ☐ Fair   lighting source is provided to all habitable areas & service rooms.
☐ Additional lighting recommended at: _____
☐ Good ☐ Fair   number of receptacles is provided to all habitable areas & service rooms.
☒ Additional receptacles recommended at: ALL BEDROOMS; presently there are
☐ _____ only 1 per
☐ _____

[Priority: MAJOR REPAIR ☒]

REPAIR/UPGRADING RECOMMENDATIONS

☒ Upgrade amperage of main service to ☒ 100 AMPS ☐ 200 AMPS presently or upon the next
    significant home improvement undertaken. ☐ _____
☒ Most (some) convenience receptacles in dwelling do not have secondary ground (i.e. 2 prong);
    add properly grounded (i.e. 3 prong) receptacles where required/desired. ☐ _____
☐ Rework poor wiring connections in basement. ☐ _____
☒ Repair/replace lighting outlets, switches at: basement; most are loose.
☐ Repair/replace receptacles at: _____
☐ Missing coverplates/loose outlets observed at: _____
☒ G.F.C.I. protected receptacles/circuits are recommended to be installed at:
    ☒ exterior ☒ garage/outbuilding ☒ bathrooms ☐ spa/whirlpool bath ☐ _____

ADDITIONAL OPINIONS: _____
_____
_____
_____

Clients
Initials _____

☐ **SEE ADDITIONAL COMMENTS PAGE / INFORMATION SHEET** ☐ _____

© Copyright (1999) CBCG (Inc.) (rev 08/99)

1-Yr. Priority Key

Functional	Monitor	N.A.	Minor Repair	MAJOR REPAIR

CENTRAL HEATING SYSTEM

GENERAL COMMENTS

Energy source:
- ☐ Oil
- ☒ Gas
- ☐ Electric

Furnace type:
- ☐ gravity air (octopus) furnace
- ☒ conventional forced warm air furnace
- ☐ mid-efficiency forced warm air furnace
- ☐ high-efficiency forced warm air furnace

☐ ☐ ☐ ☒ ☐

Approximate age of furnace = ___10___ **years**
Probability of furnace replacement within the next _10_ **years:** ☐ High ☒ Medium ☐ Low ☐ ?
☒ **Limitations: The heat exchanger is concealed within the furnace and cannot be fully reviewed.**
Chimney flue interior: ☐ Clay lined ☐ Metal lined ☒ Brick lined ☐ PVC/ABS tubing
☒ Metal lining of chimney flue recommended. ☐ _____
Furnace room ventilation: ☐ Good ☐ Fair ☒ Requires improvement _ADD WALL VENT._
Thermostat condition: ☒ Good ☐ Fair ☐ Requires replacement _____
Thermostat location: ☒ Good ☐ Fair ☐ Requires relocating _____

☒ ☐ ☐ ☐ ☐

Adequate heat source supplied to habitable areas / zones:
Basement: ☒ Yes ☐ No   Main floor: ☒ Yes ☐ No
2nd floor: ☒ Yes ☐ No   3rd floor: ☐ Yes ☐ No
Habitable room(s) not provided with heat: _____

☒ ☐ ☐ ☐ ☐

WARM AIR SYSTEM – FURNACE

Fan belt/motor operation: ☒ Good ☐ Fair ☐ Requires repair/replacement
Clean air/filtration system: ☐ Good ☒ Fair ☐ Requires repair/replacement
Central humidifier operation: ☐ Good ☒ Fair ☐ Requires repair/replacement
Burner(s)/coil condition: ☒ Good ☐ Fair ☐ Requires repair/replacement
Limit and operating controls: ☒ Good ☐ Fair ☐ Requires repair/replacement
Vent/smoke pipe condition: ☒ Good ☐ Fair ☐ Requires repair/replacement
☐ _____

☐ ☐ ☐ ☒ ☐

☒ Annual servicing and cleaning recommended ☐ Heating company insurance plan recommended
☒ Humidifier requires servicing _____ ☐ Humidifier recommended
☒ Air cleaner/filters requires servicing _____
☐ Air duct cleaning is recommended ☒ Carbon monoxide (CO) detector is recommended
☐ _____

☒ ☐ ☐ ☐ ☐

DISTRIBUTION SYSTEM – AIR DUCT SYSTEM

Condition of supply plenum: ☒ Good ☐ Fair ☐ Requires repair _____
Condition of return plenum: ☒ Good ☐ Fair ☐ Requires repair _____
Condition of branch ducts: ☒ Good ☐ Fair ☐ Requires repair _____
Condition of register/grilles: ☒ Good ☐ Fair ☐ Requires repair _____
Function of return ducts/inlets: ☒ Good ☐ Fair ☐ Requires repair _____
Air flow at supply outlets: ☒ Good ☐ Fair ☐ Requires repair _____
☐ _____

☐ ☐ ☒ ☐ ☐

HEATING FUEL STORAGE & DISTRIBUTION SYSTEMS

☐ Good condition ☐ Fair condition ☐ Remove/encapsulate asbestos wrapping around ductwork.
☐ Requires repair/replacement: _____

☒ ☐ ☐ ☐ ☐

SUPPLEMENTARY HEATING

☒ Electric baseboard heaters/space heaters have been installed at the following areas:
- rear room - main floor
☐ Supplementary heating is recommended at the following areas:

☒ **Rooms above unheated space / garages / crawlspaces:** _rear room - main floor._
NOTE: These rooms may be slightly cooler than other areas of the house during cold winter days.
ADDITIONAL OPINIONS: _____
_____

Clients
Initials _____

☐ **SEE ADDITIONAL COMMENTS PAGE / INFORMATION SHEET** ☐ _____
© Copyright (1999) CBCG (Inc.) (rev 08/99)

1-Yr. Priority Key

Functional / Monitor / N.A. / Minor Repair / MAJOR REPAIR

INTERIOR PLUMBING SYSTEM

☒ **LIMITATIONS:** The visual access to main drain lines and drains underneath basement floors is restricted. No assurances or warranty can be provided regarding proper drainage conditions or performance. Sewer back-up is beyond our ability to detect or predict.

WATER SUPPLY ☒ Municipal ☐ Private   **SEWAGE DISPOSAL** ☒ Municipal ☐ Private ☐?

☒ ☐ ☐ ☐ ☐   **MAIN SHUT-OFF VALVE/LEVER**
Location: ☒ Basement _____ ☐ _____ ☐ Location not determined
☒ Good condition ☐ Fair condition ☐ Requires repair/replacement _____

☒ ☐ ☐ ☐ ☐   **TYPES AND CONDITIONS OF WATER SUPPLY LINES**
Predominant type: ☒ Copper piping ☐ Galvanized steel ☐ _____
Visible condition: ☒ Good condition ☐ Fair condition ☐ _____
☐ Repairs required to: _____
☐ _____
☐ Removal of all galvanized water lines is required/recommended to increase water flow and
    pressure to a desirable level. ☐ _____

☒ ☐ ☐ ☐ ☐   **Water pressure:**
☒ Good water pressure ☐ Fair water pressure ☐ Poor water pressure
Functional flow:
☒ Good functional flow to 2 or more fixtures when used simultaneously.
☐ Fair/poor functional flow is evident. ☐ _____

☐ ☐ ☐ ☒ ☐   **TYPES AND CONDITIONS OF INTERIOR WASTE/DRAIN LINES**
Predominant type: ☐ Cast iron/lead ☒ Copper ☒ ABS /plastic
Visible condition: ☒ Good condition ☐ Fair condition ☐ _____
☒ No abnormal drainage conditions were observed with all fixtures. ☐ _____
☐ Repairs required to main drain lines at: _____
☐ Clogged, slow draining fixtures at: _____
☐ Improperly installed fixture drains at: _____
☒ Leaking fixture drains at: _Kitchen sink - minor leak._
☐ Fixtures with fair functional drainage that appear to be improperly vented: _____

☒ ☐ ☐ ☐ ☐   **BASEMENT/CRAWLSPACE FLOOR DRAIN**
☒ Good condition ☐ Fair condition ☐ Requires repair/replacement/cleaning
☐ Location not determined ☐ Floor drain not installed ☐ _____
ADDITIONAL OPINIONS: _____

☒ ☐ ☐ ☐ ☐   **HOT WATER TANK**
Energy source: ☒ Gas ☐ Oil ☐ Electric   **Type:** ☐ Rental ☒ Owned
☒ Hot water tank is in: ☒ Good condition ☐ Fair condition ☐ Requires repair/replacement
☒ Vent hood & flue condition (gas/oil only): ☒ Good/fair condition ☐ _____
☐ _____

☐ ☐ ☒ ☐ ☐   **SUMP PUMP/SEWAGE EJECTOR SYSTEMS**
Condition of sump: ☐ Good ☐ Fair condition ☐ Requires repair/replacement
Operation of pump: ☐ Good ☐ Fair condition ☐ Requires repair/replacement
Condition of pump discharge: ☐ Good ☐ Fair condition ☐ Requires repair/replacement
☐ _____

☐ ☐ ☒ ☐ ☐   **PRIVATE WATER SOURCE**
Type: ☐ Pond, stream, spring ☐ Well ☐ Vault, cistern   **Location:** _____
Operation of pressure tank: ☐ Good ☐ Fair condition ☐ Requires repair/replacement
Operation of (well) pump: ☐ Good ☐ Fair condition ☐ Requires repair/replacement
☐ _____

☐ ☐ ☒ ☐ ☐   **PRIVATE SEWAGE DISPOSAL SYSTEM** ☐ **NOTE:** Limitations of visual inspection is in effect.
Type: ☐ Septic system ☐ Holding tank ☐ Not determined   **Location:** _____
Percolation field free of trees, shrubs: ☐ Yes ☐ No ☐ Not determined   **Location:** _____
☐ _____
ADDITIONAL OPINIONS: _____

Clients
Initials _____   ☐ **SEE ADDITIONAL COMMENTS PAGE / INFORMATION SHEET** ☐ _____

1-Yr. Priority Key

Functional	Monitor	N.A.	Minor Repair	MAJOR REPAIR

INTERIORS

☒	☐	☐	☐	☐

WALL & CEILINGS

Predominant material type:
☐ Plaster & wood lath
☒ Plaster & gypsum lath
☐ Drywall ☐ Wood paneling

Interior wall structure type:
☒ Wood ☐ Steel ☐ Masonry & strapping
☐ Water stains noted at _____
☐ _____

General condition of surfaces:
☒ Good condition ☐ Fair condition
☐ Repair required at: _____
☐ Substantial refurbishing recommended

Alternate ceiling type:
☐ Suspended/acoustic tile ☐ _____
which were measured dry. Monitoring required.

☒	☐	☐	☐	☐

FLOOR COVERINGS

Predominant material type:
☒ Carpet   ☐ Concrete
☒ Hardwood   ☐ Wood
☐ Vinyl   ☐ Ceramic tile _____
☐ Other_____

Structural/other conditions:
☐ Repairs recommended at: _____
☐ _____

General condition of surfaces:
☐ No hazardous defects exist (normal wear)
☐ Repair required at:_____
☐ Substantial refurbishing recommended
☐ _____

☐ 2nd/3rd level floor system was not originally intended for habitable use and is presently limited in its ability to support a normal load. ☐ _____

☐	☐	☐	☒	☐

PRIMARY WINDOW OPERATION/CONDITION

Function of ventilating windows:
☐ Good operation ☐ Fair operation
☒ Minor adjustment to most/some units
☐ Major refurbishing/replacement is
   recommended

Window handles/locks/hardware:
☐ Good condition ☐ Fair condition
☒ Some localized repair/upgrading
☐ Major upgrading recommended
☐ _____

☐ Thermal windows with defective seals/condensed inner glass panes at: _____
☐ _____

☐	☐	☐	☒	☐

☐ All/most operating windows are equipped with insect screens.
☒ Few/most require to be replaced/installed   ☐ _____
☐ _____

☐	☐	☐	☒	☐

PRIMARY DOOR OPERATION/CONDITION

Function of interior doors:
☐ Good operation ☐ Fair operation
☒ Minor refitting to most/some doors
☐ Major refurbishing/replacement is
   recommended
☐ _____
☐ _____

Door hardware – general condition:
☐ Good condition ☐ Fair condition
☒ A few missing handles/repairs required
☐ Most require improvement
☐ _____

☐	☐	☐	☒	☐

STAIRWAYS, RAILINGS & BALCONIES

Condition of primary staircase(s):
☒ Good condition ☐ Fair condition
☐ Loose treads/minor repair
☐ Major repair/replacement
   recommended
☐ _____

Condition of primary railings/guards:
☐ Good condition ☐ Fair condition
☒ Loose rails/spindles/minor repair
☐ Installation of safety handrail required
☐ _____

☐	☐	☐	☒	☐

Condition of basement staircase(s):
☐ Good condition ☒ Fair condition
☐ Loose treads/minor repair
☐ Major repair/replacement
   recommended
☐ _____

Condition of basement railings/guards:
☐ Good condition ☐ Fair condition
☐ Loose rails/spindles/minor repair
☒ Installation of safety handrail required
☐ _____

ADDITIONAL OPINIONS: _____
_____
_____

Clients
Initials _____

☐ **SEE ADDITIONAL COMMENTS PAGE / INFORMATION SHEET** ☐ _____

© Copyright (1999) CBCG (Inc.) (rev 08/99)

1-Yr. Priority Key				
Functional	Monitor	N.A.	Minor Repair	MAJOR REPAIR

ATTIC/ROOFSPACES

☐ **LIMITATIONS:** The inspection process cannot predict the ability of the roof stucture to support heavy snow loads.

ACCESSIBILITY
☒ Good access ☐ Fair access to attic
☐ Attic/roof space has been
   converted into living space
☐ _____

☐ No access to attic is installed
☐ Access to roof spaces is recommended
☐ Increase size of attic access
☐ Insulate, weatherstrip attic hatch

(Priority: ☒ Functional)

VENTILATION
☒ Domed roof units ☒ Soffit vents
☐ Gable/ridge vents
☐ Attic fan(s)/turbine vents
☐ Spaced board sheathing

☒ Roof vent(s): ☐ Good condition ☐ Fair condition
☐ Additional vents recommended (low/high)
☐ Repair/replace roof vents at: _____
☐ _____

(Priority: ☒ Functional)

INSULATION: APPROX. R-VALUE
☒ R-0 to R-15 (0" – 5")
☐ R-20 to R-28 (6" – 8")
☐ R-32 to R-40 (10" – 12")
☒ Additional insulation recommended
☐ _____

TYPE
☐ Cellulose fibre
☒ Fibre glass batts/loose fill
☐ Rock wool/Vermiculite
☐ Other: _____

(Priority: ☒ Minor Repair)

CONDITION OF RAFTERS/COLLAR TIES TRUSSES/STRUCTURAL MEMBERS
☒ Good condition ☐ Fair condition
☐ Some localized repairs/defects
☐ Additional collar ties/structural support
   is recommended
☐ _____

CONDITION OF ROOF BOARDS/SHEATHING
☒ Good condition ☐ Fair condition
☐ Probability of replacement of some sheathing
   with next shingle replacement
☐ Poor condition due to inadequate ventilation
☐ _____

(Priority: ☒ Functional)

ADDITIONAL OPINIONS: _____
_____

FIREPLACES

☒ **LIMITATIONS:** Determining the condition of flue interiors and the ability of the fireplace to draw properly is beyond the scope of a visual inspection.

FIREPLACE TYPE
Masonry fireplace at: ___LIVING ROOM_____
Factory-built fireplace at: _____
Wood-burning stove at: _____
Wood/coal insert at: _____
Gas fireplace at: _____

FIREPLACE CONDITION
☒ Combustion chamber is in good/fair condition. ☐ _____
☐ Damper is in good/fair condition. ☐ _____
☒ Hearth extension is in good/fair general condition. ☐ _____
☒ Smoke chamber is in good/fair general condition. ☐ _____
☐ _____

☐ Combustion chamber requires repair at: _____
☒ Damper requires repair/replacement at: _____
☐ Hearth floor requires repair/extending at: _____
☐ Smoke chamber requires repair at: _____
☐ _____

(Priority: ☒ Minor Repair)

Flue cleaning recommended at: ___LIVING ROOM_____
Roughed-in fireplace installed at: _____
Fireplace is obsolete/disconnected at: _____

(Priority: ☒ Minor Repair)

Non-combustible base/lateral clearances from combustible materials of wood burning stoves.
☐ Good condition ☐ Fair condition ☐ _____
☐ Improvement required at: _____
ADDITIONAL OPINIONS: _____
_____

Clients
Initials _____

☐ **SEE ADDTIONAL COMMENTS PAGE / INFORMATION SHEET** ☐ _____

1-Yr. Priority Key				
Functional	Monitor	N.A.	Minor Repair	MAJOR REPAIR

BATHROOMS

☒ **LIMITATIONS:** Due to the unpredictable and latent nature of plumbing, shower and bathtub enclosure leaks, no assurances or warranty can be provided that leaks will not develop at any time after the inspection date.

☐ ☐ ☐ ☒ ☐ **SHOWER/BATHTUB ENCLOSURE CONDITION**
☐ The ceramic tile/wall surfaces are in good general condition. ☐ _____
☒ The ceramic tile/wall surfaces are in fair general condition. ☐ _____
☒ Sealant and grout touch-ups/repair required at all/most shower/bathtub enclosures.
☐ Repair/replace tile or wall surface at: _____
☐ Complete tile and wall replacement required at: _____
☐ Repair/install shower door/curtain assembly at: _____

☒ ☐ ☐ ☐ ☐ **FAUCETS/SHOWER HEAD CONDITION**
☒ Shower faucets/head assembly are in good/fair general condition. ☐ _____
☒ Tub faucets are in good/fair general condition. ☐ Faucet washers are recommended to be replaced.
☐ Shower faucet/head assembly requires repair/replacement at: _____
☐ Tub faucet requires repair/replacement at: _____

☒ ☐ ☐ ☐ ☐ **BATHTUB CONDITION**
☒ Bathtubs are in good/fair general condition. ☐ _____
☐ Bathtub requires repair/replacement at: ☐ _____
☐ Whirlpool bath is functional. ☐ Whirlpool bath electrical circuit is required to be protected by a GFCI.
☐ Whirlpool bath requires repair at: _____

☐ ☐ ☐ ☒ ☐ **TOILET CONDITION/BIDET CONDITION**
☐ Toilets are in good/fair general condition. ☐ _____
☒ Toilet is improperly installed to floor (ie) loose at: _repair/ floor slightly rotten._
☐ Toilet requires repair/replacement at: _____
☐ Bidet is in good general condition ☐ Bidet requires repair at: _____

☒ ☐ ☐ ☐ ☐ **WASH BASIN/FAUCET CONDITION & OPERATION**
☒ Wash basins are in good/fair general condition. ☐ _____
☒ Faucets are in good/fair general condition. ☐ Faucet washers are recommended to be replaced.
☐ Wash basin requires repair/replacement at: _____
☐ Faucets require repair/replacement at: _____

☐ ☐ ☐ ☒ ☐ **ELECTRICAL**
☐ Receptacles are in functional condition at all/most bathrooms. ☐ _____
☒ Installation of GFCI receptacle recommended at: _____
☐ Repair/replace receptacle at: _____
☒ Relocate light switch/replace light fixture at: _LIGHT IN SHOWER STALL NOT MOISTURE PROOF_

☐ ☐ ☐ ☒ ☐ **VENTILATION: WINDOWS / EXHAUST FANS**
☐ Ventilation is provided by a functional window and/or a functional mechanical exhaust fan.
☐ Repair/replace exhaust fan at: _____
☒ Exhaust fan installation recommended at: _BATHROOM - 2ND FLOOR._
☐ Rework window to provide proper operation/replace window at: _____
☐ Window is located in shower enclosure; protection of window is required at: _____

☐ ☐ ☒ ☐ ☐ **SAUNAS/SPAS**
☐ System/components are in good general condition. ☐ _____
☐ System/components require repair/replacement at: _____

☐ ☐ ☒ ☐ ☐ **GENERAL CONDITIONS**
The _____ bathroom is in marginal condition. Major remodelling is recommended in the near future.
☐ _____

☐ ☐ ☒ ☐ ☐ **ADDITIONAL OPINIONS** _____
_____
_____
_____

☐ **SEE ADDITIONAL COMMENTS PAGE/INFORMATION SHEET** ☐ _____

Clients
Initials _____

1-Yr. Priority Key				
Functional	Monitor	N.A.	Minor Repair	MAJOR REPAIR

LAUNDRY ROOM

☐ ☐ ☐ ☒ ☐

CLOTHES DRYER CONNECTIONS
Power source:
☒ Plug receptacle installed/240 V
☐ Direct wire connection; no receptacle
☐ No electrical connections
☐ Gas dryer connection
☐ _____

☐ Properly vented to the exterior.
☐ Duct/vent requires repair _____
☒ No venting installed _____
☐ Vented through window; rework.
☐ _____

☒ ☐ ☐ ☐ ☐

WASHING MACHINE CONNECTIONS
Power source:
☒ Plug receptacle available & properly grounded.
☐ No plug receptacle installed.
Water connections:
☒ Satisfactory connections/shut-off valve.
☐ Connections require repair/replacement/relocating.

☐ _____
☐ Replace receptacle/not grounded.

☐ No water connections installed.
☐ _____

☐ ☐ ☐ ☒ ☐

LAUNDRY TUB/FAUCETS
☐ Tub is in: ☐ Good condition ☐ Fair condition ☒ Tub requires repair/replacement
☐ Faucet is in: ☐ Good condition ☐ Fair condition ☒ Faucet requires repair/replacement
☐ New washers required ☐ _____

☐ ☐ ☒ ☐ ☐

SEWAGE EJECTOR PUMP
Pump is in: ☐ Good condition ☐ Fair condition ☐ Pump requires repair/replacement

ADDITIONAL OPINIONS: _____
_____
_____

KITCHEN

☒ ☐ ☐ ☐ ☐

COUNTER TOP CONDITION
☒ Counter top is in: ☒ Good condition ☐ Fair condition ☐ Requires repair/replacement
☐ Localized damage around faucets – replacement is imminent. ☐ _____

☒ ☐ ☐ ☐ ☐

CABINET(S) CONDITION
☒ Cabinet condition, installation & operation is in: ☒ Good condition ☐ Fair condition
☐ Repairs required to drawers/door fronts/shelving/cabinet mounting.

☐ ☐ ☐ ☒ ☐

STOVE POWER SOURCE
☒ Plug receptacle installed/240V
☐ Direct wire connection/no receptacle
☐ Gas stove connection
☐ _____

EXTRACTION FAN
☐ Exhaust fan is functional/marginal
☐ Re-circulating fan is functional
☐ Repair/replace fan ☐ _____
☒ Installation of exhaust fan recommended

☐ ☐ ☐ ☒ ☐

ELECTRICAL RECEPTACLES
☐ Good number ☐ Fair number of receptacles installed at counter level
☒ Limited number of receptacles in kitchen ☒ Additional split duplex receptacles recommended

☐ ☐ ☐ ☒ ☐

SINK, FAUCET CONDITION
☒ Sink is in: ☒ Good condition ☐ Fair condition ☐ Sink requires repair/replacement
☐ Faucet assembly is in: ☐ Good condition ☐ Fair functional condition ☐ New washers required
☒ Faucet assembly requires repair/replacement ☐ _____

ADDITIONAL OPINIONS: _____
_____
_____
_____

☐ **SEE ADDITIONAL COMMENTS PAGE / INFORMATION SHEET** ☐ _____

Clients
Initials _____

Appendix C

Where Can I Get More Information? Real Estate Resources

● ●

You're going to have lots of questions as you go through the home-buying or home-selling process. Fortunately, there are lots of people out there ready to supply the information you need.

Mortgages

The world of mortgages is complicated. No doubt, if you've already attempted doing some research, you've found a bewildering amount of information and advice out there. Buyers and sellers alike have a million questions to answer before deciding on the right financial plan for their individual needs. The following resources offer plenty of easy-to-understand and helpful information that will prepare you for the world of mortgages.

Online mortgage calculators

Most Web sites devoted to mortgage information and those of major financial institutions offer online mortgage calculators. If you are having trouble navigating a site, try using links to "Calculators," "Tools," "Mortgage," "Mortgage Centre," or "Personal Banking." You can find online calculators at the following sites:

www.bmo.com
www.canadamortgage.com
www.canadatrust.ca
www.cibc.com
www.citizensbank.ca

www.laurentianbank.com
www.nbc.ca
www.royalbank.com
www.scotiabank.ca
www.tdbank.ca

Canada Mortgage and Housing Corporation (CMHC)

The CMHC is Canada's national housing agency and serves many roles in the housing industry. It insures high-ratio mortgages to protect lenders from default, assists in public–private partnerships in housing, conducts and coordinates research into housing issues, and has Canada's largest database regarding homes and housing.

National Office

700 Montreal Road, Ottawa, ON K1A 0P7
(613) 748-2300 or Toll Free: (800) 668-2642
Fax: (613) 748-2098
e-mail: chic@cmhc-schl.gc.ca
www.cmhc-schl.gc.ca

New Brunswick

1045 Main Street, Unit 103, Moncton, NB E1C 1H1
(506) 851-2229, Fax: (506) 851-6188
e-mail: bmooney@cmhc-schl.gc.ca

Newfoundland

P.O. Box 9300, Station A, 120 Torbay Road, St. John's, NF A1A 3V6
(709) 772-5973, Fax: (709) 772-1166
e-mail: dring@cmhc-schl.gc.ca

Nova Scotia

P.O. Box 9315, Station A, Halifax, NS B3K 5W9
(902) 426-8462, Fax: (902) 426-9991
e-mail: swaldher@cmhc-schl.gc.ca

Québec

As of November 1, 2000:
1100, boul René Levesque Ouest, 1st floor, Montréal, QC H3B 5J7
Toll Free: (800) 668-2642
www.cmhc-schl.gc.ca

Ontario

100 Sheppard Avenue E., Suite 500, North York, ON M2N 6N5
(416) 218-3345, Fax: (416) 250-3203
e-mail: ckerley@cmhc-schl.gc.ca

Prairies and Northwest Territories

708 11th Avenue S. W., Suite 500, Calgary, AB T2R 0E4
(403) 515-2955, Fax: (403) 515-2930
e-mail: mrasmuss@cmhc-schl.gc.ca

British Columbia and Yukon

2600 Granville Street, Suite 400, Vancouver, BC V6H 3V7
(604) 666-2940, Fax: (604) 666-3020
e-mail: lsiracus@cmhc-schl.gc.ca

Canadian Housing Information Centre (CHIC)

It's also worth checking out this suborganization of the CMHC.

700 Montreal Road, Ottawa, ON K1A 0P7
(613) 748-2367 or Toll Free: (800) 668-2642
Fax: (613) 748-4069
e-mail: chic@cmhc-schl.gc.ca

GE Capital Mortgage Insurance Canada

GE Capital Mortgage Insurance Canada is the only private-sector supplier of mortgage default insurance in Canada. While its rates are identical to those charged by the Canada Mortgage and Housing Corporation, there are some competitive differences between the two companies. For example, GE Capital may include up to 50 percent of income from illegal suites to qualify as income, whereas the CMHC will not include any unauthorized income. You can contact GE Capital at this address:

2300 Meadowvale Blvd, Mississauga, ON L5N 5P9
(905) 858-5100 or Toll Free: (800) 511-8888
Fax: (905) 858-5292
www.ge-mi.com/canada

Canadian Home Income Plan (CHIP)

The CHIP is the major organization that currently offers reverse mortgages in Canada. Its address is:

45 St. Clair Avenue West, Toronto, ON M4V 1K9
Toll Free: (800) 563-2447
e-mail: info@chip.ca
www.reversemortgage.org/canadian.htm

Inspectors

Home inspectors are an integral part of most home sales in Canada. The inspector will offer an educated and independent opinion about the overall condition of the home, and the systems within the home.

Canadian Association of Home Inspectors (CAHI)

Formed in 1982, the CAHI maintains and regulates national standards in home inspections, and offers a Code of Ethics that its members must adhere to. The CAHI offers education services to its members and interacts with government agencies and the public as a leading authority in the home inspection field.

National Office

P.O. Box 507, Brighton, ON K0K 1H0
(613) 475-5699 or Toll Free: (888) 748-2244
Fax: (613) 475-1595
e-mail: parkway@reach.net
www.cahi.ca

Contact information for the CAHI's regional offices changes annually. Consult the regional Web sites for more information.

CAHI Atlantic

www.cahi.ca/atlantic.htm

Association des inspecteurs en bâtiment du Québec (AIBQ)

www.aibq.qc.ca

CAHI Ontario
www.oahi.com

CAHI Manitoba
www.cahi.mb.ca

CAHI Saskatchewan
www.cahi.ca/sask.htm

CAHI Alberta
www.telusplanet.net/public/moemad/home.html

CAHI British Columbia
www.cahi.bc.ca

Real Estate Associations

Provincial real estate associations are a good resource to answer any questions about specific provincial laws and regulations. These associations can often direct buyers and sellers who are searching for an agent to the applicable local Real Estate Board. Here is a list of real estate associations across Canada:

Canadian Real Estate Association

Minto Place, The Canada Building, Suite 1600, 344 Slater Street,
Ottawa, ON K1R 7Y3
(613) 237-7111, Fax: (613) 234-2567
e-mail: info@crea.ca
www.mls.ca/crea

New Brunswick Real Estate Association

358 King Street, Suite 301, Fredericton, NB E3B 1E3
(506) 459-8055, Fax: (506) 459-8057
e-mail: nbrea@nbnet.nb.ca

Newfoundland Real Estate Association

251 Empire Avenue, St. John's, NF A1C 3H9
(709) 726-5110, Fax: (709) 726-4221

Nova Scotia Real Estate Association

7 Scarfe Court, Dartmouth, NS B3B 1W4
(902) 468-2515, Fax: (902) 468-2533

Prince Edward Island Real Estate Association

75 St. Peter's Road, Charlottetown, PEI C1A 5N7
(902) 368-8451, Fax: (902) 894-9487
www.cyberhomes.com

Fédération des chambres immobilières du Québec

600 chemin du Golf, Ile-des-Soeurs, QC H3E 1A8
(514) 762-0212, Fax: (514) 762-0365
e-mail: fciq@cigm.qc.ca

Ontario Real Estate Association

99 Duncan Mill Road, Don Mills, ON M3B 1Z2
(416) 445-9910, Fax: (416) 445-2644
e-mail: info@orea.com
www.orea.com

Manitoba Real Estate Association

2nd Floor 1240 Portage, Winnipeg, MB R3G 0T6
(204) 772-0405, Fax: (204) 775-3781
e-mail: bcollie@mrea.mb.ca
www.realestatemanitoba.com

Saskatchewan Real Estate Association

231 Robin Crescent, Saskatoon, SK S7L 6M8
(306) 373-3350, Fax: (306) 373-5377
e-mail: kbacon@srea.sk.ca
www.srea.sk.ca

Alberta Real Estate Association

Suite 310, 2424-4th Street S.W., Calgary, AB T2S 2T4
(403) 228-6845 or Toll Free: 1-800-661-0231
Fax: (403) 228-4360
e-mail: drussell@abrea.ab.ca
www.abrea.ab.ca

British Columbia Real Estate Association

309 – 1155 West Pender Street, Vancouver, BC V6E 2P4
(604) 683-7702, Fax: (604) 683-8601
e-mail: bcrea@helix.net
www.bcrea.bc.ca

Yukon Real Estate Association

P.O. Box 5292, Whitehorse, YK Y1A 4Z2
(867) 668-2070, Fax: (867) 668-2070
e-mail: mail@yrea.yk.ca
www.yrea.yk.ca

Surveys

Here is a list of provincial associations of land surveyors:

Association of New Brunswick Land Surveyors

358 King Street, Suite 304, Fredericton, NB E3B 1E3
(506) 458-8266, Fax: (506) 458-8267
e-mail: anbls@nbnet.nb.ca
www.anbls.nb.ca/links.htm

Association of Newfoundland Land Surveyors

62 Pippy Place, St. John's, NF A1B 4H7
(709) 722-2031, Fax: (709) 722-4104
e-mail: info@surveyors.nf.ca
www.surveyors.nf.ca

L'Ordre des arpenteurs-géomètres du Québec

Iberville Quatre, 2954, boul. Laurier, bureau 350, Sainte-Foy QC G1V 4T2
(418) 656-0730, Fax: (418) 656-6352
e-mail: oagq@oagq.qc.ca
www.oagq.qc.ca

Association of Ontario Land Surveyors

1043 McNicoll Avenue, Scarborough, ON M1W 3W6
(416) 491-9020 or Toll Free: (800) 268-0718
Fax: (416) 491-2576
e-mail: admin@aols.org
www.aols.org

Saskatchewan Land Surveyors' Association

408 Broad Street, #230, Regina, SK S4R 1X3
(306) 352-8999, Fax: (306) 352-8366
e-mail: slsa@sk.sympatico.ca
www.gov.sk.ca/spmc/sgd/sls/slsahome.htm

Alberta Land Surveyors' Association

2501 CN Tower, 10004 -104 Avenue, Edmonton, AB T5J 0K1
(780) 429-8805 or Toll Free: (800) 665-2572
Fax: (780) 429-3374
e-mail: admin@alsa.ab.ca
www.alsa.ab.ca

Corporation of Land Surveyors of British Columbia

#306 – 895 Fort Street, Victoria, BC V8W 1H7
(250) 382-4323, Fax: (250) 382-5092
e-mail: corpbcls@islandnet.com
www.bclandsurveyors.bc.ca

Lawyers

Lawyers are involved in most real estate transactions in Canada, except in Quebec where notaries are the norm. The buyer and the seller should each have their own lawyer to act in their best interest, to review the Contract of Purchase and Sale, if necessary, and to complete the transfer of the property from the seller to the buyer.

The Federation of Law Societies of Canada

This is the blanket organization for all provincial law societies. The FLSC Web site has a link to each provincial law society Web site and e-mail address for inquiries. Many provincial Web sites list local lawyers and their specialties, or provide links to provincial legal education associations or societies that provide this information. The Federation of Law Societies of Canada can be contacted at the following address:

Suite 480, 445 boulevard Saint-Laurent, Montréal PQ H2Y 2Y7
(514) 875-6350, Fax: (514) 875-6115
e-mail: pafoley@flsc.ca
www.flsc.ca

Provincial Lawyer Referral Services

Most provinces also have a "Lawyer Referral Service" that the public can use to be put in touch with a lawyer in their region who can meet their needs.

Nova Scotia
Halifax/Dartmouth: (902) 455-1722
Outside Halifax/Dartmouth: Toll Free: (800) 665-9779

Ontario

Toronto: (416) 947-3330
Outside Toronto: Toll Free: (800) 268-8326

Manitoba

Winnipeg: (204) 943-2305
Outside Winnipeg: Toll Free: (800) 262-8800

Saskatchewan

Toll Free: (800) 667-9886

Alberta

Calgary: (403) 228-1722
Outside Calgary: Toll Free: (800) 661-1095

For a listing of lawyers and firms in other provinces and territories as well as in provinces that have a lawyer referral service, www.canlaw.net is a great Web site. The listing includes names, addresses, and areas of expertise. It is divided by province and then further divided into area or city. It also has links to real estate pages!

Finding specific lawyers or firms

If a friend has given you the name of a lawyer or firm, but you aren't sure how to find them or aren't sure if they even practise real estate law, www.canadianlawlist.com is worth a visit. This site contains a database of lawyers and their specialties that is searchable by lawyer name or firm name.

Warranties

Home warranties are essential to protect buyers of newly built or substantially renovated homes. Some provinces have provincial warranty programs, and other provinces have mandatory warranty coverage supplied by private companies. Check out the list of provincial New Home Warranty Programs for the one that applies to you.

Atlantic Home Warranty Program

Established in 1976, the Atlantic Home Warranty Program has backed over 75,000 homes in the Atlantic region.

15 Oland Crescent, Halifax, NS B3S 1C6.
(902) 450-9000 or Toll Free: (800) 320-9880
Fax: (902) 450-5454
e-mail: info@ahwp.org
www.ahwp.org

La Garantie des maisons neuves de l'Association provinciale des constructeurs d'habitations du Québec

5930, boul. Louis-H. Lafontaine, Anjou, QC H1M 1S7
(514) 353-9960 or Toll Free: (800) 468-8160
Fax: (514) 353-4825
e-mail: info-apchq@apchq.com
www.apchq.com

Ontario New Home Warranty Program

5160 Yonge St., 6th Floor, Toronto, ON M2N 6L9
(416) 229-9200 or Toll Free: (800) 668-0124
e-mail: info@newhome.on.ca
www.newhome.on.ca

New Home Warranty Program of Manitoba Inc.

675 Pembina, Winnipeg, MB R3M 2L6
(204) 453-1155

New Home Warranty Program of Saskatchewan Inc.

#4 – 3012 Louise St. E., Saskatoon, SK S7L 3L8
(306) 373-7833, Fax: (306) 373-7977
e-mail: service@nhwp.org
www.nhwp.org

Alberta New Home Warranty Program

Incorporated in 1974, the Alberta New Home Warranty program was the first new home warranty program in Canada. It has offices in Calgary and Edmonton.

Calgary Office

201, 208 – 57th Avenue SW, Calgary, AB T2H 2K8
(403) 253-3636 or Toll Free: (800) 352-8240
Fax: (403) 253-5062
e-mail: anhwp@anhwp.com
www.anhwp.com

Edmonton Office

201 – 10335 172nd Street, Edmonton, AB T5S 1K9
(780) 484-0572 or Toll Free: (800) 352-8240
Fax: (780) 486-7896
e-mail: anhwp@anhwp.com
www.anhwp.com

Homeowner Protection Office in British Columbia

Since the collapse of the British Columbia New Home Warranty Program, the Homeowner Protection Office has established warranty guidelines to help re-establish and strengthen consumer confidence for buyers of new homes and condominiums. The HPO licenses builders, oversees mandatory third-party warranties on all new homes, offers reconstruction loans to owners of leaky condos, and offers education and research programs. The HPO Web site has great links to industry associations, warranty information, industry information, government links, and British Columbia's Better Business Bureaus, and outlines relief programs available to people with leaky condominiums in B.C.

2270 – 1055 West Georgia Street, PO Box 11132, Royal Centre,
Vancouver, BC V6E 3P3
(604) 646-7055 or Toll Free: (800) 407-7757
Fax: (604) 646-7051
e-mail: hpo@hpo.bc.ca
www.hpo.bc.ca

National Home Warranty Programs

In many provinces, third-party warranties are required for new homes and
condominiums. National Home Warranty Programs is one of the major
companies that offers third-party warranty coverage for new construction
across Canada. Their Web site offers excellent information about warranty
coverage across the country.

1001 – 10405 Jasper Avenue, Edmonton, AB T5J 3N4
(780) 425-2981 or Toll Free: (800) 472-9784
Fax: (780) 426-2723
www.nationalhomewarranty.com

Home Builders

If you're buying a newly built home, it's important to find out as much as you
can about the various people associated with building it from the ground up.
This broad category includes builders, renovators, trade contractors, product
manufacturers, and lending institutions. The Web site contains links to
provincial and local home builders' associations and provincial warranty
program sites.

Canadian Home Builders' Association

The Canadian Home Builders' Association represents more than 6,000 firms
in the residential construction industry across Canada. Its Web site contains
links to provincial and local home builders' associations and provincial
warranty program sites.

150 Laurier Avenue W., Suite 500, Ottawa, ON K1P 5J4
(613) 230-3060, Fax: (613) 232-8214
e-mail: chba@chba.ca
www.chba.ca

Selling Privately

If you're selling on your own, you have some special concerns. Fortunately, lots of other homeowners have been through the selling process on their own, and (lucky you!) you can benefit from their expertise. Unfortunately, while there are many Web sites for listing or browsing homes being sold privately, there are few sites dealing with the ins and outs of private sales. The following is the most informative site we managed to find:

www.privatelist.com

It seems your best bet as a private seller is to use the Internet for advertising, and use the bookstore for research. You can also attempt to contact private sellers (friends of friends perhaps, or through a listing) and see if they will be willing to spend some time telling you about their experience and giving you a few tips.

Home Insurance

It's important to insure both the structure and contents of your home, as well as yourself in the event that you cause damage to somebody else's home. You should purchase a policy that offers both property and liability coverage.

Insurance Bureau of Canada

The Insurance Bureau of Canada can answer any questions regarding insurance matters in Canada, and direct you to the appropriate contact in your area. You can get in touch with them at their head office:

151 Yonge Street, Suite 1800, Toronto, ON M5C 2W7
(416) 362-2031, or Toll Free: (800) 387-2880
Fax: (416) 361-5952
e-mail: info@ibc.ca
www.ibc.ca

Condominiums

Owning a condominium isn't like owning a house. While there are some similarities, there are more differences — like the role of the condominium corporation, maintenance fees, and commercial property. These are details you want to work out before you sign on the dotted line and gain possession of that castle in the sky.

Canadian Condominium Institute

The Canadian Condominium Institute is an independent, non-profit organization that assists all aspects of the condominium community, through research, education, and information dissemination. You can contact their national office at:

310-2175 Sheppard Ave. E., North York, ON M2J 1W8
(416) 491-6216, Fax: (416) 491-1670
e-mail: cci.national@taylerenterprises.com
www.cci.ca

Credit Reporting

Your lending institution will perform a credit check when you apply for a mortgage.

Equifax Canada Inc.

Equifax Canada is one of the largest credit-checking agencies in Canada. You can contact them to confirm the status of your credit rating if you are curious.

Consumer Relations Department, Box 190 Jean Talon Station
Montreal, PQ H1S 2Z2.
(514) 493-2314 or Toll Free: (800) 465-7166
Fax: (514) 355-8502
e-mail: inquiries@equifax.com
www.equifax.ca

Index

● *T* ●

Notes

Notes